D1481883

Niebuhr and His Age

NIEBUHR
and His Age

Reinhold Niebuhr's Prophetic Role
in the Twentieth Century

Charles C. Brown

Trinity Press International   Philadelphia

First Published 1992

Trinity Press International
3725 Chestnut Street
Philadelphia, PA 19104

Library of Congress Cataloging-in-Publication Data

Brown, Charles C. (Charles Calvin), 1938–
   Niebuhr and his age : Reinhold Niebuhr's prophetic role in the twentieth century / Charles C. Brown.
     p.   cm.
   Includes bibliographical references and index.
   ISBN 1-56338-042-0 :
1. Niebuhr, Reinhold, 1892–1971. 2. Theologians—United States—
Biography. 3. Theology—History—20th century. I. Title.
BX4827.N5B76 1992   92-25356
230'.092—dc20   CIP

© 1992 Charles C. Brown

Cover design: Jim Gerhard

Printed in the United States of America

To my parents
Dolores S. Brown (1915–1953)
and Calvin C. Brown

Contents

ॐ

PREFACE

It was as a college student at DePauw in the later 1950s that I began to appreciate Reinhold Niebuhr's prophetic role in the twentieth century. James M. Ward, for whom Niebuhr had become a formative influence during studies at Union Theological Seminary, introduced me to Niebuhr's thought while I was a student there, and years later he encouraged me to undertake this book. Now at Perkins School of Theology, he is the author of a recent work, *Thus Says the Lord: The Message of the Prophets*, which surely would impress Niebuhr if he were here today. Niebuhr's impact on his age, including my generation, is hard to convey to those who have grown up in a subsequent era. I well remember a stampede to the lounge of my residence hall at DePauw as word spread, on April 27, 1958, that Niebuhr was on television as the guest of Mike Wallace in a special "Freedom and Survival" series.

After college I read Niebuhr regularly in the pages of *Christianity and Crisis* and the *New Leader* and turned increasingly to his books for a deeper understanding of social and political problems and of Christian faith. As a graduate student in history at the University of Missouri in the late 1960s and early 1970s I profited from discussions of Niebuhr with Clifton W. Kerr, then director of an ecumenical ministry and now associated with Eden Theological Seminary, and received encouragement from my professor, Richard S. Kirkendall, to pursue this growing interest with a view to publication. Then, aided by a bequest from my grandparents, Jay and Amelia Brown, I began this project fifteen years ago, gathering and assimilating Niebuhriana from libraries around the nation.

During the 1980s I did background study, enlarged the scope of research, and began to write the book with grant support from the Marguerite Eyer Wilbur Foundation, residing for eighteen months of this period as a Senior Fellow at its writers' center in Mecosta, Michigan. There, lodged near the home of Russell Kirk and next door to his library, I benefited greatly from his experienced advice as the author of many books, among them *Eliot and His Age*, which inspired the title for this book. Discussions with other Wilbur Fellows—especially Jan van Houten from the Netherlands, Andrew Shaughnessy from Scotland, and Marjorie Haney and Jeff Nelson of the United States—were helpful during this stay in a village of rural Michigan. A grant from the Earhart Foundation in 1991 provided funds for travel and research and for preparation of the book for publication. The grant was processed for me, as Senior Scholar of the Graduate School of the City University of New York, by staff members of its Office of Sponsored Research and its Research Foundation.

Scholarship is corporate, and this book involved the cooperation of others who read all or part of a draft of the manuscript, making helpful suggestions and correcting errors, or assisted by providing source materials and pursuing special problems of research. Ursula Niebuhr invited me to her home in Stockbridge, Massachusetts, five years ago, reminisced about Reinhold while I sat in his favorite chair, and allowed me to peruse books he had used in their personal library. Then she read my entire draft, helping to make it more rich and factually accurate as personal biography. Christopher Niebuhr joined in this, providing much detailed information about his father. Ronald H. Stone discussed this project with me helpfully during my visits with him in Pittsburgh, encouraged me to enlarge it, opened his Niebuhr files to me, and read the whole draft. Roger L. Shinn worked especially closely with me, reading the unfolding draft of the manuscript over a period of years and offering his knowledgeable and judicious comments. In mid-April of 1991 he visited at my residence in Columbia, Missouri, for extended conversation on many points, and the book was greatly improved as a result. He also helped by delving into records and library resources at Union Theological Seminary and Columbia University. Especially close also during the later years of this project was Carl Hermann Voss, who used the telephone frequently to encourage my efforts, to share his personal memories of Reinhold Niebuhr, and to discuss many problems in the writing of the book. He read portions of the manuscript, brought my work to the attention of Harold Rast at Trinity Press International, and joined his wife, Phyllis, in providing funds for extra research.

Arthur Schlesinger, Jr., also took a supportive interest in this work, conversing with me at his office about Niebuhr, reading a portion of the draft, and corresponding with me on some points. John C. Bennett read and commented helpfully on the entire draft and discussed various problems by telephone. Martin Marty invited me to his home for a Niebuhr conversation, read the whole draft, and provided some material incorporated in it. June Bingham Birge met with me, shared some of her Niebuhr materials, and read portions of the draft, making suggestions for improvements. Langdon Gilkey, Kenneth W. Thompson, and Nathan A. Scott, Jr., welcomed me for visits to discuss Niebuhr, made important points, and encouraged my efforts. William Lee Miller and Larry Rasmussen also took an interest, meeting and talking with me. Robert T. Handy and Franklin H. Littell found and sent me valuable information and material.

My research was assisted by Paul Abrecht in Geneva, Werner Kramer in Zurich, and Justin Stagl in Bonn. In the United States it was aided by Viola Braun and her son Richard, Claude Heckscher, John C. Helt, W. Lance Martin, George Michos, Victor Obenhaus, Harold Wilke, and Laurence M. Wood; and in Canada by Ian Boyd. Richard John Neuhaus provided stimulation by inviting me to a conference in New York, the proceedings of which were subsequently published in a volume he edited entitled *Reinhold Niebuhr Today*. William H. Gentz helped at an early stage by advising me on the ways of publishers. In Columbia, Missouri, local friends who helped by discussing various aspects of research and writing, and by encouraging the project, include Wayne K. Davis, Ken Green, Alan R. Havig, E. Clarendon Hyde, Dick Millspaugh, Charles F. Mullett, Charles G. Nauert, Jr., Osmund Overby, Dale A. Patrick, Ewell Reagin, and Donald L. Scruggs. Also in Columbia, Adolf Schroeder and Luverne Walton translated letters and documents from German for this book.

Many librarians provided services indispensable to my research, especially the reference staff and others at the Ellis Library of the University of Missouri, which has a superb collection of periodicals, microfilms, and reference works; Karen Luebbert and Sue Gold of the Eden-Webster Library in Webster Groves, Missouri, which has complete runs of the two journals with which Niebuhr was editorially associated for many years; and Seth Kasten, Barbara Griffis, Tanya Serdiuk and others at the Burke Library of Union Theological Seminary in New York, with its outstanding collection of theological literature and its records of Union's history. Also helpful in locating widely scattered Niebuhriana were Richard E. Bopp at the University of Illinois Library, Dan O. Clemmer, Jr., at the U.S. State Department Library, James R. Magruder at the Yale University Library, staff at the Detroit Public Library and its Burton Historical Collection, and others at the Harry S. Truman Library, the Winston Churchill Memorial and Library, and libraries of the University of Chicago, Harvard University, Drew University, Southern Methodist University, and Garrett Theological Seminary.

David Wigdor and his staff at the Manuscript Division of the Library of Congress made the Reinhold Niebuhr Papers available to me. Ann T. Knox at the library of Union Theological Seminary in Virginia cooperated in my use of the Reinhold Niebuhr Audio Tape Collection. Rudolf G. Schade at Elmhurst College, Lowell H. Zuck at Eden Theological Seminary, Paul A. Byrnes at Union Theological Seminary, Charles F. Rehkopf of the Episcopal Diocese of Missouri, Paul G. Anderson of Christ Church Cathedral in St. Louis, and Robert L. Miller of the Episcopal Diocese of Michigan cooperated in providing photographs, historical information, and other materials from the archives in their care.

David Rees and Todd Winge advised and assisted in preparing photographs for reproduction in this book. The picture of the parsonage and church in Lincoln, Illinois, is included in the illustrations by courtesy of the Library of Congress, to which it was donated by June Bingham Birge. The pictures of the old Elmhurst campus and of Reinhold Niebuhr as a student there are used by courtesy of Elmhurst College. The picture of Samuel Press is included by courtesy of Eden Theological Seminary. The pictures of Bethel Church in Detroit are reproduced by courtesy of Emmanuel Bethel Church in Royal Oak, Michigan. The picture of the Niebuhr family is used by courtesy of Ursula M. Niebuhr. The portrait of William Scarlett is reproduced by courtesy of Christ Church Cathedral in St. Louis. The cover of *Time* is reproduced by courtesy of *Time* magazine. The picture of Niebuhr with Schlesinger's *A Thousand Days* beside him is used by courtesy of Ronald H. Stone. The following ten illustrations are reproduced by courtesy of Union Theological Seminary, The Burke Library, New York City: Niebuhr ca. 1930, portrait of Henry Sloane Coffin, Union Theological Seminary as seen from Broadway at 120th Street, Niebuhr with Hubert Humphrey, Niebuhr lecturing to a class, Niebuhr with a student, Niebuhr preaching in James Chapel, Niebuhr talking with friends while walking poodles, Niebuhr ca. 1960, and Niebuhr with John Bennett.

My work in getting the main text and other parts of this book in shape for publication benefited tremendously from the counsel and patience of my editor, Harold W. Rast, and his staff at Trinity Press International. Shirley Bynum ably assisted in preparing the index.

My long endeavors were also aided and made pleasant by the personal kindness of my brother, Jerrold J. Brown, and his wife Albita; of Annette Kirk in Mecosta, Michigan; of Sarah W. Bess, C. Edward and Greta Carroll, and John and Chaille King in Columbia; of Rodney and Florence Olsen during stays in Washington, D.C.; and of Nathan and Charlotte Scott in Charlottesville, Virginia.

To all those, named and unnamed, who helped in various ways I am most grateful. Their assistance and generosity enabled me to make this a better book. Its imperfections, and whatever errors are found on its pages, are my own.

Columbia, Missouri
March 1992

CHAPTER ONE

Niebuhr's Wisdom in an
Age of Perplexity

&

The impact of Reinhold Niebuhr on the religious, political, and intellectual life of the twentieth century, and the impression he made on contemporaries, are widely attested. "He was the greatest man I knew," stated Arthur Schlesinger, Jr., who spent years in the White House and knew many of the nation's foremost leaders. Niebuhr had, Alan Paton reflected in his memoirs, "an understanding of human nature and of human society that no one has equalled in our century." John Gunther, after interviewing him once, wrote: "To ask Dr. Niebuhr a question is like hurling a paper dart into an electric fan." He continued: "The ideas rushing out of his mind, his answers to questions, are never mere verbal confetti but are like splinters off craggy granite." Walter Lippmann, after listening to Niebuhr speak at a conference on international politics, was heard to remark, "We shall not see his like again." Nathan Scott, Jr., expressing a view held by many who heard him preach and lecture and read his books, has maintained that "Reinhold Niebuhr was the most creative theologian in the history of American thought."[1]

As America in the 1930s and 1940s passed through crises at home and abroad that shook its once sanguine culture, Niebuhr emerged as mentor to an influential following of clergy, scholars, journalists, and politicians, and remained in that role as the nation faced new frustrations in the 1950s and 1960s. So engaged was he in the salient issues of those decades that an account of his life and thought not only elucidates his lasting contributions to theology and social philosophy but provides a panoramic view of the events and milieus of his age.

"We are perplexed," Reinhold Niebuhr often stated, quoting Saint Paul, "but not in despair."[2] At the core of his thought was an understanding of sin and grace pointing to creative possibilities and inevitable corruptions

— 1 —

in society; a recognition of love and justice as complements in human affairs; a dialectic of Christian faith and the disciplines of culture as sources of guidance and truth; an emphasis on making discriminate judgments in support of good causes while eschewing self-righteousness in the struggle for them; a pragmatic pursuit of proximate rather than final solutions in politics; an acknowledgment of limits in the wisdom and virtue of any nation or social group; an apprehension of mystery and meaning within and beyond the dramas of history; a sense of the importance of both organism and artifact in democratic integrations of community; and a perception that human striving and divine providence are intertwined.

When *Time*, in March of 1948, featured Niebuhr in the cover story of its twenty-fifth anniversary issue, it was in recognition of his stature as a religious and social thinker.[3] He was then in his fifties, having worked out most themes of his mature thought several years earlier, in the late 1930s and early 1940s. Raised in the parsonage of a midwestern German-American community at the turn of the century and acquiring an education culminating at Yale, Niebuhr served for thirteen years as a pastor in Detroit and then, from 1928 to 1960, taught Christian ethics at Union Theological Seminary in New York. By energetic teaching and preaching and through a constant flow of books and articles, he not only helped mold the vital center in U.S. foreign policy and domestic politics from the 1940s to the 1960s, but during the same decades led American Protestantism in recovering its biblical and theological heritage in creative relationship with modern culture.

Reinhold Niebuhr's lifetime, from 1892 to 1971, spanned the final decades of an era that expected progress through the extension of science and goodwill, and the emergence of an age that faced the perplexities of an advanced industrial society, of a world torn by upheavals, and of nuclear weapons. "Future generations," he wrote in 1947, as the Cold War emerged on the ashes of World War II, "may well look upon our own age with some degree of pity. Our lot has not been cast in pleasant places." When the contours of the dawning era became more clear by 1953, he stated: "We now know that the future is not so full of the promise of good things as the nineteenth century believed; and it may not be so ominous as was suggested in the decade just passed."[4] Influenced during his earlier life by the religious and moral idealism prevalent in America through the first third of the century, Niebuhr had broken with it in the 1930s and became increasingly recognized—after his renowned Gifford Lectures of 1939 were published as *The Nature and Destiny of Man*, and through the journal he cofounded in 1941, *Christianity and Crisis*—as the leading exponent of "Christian realism" in theology and politics. In his mature works and seasoned journalism he drew from the Old Testament prophets and Paul, from the theology of Augustine and the pragmatism of James, from the wisdom of Burke and Madison and various insights of Luther and Calvin and Kierkegaard, and from his own keen observations of Detroit before the Great Depression and of world events from the rise of Nazism through the early decades of the Cold War. In reacting against the optimism of an earlier era, he did not fall into paralyzing pessimism, but often cited a line from Arthur Hugh Clough, "If hopes are dupes, fears may be liars."[5]

While Niebuhr's pen and voice addressed primarily American religious and secular audiences, his influence has been international. One measure of it has been the translation of various books of his into German, Dutch, French, Spanish, Swedish, Czech, Polish, Japanese, Korean, and Chinese, and the appearance of nearly all in British as well as American editions. Another reflection of his reputation, both in America and overseas, was the roster of sponsors who led in funding the Reinhold Niebuhr Professorship of Social Ethics at Union Seminary when he retired from its faculty in 1960: among them W. H. Auden, John Baillie, Emil Brunner, Ralph Bunche, C. H. Dodd, David Dubinsky, T. S. Eliot, Louis Finkelstein, Harry Emerson Fosdick, Hubert Humphrey, Robert Hutchins, George Kennan, Walter Lippmann, Charles Malik, Jacques Maritain, Alan Paton, Walter Reuther, Arthur Schlesinger, Jr., Adlai Stevenson, Paul Tillich, Arnold Toynbee, and W. A. Visser 't Hooft.[6]

Reinhold Niebuhr's greatness arose not only from his unusual energy, rhetorical gifts, and sheer brilliance, but from the originality and profundity of his thought and his forthrightness in applying it to issues—religious, social, and political—during the momentous years from the eve of World War II through the turbulent later 1960s. Many of his contemporaries reached similar views, and he shared with them an atmosphere of tempered expectations, support for democracy against totalitarianism, and renewed appreciation of the Christian and humanist heritage of the West. But he developed a perspective that was distinctive in its understanding of human nature and social realities, in relating biblical faith to politics and culture while distinguishing between it and those realms, in apprehending mystery and meaning in human experience and in the pinnacles of Christian faith, and in facing the perplexities of life and history without illusions or despair.

Among many Protestants at mid-century Niebuhr was regarded as one of the "big four" theologians, the others being Karl Barth and Emil Brunner of Switzerland and Paul Tillich, who emigrated from Germany to America. He joined them in extricating the gospel from the sentimentalities of late-nineteenth- and early-twentieth-century culture, without rejecting its achievements in science and scholarship. Unlike them, he developed a less complete theology and gave more sustained attention to political problems, practically and philosophically. He also addressed a broader public within and outside the Protestant churches. A prolific contributor to religious and secular journals, Niebuhr brought characteristic insights to bear on the case for war against Nazi Germany, for a Jewish national homeland, for preserving the New Deal, for the Marshall Plan and NATO, for policies sensitive to the Third World, for the rights of black Americans, and for a U.S. nuclear deterrent and partnership with Russia in avoiding catastrophe. He anticipated such developments of the late twentieth century as the disintegration of Communism, American economic contraction, and environmental problems. As a cultural critic, he addressed issues in American education and the mass media. As a churchman, he not only spoke out on social concerns but addressed problems of interfaith relations and of preaching and worship in the local congregation.

Well read in many fields, Reinhold Niebuhr was not a specialized scholar but a thinker informed by a vast fund of learning and experience. In a lecture hall or pulpit or auditorium, he went from point to point in explosive and moving speech. Though tending to be less effective on the printed page, he often rose to an eloquence that expressed his ideas memorably, more so in books and essays than in journalistic pieces dashed off to meet deadlines, and especially in brief passages summing up a point under discussion. For example:

> There is no such thing as neutrality in human affairs. All of us are protagonists of some cause or other and pleaders of some particular interest. The most honest and sincere conciliation will come from men and groups who do not imagine themselves above the conflict but who know themselves to be in it. (1935)

Here is another such passage:

> History is today, as it has always been, filled with hours of decision in which we can relate ourselves to its promises or contribute to its disasters. It is therefore more important to seek to do our duty in watchfulness and soberness than to speculate overmuch about the perils which lie before us. (1948)

Now a shorter one:

All of us, like Abraham of old, go out, not knowing whither we go. The drama of human history is determined by God's providence and our decisions. (1952)

And finally this:

Love as a substitute for justice is odious, but love as a supplement to justice is an absolute necessity. (1958)[7]

Such aphorisms can be culled and pondered profitably, but the full dimensions of Niebuhr's thought are not expressed so succinctly. In the chapters that follow, its intricate architecture is presented through apt quotations and compact paraphrase. This book is primarily an intellectual biography, tracing the roots of his mature achievement back to long formative years, expounding his perennial themes and changing concerns in historical context, demonstrating his influence on two generations of thoughtful spirits, and assessing his legacy in terms of its continued relevance and limits. Such a study necessarily relates in some detail the thread of Niebuhr's life, but is not concerned with intimacies of family, friendships, and health. It does not treat exhaustively any single period or aspect of his work—the proper subjects of more specialized studies— but aspires instead to a broad understanding of his convictions and opinions. This account weaves together chronological and thematic approaches to Niebuhr's life and thought. It integrates a mass of material from his score of books and abundant shorter writings, his recorded lectures and speeches, his correspondence, the memories of persons who knew him well, a large body of literature about him, and many other sources.

Any endeavor to present an accurate and comprehensive account of Reinhold Niebuhr's development and achievement encounters certain problems. One of them arises from his tendency to be reticent about himself. Except for a diary kept during his pastoral years, he had little interest in autobiography, and when prodded gave rather sketchy accounts in recalling his past and sometimes was inaccurate on details. Yet his reminiscences—whether elicited by others, or mentioned parenthetically in speech or on paper, or appearing in tributes to his mentors—are richly illuminating. Where minor discrepancies or even lapses of memory occur, other evidence helps to reconstruct his development.

Another problem in rendering a full and reliable account arises from the sheer bulk of Niebuhr's published work, which includes not only a shelf of books but upward of 2,750 essays, articles, editorials, columns, book reviews, prefaces, and pamphlets. These shorter writings are essential for an accurate picture of his intellectual life as it evolved over the years in its various facets, but only some of the best have been an- thologized, while the rest are buried in diverse journals and sundry pub- lications not readily available to readers. Additional material is on tapes of lectures, sermons, and addresses. These resources have become avail- able to scholars only in recent years, through the labors of Niebuhr's bibliographer, D. B. Robertson, and the development of the Reinhold Nie- buhr Audio Tape Collection. Using this material fully, together with newly found letters and previously untapped archival documents, the present work focuses on Niebuhr as pastor, teacher, theologian, social philoso- pher, journalist, and public figure, filling gaps and correcting mispercep- tions of his evolution and views.

As the following chapters will demonstrate in more detail, Niebuhr's family heritage and his studies at the preparatory school and seminary of his denomination were formative in his mastery of German and Greek, in the beginnings of his social conscience, and in his appreciation—min- gled with criticism—of Luther. At Yale he imbibed a theology of moral idealism that began to break down as he gained pastoral and social ex- perience in Detroit. Influenced by the reforming passion of the Social Gospel in the 1920s, he became more radical in the early 1930s, attracted in the depths of the Depression to socialism as the only hopeful alternative to the failure of capitalism. But the Marxist element of that phase of his development was qualified by a decisive turn to Pauline Christianity toward the end of the 1920s, soon after his move to Union Seminary. Stimulated by Barth, Tillich, and Brunner during the 1930s, and impressed even more by Augustine and later in the decade by Kierkegaard, Niebuhr also learned much through keen observation of the behavior of economic, national, and racial groups in America and Europe during the interwar years. He found that biblical insights illuminated current history and social philosophy, while social and inward experience validated the truth of Christian faith. Developing independently of, though in conversation with, his brother H. Richard Niebuhr—a distinguished professor and the- ologian at Yale Divinity School—he foreshadowed in books of the 1930s his wiser and more definitive work of the 1940s and after.

As shown in later chapters of this book, Reinhold Niebuhr's published Gifford Lectures—expounding the mystery of sin and the meaning of grace in relation to a dialectic of faith and reason, with implications for prox- imate as well as ultimate problems of human existence—provided the substratum of his mature thought. By the early 1940s he saw that the New Deal, especially its labor laws and welfare measures, had significantly reformed American capitalism, and thereafter he became a persuasive apologist for Roosevelt's mixed economy as more just and realistic than Marxism or laissez-faire. Having opposed prewar American pacifism and isolationism in the face of the Nazi menace to Western civilization, he supported postwar containment of Stalinist Russia, helping to found Americans for Democratic Action as an organ of non-Communist liberal politics. During the early postwar years Niebuhr remained theologically creative even while devoting much time to public affairs. Despite a stroke in 1952 that slowed his pace, he made a two-thirds comeback and did some of his best work, journalistic and reflective, during the placid 1950s and the stirring 1960s. He produced more books that elaborated, complemented, and refined themes of theology and social philosophy set forth in the 1940s. Sensitive to currents of history, he saw signs of change in Soviet Russia and counseled patience and restraint while Communism slowly abated as a global threat, and he sensed that in America the time was ripe to press for belated justice to the nation's black minority.

Any account of Niebuhr's life and thought involves not only research but a framework of interpretation. In selecting texts and making sense of facts, the historian as biographer may strive for objectivity but is influenced by his or her religious beliefs, philosophical assumptions, political views, perspective on history, and areas of interest. Accordingly, some accounts of Niebuhr have emphasized his earlier period rather than the later work on which his lasting reputation rests, or have tended to politicize him without the theological dimension. As the exponent of a pragmatic Christian realism—rooted in biblical faith in dialogue with modern knowledge, politically in the center, dialectically balanced—Niebuhr has had detractors and critics among those hostile to his basic position: positivists, fundamentalists, pacifists, ideologues on the left and on the right. In recent years a variety of criticisms has come from feminists and latter-day Marxists. Some historians, with preconceived images of Niebuhr, have drawn a distorted picture of him as becoming after 1945 an uncritical champion of the American status quo and of the rigid anti-Communist posture that led to U.S. involvement in the Vietnam War. Niebuhr's role in American life was certainly misunderstood by a journalist who called him "the official Establishment theologian."[8] A growing body of literature about him in books and essays, much of it illuminating and some of it badly flawed, is discussed in an appendix of this book.

The present account allows Reinhold Niebuhr to be heard in his own words, particularly on crucial issues of his age and on salient themes of his thought. It seeks to understand him on his own terms and through the eyes of those—colleagues, students, friends, and scholars friendly to the man and his contribution—who have known and understood him. He was regarded by many as a prophet, not in the sense of speaking with canonical authority or of forecasting the future, but because, like the Old Testament prophets from whose message he drew inspiration, Niebuhr addressed his nation and its religious communities in times of crisis and decision, and did so in accents challenging pride and complacency in the name of a God who calls for justice within and among nations. Like the prophets from Amos to the sublime messenger of the later books of Isaiah, he perceived the universality of human sin and witnessed to the judgment and redemption of the holy and majestic Lord of history.

In his prophetic role, Niebuhr was well aware of the limitations and fallibility of all human thought, including his own. It is easy to find weaknesses in the vast body of his published work; yet many critics have discovered their own criticisms anticipated by Niebuhr himself, whose habit was not to revise his books, but to write new ones giving his revised judgments. The present study, while focusing on his theological insights and social wisdom and political perspicacity, takes account of some defects and limitations of his achievement. Niebuhr did not, for instance, elaborate a doctrine of the church, nor did he say much about apathy or sloth as a cause of social evil. His writings are somewhat uneven in literary quality and not without occasional mistakes on historical details and fine points of philosophy. However, as this study demonstrates, some criticisms of his work are exaggerated, whereas others rest on misunderstandings arising from lack of familiarity with the whole body of that work.

As Niebuhr's age recedes into the past, so has the immediate relevance of his commentary on once-pressing issues—such as the perilous Cold War, which has since ended with the collapse of the Soviet Union—but various international and domestic problems he addressed persist as the twentieth century draws to a close. Beyond this, Niebuhr produced a durable body of theological and social reflections provoked, like those of Augustine and Burke and Madison before him, by political and cultural crisis. He did not systematize his thought or sum it up in a single treatise or two, and some of his most trenchant insights were expressed not in books but in his running commentary on current events. The substance of his mature thought, rooted in diverse traditions and loosely woven into a whole, so defies conventional labels that the word "Niebuhrian" has come into use as the most apt term for it. In demonstrating Reinhold Niebuhr's growth and expounding his themes, the several chapters that follow point to a legacy that may help guide public and religious communities through old and new perplexities of the dawning age.

CHAPTER TWO

From His Father's Parsonage to the Motor City

The roots of Niebuhr's mature thought begin in his family's religious heritage, his student years, his pastorate in Detroit, and his experience as a young man in that city and beyond. It was not until later that he formulated the characteristic themes of his theology and social philosophy, but this formative period foreshadowed some of them.

Gustav Niebuhr and the Heritage of German Pietism

Born in Wright City, Missouri, a village some forty miles west of St. Louis, on the first day of summer in 1892, Reinhold Niebuhr grew up in the parsonage. He spent his boyhood in St. Charles, on the banks of the Missouri River, and his early teens in Lincoln, Illinois, surrounded by flat farmland in the central part of the state, where his father was pastor of St. John's Evangelical Church from 1902 to 1913. Reinhold later said of his father, Gustav Niebuhr, "I was thrilled by his sermons and regarded him as the most interesting man in town."[1]

Gustav (whose surname means "new farmer") had emigrated from Germany in 1881, leaving his family's farm in Lippe-Detmold, a principality of northwestern Germany between Westphalia and the old grand duchy of Hanover. Before coming to America, he had received instruction in the Heidelberg Catechism, for his native territory was Reformed, and had attended a famous old *Gymnasium*, or grammar school, in Lemgo, north of the castle town of Detmold, studying languages, history, and science. Like most natives of that area, he was anti-Prussian. Working as a farmhand in Illinois, Gustav became associated with the German Evangelical Synod of North America, and prepared for the pastoral ministry at the denomination's seminary in St. Louis.[2]

The Evangelical Synod was "Evangelical" in the traditional German Protestant meaning of the word, rather than its American revivalistic sense in the past or present century. Based in the Midwest, it was an offshoot of the Union Church of Prussia, into which Lutheran and Reformed churches of various German lands merged by state decree after 1817, as one territory after another was annexed by Prussia until 1870. Thus it blended traditions tracing back to Luther and Calvin, the Lutheran element predominating because of its German roots. Transplanted to America in the mid-nineteenth century as the *Kirchenverein des Westen,* or Church Society of the West, the denomination adhered to a standard expressed in these words: "We recognize the Evangelical Church as that communion which acknowledges the Holy Scriptures of the Old and the New Testament as the Word of God and as the sole and infallible rule of faith and life, and accepts the interpretation of the Holy Scriptures as given in the symbolic books of the Lutheran and Reformed Church, the most important being: the Augsburg Confession, Luther's and the Heidelberg Catechism, in so far as they agree; but where they disagree, we adhere strictly to the passages of Holy Scriptures bearing on the subject, and avail ourselves of the liberty of conscience prevailing in the Evangelical Church."[3] Thus the most ecumenical and conciliatory expressions of the two principal branches of the Reformation, framed by Melanchthon and Ursinus, were emphasized, and the ultimate authority of the Bible was affirmed.

Not only an irenic spirit but a social conscience characterized the ethos of this immigrant church, and both were rooted in its heritage of Pietism, a movement within German Protestantism emphasizing a warm devotional life and charitable missions. Led by Philipp Spener and August Francke in the late seventeenth century and Johann Wichern in the nineteenth, Pietists met for Bible study and prayer and established orphanages, schools, hospitals, and other agencies for the poor throughout Germany— a movement known as *Innere Mission.* The universities of Halle and Basel became their academic centers, and their best teachers and preachers absorbed the achievements of nineteenth-century German biblical scholarship. Pietism, Reinhold Niebuhr wrote of his denomination, "was potent in the lives of our fathers; but this pietism never degenerated into legalism or fundamentalism."[4]

The theological genius of the *Kirchenverein,* renamed the German Evangelical Synod in 1877, was Andreas Irion, a Pietist from Württemberg who studied at Basel and taught at the denomination's seminary in Marthasville, Missouri, from 1853 to 1870. Irion was chiefly responsible for an abridged version of the church's *Evangelische Katechismus*, published in 1862 and used throughout its parishes and schools, with revisions, well into the next century. With questions and answers supported by biblical texts, it focused on the Decalogue, the Apostles' Creed, the Lord's Prayer, Baptism, and the Lord's Supper. More Lutheran than Reformed and yet unionist, Irion's work, suffused by the temper of Pietism, came to be called the "E Catechism." Young Reinhold was exposed to it at home.[5]

The bearded and learned Gustav Niebuhr, ordained in 1885, took a missionary pastorate in San Francisco, where he met and married Lydia Hosto, the daughter of a pioneer missionary and an active participant in parish work. The Niebuhr family was to become uncommonly productive of theologians, not only Reinhold but his older sister, Hulda, and younger brother, Helmut Richard, becoming influential seminary professors and authors. Reinhold later described the conditions of their life as "genteel poverty." Gustav himself became an intellectual and organizational leader in the Evangelical Synod, and members of its clergy often visited the Niebuhr parsonage in Lincoln.[6]

Among Gustav's scholarly contributions was a review in 1902 of Adolf von Harnack's *Das Wesen des Christentums*, the most widely read book of the most influential religious scholar of the time, translated into English as *What Is Christianity?* A professor at the University of Berlin whose lectures and seminars drew students from all over the Western world, Harnack popularized the prevailing "liberal" theology as set forth a generation earlier in Germany by Albrecht Ritschl. A dominant influence among Protestants in Europe until World War I and in America until 1930, Ritschlian theology emphasized the influence through Christ of moral values and the worth of each soul to a loving God, while disregarding the seriousness of sin, the holiness and justice of God, and the deeper meaning of the cross. It identified Christianity with the ideals of nineteenth-century Western culture and hoped to realize the kingdom of God in social progress. Gustav Niebuhr's review of Harnack's book, while appreciative, was not entirely favorable. "Harnack's Christ," he wrote, ". . . is for us too small, too limited"; his interpretation failed to see "the prophetically preparatory and almighty fulfilling hand of God." Reinhold—who in his mature years attacked the optimism of Harnack and Ritschl—later recalled that his father "introduced his sons and daughter to the thought of Harnack without fully sharing the liberal convictions of that theologian."[7]

Gustav studied the Bible daily in its original languages, and tutored Reinhold in Greek. His personal library included a multivolume set of

Luther's *Werke*, which Reinhold later inherited and used. Like Luther, the elder Niebuhr believed that the Bible as the Word of God is understood in the personal experience of grace, manifested in good works. The son must have been impressed by his father's social interests, inspired by the Pietist tradition of *Innere Mission*, which included the founding of asylums for epileptics and the retarded, still in service as the Emmaus Homes in and near St. Charles, Missouri, and the management of a deaconess hospital for the poor owned by St. John's in Lincoln. An admirer of Theodore Roosevelt, Gustav believed in public responsibility in such areas as child labor law. In an article published in 1913, he declared that Jesus' parables of the salt and the leaven pointed to exercising "a direct and wholesome influence on the human race," and that "this includes, most assuredly, all social and political conditions."[8]

On the wall behind the pulpit of St. John's Evangelical Church in Lincoln, where Gustav was pastor, were the words *Gott mit uns* (God with us), and above on the alcove in which altar and pulpit were set, *Ehre sei Gott in der Höhe* (Glory to God in the highest). There Reinhold was confirmed, his father officiating, on Palm Sunday, 1906. German was the language of services and of the Niebuhr home in the parsonage next door—a large, porch-lined frame house on Fifth Street. In the town where Reinhold grew up, however, English was spoken at the Chautauqua events he attended each summer, as it was in the public school. His studies as a freshman at Lincoln High School included English, Latin, civics, algebra, and zoology. His grades were in the 90's, the highest in Latin, with averages of 95 and 97.[9]

ELMHURST, EDEN, AND YALE

Intending to follow in his father's footsteps, Reinhold applied at age fifteen for admission to the Evangelical Synod's *Pro-Seminar*, a preparatory school in Elmhurst, Illinois, for young men intending to go on to seminary or to teach in the denomination's elementary schools. As part of the application procedure, he submitted a brief autobiography, handwritten in German and translated here:[10]

> I was born on June 21, 1892, in Wright City, Missouri, as the fourth child of my parents. When I was 2½ years old, we moved to St. Charles, Missouri, and there I attended the German school for three years. When I was 10 years old, we moved to Lincoln, Illinois, where we are living now. For the past five years I have been attending the free school and have passed the first year of high school. I was permitted, while I was in the 8th grade, to

take two high school subjects, so that I now have slightly more than one year of high school education. Last year I was confirmed in St. John's Church. My confirmation motto reads: "I have loved you with an everlasting love; therefore I have continued my faithfulness to you." Three times I have had private confirmation instruction, for two years with my brothers and sister, and the last year alone.

Reinhold Niebuhr

The motto quoted above, assigned by Gustav as pastor, is Jeremiah 31:3. Reinhold also submitted, as required by the school, this letter to its director, Daniel Irion, the son of Andreas Irion:

Lincoln, Ill. June 17, 1907
Rev. D. Irion, D.D.   Elmhurst, Ill.
Dear Director:
   Since it has always been my wish to become a pastor, I herewith request admission to the Evangelical Pro-Seminar. I promise that I will obediently follow all instructions and requirements of the institution. In the hope that I will find acceptance, and that I may become a tool of the Lord, I remain your devoted

Reinhold Niebuhr

Founded in 1871 in a west Chicago suburb, the school, now Elmhurst College, then offered a curriculum including nearly all elements of a German *Gymnasium*. A large, towered brick building, now called Old Main, dominated the parklike grounds, and some one hundred fifty young men from various parts of the country studied under a faculty of eight during Niebuhr's three years there, from 1907 to 1910. By his final year, Elmhurst was accredited with standing somewhat above high school level. The prescribed course of study, taught in German but involving some work in English, included three years each of religion, Greek, Latin, German, English, history, science, and mathematics.[11]

The content of young Niebuhr's studies is described vividly in Elmhurst's *Jahrbuch*, the school's annual catalog. His religion classes, taught by Irion—who headed the institution from 1887 to 1919—focused on the Bible and the *Evangelische Katechismus*. His study of Greek progressed through selections from Homer's *Odyssey* and Plato's *Apology* to New Testament Greek, and finally the reading of Mark's Gospel with Irion. Latin classes read selections from Cicero, Sallust, Livy, and Virgil. English classes did theme writing and read, among other literature, dramas of Shakespeare, selections from Milton and Addison, Burke's *Speech on Conciliation with America*, and Lowell's *Vision of Sir Launfal*. Reinhold's history classes did not devote much time to American history but, using Weber's

Weltgeschichte, focused in two years on the Middle Ages, the Reformation, Stuart and Cromwellian England, France in the age of Louis XIV ("Ludwig XIV" in Elmhurst's catalog), the French Revolution and Napoleon, the rise of Prussia, and Germany under the Kaiser. Other studies included zoology, botany, physics, advanced algebra, and geometry. Niebuhr also participated in sports and, a performer since boyhood, took part in a Shakespearean drama.[12]

Such a program was typical of preparatory schools then, but Elmhurst's curriculum was unusual in its emphasis on German language and literature, through which it sought to impart a grasp of Germany's rich cultural heritage and a thorough knowledge of a language important for theological study. Reinhold's classes, progressing from grammar to literary works, were taught by Professor Hermann Brodt. They studied medieval German folk songs and love poems, read selections from Luther and from Klopstock's *Messias*, and studied Grimmelshausen's *Simplicissimus* and Lessing's *Minna von Barnhelm*. Then, during his senior year, they studied literary history in the age of Goethe and Schiller, reading such works as Goethe's *Hermann und Dorothea* and *Götz von Berlinchingen* and Schiller's *Wilhelm Tell* and *Die Braut von Messina;* and went on to study the Romantics, poets of the Wars of Liberation, dramatists of 1815–30, the Swabian poets, and Platen, Chamisso, Rückert, and Heine.[13]

As an enclave of German-American culture, Elmhurst had limitations for the son of an immigrant who aspired, as Niebuhr did a few years later, to study at Yale. There he felt his weakness in English and lack of a college experience such as others had. But Elmhurst did provide him with foundations for further study and prepared him in languages, especially German, crucial to his later achievements as he read, before English translations became available, works of Troeltsch, Tillich, Brunner, and Kierkegaard (whose works were translated from Danish into German well before their translation into English). After graduating from Elmhurst, Niebuhr a decade later urged its transformation into a college and assisted a fund drive for a new library. His brother H. Richard, who also attended the institution, became president of Elmhurst College from 1924 to 1927 and raised its standards to a four-year liberal arts program. A later Elmhurst president, Robert C. Stanger, once a music teacher of Reinhold Niebuhr, remembered him well: "A brilliant student, Reinhold graduated as valedictorian of the Class of 1910. He was a very energetic and effervescent type of person."[14]

In the fall of 1910 Reinhold entered the Evangelical Synod's seminary in the north St. Louis suburb of Wellston. Then known as Eden College, so named because of its proximity to Eden station on the Wabash Railroad, it had relocated from the remote river town where Andreas Irion had taught a half-century earlier. Niebuhr's three years at Eden were significant because of the lasting influence of his favorite professor, Samuel D. Press. An American-born son of South German Pietists, Press had studied at Elmhurst and Eden, held pastorates in Texas, and studied at Berlin in 1902 under famous scholars, including Hermann Gunkel, Reinhold Seeberg, and Harnack. "Harnack's theology," he later wrote, "never became mine, but I cherished the man and his great scholarly mind throughout my life." Eden's first faculty member to hold classes in English, Press taught there for decades, later becoming president of the seminary, which subsequently named after him its main building on its present site in the St. Louis suburb of Webster Groves.[15]

As a student at Eden, Reinhold, who regarded Press as his "Mark Hopkins," took his course described in the catalog as "Old Testament Exegesis according to the Hebrew text: The Book of Amos, Two hours a week in the first semester and one in the second semester, the other being devoted to a study of modern sociological problems." As implied, it presupposed ability to read Hebrew, which Niebuhr studied at Eden, and related the prophet's message to current conditions. He also took Press's course in the Epistle to the Romans, a curricular emphasis at Eden reflecting the Pauline piety of the Evangelical Synod which distinguished it from the thoroughgoing theological liberalism of the age. Among other courses taught by Press and taken by Reinhold were "American Theology," focusing on Jonathan Edwards and the Calvinist tradition; and "Social Service"—inspired by Press's study in Germany of *Innere Mission*—involving students, including Reinhold, in seeking the best location for a new settlement house, which became the Caroline Mission in St. Louis.[16]

Niebuhr later described Press as "the revered teacher of many of us," who combined "rigorous biblical scholarship" with "vital evangelical piety," and commented that "he first made both the prophet Amos and the apostle Paul a real influence in my religious life." Returning to Eden Theological Seminary on February 19, 1941, for a dinner honoring Dr. Press on the occasion of his retirement, Niebuhr—whose first volume of Gifford Lectures was about to appear—was the featured speaker. "He always took the Bible seriously," Niebuhr said of his former teacher, "but not absolutely literally the way some Biblicists take it and kill the spirit by the letter." He further stated, "I remember his Amos class better than any other course," adding that "all theology really begins with Amos." Press, he went on to say, steered a path between the error of reducing the gospel to a body of moral teaching and the more extreme type of orthodox reaction against that error: "There never was a question in his mind about any contradiction between Christ and Paul—between the Gospel and the Epistles." Confessing that he had himself been "tinctured" by the prevalent religious moralism that Press avoided, Niebuhr said in his speech that evening:

> I will admit contritely that it took me years to discover what these things meant, and I didn't discover them first of all by studying Martin Luther, not even by studying St. Paul, but first by discovering that the simple explanations I had about life and the meaning of the Gospel ... broke down.[17]

Niebuhr's first published piece, entitled "The Attitude of the Church Toward Present Moral Evils," appeared during his first year at Eden in the seminary's student journal, the *Keryx*. "To make more men Christian and all Christians truer," wrote the youthful Reinhold, was the only way to develop temperance, charity, and scruples, and so curb "dishonesty in business, the ever widening breach between rich and poor, and above all the curse of the saloon." An older Niebuhr saw more deeply and differently into moral problems, but it was an earnest and well-written essay. During his middle year Reinhold led Eden successfully in a student debate with Concordia, the neighboring seminary of the Missouri Synod Lutherans, on arbitration as a method of settling international disputes. In his senior year he became editor of the *Keryx*. Then in April of 1913, toward the end of the academic year, Gustav Niebuhr died unexpectedly of a diabetes attack, and Reinhold—undoubtedly stunned—went home for the funeral and helped temporarily at the parish in Lincoln. Two months later, at the age of twenty-one, he graduated from Eden as valedictorian and was ordained into the ministry of the Evangelical Synod.[18]

Postponing appointment to a pastorate, Niebuhr, encouraged by Press, made plans for advanced study at Yale Divinity School, which admitted him with a scholarship. Before enrolling, however, he spent the summer of 1913 filling the vacancy, resulting from his father's death, at St. John's. At a service on August 17 he preached a sermon taking as its text Matthew 10:39: "He that findeth his life shall lose it, and he that loseth his life for my sake shall find it." He began by noting, as he often did years later, its expression of the paradox that self-sacrifice leads, as an unintended consequence, to self-realization; but then went on to apply the gospel in a way he later regarded as simplistic. "The world," he declared, "owes every man who is industrious, even if he can only work with his hands, a decent living. Not half the working men are getting it." The problem, he continued, must be solved by love: "There can never be a real solution" unless capitalists "voluntarily release some of their fat profits" to employees. Thus, "our text does not only solve the personal but the social problem." Also during that summer at home, Reinhold read, as he prepared to leave for Yale, the book his father had reviewed, Harnack's *What Is Christianity?*[19]

Arriving in New Haven and enrolling at Yale in September of 1913, Niebuhr was thrilled by the great academic center in the East. Within days he wrote Professor Press, who took a fatherly interest in him after Gustav Niebuhr's sudden death, "I am certainly delighted with the place and do not think I could have found a better place for my purpose." His letter continued, "The old New England religious life dominates the university." Dean Charles Reynolds Brown of the Divinity School, he wrote, "complimented the thorough work that is done in Eden according to the catalog, which he examined. He thinks if it lacks in any department it is philosophy, and thinks I am doing well to specialize there." The dean, he went on to explain, credited his Eden studies heavily toward B.D. candidacy at Yale, so that he could complete the degree in nine months. In the same letter and another in October, Niebuhr wrote that his courses, taken in the Graduate School as well as the Divinity School, required "an immense amount of reading" and included philosophy of religion with Douglas Clyde Macintosh, New Testament theology with Frank C. Porter, the Johannine writings with Benjamin Bacon, history of philosophy with Charles Bakewell, and history of ethics with Ilias Hershey Sneath. "The hardest course," he added, "is that in Epistemology, but it is very interesting." He also grew homesick: "In spite of the nice way I have been received, I feel lonely sometimes."[20]

In November, Niebuhr again wrote Press: "Yale is indeed very liberal. Although there is no special unity in the theology of the different professors, I believe you could call the general tendency of their theology akin to Ritschlianism. . . . Practically every one has studied under Harnack in Germany." The Social Gospel, as developed in America by Walter Rauschenbusch, himself influenced by the nineteenth-century legacy of Ritschl, was then current in seminaries such as Yale, but seems to have made no impression on Niebuhr, who made no mention of Rauschenbusch in any of his letters to Press.[21]

In the spring of 1914 Niebuhr wrote his B.D. thesis, under Macintosh's supervision, on "The Validity and Certainty of Religious Knowledge." In preparation he read some fifty books, including three volumes of William

James, which he purchased and kept for the rest of his life: *The Varieties of Religious Experience, The Will to Believe,* and *Pragmatism.* His thesis began by observing that science and biblical scholarship had made some older concepts of revelation and authority no longer tenable. It went on to explore such options as Comtian positivism and Hegelian idealism, and concluded that the one failed to recognize moral purpose in the universe, while the other tended to pantheism and had no room for human freedom: "The God of the Absolute hardly makes religious experience more possible than the worst naturalism." A more satisfactory philosophy, the thesis continued, was that of James, whose revolt against metaphysical determinism allowed no "moral holiday" and whose defense of "the will to believe" acknowledged personal values as more true than anything else in existence. The American philosopher, furthermore, left room for religious faith: "James' reason for believing in the transcendent God of religion" was "his belief that religious experience established the reality of such a God," while at the same time he rejected as "overbelief" the notion "that God is in control of all the events of time." Niebuhr's thesis, touching on such different thinkers as Aquinas, Kant, and Bergson, exhibited a special affinity for James. It concluded that religious ideas "are based upon what man believes to be necessary for the existence of personality in the universe," and that the experience of "God in our hearts" is the "supreme reason for certainty" of religious truth. Apart from its central theme, the thesis reveals the impression that James's *Pragmatism* made upon him. Stating that "we may test the truth of ideas by the manner in which they 'work,' " Reinhold went on to say: "Pragmatism at its best . . . does not give us a new conception of truth. It provides us only with a new method of obtaining it or, more correctly, explains a very old method."[22]

Besides studies, Niebuhr found time to attend special lectures, including one by Hastings Rashdall of Oxford and a series on German literature by an exchange professor. He was often called upon to help others with German books not yet translated, and earned needed funds by preaching in a nearby church. Having completed his B.D., he chose to return to Yale in the fall of 1914 for another year. During the intervening summer, the outbreak of war shattered a century of peace in Europe and shocked some of Harnack's own theological students into reconsidering the confident assumptions of moral progress they had learned from him. But the European war hardly shook the sunny temper of American culture or the optimistic theology and philosophy of the Yale faculty. Since Niebuhr lacked a college degree, having grown up in a German-American culture that sent him to Elmhurst, Dean Wilbur Cross of the Graduate School proposed to give him an M.A. degree if he maintained straight A's during his second year. His courses included one titled Platonic Idealism with Bakewell, religion and contemporary philosophy with Macintosh, Old Testament theology with Bacon, and church history with Williston Walker, his most famous professor at Yale.[23]

Niebuhr wrote his master's thesis, again under Macintosh, on "The Contribution of Christianity to the Doctrine of Immortality," reading a pile of books on the subject. After a preliminary inquiry into the New Testament account of Christ's resurrection, in which he concluded that the appearances of the risen Lord were "objective though not corporeal," Niebuhr in his thesis turned to the question of how Christianity added to, or modified, existing beliefs about immortality. First he traced Jewish ideas, beginning with the early notion of a shadowy existence in Sheol, continuing in the psalmist's affirmation of justice after death, and later tending toward more individualistic and otherworldly accents in apocalyptic literature. Then he surveyed Greek concepts, from the notion of a gloomy afterlife in Hades, through the rise of religious cults emphasizing moral rewards and punishments, to Plato and Aristotle's view of the soul or intellect as inherently immortal. He noted as a Christian inheritance the Hebraic view of body and soul as a unity, in contrast to the Greek distinction between them. Christianity, Niebuhr maintained, went beyond the best Greek thought in developing the Hebraic appreciation of individuality in this life and the next. Jesus, comparing God to a shepherd caring for one lost sheep, "revealed the value of personality more fully than ever before by his emphasis on the individual in whom the real richness of personality dwells." Paul "retained the Jewish emphasis on individuality in the after life by his belief that the body would be resurrected in some form, though not in the flesh." The latter point, a chief conclusion of his thesis, appeared in Niebuhr's mature works, but in a deeper theological context. His master's thesis elsewhere reflected the extent to which Ritschlian theology had entered his thought, for in it he alluded to "the life and death of Christ" in terms of its "moral effect upon mankind," and asserted that "God's mercy, existing in and through his justice, is so reasonable and believable" as not to require revelation through the cross. Although Niebuhr did not quite maintain the dean's special standard, continuing the B+ average of his first year, Yale was sufficiently impressed to confer a master's degree on him in June of 1915.[24]

Though invited to pursue a doctorate at Yale, Niebuhr instead took a pastorate. This he did because of an obligation as an ordinand of his denomination, because of financial responsibility for his widowed mother, and because, as he later put it, "epistemology bored me . . . and frankly the other side of me came out: I desired relevance rather than scholarship." His experience at Yale was broadening, especially in exposing him in some depth to the field of philosophy and in impressing him with the thought of James. It also instilled in him the habit of reading original sources. "This constant demand for original research in the sources themselves," he wrote in 1914, ". . . was rather new to me. In the course of a year one is required to wade through an endless number of books and this first-hand knowledge of prominent writers is more educative than any of the classroom work." At Yale, too, he imbibed much of Ritschlian theology. Commenting years later on his subsequent rejection of it, Niebuhr remarked, "I was up against an industrial city, and I saw that human nature was quite different than I had learned at Yale Divinity School." The city was Detroit, where the Home Mission Board of the German Evangelical Synod assigned him to a newly organized parish.[25]

BETHEL'S PASTOR: EARLY YEARS

In August of 1915, at the age of twenty-three, Niebuhr arrived at Bethel Evangelical Church, on what was then the northwest edge of Detroit, to begin a pastorate that lasted for thirteen years and was crucial in the development of his mature thought. "In my parish duties," he commented long afterward, "I found that the simple idealism" of prevailing liberal theology "was as irrelevant to the crises of personal life as it was to the complex social issues of an industrial city." From the beginning he kept a diary, later published in part as *Leaves from the Notebook of a Tamed Cynic*, in which he recorded the candid and perceptive observations of a maturing young pastor. His mother, Lydia, who had remained in Lincoln, joined him in Detroit, where she not only kept house for him but supervised the Sunday school and parish organizational activities. Thus she, as Niebuhr stated toward the end of his ministry there, "shared with me the work of a Christian pastorate." Her help freed him for part-time endeavors, in writing and preaching, beyond Bethel Church.[26]

The parish, which maintained a small brick church at Linwood and Lothrop Avenues, had sixty-five members when Niebuhr came there. It was one of thirteen hundred congregations of the Evangelical Synod, whose seventy-fifth anniversary on October 15, 1915, was the occasion for one of the young pastor's first sermons. Preaching twice that day, in German and in English, Niebuhr took as his text John 17:21, "That they all may be one," his denomination's motto. Recalling the Synod's roots in the union of Lutheran and Reformed churches decreed by the king of Prussia nearly a century earlier, he went on to emphasize that "truth is many-sided, even Christian truth." Protestant differences were ones of emphasis: "The Calvinist emphasizes the sovereignty of God and the Methodist the freedom of man. The Reformed makes the sermon the central force of the worship and the Lutheran the sacrament. . . . We ought to be tolerant with people who see the truth a little differently than we do and who worship with slightly different forms."[27]

Niebuhr quickly discovered that the scholarly standards and progressive social interests of mentors such as his father and Samuel Press were not universally shared in his denomination, and wrote Press unhappily about the "standpattism of some sections of our church." His analysis of the problem appeared in his first nationally published magazine article, "The Failure of German-Americanism," in 1916. America's sympathy with the Allies in the war against Germany, he observed, resulted in tension with its German-American population, whose characteristics accordingly invited examination. Although German immigrants and their descendants had fought loyally in earlier wars, produced such a statesman as Carl Schurz, and contributed to economic development, they tended on the whole, Niebuhr held, to provincialism and indifference to national problems. The typical German-American, unlike many fellow citizens, did not join in efforts to reform relations between capital and labor, "in spite of the fact that he comes from a country that has been a clinic for the world in the methods of humanizing industry." Similarly in religion, he was slow to accept modern scholarship. Perhaps, suggested Niebuhr, this situation arose from the fact that so many German immigrants were peasants unaffected by the universities of their fatherland, and came to America before modern Germany was born. The German-American failure consisted in an attempt "to perpetuate customs and ideals long since discarded in Germany itself."[28]

So Niebuhr saw the limitations of German-American culture while still adjusting to his new parish responsibilities. Several months later, when the United States entered the war on the side of Britain and its allies, his denomination's ties with Germany involved it in conflicting loyalties between the older, German-born generation and the more Americanized generation to which he belonged. The young Detroit pastor was asked to head a commission set up by the Evangelical Synod to maintain contacts with its men in military service. This he agreed to do, distributing materials to soldiers from his office at Bethel and visiting army camps.

The work made Niebuhr feel that he should resign the job and become an army chaplain—a course from which he was dissuaded only by appeals from the Synod's president, John Baltzer. Caught up in the hopes for a better world as the goal of American intervention, he wrote in his diary early in 1918, "I think that if Wilson's aims are realized the war will serve a good purpose." In a message to his Synod's clergy, he gave as his view that "as wars go, there has never been one . . . that was as full of purpose to use the sacrifices of war for its final abolition." He subsequently regretted that, in reacting against German-American criticism of the United States, "I was more than ordinarily patriotic during the war." Furthermore, he soon shared in the disillusionment with the Versailles Treaty, holding that Wilson at Paris trusted too much in words while the "sly Clemenceau . . . helped by Mr. Lloyd George" undermined his aims by writing into the terms of peace large reparations demanded from Germany.[29]

Yet the distant battlefields in Europe and their immediate aftermath had no great impact on him. More important in shaping his mind then was his experience as a pastor facing, in his words, "human problems on all levels of weal and woe." An experience he often recalled was his visits to two dying old ladies, one of whom was "in a constant hysteria of fear and resentment" over her illness, while the other faced death serenely: "I stood weekly at her bedside while she told me what passages of Scripture, what Psalms and what prayers to read to her; most of them expressed gratitude for all the mercies of God which she had received in life." This experience, early in his ministry, brought to his mind Matthew 24:41: "Two women shall be grinding at the mill; the one shall be taken, and the other left." It led him to perceive that, as he later stated, "the Church is a curiously mixed body consisting of those who have never been shaken in their self-esteem and self-righteousness . . . and of the true Christians who live by 'a broken spirit and a contrite heart.' Whether we belong to this latter group, which makes up the true but invisible Church, no one but God can know."[30]

Niebuhr's pastoral responsibilities involved him not only in visiting the sick but also in concern for the parish's Sunday school, in which he sometimes taught a class of youth. His sister, Hulda, then pursuing studies at Boston University and later a noted author of books for Sunday schools, prepared materials for Bethel. Early in his ministry, Niebuhr pointed out in a sermon that the Sunday school is a uniquely American development, stressed its importance in a society so diverse that public schools cannot undertake religious instruction as in more homogeneous European nations, and affirmed his denomination's commitment to a catechetical and educational approach to Christian nurture. Addressing Sunday school teachers of his denomination in 1917 and again in 1919, he spoke of the Bible as "our text book" and of the need to use with it "some extra-Biblical material," cautioning against a didactic approach: "It is easy to tell a child something, but it requires pedagogical talent to help it discover the truth." Besides teaching young people at Bethel, he also served as scoutmaster for a troop of boy scouts.[31]

Midway through Niebuhr's pastorate, the parish built a much larger church nearby—an English Gothic edifice of red bricks and limestone trim, with a large, pointed window in front and a belfry to its right—on the south side of West Grand Boulevard near Linwood, in a fashionable neighborhood. Completed early in 1922, it had an interior of oak and plaster, with a pew capacity of 750 and a carved center-front pulpit—behind which a raised-tile reredos, above the organ loft in the chancel, depicted Jesus attended by Mary and Martha. Light flooded into the nave through the front window in the gallery above the narthex. In the west wing was the pastor's study, and in back and below were classrooms and other facilities. The growing congregation—mostly middle class but including auto workers and two millionaires—drew members from beyond its original core of German-Americans, and English completely replaced German in its services. Bethel Evangelical Church grew tenfold, to 656 members, during his thirteen years there, while Detroit itself, burgeoning with the expanding automobile industry, tripled in population during the same period. Niebuhr was, as he put it retrospectively, "trying to be helpful in fashioning a 'community of grace' in the barren anonymity of a large city."[32]

THE HARD REALITIES OF EUROPE AND DETROIT

Detroit exposed Bethel's pastor to the problem of industrial justice addressed by the Social Gospel in the decades before World War I. Niebuhr's interest in this area began to focus in 1920, when he wrote in a nationally published article:

> The changes that are necessary in our economic order will require the sacrifice of many privileges and rights on the part of the holding classes. They will make such a sacrifice willingly only if their vision is broadened and their conscience sensitized by such agencies as the church. . . . While the conversion of the individual employer and member of the holding classes

to a new social viewpoint is precisely what the world needs and the church can best accomplish, it must be emphasized that democracy in industry . . . must be granted to workers as their right and not as a gift.

The social conscience Niebuhr had acquired from his Pietist heritage became transformed to include not only charitable endeavors but promotion of legislation protecting industrial workers and their families. At first he emphasized such reform as an act of unselfishness on the part of privileged classes, without envisaging the need for pressures by workers themselves, as Washington Gladden and Walter Rauschenbusch had done in fathering the Social Gospel, the latter calling for a push by "the tramping hosts of labor."[33]

As the reform spirit of Progressive politics yielded to the complacent "normalcy" of the 1920s, the Social Gospel lost direction as well as influence, surviving only among some clergy, settlement workers, and denominational bureaucrats. Its remnant in Detroit was led by Charles D. Williams, bishop of the Episcopal Diocese of Michigan since 1906, with whom Niebuhr became associated in the early 1920s. A mentor to Bethel's pastor, the bishop a few years earlier had written a book entitled *The Christian Ministry and Social Problems*, dedicated "to Walter Rauschenbusch . . . by one who has found in the writings of that man of God a chief source of inspiration in preaching the Gospel of the Kingdom." Like Rauschenbusch, Williams emphasized Jesus' concern for righteousness on earth, and he held that charity should not be a substitute for justice. In sermons, he sought to arouse sensitivity to social and economic conditions and a passion for justice, without advocating specific methods of reform on which people may sincerely disagree. Outside the pulpit, he took stands on labor issues that made him unpopular with the Detroit establishment. Williams, as Niebuhr later recalled, "dared to insist that workers required collective bargaining in a city in which all the new industrialists were insistent that the future of the auto industry required the kind of autocracy which had grown up with the rising industry." In a eulogy after the Episcopal leader's death in 1923, Bethel's pastor stated:

The most outstanding characteristic of Bishop Williams' life was his utter fearlessness. Had he been without this virtue, he could never have insisted so relentlessly upon the social implications of Christ's gospel. . . . Nowhere has the prophet of a social gospel a more difficult time than in America. The vast wealth of our nation has inclined our people to complacency and has obscured for a time the inequalities and iniquities which characterize our modern industrial civilization.

The late bishop, he concluded, was "a prophet" who challenged that complacency.[34] About this time, it appears, Niebuhr came to share Williams's appreciation of Rauschenbusch, buying and marking current editions of his *Christianity and the Social Crisis*, which had created a stir when it first appeared in 1907, and *A Theology for the Social Gospel*, Rauschenbusch's final book of ten years later.

The indifference of most middle-class Americans to the injustices of industrial capitalism became a central concern of Niebuhr. He turned to the subject now and again in the *Christian Century*, which became in the editorial hands of Charles Clayton Morrison the chief organ of liberal American Protestantism in the 1920s and 1930s. In his first signed piece for that journal in 1922, Niebuhr pointed out that, while national leaders of the Protestant churches increasingly accepted labor's right to strike, most of their members opposed it, for "middle classes enjoy the comforts which the high productivity of modern industry secures for them" and "blame not the entrenched but the attacking party for the conflict which disturbs their comfort." As long as the possessing classes rule economic and industrial life as they do, he went on to say, "labor will not only be provoked to use the weapon of the strike but will be compelled to avail itself of its power to equalize its unequal struggle with capital." His emphasis through the mid-1920s, however, was less on labor organization than on sensitizing American middle classes to the realities and complexities of modern industrial society—a characteristic accent of the Social Gospel. As editor of the *Christian Century*, Morrison encouraged Niebuhr to write pieces regularly for its pages. "Just send them in," he wrote early in 1923, "and as many as possible, and as often as possible. You have the right touch."[35]

While Detroit exposed Niebuhr to industrial problems, his first trip to Europe—with an American study group organized by Sherwood Eddy in the summer of 1923—enlarged his understanding of world affairs, especially the tangled problem of German reparations and Allied war debts. Although America enjoyed prosperity during the Harding and Coolidge years, Germany's Weimar Republic, born in the defeat of the Kaiser's empire, suffered economically under pressure to pay reparations. France, especially, had insisted on reparations at Versailles, and occupied the Ruhr after Germany declared its inability to fulfill payments. In the industrial cities of Essen and Düsseldorf, Niebuhr saw the abusive treatment of Germans by French forces. Returning to Germany a year later with the same group, he found conditions improved as a result of the Dawes Plan, which scaled down reparations, provided loans to Germany, and secured

French evacuation of the Ruhr. Yet, as he reported in a denominational journal, the American-sponsored adjustment of treaty terms still demanded thirty-three billion dollars from Germany, placing it in "perpetual economic servitude." Conceived by bankers who had money to lend the Germans and who would benefit as the French used reparations to repay American loans, it showed that "self-interest is the mainspring of our action."[36]

The tours abroad, with stops in Britain as well as Germany, enriched Niebuhr's sense of conditions and traditions in those countries. He saw the Krupp steelworks in Essen, attended services at the great Catholic cathedral in Cologne and at Lutheran churches elsewhere in Germany, visited relatives on his ancestral estate in Lippe-Detmold, met William Temple at a labor gathering in Oxford, and visited York Minster and its environs. In articles appearing in the *Atlantic Monthly* as well as the *Christian Century*, he related and reflected on what he had observed. Germany's politics, he explained, involved "a triangular conflict" among nationalists, industrialists, and socialists. The nationalists were mostly rural traditionalists who wished to restore Prussian authoritarianism and blamed the unpopular peace terms on the government; the industrialists governed in coalition with moderate Catholic and middle-class parties committed to republicanism and peace under Stresemann's leadership; and the socialists supported those goals but were alienated from the rest of the nation by traditional Lutheran indifference to injustice suffered by industrial workers. The labor movement in Germany, he pointed out, was overwhelmingly Marxist, its millions of members "out of the church and hostile to it"; only one sixth of trade unionists were professedly Christian, nearly all of them Rhineland Catholics. He also noted, in the mid-1920s, the emergence of "a noisy right wing" of the nationalists, which had formed its own party under Hitler and, cursing Jewish influence in German political and economic life, espoused "violent anti-Semitism." Britain, on the other hand, Niebuhr found in a much healthier condition, for Anglicanism was long sensitive to social problems, while the British Labor Party, nourished in nonconformist chapels, was free of Marxist dogmas. Americans, meanwhile, were singularly oblivious to the defects of their civilization:

> Its obvious defects are obscured by the sheer physical abundance in which we revel; and the tragic consequences of international strife . . . fail to challenge our conscience because of our geographic isolation. Nor do the more covert cultural defects of our modern life seriously disquiet the soul of a

people who are still given to the naive enjoyment of their mechanical paradise.[37]

Returning from abroad in the fall of 1924, Niebuhr was persuaded by Jane Addams to chair a large Detroit rally for La Follette's insurgent presidential candidacy. When, several months after the Coolidge landslide of that year, La Follette died, Niebuhr wrote: "We have at least the virtue of respect for integrity and burning moral zeal. That is why Senator La Follette is mourned as no ordinary senator." In 1925, while the business creed continued to prevail at the White House as well as on Main Street, Bruce Barton's *The Man Nobody Knows* appeared, portraying Jesus as a successful carpenter and expert advertiser of ideals cherished by the business community. Reviewing the book, Niebuhr declared, "There is something almost pathetic in the naive delight of the author in his discovery of a certain kinship between Jesus' ideals of service and the sadly diluted idealism of modern business enterprise."[38]

It was the heyday of Henry Ford, who became a folk hero as his Model T rolled off the assembly lines in Detroit and put the nation on wheels. Less visible to the public were the hardships of Ford workers and their families. After visiting the coke oven in the Rouge plant, five miles southwest of Bethel Church, Niebuhr wrote in his diary: "The heat was terrific. The men seemed weary. . . . Their sweat and their dull pain are part of the price paid for the fine cars we all run." In pieces for *Christian Century* readers in 1926 and 1927, he presented facts contradicting Ford's self-promoted image as a benevolent industrialist: his supposedly generous five dollars a day obscured assembly-line speedups that exhausted older men, retooling layoffs without pay, the absence of any pensions, the discharging of sick employees and then rehiring them at beginning wages, and the burdening of local charities with Ford workers unable to make ends meet. Among Ford's critics was Samuel Marquis, a local clergyman who wrote a book about his experiences; but Ford himself, according to Niebuhr, bought up all copies from bookshops and libraries, making it virtually unobtainable. Despite the efforts of Niebuhr and others to publicize the sufferings of Ford's workers, the public in 1927 celebrated his Model A, with its improved transmission, in the song "Henry's Made a Lady out of Lizzy." Niebuhr, aware of the consequences of the long shutdown for retooling, wrote in *Leaves*:

No one knows how many hundreds lost their homes in the period of unemployment, and how many children were taken out of school to help fill the depleted family exchequer, and how many more children lived on short rations during this period. . . . No one bothers to ask whether an industry which can maintain a cash reserve of a quarter of a billion ought not make some provision for its unemployed.

He later credited the billionaire automobile industrialist for educating him in the abuses of laissez-faire capitalism: "I cut my eyeteeth fighting Ford."[39]

Detroit in those years was an open-shop city, its business community solidly opposed to unions. When in October of 1926 the A.F.L. held its annual convention there, some churches had invited labor speakers, and William Green, president of the labor federation, was to speak at the YMCA, but the Detroit Board of Commerce brought financial pressures on the "Y" and all but a few churches to cancel the arrangements. Bethel, led by its pastor, was one that resisted. In later years Niebuhr explained to seminary classes that he allowed the labor speaker to use a basement room, reserving the pulpit for its prophetic function. In a *Christian Century* report at the time, he pointed out that the Federal Council of Churches stepped in by sending Worth M. Tippy to Detroit to protest the indignities to which Green and the federation were subjected. Actually, as he noted in retrospect, the A.F.L. was hardly capable of organizing auto workers, for it was a crafts union with no experience in mass-production industries: industrial unionism had to await the rise of the C.I.O. a decade later.[40]

Meanwhile, racial tensions developed in Detroit as the black population, augmented by migration from the South, increased eightfold during the period from the war to 1925. During the summer and fall of that year riots occurred after a black physician moved his family into a white neighborhood. The mayor responded by appointing a biracial committee on race relations, chaired by Niebuhr, which reported its recommendations based on findings of the city's research bureau. The committee's report, published in 1926 and reflecting the views of its various members as well as Niebuhr's style, emphasized housing and employment problems, calling for more civil attitudes in racially mixed neighborhoods, for banking practices favorable to home ownership by blacks, for better public sanitation and street repair in black districts, and for support of black women seeking jobs. The report also recommended more black policemen and teachers, summer camp facilities for blacks, and a new building for the Urban League. Its recommendations were moderate, conciliatory, and farsighted, but went mostly unheeded by Detroit's white community. Discussing the report in a *Christian Century* article, Niebuhr wrote that it "reveals the Negro population in this most prosperous of cities to be in a miserable state." Realtors, he pointed out, exploited blacks by selling them lots in areas without prospect for sewers or sidewalks, and bank officials restricted credit to responsible blacks on the assumption that all were as shiftless as some with whom they had dealings. "Out of such social investigations," he declared, "it is possible to draw more than one theological conclusion and one of them is that the natural virtue of man has been greatly overestimated." Niebuhr himself worked with black clergy to invest their churches' endowments in banks that would employ blacks as tellers. His involvement moved some blacks to attend services at Bethel Church.[41]

In Detroit, Niebuhr not only acquired understanding of conditions in the black ghetto and in the ununionized auto industry, but also gained an appreciation of Jewish and Catholic traditions. His work on the mayor's committee engaged him closely with one of its members, Fred Butzel, a Jewish lawyer whose intelligent civic conscience he would remember. "Through him I established contacts with the Jewish community," he recalled, "and from him I learned another aspect of American democratic life—the cooperation across religious lines." Toward the close of his Detroit years Niebuhr wrote in *Leaves:* "The more I make contact with the Jews the more I am impressed with the superior sensitiveness of the Jewish conscience in social matters." Contacts with Detroit's Catholic population, many of them Polish immigrants, prompted him to write in a *Christian Century* piece that Protestants should seek "humbly and patiently to discover what is true and good in a Christian tradition so markedly different from our own and yet so obviously vital in the lives of many people."[42]

BETHEL'S PASTOR: LATER YEARS

Niebuhr's parish by the mid-1920s had an associate pastor, needed as Bethel grew and its pastor's reputation led to out-of-town engagements. Sherwood Eddy, who had conducted the European study tours and was a national YMCA leader—offered in 1923 to pay an assistant's salary from his inherited wealth in order to free Bethel's pastor for weekday preaching in college chapels. The first to serve on Eddy's payroll at Bethel was Theodore Braun, who had roomed with Reinhold's brother Richard at Yale Divinity School and would stay at the parish in Detroit for two years. "During this time," Braun later recalled, "Reinie Niebuhr did not relinquish his responsibility for the care of the parish, but returned regularly on weekends. . . . Often he did more pastoral visiting on a weekend than I had done all week. Many individuals testified gratefully to the help he gave them in times of sorrow and distress." Niebuhr, Braun's wife Viola reminisced, "was always home on Saturday, working on his sermon for Sunday, spending the afternoon visiting the sick in homes and hospitals. He was a true pastor, very popular with youth as well as oldsters. His services were always formal and well-planned. He knew all his members by name." Children felt they were his special friends, recalled Braun: "I remember well the Sunday morning at the close of the service when Reinie was walking out the center aisle to greet people as they left the sanctuary. Suddenly the reverent hush was broken by the eager voice of a little child above the muted tones of the organ: 'Here I am, Mr. Niebuhr! Here I am!' " Often staying up late at night to write articles for the *Christian Century*, Niebuhr would be at his office early the next morning. He had, in Braun's words, "tremendous physical stamina," and "despite his wide-ranging activities, he maintained close personal relationships." Braun was followed during Niebuhr's last three years at Bethel first by Harold Pflug and then by Ralph Abele as associate pastor.[43]

Niebuhr's sermons during these years often took as their biblical text a parable of Jesus, sometimes a psalm or the book of Job or Paul's poem on love in Corinthians. Twice, in the fall of 1926 and the spring of 1928, he preached a series on the prophets, from Amos to Second Isaiah. In a sermon entitled "Tyrant Servants," with Mark 2:27 as its text, he declared that, just as the Pharisees' legalism made the Holy Day burdensome, so modern Americans' "delight in making and owning things" made industry an end in itself, a vast machine that "de-humanized the mechanic" and produced "the doubtful blessing of an automobile." His preaching in Bethel's center-front pulpit was, by all accounts, moving. Congregational prayers were printed in the Sunday bulletin, composed by him or drawing on resources such as the 139th Psalm or the Anglican Book of Common Prayer. On some occasions his brother Richard came as guest preacher. Niebuhr also developed an evening program, reaching out to people in the community who were not members of the church, with topics such as Dante, Don Quixote, social problems in Detroit, and Christianity and Judaism. This he described in *Leaves*:

> I give a short address or sermon upon a more or less controversial moral issue, or upon a perplexing religious question, and after closing the service we have a half-hour to forty-five minutes of discussion.

These "open forums," as Braun called them, drew persons from all over Detroit, and a remnant usually stayed until Niebuhr sent them home. An incident that long remained vivid to Niebuhr occurred at Bethel:

> I remember when I was a young parson, two Sunday school girls were playing under the window of my study. One said, "Let's not make too much

noise; we will disturb Mr. Niebuhr." And the other little girl said, "Who is Mr. Niebuhr?" The first child answered, "Don't you know? He is the pastor in this church. He knows all about God."

In recalling this, Niebuhr pointed out that biblical faith affirms both the hiddenness and the disclosure of God, and that, for Christians, the revelation through Christ does not completely dissolve mystery. Clergy and theologians, he added, do well not to pretend to knowing more about God than anybody can know.[44]

Although Niebuhr's preaching and writing during these years focused heavily on social wrongs, he maintained a self-critical stance. As he wrote in *Leaves:* "One who has lost his illusions about mankind and retains his illusions about himself is insufferable. Let the process of disillusionment continue until the self is included." Nor did he fail to appreciate private morals in Christian life, or the virtues of his middle-class parishioners: "The same middle classes which seem so blind to the larger problems of society have, after all, the most wholesome family life of any group in society." Again in *Leaves:* "The spiritual amenities and moral decencies which the churches help develop and preserve in the private lives of individuals are worth something for their own sake."[45]

During his pastoral years Niebuhr became close to Lynn Harold Hough, widely known for his learning and eloquence. From 1920 to 1928 Hough was minister of Central Methodist Church in downtown Detroit, a very large and beautiful edifice to which people throughout the city came to hear him preach at crowded services. He introduced Niebuhr to a monthly discussion group of clergy known as "Wranglers." As president of the Detroit Council of Churches, the eminent Methodist sided with Niebuhr in the A.F.L. affair, rebuking the Chamber of Commerce for seeking to intimidate the churches. Associated with Irving Babbitt and Paul Elmer More in the literary movement known as the New Humanism, Hough was himself the author, among other books, of *Evangelical Humanism* (1925), which Niebuhr especially appreciated for its way of joining "the light which shines from Athens and the Light which came forth from Judea." Its theme of Christianity and humanism in partnership and tension found expression in *Leaves:* "A reasonable person adjusts his moral goal somewhere between Christ and Aristotle, between an ethic of love and an ethic of moderation. I hope there is more of Christ than of Aristotle in my position. But I would not be too sure of it." Hough dedicated his next book, *Imperishable Dreams* (1926), "to my friend, Reinhold Niebuhr, in whose words and writings the younger generation has achieved an almost disconcerting sincerity and a penetrating power of analysis which searches the conscience and refuses the comfort of even the most delicate and gracious self-deception." Hough went on to become dean of Drew Theological Seminary, producing a shelf of books, and when he retired in 1947 Niebuhr stated:

> Many of us appreciated Dr. Hough's ministry the more because we had an aversion to the cheapness and vulgarity of the evangelistic preaching of the day, and wondered whether any other kind of preaching could hold or influence any large number of people. . . . His sermons were always directed to real issues, personal and social. But they brought to bear upon them the wisdom of the Christian ages, and constantly related the insights of the non-Christian classics to Christian faith as well.

He recalled that "it was a sermon on St. Augustine by Dr. Hough which sent me back to a more careful study of this, probably the greatest, Christian theologian of the ages, a study which has remained rewarding through all the years." A reference in Niebuhr's diary dates that sermon in 1926; a year later, mention of Augustine's "elaborate theological structure" appeared in his first book. He used the Marcus Dods translation of *The City of God*, returning to it with deeper comprehension years after Hough had first inspired him to read it.[46]

Niebuhr's heavier reading during his Detroit years included Ernst Troeltsch's *Die Soziallehren der christlichen Kirchen und Gruppen*, which later appeared in English as *The Social Teaching of the Christian Churches*. Reinhold shared an interest in that early-twentieth-century scholar's work with his brother Richard, who wrote his dissertation at Yale in 1924 on Troeltsch's philosophy of religion. It was Troeltsch's presentation of Max Weber's view of the relationship of Protestantism to capitalism that prompted Niebuhr to read the latter's as yet untranslated essay "Die protestantische Ethik und der Geist des Kapitalismus," which had stirred controversy in Europe with its thesis that Calvinism had generated the spirit of capitalism. At first impressed by its plausibility, Niebuhr by 1926 accepted R. H. Tawney's critique and modification of the Weber thesis in *Religion and the Rise of Capitalism*. Tawney, he wrote in reviewing the book, proved that the early Protestant Reformers had no conscious intention of creating the secular forces of modern capitalism:

> So strenuous in fact were Calvin and his associates in reproving the avarice and greed of the new commercial classes that . . . Beza, Calvin's associate, was accused of stirring up class hatred against the rich. Yet Calvin did amend the canonical prohibition against interest and faced the new complexities of economic life by permitting moderate interest charges. . . . Even Puritan-

ism, which derived from Calvinism, cannot be accused of easy connivance with the sins of a new commercialism, as the records of our own New England colonies prove. . . . The fact is that the Reformation only hastened processes in the economic and social life of Europe which antedate the Reformation by a century.

Niebuhr also found time, amidst pastoral duties and preaching on the college circuit, to read such other recent books as Lynn Thorndike's *A Short History of Civilization*, Oswald Spengler's *Der Untergang des Abendlandes* (before its translation as *The Decline of the West*), Alfred North Whitehead's *Science and the Modern World*, and Miguel de Unamuno's *Tragic Sense of Life*.[47]

Niebuhr's own mind was filled with unresolved tensions, his early idealism colliding with experience, as he wrote his first book, published late in 1927 under the title *Does Civilization Need Religion?* Essentially a statement of the Social Gospel, grounded in the still dominant Ritschlian theology of the American Protestant milieu in the 1920s, it called for a fusion of religious goodwill and reason to solve urgent problems of modern civilization—a strategy Niebuhr five years later criticized as inadequate in *Moral Man and Immoral Society*. "The task of making complex group relations ethical," he wrote in this early volume, "belongs primarily to religion and education" rather than to statecraft; unruly group behavior "can be subdued only by the most astute intelligence united with a high moral passion." The social ethic set forth in its pages rested on the liberal theology that Niebuhr as a young man had brought to Detroit from Yale Divinity School. "The significance of Jesus for the religious life of the Western world," he wrote, "is due to his attainment and incarnation of a spiritual and moral ideal" not to be compromised in human social existence; in the religion of Jesus "the appropriation of divine grace is a necessary part of the moral adventure," but in Paul's religion "it is separated from the moral enterprise and easily becomes a substitute for it." The assumed tension between Jesus and Paul, the view of Jesus as moral exemplar, the reliance on morally robust religion and educated intelligence to improve society—these were characteristic of the legacy of Ritschl and Harnack in early twentieth-century Protestant liberalism. Yet in this same book were other passages revealing cracks in the optimistic religious moralism it expressed, pointing toward Niebuhr's later Christian realism. Human beings, he wrote on one of its pages, "are never as good as their ideals." The modern churches, he stated on another page, "give themselves to the pleasant hope that time and natural progress will bring inevitable triumph to every virtuous enterprise." Elsewhere in the volume

Niebuhr pointed out "the brutalities of the economic conflict, the disillusioning realities of international relations, the monstrous avarice of nations, and the arrogance of races." It is easier, he observed, "to act as an ethical individual in a comparatively simple social group, such as the family, than in a very large and complex social group." Selfish economic groups, he perceived, "are not inclined to abridge their power if someone does not challenge their right to hold it." Despite such realistic notes, the book closed by emphasizing a strategy for social redemption through "religiously inspired moral idealism."[48]

A decade later, while preparing his Gifford Lectures, Niebuhr wrote retrospectively in a *Christian Century* piece that his first book contained "almost all the theological windmills against which today I tilt my sword." Despite its faults, *Does Civilization Need Religion?* was a notable exception to the sanguine temper of American religion in the 1920s. Niebuhr's comment on one page that religion in this country had "evolved a sentimental over-estimate of human virtue" caught the attention of Bernard Iddings Bell, a prominent Episcopal clergyman and educator, then president of St. Stephens (now Bard) College. "This man," Bell wrote in *Saturday Review*, "seems to know more than most parsons do about the twentieth century." He found Niebuhr's book "a pleasant relief in a flood of volumes about religion almost all of which are either sentimental or deadly dull." Within a few years, nevertheless, Reinhold Niebuhr moved well beyond positions taken in that book, and was happy to see it go out of print.[49]

In the spring of 1928 Niebuhr, by then widely known as a journalist and preacher, decided to resign his pastorate in order to accept a position, beginning in the fall of that year, on the faculty of Union Theological Seminary in New York. Already a distinguished center of Protestant scholarship, Union sought, under the leadership of Henry Sloane Coffin as president since 1926, to give more emphasis to preparing young men for the clergy. Through Sherwood Eddy, Niebuhr came to Coffin's attention as an experienced pastor whose mind and talents would be an asset to the seminary. Certain faculty apparently objected that Niebuhr lacked a doctorate, but a majority joined Coffin in support of the appointment, recognizing the need for the kind of educated and experienced perspective that he had to offer. While Niebuhr appreciated the contributions of scholarly specialists, he believed that generalists are also needed in church and society, and reflected on this in a column he began to write for *The Detroit Times* early in 1928:

As the body of knowledge enlarges each scholar must be content to master a relatively smaller and smaller area of it. Nothing will probably be able to stop the general drift toward specialization. . . . While this tendency makes for productive and professional efficiency the loss in spiritual, social, and moral values is tremendous. If we are not careful, we will all develop into a society of undereducated experts who know a great deal about a small area of life and very little about life itself.

On April 23 his resignation as pastor of Bethel Church was front-page news. "The call which I have received from Union Theological Seminary," he stated, ". . . offers me a field of usefulness so much in harmony with my own inclinations that I feel compelled to accept it." Niebuhr's parishioners remembered him as warm, friendly, and gentle. Otto Pokorny, Bethel's president in the year of his departure for Union, later recalled: "He was youthful and he had that spirit that would grip some fellow that was interested in the problems of the world. The members became very devoted to him."[50]

At Union Seminary eleven years later, in the same *Christian Century* article disavowing most of his first book, Niebuhr wrote that "such theological convictions which I hold today began to dawn upon me during the end of a pastorate in a great industrial city." These convictions, he went on to say, "have been further elaborated in a teaching position in a theological seminary. Greater leisure has given me opportunity to discover the main currents and emphases of the classical ages of Christian thought, and to find insights there which have been long neglected and which are yet absolutely essential to modern man, or indeed to man of any age."[51] Those insights came to him as he developed, through experience during his years in Detroit, a deeper sense of sin as a social and personal reality. The Pauline understanding of grace had been part of his Pietist heritage in the Evangelical Synod, but its integration in his life and thought had to await the dissolution, during those years, of his youthful moral idealism. As he turned to theology in the years ahead, he did so with a certain freedom and a social conscience nurtured in the non-doctrinal character of Pietism and its emphasis on faithful living. Long formative years, from his father's parsonage to his pastorate in the Motor City, had prepared Reinhold Niebuhr for future greatness.

CHAPTER THREE

Toward Christian Realism
in Social Ethics

୫

The lines of Niebuhr's mature achievement began to take shape during his early teaching years at Union Seminary, in a milieu influenced by theological ferment in Europe, the shaking of old economic certitudes in America by the Great Depression, and the ominous rise of Nazism. During the early and middle 1930s he led the way toward a realism in social ethics based on Christian insights and contemporary experience. But his greatest contributions still lay in the future.

UNION SEMINARY AND THE WORLD

In September of 1928, Reinhold Niebuhr, then thirty-six, moved with his mother to upper Manhattan to begin his teaching career as an associate professor of philosophy of religion at Union Theological Seminary. The seminary's edifice—a five- to seven-storied quadrangle covering two city blocks, with a large inner courtyard and a massive tower at the northwest corner of Broadway and 120th Street—was a fine example of Collegiate Gothic Revival architecture in two-toned stone. Situated in the neighborhood of Morningside Heights, it was surrounded by famous institutions and landmarks, including Columbia University on the southeast, Jewish Theological Seminary on the northeast, Riverside Church—then being built for Harry Emerson Fosdick's congregation by John D. Rockefeller, Jr.—on the west, and Barnard College on the south. Underneath Broadway the subway sped south to Times Square. Two blocks west lay Riverside Park and Grant's Tomb, overlooking the Hudson River. The seminary and its environs were an island of relative calm in the bustling city. Founded in 1836 under Presbyterian auspices, Union became nondenominational in 1892, and in 1910 moved into the large and newly built structure where it has remained. Its faculty had included such notable scholars as Philip Schaff, Charles Briggs, and Arthur McGiffert. When Niebuhr arrived, it was already the foremost divinity school in America, and a crossroads of international Protestantism.[1]

The environment at Union in 1928 was similar to that at Yale fifteen years earlier. William Adams Brown, a former student and disciple of Harnack, taught systematic theology. Harry F. Ward, an ardent proponent of the Social Gospel, taught ethics. Harry Emerson Fosdick, Union's best-known faculty member then, taught homiletics and a popular course on "The Modern Use of the Bible"; he also served his large congregation and led the cause of biblical scholarship and modern science in the battle against fundamentalism during the 1920s. A few years earlier Niebuhr had written about "the ripe scholarship and moral earnestness of Union with its fine sense for the social mission of our faith." Many years later he remarked in class, more critically: "When I came here, this was absolutely a paradise of Social Gospel liberalism." The sanguine theology of Ritschl and Harnack, envisaging a better world in which people and institutions increasingly followed the teaching and example of Jesus, had been shattered in Europe during World War I, and the Swiss theologians Karl Barth and Emil Brunner led Protestant thought in discovering anew the meaning of Christian faith as interpreted by Paul, Luther, and Kierkegaard. But among Americans, who had suffered far less from the war than their European cousins, nineteenth-century optimism about human nature and history persisted until the trauma of World War II.[2]

The dominant theology at Union in the 1920s, professedly Christian but colored by cultural optimism, was known as evangelical liberalism, familiar to many through the sermons and books of Fosdick. Before arriving at Union, Niebuhr had reviewed Fosdick's *Adventurous Religion* in a piece entitled "How Adventurous Is Dr. Fosdick?" The review agreed with Fosdick's affirmation of religious faith against skeptics who thought that science required its abandonment and obscurantists whose formulations of faith outraged the modern mind, but Niebuhr went on to challenge him to move beyond such issues to a heroic criticism of the injustices of modern civilization. Soon after Niebuhr's arrival at the seminary, Fosdick invited him to preach at Riverside Church and, as Niebuhr recalled, afterward in his office "told me, without referring directly to my attack upon him, that it was his conviction that each generation had only one battle in its system and would have to trust to the next . . . subsequent battles." Fosdick's graciousness impressed Niebuhr, who subsequently apologized for his criticism in an evening talk at Riverside Church.[3]

With Niebuhr's appointment, Union was on the threshold of an altered climate: he was the first of a new generation of faculty, recruited by the seminary's urbane and aristocratic Presbyterian president, Henry Sloane Coffin, who became receptive to new currents in European theology. In the fall of 1928 Niebuhr met Emil Brunner, who had earlier spent a year as a European fellow at Union and then visited it on a lecture tour of American seminaries, where the movement he and Barth led became known as neo-orthodoxy. A professor of theology at the University of Zurich, Brunner had published a year earlier his influential *Der Mittler,* subsequently translated as *The Mediator,* on the atonement of God's act in Christ. After Brunner's lecture Niebuhr sat with him in a small circle for an evening of discussion, which Brunner later recalled: "What I said in my lecture about sin led to an animated and passionate discussion. The concept of sin in those days had almost disappeared from the vocabulary of enlightened theologians. But I sensed how this basic term seemed to stimulate Niebuhr and set fire to his imagination." Emil Brunner's lectures in America at that time appeared in print a year later as *The Theology of Crisis,* and Reinhold Niebuhr read it. During the same autumn of Brunner's visit, Barth received American attention in translation. Over the past decade his *Römerbrief* had stirred theological faculties in Germany with a fresh exposition of Paul's Epistle to the Romans, and led to his leaving Switzerland for university chairs in Göttingen and Bonn. His first book translated into English was *Das Wort Gottes und die Theologie,* which appeared late in 1928 as *The Word of God and the Word of Man.* Niebuhr, in a *Christian Century* piece, wrote that "we finally have direct contact with this man Barth." The Swiss thinker was not a fundamentalist, he pointed out: "The Barthian school accepts the results of Biblical criticism and has no magical conceptions of revelation. Neither has it any quarrel with the physical sciences and evolution." Niebuhr's assessment was partly favorable and partly critical. "In so far as Barthian theology reintroduces the note of tragedy in religion," he commented, "it is a wholesome antidote to the superficial optimism of most current theology." On the other hand, it could be a liability: "It is quite possible that such a religious consciousness of sin has the moral limitation that it pre-occupies the soul with an ultimate problem of life to such a degree that it loses interest in specific moral problems and struggles which must be faced day by day." Such remained Niebuhr's view of Barth; in time, he acquired a preference for Brunner.[4]

It was during Niebuhr's first year at Union that he finally broke with the American Protestant tendency of the past three decades, rooted in the Ritschlian theology of Christ's moral influence, and accepted Paul's doctrine of grace through faith. In a piece in early 1929 on "The Terrible Beauty of the Cross," he wrote in a Pauline vein:

> Only a tragic and suffering love can be an adequate symbol of what we believe to be at the heart of reality itself. To believe in a God of love without understanding that aspect of his love which the cross reveals is to sink into sentimentality and romanticism.

Niebuhr's acceptance of Pauline Christianity by 1929 is clear in an essay, "Christianity and Redemption," which he wrote for a book edited by Lynn Harold Hough. Religion at its deepest, he began, is more than reverence before the majesty of nature or gratitude for its beneficences; rooted in the moral imagination and aware of frustration and sin, it "springs from a sense of need and culminates in an experience of redemption." Those who disavow Paul in favor of Jesus "do not realize that Paul was not the author, but only an effective champion and expounder, of the religious experience of grace, and that this experience is a necessary element in vital religion." The supposed tension between Jesus and Paul, he saw, did not exist. Christ's suffering love on the cross is a source of human renewal as well as divine forgiveness: "True religion redeems men, partly by helping them to be victorious over sin and partly by reassuring them in their inevitable failure to gain victory." There in embryo was Niebuhr's later theme of grace as power and pardon. That theme recognized the persistence and universality of sin, especially as pride—an emphasis in his later work on which he touched in 1929 after reading G. K. Chesterton on the subject in a London newspaper. "If I had only one sermon to preach," he quoted Chesterton, "it would be a sermon on pride." Citing racial and national pride, displays of power by industrialists, and expansive egos among professors and clergy, Niebuhr observed: "Any careful analysis of life reveals that a goodly portion of the misery which we bring upon each other in our social intercourse is due to pride."[5]

In the late 1920s, Niebuhr not only began to apprehend sin and grace more deeply but, in New York City, experienced metropolitan life on a scale even larger than Detroit, in contrast to the small-town experience of his boyhood. Noting both fine cultural institutions and brazenly vulgar amusements in the city, he wrote in the Detroit newspaper column which he continued for a time after moving to Manhattan: "When millions of people are brought together in one small area, both their vices and their virtues are cumulated." His response to urban existence tended to be rather critical:

The city wants to standardize us all. It is not content until we wear the same clothes . . . and, alas, it tries to coerce our opinions until the person with a touch of individuality still maintained is thought to be "queer". . . . There is no use revolting against the city. Modern civilization will continue to increase its size. But any one who accepts the city without attempting to counteract its destructive influences and to build up immunities to its unwholesome tendencies is missing a part of life. Some day American people will stop taking puerile pride in the numerical growth of their cities and will work upon the task of humanizing them.

It is well, he suggested, to escape the whirl and artificialities of the city, when possible, and stroll through forests or listen to the sea, and so "meditate upon the mysteries of the power in the universe that lies outside of man." Such occasions can be good for the soul:

Discipline in meditation and inner quiet is worth while on a purely humanist level, but it is well to remember that religious knowledge and inspiration comes in this manner. "Be still and know that I am God," says the Psalmist. Only those who try to penetrate to the center of their own lives can ever catch a glimpse into the center of all life. Most of the irreligion of our day is due to its hectic character, its multitude of distractions.[6]

While experience of the city prompted such reflections, Niebuhr's primary concern remained the problem of justice in modern industrial society. By the time he left Detroit his commitment to the right of labor to organize was not only firm but well expressed in his newspaper column:

Capital combines in larger and larger units and the men who work for these large aggregates of capital are impotent to obtain just bargains when they barter their labor individually. . . . Group action always destroys some individual liberties and virtues, but it is better to risk these dangers than to permit the idea of individualism to run riot and to issue inevitably in the liberty of the strong to exploit the weak.

Though earlier sympathetic to the cause of Prohibition, Niebuhr had criticized a religious moralism more interested in outlawing alcoholic beverages than in reforming unjust industrial and social structures. As for the liquor issue, he came by 1928 to oppose the experiment of Prohibition as an unworkable legacy of the nation's Puritan past; experience, he held, proved the Volstead Act too sweeping and without the consensus needed to enforce any law.[7]

As the presidential election of 1928 approached, Niebuhr much preferred Al Smith to Herbert Hoover, applauding the former's "challenge of the Coolidge prosperity dogmas," but he joined others in endorsing

Norman Thomas, who succeeded Eugene V. Debs as the quadrennial Socialist candidate. Not yet a member of the Socialist Party, he was initially drawn to Thomas, whom he knew and admired, more for his articulate support of many reforms than because of interest in the socialist goal of public ownership of major industries. Meanwhile, a year before the stock market crash of October 1929, Niebuhr described the basic condition which, it is widely agreed, caused the Depression. Writing in the *World Tomorrow*, a religious journal of pacifist and socialist tendencies edited by Kirby Page with his assistance, he commented that "as industry continues to perfect its machines, it arrives at a production capacity which the wants of the community cannot absorb." Penetrating to the root of the problem, he continued: "With his present buying power the worker cannot absorb the products of his own toil." After Hoover's landslide election and the onset of the Great Depression, Niebuhr joined Thomas's party and was even a candidate on the Socialist ticket for the New York State Senate and for Congress in the early 1930s.[8]

The Depression had begun when, during the summer of 1930, Niebuhr left for extensive travels, first through the American South and then through Germany and Russia. Relating to *Christian Century* readers his experience in mill cities and mountain retreats of the South, he wrote that "there is no question about the charm of Southern people," whose hospitality and manners were "perhaps . . . the remnant of an agrarian civilization." At the same time, he deplored "ubiquitous evidences of Jim Crowism," such as iron fences erected in railroad stations to separate blacks from whites and hotels where blacks were not allowed to sleep or eat. Racial segregation, he wrote, breeds misunderstanding and hatred; anyone who "crossed the color line long enough to explore the mind and heart of an intelligent Negro" would see "how much spiritual agony is caused by this publicly proclaimed contempt of one race for another." Two years later in his book *Moral Man and Immoral Society*, Niebuhr advised nonviolent resistance to the indignities of Jim Crow—a strategy that may have occurred to him while following developments in India, where Gandhi perceived the efficacy of peaceful pressure against British rule. "Gandhi," he wrote, after seeing the man himself, in loincloth and shawl, in London in 1931, "has laid a foundation for . . . Indian independence which is bound to bear fruit in time."[9]

Before leaving for Germany, where he continued to keep a watchful eye on developments, Niebuhr published an article in the *Atlantic Monthly* expressing concern that the United States still regarded war debts as a bankers' problem rather than a political one linked to German reparation payments. Americans, he maintained, emerging after the war as the wealthiest nation in the world, were "awkward imperialists":

> Europe, seething with resentment, suggests a more generous settlement of the war debts. We insist that we can tolerate nothing but a "businesslike" settlement of this problem. . . . We are a business people who know nothing about the intricacies of politics, especially international politics, and . . . make no calculations of the reactions to our attitudes in the minds of others.

U.S. demands for debt settlement, payable through reparations pressed out of Germany, had the effect of increasing German distress when American loans to that country dried up in the Depression. Traveling through southern Germany and the Rhineland in July of 1930, Niebuhr explained the German political situation to American readers: a treasury deficit created by growing unemployment was aggravated by continued pressure for reparations, and payment of the latter was a burden for the governing coalition, then led by Brüning and challenged by the Nazis and others in elections to be held in September. Hitler's party, he observed, announcing rallies on posters with the words *Juden haben keinen Zutritt* (Jews keep out), gathered strength "chiefly on the strange idea that the problems of Germany could be solved if the Jews were eliminated from its political life." From Munich, Niebuhr wrote to John Bennett, his friend and future colleague at Union, "The political conditions of Germany are growing worse daily. Parliamentarism will probably survive, but the bad economic conditions are playing into the hands of both fascists and communists."[10] Weeks later the election results allowed Brüning to carry on with diminished support, while Communist seats in the Reichstag increased from 54 to 77 and Nazi seats soared from 12 to 107—almost one fourth of the total.

In August of that year Niebuhr journeyed on to Russia, where the first of Stalin's five-year plans was under way. Reporting again to readers back home, he observed that the state-run economy, with its poorly managed factories and queues of people in Moscow waiting for scarce and shoddy goods, gave one an "impression of inefficiency." Noting the contrast between the splendor of the czar's former palace near Leningrad and the miserable huts along the way to it, he wrote that the class hatred in Marxist dogma had a vitality in Russia "achieved nowhere else" because of "the bitterness which centuries of oppression distilled in the hearts of the peasants and workers." That dogma insisted upon equality at the expense of liberty, using political pressures that "reduce the cultural life to a deadening uniformity of expression." The Soviet experiment, he concluded, was no model for the West: "Russia is so totally different from anything we know in the Western world that nothing could be quite so unscientific as to imagine that what succeeds in Russia will succeed among us."[11]

Returning home by the end of the summer, Niebuhr began the academic year of 1930–31 newly appointed as Dodge Professor of Applied Christianity. In a letter informing him of the appointment, President Coffin of Union Seminary—called "Uncle Henry" by students and faculty alike—wrote that "the Board of Directors unanimously and with enthusiasm agreed to the suggestion of the Faculty and adopted the recommendations of the Finance Committee that you should be Professor in the Dodge chair." Niebuhr's salary during his first two years at Union had been provided to the seminary by Sherwood Eddy; initially he taught a course called Religion and Ethics and cotaught two others with Harry Ward, while also assisting Kirby Page editorially at the *World Tomorrow*. Thereafter he held for three decades a chair endowed in 1892 in memory of William E. Dodge, a Presbyterian layman and businessman who had long served on the seminary's board of directors. Looking back on his first decade of teaching, Niebuhr commented that he felt inadequate at first but grew in biblical and theological learning through "the pressure of academic discipline and my companionship with the distinguished members of the Union faculty." He became particularly close to John Baillie, a scholarly Scot who taught systematic theology at Union from 1930 to 1934, when he took a position in the divinity school at the University of Edinburgh. Baillie subsequently had a part in inviting Niebuhr there to give the Gifford Lectures, and included in his edifying *Diary of Readings* passages from his American friend. During Niebuhr's early years in the Dodge chair he taught, alternating with Harry Ward, a two-semester course called Historical Introduction to Ethics, tracing developments in pre-Christian cultures as well as through centuries of church history. Troeltsch's *Social Teachings of the Christian Churches*, which he had earlier read in German, became a resource for the course, and in 1931 Niebuhr commended Olive Wyon's English translation of "this most important analysis of the relation of the Christian religion to the social and economic forces of the various ages." Sometimes he taught, among other courses, one called Ethical Viewpoints in Modern Literature.[12]

It was in the fall of 1930 that Reinhold Niebuhr met Ursula Keppel-Compton, who came to Union on a fellowship from Britain, having completed a B.A. degree at Oxford. The daughter of Anglican parents, she had grown up in Southampton, where her father practiced medicine, and had studied history before going to Oxford. There, residing at St. Hugh's

College, founded for women in 1886, she shifted from history to theology. With B. H. Streeter as tutor, she pursued biblical and patristic studies, including much work in New Testament and the early church fathers as well as Saint Augustine. C. H. Dodd, the eminent New Testament scholar whose lectures she attended, was her examiner in Greek in the theology school, in which she took first class honors. After several months of courtship in the neighborhood of Morningside Heights, Niebuhr at the age of thirty-nine married the young Englishwoman, then twenty-four, at Winchester Cathedral in December of 1931. Reinhold and Ursula Niebuhr eventually settled in the seminary's new faculty apartment building at 99 Claremont Avenue, facing the north end of the west side of Union's quadrangular edifice. Thus began a marriage of forty years which included sharing of books and friends. One of Ursula's first gifts to Reinhold was a 1704 edition of selected works of Augustine.[13]

Niebuhr's clearest and fullest statement of his theology and ethics at this time, foreshadowing the lines of his developing Christian realism, appeared in an international symposium edited by W. A. Visser 't Hooft, the Dutch ecumenical leader, in a volume entitled *A Traffic in Knowledge*, published in Britain in 1931. In an essay on "The American Approach to the Christian Message," he combined the insight of Continental neo-orthodoxy on the uniqueness of Christian faith with Anglo-American concern for its social relevance. Barthian theology, he began, had extricated the truth of the gospel from the mind of modernity, but in reacting to recent tragedy became too pessimistic in its emphasis on human sin and divine transcendence:

> To regard man from the perspective of God's holiness is a wholesome corrective to the inclination to moral complacency in man; but to regard his actions only from that perspective means to erase important moral distinctions. The fact that even good men fall short does not prove that the difference between good men and bad men is unimportant from any historical standpoint.

Such distinctions are important to all moral effort, Niebuhr held. He went on to state the meaning for faith of the revelation in Christ:

> He incarnates the perfect love ideal which is the logical culmination of all ethical striving. In that sense he is the ideal which we must realize. But since all human effort falls short of this ideal, He is also the occasion for the discovery of our imperfection and the realization that our final trust must be in the mercy of God. . . . Those who accept the assurance of grace in Christ are able to live in the spirit of serenity without falling into com-

placency. They are constantly convicted of their imperfections and constantly assured of the love of God which accepts the truly contrite heart.

The gospel, he continued, can become a leaven for society, helping to resolve the industrial problem through a realistic ethic which understands the inevitability of conflict and pressures in the struggle for justice, and imparts among religiously sensitive contenders contrite recognition of how much their ideas and actions serve their own interests. Such an ethic, Niebuhr concluded, will avoid undue optimism or pessimism:

> It is not to be supposed that any social order which may emerge out of the moral strivings of this or any other age will ever approximate the Kingdom of God of Christian faith. That Kingdom is . . . the impossible goal which, because it is never reached, makes men conscious of the imperfections of their social order. . . . Vital Christianity worships a transcendent God Whose will is never perfectly done in history; but it also requires that the attempt be made.

It was a pensive and lucid essay, in which Niebuhr by 1931 began to develop some major themes of Christian realism: the need for moral distinctions while recognizing the universality of sin, contrition as a morally fruitful response to Christ's suffering love, the kingdom of God as a goal of human striving though never realized in history.[14]

SEARCHING FOR JUSTICE IN THE DEPTHS OF A DEPRESSION

As the Great Depression deepened in the early 1930s—with growing joblessness, bankruptcies, and breadlines—Niebuhr observed conditions keenly. He noted that, in some parts of the country, race relations became aggravated as whites sought to force blacks out of jobs: "They ought not succeed because the Negroes are already bearing more than their fair share of the unemployment situation." The economic crisis was entering its third year as he read Frederick Lewis Allen's *Only Yesterday*, with its vivid—if exaggerated—account of superficiality in the booming 1920s, causing him to reflect on the contrasting plight of a large portion of the population "facing insecurity, eviction from its domiciles, undernourishment for its children, and every other disadvantage of poverty." He went on to emphasize "the difference between genteel and abject poverty":

> Those who have had their incomes cut from ten thousand to five thousand dollars per year, or from five thousand to three thousand, may well make virtue of necessity and rediscover the advantages of an economy which does not offer undue temptations to excesses. But that is a much easier

achievement than to address oneself to the task of building a society in which ... all men will have an income which can afford life's basic necessities.[15]

In 1932 Niebuhr, summering with his wife at a friend's cottage in Heath, Massachusetts—a village in the Berkshires near the Vermont border, where they often returned in summers to come, prepared for publication a slim volume entitled *The Contribution of Religion to Social Work*, comprising his Forbes Lectures at Columbia University's New York School of Social Work in 1930. His contacts with social workers, successors of Jane Addams and the settlement house movement, had begun in Detroit, though seeds of his interest can be traced to the social missions of his denomination. Such contacts continued in New York through his friendship with Gaylord White, who headed the Union Settlement on East 106th Street, a link between the seminary and social workers. Niebuhr began his brief book by tracing philanthropy from the early church to its modern forms, and then pointed out its limitations: "Charity flows only where human need is vividly displayed and where it is recognized in intimate contact." It "cannot do justice to social needs which arise out of the maladjustments of a mechanical civilization and are obscured amidst the impersonal relationships of an urban civilization."[16]

Charity, Niebuhr went on to say, is often an expression of power by those who possess excessive privilege, or of sentimentality by middle-class people who neither wield power nor suffer from it. Though necessary and helpful, private charities cannot possibly "meet the needs of the unemployed" nor initiate "an adequate housing scheme for the poor ... within the limits of private enterprise." True religion, he held, contributes to the goals of social work in five ways: It heeds the "rigorous demand for social justice" of "the eighth-century prophets of Israel"; it is, amidst the moral decay of urban culture, potent in preserving "traditional disciplines" in many lives, while "bringing order out of confusion" in others through the therapy of grace; it gives people "serenity and poise" for dealing with the vicissitudes of life; and it can help to heal family frictions through "mutual forbearance and forgiveness" as taught by Jesus. Summoning social workers to appreciate the meaning of biblical faith in the lives of many to whom they minister, Niebuhr expressed a deep insight in this memorable passage:

> The ultimate affirmation of religion about the goodness of God remains, of course, a hypothesis of faith which can never be proved to those who are preoccupied with the chaos and evil which life reveals; neither can it be disproved to those who have felt it validated in their inner experience.[17]

Overshadowing this insightful little book, Niebuhr's *Moral Man and Immoral Society*, also written during the summer of 1932 at Heath, appeared in the following winter, with much impact. Its main theme was that relations between human collectives, lacking the higher moral potential of personal relationships, are determined as much by power as by ethical or rational considerations, and so require the countering of power by power for the sake of justice. The divergent interests, aggrandizing tendencies, or assertive impulses of classes, nations, and races, he maintained, produced conflicts carried on by the threat or use of force, more often by the covert coercion of threatened force. The book opposed certain prevailing notions, as Niebuhr explained in its opening pages:

> Inasfar as this treatise has a polemical interest it is directed against the moralists, both religious and secular, who imagine that the egoism of individuals is being progressively checked by the development of rationality or the growth of a religiously inspired goodwill and that nothing but the continuance of this process is necessary to establish social harmony between all the human societies and collectives.

Such optimism, he pointed out, was current among two groups. One consisted of philosophers and social scientists influenced by the Enlightenment, who thought social problems could be solved through education and by experts, without perceiving that classes and nations use reason to expand and justify their power. The other included preachers and theologians who expected the kingdom of God to evolve in society through love, an illusion strong in America, where an expanding economy and relative isolation had long obscured class tensions and international conflict. While recognizing that "social intelligence and moral goodwill" may "mitigate the brutalities of social conflict," Niebuhr held that "when collective power . . . exploits weakness, it can never be dislodged unless power is raised against it."[18]

The book, reflecting the times, focused mostly on problems of economic justice. Inequality of privilege, Niebuhr held, arose from difference of ability and function, but those differences do not justify the degree of inequality created in society. Privileged classes are too inclined to regard their advantages as the reward for special function, and to accept disparities arising from unequal educational opportunities and centralized economic power. Karl Marx, he pointed out, was "realistic in maintaining that disproportion of power in society is the real root of social injustice" and correctly predicted business crises caused by lack of consuming power, but Marx failed to foresee the rise in European democracies of parties that "forced the state partially to equalize the inequalities created by concentration of capital." Conditions in Russia, where a moribund regime collapsed in war amidst suffering of peasants and workers, "conformed to the formula of Marxism much more perfectly than will probably ever be the case in the industrial civilization for which the formula was designed." Soviet rule replaced old injustices with a system in which "abuse of power by communistic bureaucrats is very considerable," and refuted Marx's illusion of a transitory dictatorship on the other side of revolution. Experience, Niebuhr held, commended reform on the British model of concessions by privileged classes under pressure from advancing classes.[19]

Turning to the behavior of nations and races, Niebuhr observed that national loyalty may become "the expression of a sublimated egoism" when "the man in the street," thwarted by his limitations and checks on his ambition, "projects his ego upon his nation" and so "transmutes individual selfishness into national egoism." Such unqualified patriotism produces imperial impulses that can be partly checked by "a body of citizens more intelligent than the average, who see the issues between their own and other nations more clearly." Yet nations, like classes, display a will to power and hypocrisy by clothing their interests in some universal moral value, he maintained. As for racial and other oppressed minorities within a nation, Niebuhr recommended resistance through boycotts or strikes or civil disobedience—nonviolent methods which reduce animosities and prevent the other side from posing as champions of peace and order. "The emancipation of the Negro race in America," he stated presciently, "probably waits upon the adequate development of this kind of social and political strategy."[20]

In *Moral Man and Immoral Society*, then, Niebuhr sought to make efforts for justice, especially its economic aspects in an industrial era, effective by taking into account factors of interest and coercion in the relations of large-scale groups. In doing so, he emphasized the political nature of the problem, in which force is mingled with morality: "Politics will, to the end of history, be an area where conscience and power meet, where the ethical and coercive factors of human life will interpenetrate and work out their tentative and uneasy compromises." In this book Niebuhr took a position somewhat reminiscent of that expressed twenty-five years earlier by Walter Rauschenbusch in *Christianity and the Social Crisis*, with its call for an alliance of the churches with the working class in the struggle for justice; but he differed from Rauschenbusch in seeing a sharper conflict between labor and capital and in discerning a gap between love and justice too great to speak of "Christianizing the social order." If Niebuhr in these pages employed nontheological language, it was partly because his interest in theology was in an early stage and partly because he wished to address humanist as well as Christian circles, and so kept implicit the Pauline convictions evident in essays of the previous three years.[21]

The book was widely reviewed in America and Britain, winning a following among like-minded realists and provoking consternation among those clergy and educators who still believed in the efficacy of goodwill or intelligence alone to bring about a more just society. Among individuals influenced by *Moral Man and Immoral Society* was R. H. S. Crossman, later editor of anti-Stalinist testimonies in *The God That Failed* and a member of Harold Wilson's cabinet, who recalled: "It was the most exciting shock intellectually that I had as a young man, and I'm still recovering from it." Niebuhr's brother Richard, who had joined the faculty of Yale Divinity School in 1932, wrote to express esteem for the book despite some disagreement with it: "I just wanted to say that, though I don't see eye to eye with you, I think I understand you and that in your battle I am an ally if not a soldier in the same division, and that I rejoice in your valiant attack." Within a year of the book's publication, Niebuhr criticized its final paragraph, in which he had suggested that utopian illusions are a spur to constructive social action: "That suggestion was probably the greatest mistake in my book. It is true that these illusions are serviceable but . . . it would have been better to close on a warning against their danger." Decades later he remarked that his book of 1932 might better have been entitled *The Not So Moral Man in His Less Moral Communities.*[22] Although he moved well beyond its themes, in matured social philosophy as well as in theological depth, *Moral Man and Immoral Society* was a ground-breaking work and has remained one of his more influential books.

Niebuhr sought to implement his ideas on reducing the power of privileged classes by supporting Norman Thomas for President again in 1932. Losing confidence in both major parties, he had joined the League for Independent Political Action, formed three years earlier by Paul Douglas, with a view to promoting a third party committed to progressive taxation, protection of labor unions, social security, and other reforms. The League now endorsed Thomas, whose party's program included that agenda as well as public ownership of major industries. The latter proposal was more radical, but many then favored it as an alternative to a system that seemed discredited as the Depression grew steadily worse. Endorsing Thomas as a man of stature with "ability to call into being, and to lead, a powerful socialist movement," Niebuhr wrote in the *World Tomorrow:* "Modern society no longer faces the problem whether or not it will have social ownership. The only problem which it faces is whether it can achieve this goal without catastrophe and social convulsion." While Franklin Roosevelt won by a landslide in November, some nine hundred thousand Americans voted for Thomas, among them Niebuhr, who viewed the squire of Hyde Park as too mild an alternative to Hoover's "intransigent conservatism." In later years Niebuhr became an eloquent apologist of Roosevelt's New Deal, but after FDR's first hundred days produced the NRA, with its wage and price codes under the aegis of government-business partnership, he had only faint praise, commenting that "the gains for labor are there" but "will hardly increase consumption capacity very much."[23]

The coming of the New Deal in America coincided with a development in Germany that Niebuhr observed on the spot: Hitler's climb to power as the Third Reich supplanted the Weimar Republic. Visiting Germany again in the summer of 1933, he wrote informed and incisive analyses of Nazi rule rare in America at the time. Nazism, he declared, was "a devil's brew." It drew strength from "the fears of the privileged classes, the nationalistic resentments of an entire nation, and the impatience of the young people." Amidst economic despair and the frustrations of an unjust peace, Hitler skillfully united "the capitalists, who were afraid of a Communist revolution, and the impoverished lower middle classes." The big industrialists funded his private army of storm troopers and his propaganda machine, while unemployed youths, bankrupted storekeepers, and others supplied millions of votes as he vented their resentments by blaming the Jews for all the miseries of Germany. Hitler's "virulent anti-Semitism" was the reverse side of the "extravagant nationalism" he proclaimed.[24]

The Nazis, Niebuhr observed, with representation in the Reichstag increased to 30 percent, came to power by manipulating the organs of state, and then muzzled the press, imprisoned their foes, outlawed labor unions, imposed monolithic rule on all aspects of life, and persecuted the Jews. By mid-1933 their harassment of Jews proceeded with "primitive ferocity" as Jewish professional and business men were forced from their jobs, and beatings and killings by police took place. About such developments, however, most Germans were kept "completely in the dark." Calling in the pages of the *Christian Century* for a worldwide protest against Nazi inhumanities, Niebuhr made common cause with his friend

Stephen Wise, the Zionist leader and rabbi, who meanwhile led a massive anti-Nazi rally in New York.[25]

While in Germany that summer, Niebuhr conveyed to Paul Tillich a joint invitation from Union Theological Seminary and Columbia University to join their faculties—a maneuver initiated by Coffin and by Horace Friess of the Department of Philosophy at Columbia. Tillich, recently suspended from his post at the University of Frankfurt for protesting the beating of students by Nazi thugs, had expounded a social and existential Protestantism that mediated between his native Lutheran orthodoxy and the cultural humanism and socialist secularism of Weimar Germany. Months earlier Niebuhr had reviewed appreciatively Tillich's *The Religious Situation*, newly translated by his brother Richard, stating:

> Essential religion is, for Tillich, the recognition of the transcendent and unconditioned, and its use as a point of reference for a criticism of the finite and conditioned. The essence of irreligion is therefore the sense of self-sufficient finitude.

The secular illusion of realizing the eternal in time pervaded capitalist and proletarian culture, he commented. Niebuhr concluded the review by expressing hope that more of Tillich's works would be translated, especially his *Religiöse Verwirklichung*. The substance of the latter, which Niebuhr read in German after its publication in 1929, eventually appeared as part of Tillich's *The Protestant Era*, one of his best-known books. In the fall of 1933 at the age of forty-seven, Tillich arrived in New York, was tutored in English by Niebuhr's bilingual student Carl Hermann Voss, and thereafter remained in America while continuing his career as a philosophical theologian.[26]

Besides German and Swiss theologians, Niebuhr during his early years at Union read a diversity of other authors. Reviewing Walter Lippmann's *A Preface to Morals* in 1929, he commended the book for its recognition of "insights of the past and present converging in an ethic of disciplined freedom," but, unlike Edmund Wilson and others who acclaimed Lippmann for basing morals in experience apart from religious insight, Niebuhr saw that as the book's weakness: "Ethical sensitivity may flourish for a time in an atmosphere of humanism, but only as long as the dying sun of religious faith augments the pale light of the humanist's moon." In his review of José Ortega y Gasset's *The Revolt of the Masses* in 1932, Niebuhr wrote that it probed insightfully into distempers of modern civilization caused by the rise of industrial technology and, with it, specialists and standardized men without principles. Leon Trotsky's *History of the*

Russian Revolution, which appeared in the early 1930s, impressed Niebuhr with the exiled Bolshevik's thesis that conditions in 1917 were ripe for the Soviets' triumph when Lenin raised the standard of revolt against a government lacking will and power to reform the czarist order. Reviewing an English translation of Adolf Hitler's *Mein Kampf* after returning from Germany in 1933, he noted the Nazi leader's Machiavellian realism and, deleted from the translation, his cynical ideas on the use of propaganda. Hitler's life, Niebuhr saw, illuminated his rise to power: "His prejudices and fanaticisms are indigenous to the lower middle class soil from which he sprang; and where they transcend this class they merge into the temper and express the aspirations and illusions of a defeated, frustrated, and aggrieved people."[27]

The Nazi experience in Germany and the unresolved economic crisis in America were much on Niebuhr's mind when, late in 1933, he completed his next book, *Reflections on the End of an Era.* One of his few volumes that have not become a lasting part of the Niebuhr corpus, it predicted a drift toward fascism, followed by a socialist upheaval. Though understandable in light of trends abroad and uncertainties at home during the months from late 1932 to early 1934, the book's catastrophic note was refuted as the New Deal prevailed over alternatives on the left and the right. Long afterward Niebuhr commented that its pages were "too much influenced by the Marxist apocalypse." He was one of many thoughtful Americans attracted in some degree to Marx during the 1930s, when the failure of capitalism gave his doctrine plausibility. Marxism, whether in its communist or its democratic form, was then widely espoused in New York intellectual circles, and Niebuhr regarded Sidney Hook, a democratic socialist who taught in the city, as Marx's ablest interpreter in America. But Niebuhr was never a pure Marxist; his socialism, like that of Tillich and of many in the British Labor party, was qualified by Christianity. In *Reflections on the End of an Era,* Niebuhr sharpened his critique of Marx's doctrine: it was a secularized version of the biblical concept of the kingdom of God, and promoted a vindictiveness toward opponents which wrongly identified capitalism with evil itself. In the same book, he even began to question the indigenous semi-Marxist social system he then favored: "A society which establishes an economic equilibrium through social ownership" may "create a new disproportion of power through the necessity of strengthening the political force which holds economic life in check." It was this concern that finally led him to reject the socialist idea.[28]

Niebuhr never advocated violence as a method of bringing about change, but in those years of class tension it was conceivable that strides toward justice would have to be defended against violent reactionary opposition. For that reason he withdrew, early in 1934, from the Fellowship of Reconciliation, which he had served as chairman. Formed on Quaker principles during World War I, the FOR had grown in the 1920s as thousands of Protestant clergy, Niebuhr among them, swelled the ranks of pacifism in the disillusioning aftermath of the war. Although he had noted his revulsion to war while visiting the Ruhr years earlier, Niebuhr did not share the absolute pacifism of many FOR members. Opposing nonresistance to evil as utopian, he supported strikes and boycotts, and in 1932 he favored economic sanctions against Japan for aggression in Manchuria. In 1934 he still disavowed participation in armed international conflict, but the pragmatic grounds on which he then broke with consistent pacifism foreshadowed his support of war when, several years later, Nazi aggression threatened civilization with an evil worse than war itself.[29]

Ethics in a Theological Context

By the mid-1930s the winds of Continental theology blew across the Atlantic more strongly, especially after Barth's early work became available in English as *The Epistle to the Romans* in 1933. Reflecting on this period years later in a special talk at Union, Niebuhr said, "I remember how much Karl Barth's *Romerbrief* influenced all of us and how creative it was." While the great Swiss theologian effectively recovered Paul's theology from the complacent religious culture of the nineteenth century, he added, Barth unfortunately accentuated the weakness of German Lutheranism in stressing the transcendence of grace over the struggle for justice. Aloof from politics while Hitler rose to power, Barth inspired the Barmen Declaration of 1934, opposing nazification of the German church, and then fled to Basel in his native land. His leadership, Niebuhr observed at the time, "stiffened to a very great degree" Protestant resistance to the pretensions of the Nazi state, but Barth remained essentially apolitical. Visser 't Hooft, writing Niebuhr in 1931, had pointed out that the Barthian movement included many who were more sensitive to social and political matters. One was Emil Brunner, whose *Das Gebot und die Ordnungen*, a treatise on the relation of the biblical love commandment to problems of private morality and public justice, was published in 1932 and banned by the Nazi regime. Reading Brunner's book in 1934, before its appearance in English as *The Divine Imperative*, Niebuhr saw in it "valuable insights":

> He recognizes, for instance, that political action cannot be "Christian" in any exact sense and that the effort to have a . . . peculiarly Christian approach to any cultural or political problem will destroy the unity between Christian and non-Christian action which is necessary for the success of any secular enterprise.

Another insight of Brunner was that Christians are "justified by grace" in doing things necessary in an imperfect world of coercive political solutions. Although Niebuhr regarded Brunner's approach to social change as too conservative, he stated in reviewing the English translation three years later that it was "the most important book in Christian ethics to appear since Troeltsch's *Social Teaching of the Christian Churches.*"[30]

While reading Brunner and others across the ocean, Niebuhr often conversed with Paul Tillich after his coming to Union. On one occasion as they talked in the Union quadrangle, Ursula has recalled, art—which interested Tillich for its implicit religious meanings—came up, and Reinhold described himself as "artistically a moron." Tillich, just learning English, thought he belonged to a school of art criticism by that name. The anecdote is not only an amusing instance of Tillich's difficulties with a new language but a case of self-deprecating exaggeration on Niebuhr's part, for he had visited great art museums abroad. Sometimes the two walked along Riverside Drive; their conversations stimulated Niebuhr as he prepared his Rauschenbusch Lectures, delivered at Colgate-Rochester Divinity School in the spring of 1934 and published as *An Interpretation of Christian Ethics*, with a preface acknowledging Tillich's contributions to its theme.[31]

Before that book appeared, Niebuhr wrote a *Christian Century* piece, "Marx, Barth, and Israel's Prophets," which distinguished, as Tillich did, the biblical dialectic of God and history from the secular utopianism of Marx and the transcendentalism of Barth:

> The significant fact about Hebrew thought is that it neither lifts God completely above history nor identifies him with historical processes. . . . The transcendent God worked in history, and the prophets pointed out how he worked. Evil and injustice would be destroyed and good would be established. History was a constant revelation of both the judgment and mercy of God.

While Marx reduced the prophetic interpretation of history to a logic working toward an earthly paradise, Barth transmuted it into a moral defeatism regarding history as irrelevant to the meaning of life. "In prophetic religion," Niebuhr emphasized, "there is a more genuine dialectic in which the movements of history are in one moment the instruments of God and in the next come under his condemnation."[32]

An Interpretation of Christian Ethics, published toward the end of 1935, was Niebuhr's first effort to provide an explicitly theological framework for ethics. Its central theme was that, as human life is lived in tension between the norm of love and the reality of sin, justice is necessary as an institutional approximation of love, while love remains an ultimate standard and a complement of justice in society. The relation of love and justice, Niebuhr began, is rooted in biblical faith, which affirmed "the organic relation between historic human existence and that which is both the ground and the fulfillment of this existence, the transcendent." According to the prophets and Jesus, "the God who transcends the created world also convicts a sinful world" and initiates "an ultimate redemption" not above history but "within and at the end of it." Thus the kingdom of God as the reign of love is "always a possibility in history" but also "beyond every historical achievement." As historical possibility, love according to the Christian gospel is the fruit of gratitude and contrition, but it stands in juxtaposition to the fact of sin arising in human freedom. Living at "the juncture of spirit and nature," the human creature "makes pretensions of being absolute in his finiteness," which is the essence of sin and the root of the boundless pretensions of nations and classes.[33]

In a world of conflicting egoisms, Niebuhr held, the sublime ethic of the Sermon on the Mount is an ultimate ideal not immediately relevant to political and economic problems. Its social relevance consists in pointing to equality as "the regulative principle of justice," for "in the ideal of equality there is an echo of the law of love, 'Thou shalt love thy neighbor *as thyself.'*" Thus an adequate concept of justice involves not only prohibition of theft and murder but the obligation "to organize the common life so that the neighbor will have fair opportunities to maintain his life." So Niebuhr argued in a memorably titled chapter, "The Relevance of an Impossible Ethical Ideal." Corrective and distributive justice, he continued, requires "critical intelligence"—a legacy of the Enlightenment which may be appropriated without its secular utopianism. Neither Marxist visionaries nor Protestants of the more conventional or sentimental type perceived the need for mechanisms of justice: "A profound religion will not give itself to the illusion that perfect justice can be achieved in a sinful world. But neither can it afford to dismiss the problem of justice or to transcend it by premature appeals to the good will of individuals." Acts of charity "are never substitutes for, but additions to, the coercive system of social relationships through which alone a basic justice can be guaranteed." Yet even the best system of justice cannot "dispense with the refinements which voluntary and uncoerced human kindness and tenderness between individuals add to it." Finally, Niebuhr emphasized, Christian faith provides a perspective by which those involved in struggles for justice, contritely aware of their own sin, will preserve toward their opponents "the spirit of forgiveness."[34]

When *An Interpretation of Christian Ethics* appeared, Wilhelm Pauck, then at Chicago Theological Seminary, reviewed it as "the richest of Niebuhr's works and one of the most rewarding in recent literature." The author was "not a single voice in the wilderness," but inspired a younger generation who "are willing to be confronted . . . with the challenge of prophetic religion." His theme, Pauck added, needed further elaboration: "particularly the theological convictions which underlie his ethics will have to be clarified by more systematic considerations." Niebuhr himself, responding many years later to friendly criticism by Paul Ramsey, remarked that "I was only dimly feeling my way in this book toward a realistic and valid Christian ethic." Yet it presented fresh insights and a theme basic to his later thought. "I still believe, as I believed then," he stated in a new preface of 1956, "that love may be a motive of social action but that justice must be the instrument of love in a world in which self-interest is bound to defy the canons of love on every level."[35]

FAITH AND POLITICS IN A DISJOINTED TIME

While Niebuhr prepared his book on Christian ethics for publication, Congress in the summer of 1935 passed the Social Security Act and the Wagner Labor Relations Act, landmarks of the New Deal which Niebuhr in time came to recognize as key embodiments of the mechanisms of justice and power balancing he advocated. Meanwhile, Roosevelt launched the WPA, creating public service jobs for millions of unemployed Americans. While the Depression persisted, American capitalism was being reformed and public confidence in the system increased. But trouble soon developed abroad in 1936, as Mussolini's Italy took Ethiopia, Hitler's Germany remilitarized the Rhineland, and civil war broke out in Spain; then in 1937 Stalin conducted a bloody purge that shocked Westerners, and a militarizing Japan invaded China. In America, meanwhile, turbulence accompanied the drive to unionize heavy industry. FDR, reelected by a landslide, began his second term in a time of new troubles. In this climate, Niebuhr continued to comment on events, to read heavily, and to teach and preach.

By the mid-1930s a perceptible change began to occur within American Protestantism, reflected not so much in Niebuhr's then rather small following as in a notable sermon preached by Harry Emerson Fosdick at Riverside Church on a Sunday morning in October of 1935 and heard in countless homes on "National Radio Vespers." Still affirming the validities of science that he had defended in the battle against fundamentalism, Fosdick declared that the Protestant churches must go beyond their acceptance of modern science to recover the biblical sense of personal and social sin and of the transcendence of God that was lost in religious adjustment to the shallow, optimistic, man-centered culture of the late nineteenth and early twentieth centuries. In such a recovery, he maintained, "the watchword will be not, Accommodate yourself to the prevailing culture! but, Stand out from it and challenge it!"[36]

While Fosdick's differences with an earlier religious optimism grew deeper, John Dewey—then in his seventies at Columbia University—clung to a secular rational version of that same optimism. In *Liberalism and Social Action*, published in 1935, he affirmed his confidence that "organized intelligence," so successful in devising modern industrial technology, could create a more just society. Attacking Dewey's book, Niebuhr held that its author placed excessive faith in reason. While sharing Dewey's commitment to democracy and regarding intelligence as socially helpful, he pointed out that Dewey, in supposing that rational persuasion can induce conflicting groups to resolve their differences, failed to "perceive the perennial and inevitable character of the subordination of reason to interest." He had made the same criticism of Dewey's rationalistic naturalism in *Moral Man and Immoral Society*, and later repeated it as Dewey continued to identify the interested self with its reason and so relied on methods of science to solve social problems.[37]

Meanwhile, Niebuhr in the fall of 1935 became editor of *Radical Religion*, newly founded as the quarterly journal of the Fellowship of Socialist Christians, a group—then with some five hundred members—formed in the early 1930s under his leadership. Organized for discussion and commitment of membership dues to social causes, the FSC began its publishing venture after the *World Tomorrow*—torn and weakened as Niebuhr, Sherwood Eddy, and others dissented from the pacifist editorial line of Kirby Page—ceased publication in 1934. The new journal, exploring socialism as an option for Christians, pursued that purpose through the later 1930s, but focused increasingly on the urgent problem of supporting democracy against the rising tide of fascism. Early in 1936 Niebuhr, as editor, wrote: "The German military occupation of the Rhineland finds England hesitant and equivocal." Hitler's move "brings the next war nearer"—indeed, "German hysteria threatens to engulf the whole continent in a great war and may possibly tempt Japan to spread the war in Asia."[38]

As the presidential election approached in the fall, Niebuhr noted that Roosevelt had "allowed social services to be established which no administration will dare to destroy." Though still a socialist, he saw that Thomas had no chance in 1936. Speaking during the campaign in a hall of Pierson College at Yale, he urged FDR's reelection as preferable to the Republican alternative. Yet he remained lukewarm to the New Deal, opining months later that Roosevelt was "more renowned for his artistic juggling than for robust resolution," and writing in 1938 that "no final good can come of this kind of whirligig reform." Looking back years later, after he had come to view FDR's legacy more favorably, Niebuhr wrote Arthur Schlesinger, Jr.: "My negative attitude toward Roosevelt is really a scandal considering that he elaborated a pragmatic approach which I should have appreciated long before I did."[39]

Though slow to appreciate the New Deal, Niebuhr commented perceptively on other developments as FDR's second term began. "The real source of fascism," he wrote in 1937, "lies in the social resentments and the political confusion of lower middle class life." Demagogues, he noted, promised petty bourgeois groups some form of economic equalization without disturbing property rights, and appealed to racial or national resentments among them, but so far they were more successful in Europe than in America. As Franco's forces threatened the Spanish parliamentary government, he shared the wide sympathy for the latter in a conflict between "the fascist and the democratic way of life." He viewed the Moscow trials as a "sorry business," in which Stalin produced the doubtful evidence of self-accusation against alleged traitors in his regime. Nor did Trotsky impress him as an alternative to Stalin: "He suggests no basic changes in structure. His appeal finally implies no more than an assertion of his own integrity against Stalin's dishonesty." When Japan began war on China, he saw it as "part of a long-term plan on the part of Japanese imperialism to set up a vast empire." Criticizing pacifist and isolationist sentiment for neutrality, he called for economic pressures against Japan. Closer to home, after General Motors and Chrysler accepted unionization in the wake of sit-down strikes, Niebuhr commented that Henry Ford "seems destined to end his career in industrial situations reminiscent of the Homestead strikes in Carnegie's history. Let us hope that the operation of the Wagner Act will render his folly impotent."[40]

Whether discussing current events or religious and philosophical issues, Niebuhr used the word "liberalism" in ways that depended on context for meaning. In the pages of *Radical Religion* he sought to clarify matters. The term connoted, on the one hand, a deep tradition in our culture: "It is the spirit of tolerance and fairness. Without this spirit life would be reduced to a consistent inhumanity." On the other hand, it had become associated with religious and secular versions of the notion, still prevalent in America then, that civilization is improving morally, with the prospect that injustice and war will yield to educational efforts and appeals to goodwill: "It is a blindness which does not see . . . the perennial source of conflict between life and life . . . and the tortuous character of human history." It was liberalism in the latter sense that he criticized, whether secular thought from Rousseau to Dewey or nineteenth-century theology from Schleiermacher to Harnack. In his most recent book he had pointed out that the latter tradition, despite its sentimental moralism, had helped "to free what is eternal in the Christian religion from the shell of an outmoded culture" by accepting "a critico-historical analysis of its sources." Thus he valued "liberal" contributions to biblical studies and "liberalism" as democratic tolerance and fairness, while attacking "liberal" illusions about human nature and history.[41]

During these years Niebuhr read widely and deeply in theology. His earlier reading had included Saint Augustine, whose work he and Ursula discussed in the early years of their marriage and who is mentioned in his early books, but there is no clear evidence from his writings that Augustine became an influence until 1936. In that year Erich Przywara's *An Augustine Synthesis*, integrating passages from many works, was published; Niebuhr acquired a copy and marked it up. It was one of various texts he used. His appreciation of Augustinian Christianity is clear in an article of 1936 on Anglicanism. Familiar with its liturgy through visits to England as well as occasional attendance with Ursula at services of the Cathedral of St. John the Divine in New York, Niebuhr wrote:

> The Book of Common Prayer is not a theologically neutral prayer manual. It is informed by a definite theological tendency, which could be defined most briefly as Augustinianism. The Anglican service significantly begins with a prayer of general confession. . . . Such a prayer . . . can be prayed with sincerity only if the Augustinian interpretation of human nature is accepted—*i.e.,* if the doctrine of original sin is believed.

We do well to reject that doctrine, he went on to say, if it is meant as a description of the transmission of sin from Adam, but that myth points to a deeper truth:

> The specific truth, in the myth of the fall of man and in the doctrine of original sin, is that all human ideals, even the highest, are corrupted by self-interest. . . . Put in terms relevant to contemporary social and political life, it means that the social and political ideals of every nation and class are partly determined, and must be explained, in terms of the special interests of those groups.

Niebuhr's appreciation of the works of Luther and Calvin did not begin until later in the decade; as he stated in retrospect, "I was first influenced not so much by the Reformers as by the study of St. Augustine."[42]

Meanwhile, as Barth turned to his vast work of systematic theology, Niebuhr lost interest. Reviewing an early volume of Barth's *Church Dogmatics* in 1936, he found it, though insightful, "not only difficult, but dull," taking several hundred pages "to iterate and re-iterate a rather simple dogma of the 'qualitative difference' between the human and the divine." The current works of Tillich and Brunner appealed more to him. After Tillich's volume *The Interpretation of History* appeared in 1936, he commended not only its autobiographical part, "On the Boundary," but its exposition of a dialectic more profound than modern naturalism or Barthian theology:

> The "Unconditioned", to use his favorite phrase, is involved in every moment of history. . . . The church is the place in human society in which the tension between God and the world, between the eternal and history is known and in which life is lived and judged in terms of that tension.

Tillich's concept of "the demonic," he noted, was a Pauline-Augustinian emphasis as against the Pelagian idea that moral striving may achieve freedom from sin; and his concept of *"kairos"* was a biblical insight on qualitatively fulfilled time, neither utopia nor timeless bliss. "His terms may be abstract," concluded Niebuhr, "but his thought is not. It deals in terms of rigorous realism with the very stuff of life."[43]

Brunner, whose influence on Anglo-American Protestantism surpassed Barth's in the later 1930s and the 1940s, had earlier collaborated with Barth in editing *Zwichen den Zeiten*, a journal published in Germany from 1922 until its suppression by the Nazis in 1933. Their theological alliance, however, ended in controversy, as Niebuhr observed in 1937:

> Their common emphasis was one in which the whole tradition of liberal Christianity was challenged as being merely a derivative of modern culture,

with its humanistic, naturalistic, and optimistic world view. Against it they proclaimed a theology of revelation which insisted that Christian faith must begin with the Biblical revelation as a basis and not seek to arrive at religious certainty by the ordinary processes of knowledge. . . . In recent years this partnership has been dissolved because Brunner tried to leave a place for "natural theology" in his system.

Brunner in a publication of 1934 had held that, though salvation from sin is possible only through Christ, the world of nature and human conscience contain traces of the knowledge of God apart from biblical revelation, and that creation includes a uniquely human "point of contact" or capacity for receiving the revealed word of God. Attacking Brunner in a polemical pamphlet, Barth insisted that the Bible is the only source of knowledge of God. Their dispute stirred wide interest, and Niebuhr, regarding Barth as too biblicist, eventually stated that in this debate "Brunner seems to me to be right and Barth wrong." Brunner, he wrote in 1937, "is a profound and searching thinker, fully versed in every historic philosophical problem."[44]

Niebuhr's reading in the mid-1930s also included William Temple's *Nature, Man and God* and Étienne Gilson's *The Spirit of Medieval Philosophy*, both of which he reviewed. Temple's treatise, he explained, presented an organic view of reality in which mind apprehends the world process as a unity, implying personality as creator. Its close reasoning "is adequate proof that theism cannot be dismissed as simply as is the wont of most American academicians." Gilson's work, in his view, was a masterful and lucid account of medieval thought culminating in Thomas Aquinas's synthesis of Christian faith and Aristotelianism. "Augustine," Niebuhr commented in his review, "is not so certain that faith and reason can be brought into a perfect synthesis." Those two books had been prepared as Gifford Lectures, famous throughout the world. Early in 1937 Niebuhr himself was appointed to the Gifford lectureship in Scotland for the year 1939. "I will have to put myself into slavery of these lectures for years to come," he wrote a friend.[45]

Meanwhile, more immediate work involved Niebuhr as a participant in the Oxford Conference on Church, Community, and State in the summer of 1937—an international gathering of Protestant, Anglican, and Orthodox leaders. His visit to England then was one of several before and after that occasion. Niebuhr had acquired a vivid appreciation of the British genius for reconciling social advances and traditional institutions. A year earlier he wrote that, while the Germans were politically inept in their tendency to extremes of intellectualism or romanticism, the English possessed a historical wisdom that united organic and rational factors in a constitutional monarchy. Expanding on this in a lecture in London before going to Oxford, he stated:

> Human beings do not live in abstract universal societies. They live in historic communities; and the peace, order, and justice of such communities, such as it is, is the product of ages of development, a fact which justifies Edmund Burke in regarding historic rights and duties as more important than abstract rational rights and duties.

Conditions for peace, he declared, justify "a qualified religious reverence toward historic centers of power which maintain a tolerably just relationship to the community," but the same power needed for order so tempts those who wield it to injustice that "an unrelenting critical attitude toward all government" is required. Instrumental in arranging this lecture was Niebuhr's friend Sir Stafford Cripps, eminent barrister and Labour member of Parliament and later minister in the Churchill and Attlee governments.[46]

The Oxford Conference, held for two weeks in July, was a historic assemblage of delegates from churches in many lands for consideration of papers, addresses, and reports by leaders of thought in the churches. Among its participants as speakers, writers, or delegates were W. A. Visser 't Hooft and Emil Brunner from the Continent, William Temple and Olive Wyon from Britain, and John R. Mott, Henry P. Van Dusen, and John C. Bennett as well as Reinhold Niebuhr from America. A project of the ecumenical Life and Work movement, it was planned by J. H. Oldham, a British churchman who had been impressed by Niebuhr's *Moral Man and Immoral Society* and invited him to speak. A sense of ambiguity and perplexity in human affairs, and of need for theological understanding of social and political issues, prevailed at Oxford, in contrast to the sanguine and untheological outlook of a similar conference in Stockholm twelve years earlier. Those present felt the gathering world crisis by the absence of German Lutherans, barred from attending by the Nazi regime. In a stirring address to an audience of eight hundred, Niebuhr drew rounds of applause while delivering extemporaneously the substance of his prepared text, entitled "The Christian Church in a Secular Age." All forms of modern secularism, he declared, whether bourgeois humanist or Marxist or Nazi, contained an implicit or explicit self-glorification. The Christian gospel, on the other hand, called for contrition:

> It is a gospel of the Cross; and the Cross is a revelation of the love of God only to those who have first stood under it as a judgment. . . . It is in the

Cross that we become conscious how, not only what is worst, but what is best in human culture and civilization is involved in man's rebellion against God.

Noting that Augustine wrote *The City of God* when the Roman world had become the victim of barbarians, he suggested that the truest interpretations of Christian faith may come in such crises, when a proud culture is humbled. A profound faith, understanding life in its beauty and terror, will not seek to save the world by telling it to be more loving, but will strive for a tolerable justice in a bent world:

> The Christian gospel which transcends all particular and contemporary social situations can be preached with power only by a Church which bears its share of the burdens of immediate situations in which men are involved, burdens of establishing peace, of achieving justice, and of perfecting justice in the spirit of love. Thus is the kingdom of God which is not of this world made relevant to every problem of the world.

The address marked the beginning of Niebuhr's personal impact on the ecumenical movement. It was for many British participants at the conference their first encounter with him, and led in time to a quip (in allusion to C. H. Dodd, Oxford's great biblical scholar), "Thou shalt love the Lord thy Dodd, and thy Niebuhr as thyself."[47]

Meanwhile, in America, Niebuhr gave practical expression to his social concerns in various ways, including support of humanitarian projects in the South. Earlier he had visited and raised funds for the Highlander Folk School in the mountains of eastern Tennessee, founded in 1932 by Myles Horton—an interracial center long influential in teaching leadership skills to union organizers and civil rights activists. Then in 1936 Niebuhr joined others in a pilot project for raising living standards among Southern share-croppers, the Delta Cooperative Farm in the riverine bottomlands of northwestern Mississippi. There a group led by Sherwood Eddy acquired some two thousand acres on which impoverished sharecroppers were invited to form a cotton-producing co-op. Within a year thirty families, black and white, who had been evicted from nearby plantations for joining a tenant farmers' union settled on terms enabling them to develop and buy the farm. Niebuhr, who as president of the governing board visited the site in 1937, described it to *Christian Century* readers as "an effort to abolish landlordism." Explaining how many croppers lived in "more acute poverty and injustice than that of slavery days," he noted improved conditions on the co-op. The venture, however, ran into red ink as a result of various problems, from caprices of nature to inexperience and tension within the community, and a few years later the property was sold to individuals. Eddy concluded that producers' co-ops were unworkable, and the experience may well have given Niebuhr an appreciation of employers' problems. The Delta Farm did help to focus attention on the plight of sharecroppers, at a time when the New Deal introduced a program enabling some of them to buy farms through low-interest loans.[48]

Serving on the board of the Delta Farm with Niebuhr and Eddy was William Scarlett, Episcopal bishop of Missouri from 1930 to 1952, whose involvement on behalf of urban and rural poor had been inspired by Washington Gladden and Walter Rauschenbusch. Niebuhr and Scarlett, who first met as members of Eddy's study group touring the Ruhr in 1923, became lifelong friends. In the fall of 1937 Niebuhr published and dedicated to Eddy and Scarlett a volume of essays, originally preached as sermons in university chapels, entitled *Beyond Tragedy*. Written from sermon notes while he sailed to England and back, the book was a lucid presentation of themes developed from biblical texts: faith as trust in the meaningfulness of existence grounded in a God who transcends the world and ultimately overcomes the tragedies of history; the sin of pride as false security in human capacities and achievements or a grasping for power that results in injustice; God's working out his purposes in history through judgment of human pretensions and opportunities for repentance in response to the vicarious suffering of Christ; the kingdom of God as not purely otherworldly but a divine fulfillment of history in eternity. In each "sermonic essay" Niebuhr artfully developed his points from a biblical text. For example, taking Genesis 11:1–9 as a starting point, he wrote:

> The very character of a Tower of Babel, and the primary cause of its always tragic history is that its limitations, and its pretentious disregard of those limitations, are not seen from the inside, *i.e.*, by those groups who have compounded partial insights and particular interests with eternal and universal values.

The book moved many at the time it appeared, and has since endured for the power of its themes and its clarity of expression. Richard Niebuhr, whose own strictures on religious sentimentalism appeared that year in *The Kingdom of God in America*, wrote Reinhold that *Beyond Tragedy* was "the best book, the profoundest you have written and I think about the best theology which has appeared in America for a generation or two."[49]

Niebuhr's preaching, often done on weekends away from Union Seminary, was, as he put it, an "avocational interest as a kind of circuit rider in the colleges and universities." In the pulpit he had few peers, but he realized also the function of liturgy, commending it as better than the formlessness of pastoral prayer in most American Protestant churches. In a *Christian Century* essay in 1935, he wrote:

> Formal liturgy does not necessarily preserve vital religion. But it is like well-cultivated garden beds in which seeds may be dropped and spring to life. The individual worshiper may find in it the occasion for, and prompting to, religious aspiration which may be all the more effective because the form of liturgy is beautiful enough to carry religious emotion and not sufficiently specific to interfere with the particular moods and needs of worshipers.

If pastoral prayer is substituted for liturgy, he maintained, its style should cloak the pastor's personality, and it should include praise, thanksgiving, contrition, and intercession, naming personal and social sins and special needs among the neglected and mistreated members of society.[50]

"WHEN THE BEER IS SERVED AT REINIE'S"

Niebuhr preached not only in chapels from Harvard to the University of Chicago but, more regularly, at well-attended services in James Chapel of Union Seminary—handsomely built in English Gothic Revival style, with rich and warm and dark woodwork, a fine hammer beam trussed roof, and a chancel with a big stained-glass window and a Celtic cross suspended above it. His sermons, delivered in a forceful voice from rough notes, usually expounded the meaning of a text from the Prophets, the Gospels, or Paul. As a classroom teacher, Niebuhr—tall, bald, and blue-eyed—often paced the floor or leaned on the wall, told students what he thought of viewpoints under consideration, and always took questions toward the end of the hour. One scholar who studied with him during the early years has recalled "the marvelous rapport and ease with which he related to students." From 1934 onward he took over the basic ethics course previously taught alternately with Harry Ward, whose then thoroughgoing Marxism and humanistic view of Jesus were incompatible with Niebuhr's deepening Pauline realism. By the later 1930s enrollment rose in Niebuhr's classes and dwindled in Ward's; their differences were fictionalized in Edmund Fuller's *Brothers Divided,* a novel set in New York at a metropolitan seminary resembling Union.[51]

Outside the classroom, Niebuhr often conversed with students and colleagues in the seminary's refectory and enjoyed walks on Riverside Drive with Ursula and with friends or neighbors. His office for many years was Room 701 on the seventh floor of Union's tower, high above

the rotunda and main entrance, with windows overlooking both Broadway and 120th Street, now Reinhold Niebuhr Place. There he met individually with students and handled daily business, but he reserved
serious study and writing for quiet intervals in the sixth-floor apartment
he shared with Ursula at 99 Claremont Avenue, across the street from
the seminary. At their home, on Thursday evenings at stated times each
semester, the Niebuhrs invited everyone to an open house for informal
discussion and doughnuts with cider or beer. Ursula has described the
occasions, with normally some fifty students crowded into the living and
dining rooms, as "a free for all" but mostly "Reinhold's show," since
"they wanted him to talk." The subject invariably was theology and
politics. Niebuhr's openness and interest in students led most of them to
call him "Reinie." The evening gatherings gave rise to a student song, to
the tune of "When the Roll Is Called up Yonder":

> When it's eight o'clock on Thursday night
>   and books become a bore
> Then we'll leave our desks and climb the golden stair.
> We will gather at the master's feet
>   a-sitting on the floor.
> When the beer is served at Reinie's, we'll be there.

One student of those days, who came to the open houses while taking
Niebuhr's courses, has recalled that Niebuhr often began responding to
something said by saying, "It isn't as simple as that."[52]

Social and religious truth was for Niebuhr complex and often dialectical, found in the interaction of different and usually opposing ideas that
need each other for completion. In 1937 John Bennett—who had studied
at Oxford and Union, become associated with Niebuhr's circle, and taught
at other seminaries before joining the Union faculty in 1943—assessed
Niebuhr's contribution in the first of several lucid essays on the subject
over the decades. In order to understand him, Bennett began, one must
grasp his efforts to sort truth from error in such diverse traditions as
Lutheranism, liberalism, and Marxism; his criticism of tendencies in any
one of them might seem one-sided, "but if you read his work as a whole
you find that no thinker could be more balanced." His bilingual background put him in touch with the best Continental theology: "He has
mediated to America insights which have become commonplaces of European Christianity. He might be described as the soul of Europe hovering
over American thought." His realism was penetrating: "Underlying all of
Niebuhr's thought is his keen perception of the stubbornness of evil in

the human situation. He has torn the masks off modern life more successfully than any other religious thinker in America." A friendly critic, Bennett noted some rough edges in his work at that time, including a polemical tendency that sometimes obscured valid elements in historical movements he criticized, and insufficient allowance for forms of sin other than pride. Yet Niebuhr was, in his estimation, "the most significant influence in contemporary American religious thought."[53] In his tenth year at Union Seminary, back from the Oxford Conference, Reinhold Niebuhr turned to the task of further study and a fuller and more systematic exposition of theological and ethical themes in his forthcoming Gifford Lectures.

CHAPTER FOUR

The Magnum Opus: Human Nature and Destiny

❧

Niebuhr prepared his Gifford Lectures, delivered in the spring and fall of 1939, and revised them for publication in two volumes as *The Nature and Destiny of Man,* appearing in 1941 and 1943, while clouds of war gathered and the spread of Nazi tyranny precipitated the most terrible conflagration in the annals of humankind. He was deeply engaged in world issues preceding and following the outbreak of World War II, as related in the next chapter. The present chapter focuses on his "magnum opus."

THE GIFFORD LECTURES

Established through the munificence of Adam Lord Gifford, a wealthy Scottish lawyer and judge, the Gifford Lectures had their inception in 1888, entrusted to the Universities of Edinburgh, Glasgow, St. Andrews, and Aberdeen. Intended by their founder as a forum for discussion of "natural theology" but broadening in scope over the years, they grew in fame after William James's lectures were published in 1902 as *The Varieties of Religious Experience.* Other Gifford lecturers, before Niebuhr, had included Alfred North Whitehead, John Dewey, Albert Schweitzer, Werner Jaeger, and, as mentioned earlier, Étienne Gilson and William Temple. Subsequent lecturers, after World War II, have included Emil Brunner, Christopher Dawson, Gabriel Marcel, Arnold Toynbee, Paul Tillich, Rudolph Bultmann, and John Macquarrie, to name only some of them. Niebuhr's invitation to give the annual lectures, at Edinburgh University in 1939, came from a committee in whose decision John Baillie, professor of theology and later principal of New College at the university, played a role.[1]

Before being asked to deliver the Gifford Lectures, Niebuhr had already acquired much of the immense learning reflected in them, but the invitation spurred him to heavy studies while he prepared them before their delivery in Edinburgh, and still more before they finally appeared in print. "I am busy reading for my Giffords," he wrote William Scarlett after returning from the Oxford Conference to the cottage in Heath in the summer of 1937. He did, as Paul Tillich remarked to a friend in the late 1930s, a vast amount of reading. Its scope, as seen in the published version of his lectures, was encyclopedic. Niebuhr kept no record of his reading then, and some of it included books with which he was already familiar, but it is clear that he studied the works of Saint Augustine more thoroughly than before and began reading Kierkegaard for the first time. Furthermore, he read, or read anew, many other theological works of the past, including those of Luther and Calvin, and delved deeply into philosophy from Plato and Aristotle to Kant and Heidegger. Among contemporary works on the history of ideas, his reading ranged from Charles Norris Cochrane's *Christianity and Classical Culture* to Carl L. Becker's *The Heavenly City of the Eighteenth-Century Philosophers.*[2]

A recent theological work that clearly impressed Niebuhr during those years was Emil Brunner's *Der Mensch im Widerspruch* (1937), which he read before its appearance in English as *Man in Revolt*. In a letter to Brunner in March of 1938, he wrote:

> I have been wanting to write to you for some time to tell you how much I appreciated your book *Der Mensch im Widerspruch*. It is in every respect a profound and scholarly work that throws needed light on many questions of Christian anthropology that seem to me never to have been considered before. I have studied the book with mingled feelings, partly because I learned so much from it and partly because it took the wind out of my sails as it dealt with some matters like the historicity of "the fall" for instance, which I had expected to deal with in the Gifford Lectures on which I am working. You have made really a great contribution in this book.

In reply, Brunner stated:

> Your letter made me very happy. It was the first echo of my book from the other side of the ocean. That it was so very positive gives me hope.

He went on to say:

> We must stand fast together. It is my firm conviction: everything is at stake. Neither Fundamentalism (or the European neo-orthodoxy which tends toward Fundamentalism) nor Liberalism can advance the Church of Christ,

but only a theology that is as free, as Biblical, as candid, as aggressive as you and I, regrettably, don't have yet, but know, at least, to be our goal.

I don't seriously believe that I have taken the wind out of your sails with my book. If you begin where I have left off, more remains for you to do than I have done.[3]

Brunner's book was a study of the Christian doctrine of man, understood as created in the divine image for love of God and neighbor, but prone to contradiction of that image in self-centered or escapist tendencies arising in the human situation of existential dread. It was primarily an analysis of sin, emphasizing with Kierkegaard the paradox of its inevitability and yet of human responsibility for it, and a critique of Greek rationalism and modern naturalism as alternatives to a Christian understanding of human life as a personal unity of body and soul in rebellion against the God-given norms of its existence. Niebuhr was working on the same theological problems, approaching them in the Augustinian Protestant tradition in which Brunner also stood during the interwar period in which both—first Brunner, then Niebuhr—discovered Kierkegaard. Consequently, the first volume of his published Gifford Lectures, setting the Christian view of human nature against ancient and modern alternatives and presenting an existential analysis of sin as pride and sensuality, resembles Brunner's *Man in Revolt*.

By midsummer of 1938 Niebuhr shared his first two chapters with Henry Sloane Coffin. "This is far and away the most solid thing which you have done, and it is splendidly done," Coffin commented, adding suggestions to smoothen sentences. During the fall of that year Union Seminary was buzzing as Niebuhr gave a preliminary version of his forthcoming lectures, but it was not until after delivering them in Scotland that he put them together in a yearlong course sequence during 1939–40. He went on leave during the spring and early fall of 1939 for the Gifford Lectures, scheduled for two three-week periods, from April 24 to May 14 and from October 11 to November 1, each series including ten lectures. Sailing on the *Queen Mary* liner, he arrived in Britain weeks before the first series, accompanied by Ursula and their young son, Christopher, and baby daughter, Elisabeth. The family took a train to Edinburgh, the venerable Scottish capital, situated on the Firth of Forth and dominated by its castle on a high rock. Niebuhr's lectures, delivered in Rainy Hall of Edinburgh University, held the attention of an audience of some 250 people. John Baillie, who arranged for his family to stay at 45 Dick Place in a pleasant suburb, heard him speak each afternoon through the whole series. Afterward Baillie wrote that he "did not read his lectures, but delivered them extempore from skeleton notes," a practice unusual among Gifford lecturers that "added greatly to the interest and effectiveness of the occasion." One woman, he recalled, commented after one of the lectures with these words: "I dinna understand a word ye say . . . but somehow I ken that ye're makin' God great." Baillie himself found the lectures comprehensible as delivered, and readable in their later published form.[4] The first series became volume one, and the second volume two, of *The Nature and Destiny of Man*. Its magisterial theme will be expounded later in this chapter.

Halfway through the first series, Niebuhr wrote from Edinburgh to Bishop Scarlett in St. Louis: "The lectures have gone fairly well, I think, though the canny Scots do not let you know what they think of your stuff." By the end of that series, however, his auditors seem to have expressed their enthusiasm openly, for Niebuhr wrote his mother and sister, who since 1932 had shared an apartment in Manhattan, where Hulda was director of Christian education at Madison Avenue Presbyterian Church: "My general approach has many more kindred spirits over here than in the U.S.A., so that the warmth of response is really quite overwhelming." After the lectures he preached at the Church of St. Mary the Virgin in Oxford, writing Scarlett that it was "one of the most thrilling experiences, though I am little much of a Protestant to preach in Newman's pulpit." He also attended a theological conference presided over by the Archbishop of York, William Temple, whom he found "humble, gracious, and charming as ever." Then, during the summer of 1939, the Niebuhrs stayed at a place known as Moat House in the country village of Wivelsfield, in Sussex, forty miles south of London. There Reinhold worked on the second series of his Gifford Lectures; it was, as he wrote Scarlett from Wivelsfield, "a rather big chore." The British, meanwhile, had begun preparations for war after German troops marched into Prague in March, and air raid drills were held through the summer. Then in September, when Hitler struck at Poland, Britain and France declared war. While engaged in the greatest scholarly project of his life, Niebuhr took time to report on these grim developments in a series for *Christian Century* readers entitled "Leaves from the Notebook of a War-Bound American." Because of the war, Ursula returned home with the children, along with many other American nationals then in Britain, while Reinhold stayed for the second series of his Gifford Lectures. At one point while he lectured, those present could hear German warplanes and antiaircraft fire at a nearby naval base. It was during the initial phase of the war, before

German forces advanced into western Europe, that he completed his lectures in Edinburgh.[5]

After returning home, Niebuhr devoted much of the next year, while Hitler's armies took Paris and the Battle of Britain raged, to revising his first series of Gifford Lectures for publication. Then, before he revised the second series, certain scholarly events engaged his interest. In 1940 Charles Norris Cochrane's *Christianity and Classical Culture* appeared, making quite an impact as an Augustinian critique of Greco-Roman thought. This book by a Canadian scholar of Greek and Roman history, Niebuhr remarked in reviewing it, "has given me more unalloyed pleasure than anything I have read in the past decade." Cochrane, he observed, interpreted Rome's decline as caused basically by inadequacies in classical philosophy, though without obscuring other factors of decay after the Augustan principate overcame the chaos of the late republic:

> Professor Cochrane's basic criticism of the classical mind is that its fundamental categories are unable to comprehend the realities of history. Whether it thinks in terms of mind or matter, of the causal chains of nature or of rational forms as the ultimate reality, it cannot deal with the uniqueness of the historical occasion or comprehend the freedom of personality as it acts in history. History is, as a matter of fact, a curious compound of freedom and fate, which can be given meaning only in terms of some concept of providence which the classical mind cannot achieve.

Greco-Roman philosophy, in other words, did not understand history because classical thought alternated between a Platonism that reduced its vicissitudes to chance and a naturalism that reduced them to determinism; the gulf between nature and the Eternal can be bridged, and history understood as meaningful, only through the Christian doctrine of the Trinity as developed in the age of Constantine and after. Cochrane's account of ideas and events in the Roman Empire concluded with a treatment of Augustine's interpretation of history that impressed Niebuhr "because it has its eye upon what is essential and is not lost in theological minutiae." The modern age, he concluded his review, "requires an Augustinian reformulation of the problem of life and history." Niebuhr marked heavily and kept his copy of Cochrane's book.[6]

During the late 1930s and early 1940s, meanwhile, several of Kierkegaard's major works appeared for the first time in English translation from the Danish. Until then, only German translations existed, and in preparing his Gifford Lectures, Niebuhr relied especially on one of them, *Der Begriff der Angst*, before its publication in English as *The Concept of Dread*. When in 1941 Kierkegaard's *Concluding Unscientific Postscript*—his sustained attack on Hegelian philosophy published in Denmark almost a century earlier—appeared in English, Niebuhr reviewed it:

> Gradually the core of Kierkegaard's thought is being made available to American readers. . . . No work of the Danish philosopher will give . . . a more comprehensive view of his thought than this *Postscript*. In it we find Kierkegaard's polemic against speculative philosophy, and his indictment of philosophical systems, developed from every angle.

Kierkegaard, he continued, criticized Hegel for seeking "to give us a complete system of reality from an obviously finite perspective," for the Dane saw vividly the situation of the existing individual:

> The anxieties which make his reason something less than pure . . . are the anxieties of a spirit which both transcends and is involved in the natural process. The solution for the problem of the uniqueness, finiteness, and insecurity of the individual and the relativity of his knowledge is . . . a frank acceptance of the real situation: "My thesis is that subjectivity, inwardness is the truth."

The inwardness of Kierkegaard, Niebuhr went on to say, expresses itself in faith as the discovery of God in the human situation above and yet within nature:

> All those who think that religious faith is a substitute in the lives of simple people for what sophisticated people achieve by philosophy would learn a great deal from Kierkegaard's discussion of despair as the ultimate consequence of trying to comprehend the world from the standpoint of the finite self and of faith as the possibility on the other side of despair.

He had already read Kierkegaard's *The Sickness Unto Death* in German; when it appeared in English in 1942, he described it as "one of the profoundest of his religious treatises," but went on to join a criticism to his appreciation of the Danish thinker: "Kierkegaard's religious individualism rises to the point of destroying the meaning of life in its social context."[7]

Meanwhile, the older legacy of Saint Augustine remained a pervasive influence on Niebuhr's thought. His Gifford Lectures made abundant references to such works of the great church father as *The Confessions*, *On Nature and Grace*, *The Spirit and the Letter*, *On the Trinity*, *The Enchiridion*, and, above all, *The City of God*. That masterpiece was "one of the most important books of our spiritual history," Niebuhr wrote in a major magazine piece in the grim year of 1942:

> In it he maintained that decay of Rome was not the end of all things, and certainly not a cause for despair. On the contrary he affirmed that the

Christian religion contained an interpretation of life and history that made it possible to anticipate and to discount the periodic catastrophes of history.

Augustine's doctrines of history and selfhood deeply influenced Niebuhr's thought, as expressed in the two volumes of his Gifford Lectures. He completed work on the second volume, with some stylistic help from Henry Sloane Coffin, in August of 1942 at Heath, Massachusetts, where the Niebuhr family continued to spend summers.[8]

The general theme of *The Nature and Destiny of Man* is the need for a synthesis of Renaissance and Reformation insights concerning the possibilities and limits of human existence, implicit in a Christian understanding of the paradox of grace as renewal of life and forgiveness of sins. Such an interpretation of life and history must commence with a consideration of the human situation and the mystery of sin. The themes of Niebuhr's magnum opus are expounded in the following synopsis.

CLASSICISM, MODERNITY, AND A CHRISTIAN VIEW OF HUMAN NATURE

Volume one of *The Nature and Destiny of Man* opens with a chapter treating the classical, Christian, and modern views of human nature. Turning first to that of classical antiquity—that is, of the Greco-Roman world—Niebuhr stated:

> The classical view of man, comprised primarily of Platonic, Aristotelian, and Stoic conceptions of human nature, contains, of course, varying emphases but it may be regarded as one in its common conviction that man is to be understood primarily from the standpoint of the uniqueness of his rational faculties.

In Plato and Aristotle, he continued, "mind" is the ordering principle of the soul and practically identified with God, while the body is sharply distinguished from it and regarded as evil. While Stoicism differs as a pantheistic philosophy, it similarly regards man as essentially reason, and reason as a spark of the divine, while holding a negative view of bodily impulses. Less typically among the Greeks, Democritus and Epicurus viewed humankind wholly as part of nature. The mind-body dualism so characteristic of Greek and Roman classicism equated rationality with virtue, and resulted in reducing history to a realm of meaningless recurrences. An exception to the classical emphasis on mind as virtuous, Niebuhr noted, is Greek tragedy, for the dramas of Aeschylus and Sophocles portrayed the vitalities of life in creative as well as destructive conflict with the rational virtues, or with each other in society, and so are closer to the Christian view in measuring the human spirit.[9]

The Christian understanding of human nature, Niebuhr pointed out, appreciates the unity of body and soul as part of the goodness of creation. It further regards the human person as made in the "image of God," endowed with a spirit that includes not only rational capacity for surveying the world and forming concepts but also self-transcendence, by which the self as subject views itself as object. Mystical religions and philosophies also recognize this self-transcending depth of the human spirit, but seek absorption of the individual in an undifferentiated realm of ultimate reality. Christian faith, however, apprehending God's self-disclosure culminating in Christ, preserves individuality in viewing man as a personal unity of will "known and loved of God" who "must find himself in terms of obedience to the divine will." This high estimate of human stature, Niebuhr continued, contrasts with the low estimate of human virtue in Christian thought, which regards man as a sinner in rebellion against God:

> Sin is occasioned precisely by the fact that man refuses to admit his "creatureliness" and to acknowledge himself as merely a member of a total unity of life. He pretends to be more than he is.

The law of human nature is love, a harmonious relation of lives in obedience to God:

> This law is violated when man seeks to make himself the centre and source of his own life. His sin is therefore spiritual and not carnal, though the infection of rebellion spreads from the spirit to the body and disturbs its harmonies also.

One purpose of the present volume was to analyze the Christian idea of sin more fully in later chapters.[10]

Turning to the modern view of human nature, as seen by such varied thinkers as Bacon, Montaigne, Descartes, Kant, Hegel, Nietzsche, and Freud, Niebuhr observed an unresolved conflict between idealistic rationalism and romantic or rationalistic naturalism. By regarding humankind in terms of mind or nature, modernity had dissipated the idea of individuality which the Renaissance drew from Christianity, he held. The rationalism and naturalism of recent centuries, furthermore, was too optimistic about human nature:

> Modern man has an essentially easy conscience; and nothing gives the diverse and discordant notes of modern culture so much harmony as the

unanimous opposition of modern man to Christian conceptions of the sin-
fulness of man. . . . Either the rational man or the natural man is conceived
as essentially good, and it is only necessary for man either to rise from the
chaos of nature to the harmony of mind or to descend from the chaos of
spirit to the harmony of nature in order to be saved.

This optimism, he added, results in a philosophy of history expressed in
the idea of progress—a notion that human society can move toward perfection through some force in nature, increasing rationality, or elimination
of specific evils in religious, political, economic, or cultural life. Such
historical optimism grew on Christian soil, with its Hebraic sense of a
meaningful history, but is a secularized version of the biblical interpretation in which the doctrine of sin is excluded.[11]

Discussing in the next three chapters such modern philosophies as
Kantian rationalism, Rousseauistic romanticism, Hegelian idealism, Comtian scientism, and Marxist materialism, Niebuhr held that none of them
fully recognizes that human beings have "a freedom of spirit which transcends both nature and reason." Thus, though containing some truth,
they do not see human nature in sufficient depth, losing the self in the
universality of mind or some natural force. A recent version of such confusion, Niebuhr noted, is John Dewey's faith that organized intelligence
can achieve the same results in human relations achieved by it in the
mastery of nature: that assumption overlooks the fact that such an effort
has its own social locus and so cannot impartially resolve conflicts of
interest. Despite the social chaos, political tyranny, and international anarchy that fill contemporary history, modern man remains confident of
his goodness and "considers himself the victim of corrupting institutions
which he is about to destroy or reconstruct, or of the confusions of ignorance which an adequate education is about to overcome." Attributing
evil to faulty political or economic organization or to social anachronisms,
the French Enlightenment and its successors have failed to see that "a
particular manifestation of evil in history" is "but the fruit and consequence of a profounder root of evil." Such modern explanations may
point the way to mitigating certain social ills, but ignore tendencies in
human nature that produce historical evil.[12]

Before focusing on the Christian doctrine of man, Niebuhr devoted a
chapter to biblical revelation, with its "twofold emphasis upon the transcendence of God and upon His intimate relation with the world." The
historical revelation of God discerned by faith in special events, he pointed
out, assumes a general revelation in the world and in personal experience.
The latter includes a sense of dependence on the ultimate source of ex-

istence, a sense of moral obligation and guilt, and a longing for forgiveness. These elements are dim counterparts of the biblical doctrine of God as Creator, Judge, and Redeemer. In biblical faith, God's creation of the world is regarded as revealing his majesty and power, for the causal relations of the natural order cannot explain its givenness in totality. The world as created is good, though not God; thus "the foundation is laid for the Biblical emphasis upon the meaningfulness of history." But God, Niebuhr went on to say, is not fully known apart from specific self-disclosures of his character in historical events. The catastrophes of history experienced by ancient Israel and her neighbors, as interpreted by the prophets, were divine judgments on human pride, whether as the pretended virtue of God's covenant people or as the false self-sufficiency and grasping for power of surrounding empires. The Old Testament is more clear about God's judgment than about his mercy and how the two are related. From a Christian standpoint, Niebuhr emphasized, the life and death of Christ become the final revelation of God's character by so relating his judgment to his mercy that divine wrath is overcome, though not abrogated, by divine forgiveness. In the sacrifice on the cross, human sin becomes more vivid "by the knowledge that God is himself the victim" of it. The meaning of the revelation in Christ, once apprehended by faith, is validated in human experience. Explicated in the doctrine of the atonement, it is "an absolutely essential presupposition for the understanding of human nature and human history."[13]

In the last half of volume one, Niebuhr elaborated in five chapters a Christian interpretation of human nature in terms of its self-transcendent freedom and creaturely finitude, its proneness to sin as pride or sensuality, and its God-given norms of faith as trust and of love as the fruit of faith. Augustine, he pointed out, was the first Western thinker to comprehend the capacity of the human spirit to transcend time and even itself through memory, the storehouse of recallable experience at which he marveled in his *Confessions* and *On the Trinity*. Standing outside the world and itself as "image of God" *(imago Dei)* but not deity, it can find its true home only in God, whose mystery Augustine emphasized in words Niebuhr quoted: "For if thou dost comprehend, He is not God." The self, transcending nature as a free spirit, is nevertheless a finite unity of body and soul, in Kierkegaard's phrase "the conscious synthesis of the limited and the unlimited." Human selves, Niebuhr continued, are not evil in their finitude but meant to accept it in reverence and humility:

> The fragmentary character of human life is not regarded as evil in Biblical faith because it is seen from the perspective of a centre of life and meaning

in which each fragment is related to the plan of the whole, to the will of God. The evil arises when the fragment seeks by its own wisdom to comprehend the whole or attempts by its own power to realize it.

While Greek philosophy and early Hellenistic Christianity sought to overcome finiteness and mortality as evil, Augustine recovered the biblical truth that "sin has its source not in temporality but in man's willful refusal to acknowledge the finite and determinate character of his existence."[14]

Niebuhr's treatment of sin, integral to the larger theme of his treatise, appeared in chapters seven, eight, and nine of volume one. "The Bible," he began, "defines sin in both religious and moral terms," as a human effort to usurp the place of God and as injustice which the proud in their power impose on others. Sin arises in the human situation of finiteness and freedom, "standing in and yet above nature." In probing this, Niebuhr found Kierkegaard's *The Concept of Dread* a profound analysis of existential anxiety as "the inevitable concomitant of the paradox of freedom and finiteness in which man is involved" and as "the internal precondition of sin." Both free and bound, humankind are anxious in awareness of their finitude and, lacking perfect trust in the security of God's love, tend to prideful self-assertion. They are also anxious, however, to realize the possibilities of freedom. Thus basic human anxiety has creative as well as destructive aspects, as man seeks "both to realize his unlimited possibilities and to overcome and to hide the dependent and contingent character of his existence." So it is that human creativity is involved in sin, arising in anxiety as pride or sensuality:

> Man falls into pride, when he seeks to raise his contingent existence to unconditioned significance; he falls into sensuality, when he seeks to escape from his unlimited possibilities of freedom . . . by losing himself in some natural vitality.[15]

Sin as pride, observed Niebuhr, is more basic than sensual sin in biblical and Christian thought. Augustine, he noted, defined it in *The City of God* as "undue exaltation, when the soul abandons Him to whom it ought to cleave as its end and becomes a kind of end in itself." Niebuhr analyzed pride by distinguishing three kinds, sometimes overlapping in actual life: pride of power, of knowledge, and of virtue. The first is found among individuals or groups wielding extraordinary social power who imagine themselves "secure against all vicissitudes" or among those less established who seek "sufficient power to guarantee their security" always "at the expense of others." In the later 1930s, a historically secure but too confident Britain, and an insecure and aggressive Germany, symbolized such pride. The ancient pharaohs, hoping to immortalize themselves in pyramids, and bourgeois moderns greedy for physical comfort and security, illustrate pride as will-to-power in a mild form. Turning to pride of knowledge, Niebuhr held that it is "an attempt to obscure the known conditioned character of human knowledge and the taint of self-interest in human truth." Instances of intellectual pride are Hegel's claim that his thought was final, the blindness of Marxism to the taint and limitations of its own viewpoint, and the failure of a naturalistic age to recognize the limits of scientific knowledge. The third kind of pride Niebuhr defined as "the pretension of finite man that his highly conditioned virtue is the final righteousness and that his very relative moral standards are absolute." It is the sin of self-righteousness criticized by Jesus, Paul, and Luther and has been a source of much cruelty in history. Finally, there is an explicit form of moral pride in spiritual pride, reached when "partial standards and relative attainments . . . claim divine sanction." Catholicism and Protestantism have at times succumbed to it; so have Jacobinism and Stalinism in making unconditioned claims implicitly religious. Pride, Niebuhr added, whether of virtue or knowledge or power, involves the self in efforts to deceive itself and others in order to believe its pretensions.[16]

The pride of large-scale groups, especially of nations, Niebuhr held, is "a more pregnant source of injustice and conflict than purely individual pride." The insight of the Hebrew prophets, beginning with Amos, that such pride stands under divine judgment has no parallel in Plato and Aristotle or even in Stoic universalism:

> The conviction that collective pride is the final form of sin is possible only within terms of a religion of revelation in the faith of which a voice of God is heard from beyond all human majesties and a divine power is revealed in comparison with which the "nations are as a drop of a bucket" (Isa. 40:15).

While sin as pride was the primary concern of the prophets from Amos onward, they saw that it was invariably accompanied by injustice, and discerned the judgment of God not only on Israel but on its proud conquerors. Biblical faith, Niebuhr emphasized, not only recognizes the universality of sin but regards moral distinctions as significant:

> While all modern nations, and indeed all nations of history, have been involved in the sin of pride, one must realize, in this as in other estimates of human sinfulness, that it is just as important to recognize differences in the degree of pride and self-will expressed by men and nations, as it is to know that all . . . are sinful in the sight of God.

Thus Paul's assertion that "all have sinned, and come short of the glory of God" (Rom. 3:23) is complemented by Amos's strictures on those who "oppress the poor" and "lie upon beds of ivory" (Amos 4:1; 6:4) and by the note struck in Mary's Magnificat: "He hath put down the mighty . . . and exalted them of low degree" (Luke 1:52). Distinctions must be made, insisted Niebuhr, between oppressors and their victims, liars and honest individuals, debauched sensualists and self-disciplined workers, despite the involvement of all in sin.[17]

Turning to sin as sensuality, Niebuhr observed that it destroys harmony within the self, while pride results in disharmonies outside the self, but that such sins as sexual promiscuity and drunkenness, because more obvious than pride, "have always been subject to a sharper and readier social disapproval." Noting that Augustine, Aquinas, and Luther each viewed sensuality as derived from pride, or inordinate self-love, he offered a psychologically more convincing analysis of it as an admixture of ego-enhancing self-love and an effort by the self to escape itself: "The self, finding itself to be inadequate as the centre of its existence, seeks for another god amidst the various forces, processes, and impulses of nature over which it ostensibly presides." Thus one may seek in intoxication a sense of self-importance or an escape from guilt and the tension of conscious life; or the self in sexual passion both asserts its ego and seeks escape in idolatry of another. Sex as such is not sinful, but human sexual relations are an occasion for self-love and flight from self as well as creative self-giving. At worst, in commercialized vice, it is a means of momentary escape from life through a plunge into nothingness. Sensuality, Niebuhr concluded, whether in sexual license or drunkenness or gluttony or luxurious living or some other form, is a futile assertion of the self, an effort to escape the self in some other person or process, and finally an attempted flight into subconsciousness.[18]

Sin in any of its aspects, Niebuhr continued, is a mystery in which "man sins inevitably, yet without escaping responsibility for his sin." Augustine stated this truth in words Niebuhr quoted from *On Nature and Grace*: "Man's nature was indeed at first created faultless and without sin; but nature (as man now has it, in which every one is born from Adam) wants the Physician, being no longer in a healthy state. All good qualities . . . it has from the most High God. . . . But the flaw which darkens and weakens all these natural goods, it has not contracted from its blameless Creator . . . but from that original sin which it committed of its own free will." Thus Augustine sought to express the paradox of human responsibility for sin despite its inevitability, which his Pelagian critics attacked as illogical, holding that sin is avoidable if the will is free. The Augustinian paradox, Niebuhr insisted, is attested in the self's interior experience of remorse or sorrow for sin, to which it still remains prone. Yet Augustine, he pointed out, as Kierkegaard had done, obscured the individual's responsibility for sin by implying that it is a taint inherited from Adam. It is, again, in anxiety—or what Kierkegaard called "the dizziness of freedom"—that temptation occurs, but sin arises as self-love in disobedience to the divine will and "thus points to the prior sin of lack of trust in God." That, he added, "is the meaning of Kierkegaard's assertion that sin posits itself."[19]

Humanity even in its state of sin, Niebuhr maintained in the concluding chapter of volume one, retains some echo of the ideal possibilities of life in myths of a lost perfection, which point to "what man is truly and essentially." Christian theology expresses this in the concept of "original righteousness" *(justitia originalis)*, the law of human nature as free spirit, while Stoicism does so in its idea of natural law as the norm for humankind in its worldly life. Original righteousness, according to Niebuhr, consists of "faith, hope, and love" or "love of God and neighbor": faith and hope mean trust in the love and providence of God, while love is a derivative of faith and a requirement of human relations. Natural law, defining harmonies of life discerned by reason, is inadequate without faith and love as final norms under which human life stands. Differing with Barth, he held that, while love and trust are not simple possibilities, sin does not destroy but only corrupts the original perfection—or "image of God"—in human life, known in moments of self-transcendence. Whether or not "original righteousness" can be realized in history, Niebuhr stated, would be considered in volume two.[20]

A Synthesis of Renaissance Values and Reformation Insights

Volume two of *The Nature and Destiny of Man* commences with a discussion, in three chapters, of the meaning of life and history as illuminated by Christ. Such meaning, Niebuhr emphasized, is only possible wherever history is viewed as potentially meaningful and awaiting full disclosure and fulfillment of its meaning. But wherever meaning is sought merely in nature or in emancipation to a supramundane realm, Christ can have no meaning, because the historical dimension of life is regarded as meaningless. Such was the case among the Greeks in Epicurean naturalism or, more typically, in the Platonic quest for escape from temporal process to a realm of pure being; a more consistent and mystical disavowal of mean-ing in history appears in Buddhism. On the other hand, Niebuhr contin-ued, ancient Egyptian and Babylonian culture, taking history more seri-ously, developed hopes for a messianic king who would bring about the triumph of good over evil in history. Such hope became a strand in late Hebraic religion, looking for history's culmination in "the triumph and the vindication of the righteous"; but the prophets, discerning sin even in the righteous, raised without answering "the question of how God will complete history by overcoming the perennial evil in every human good."[21]

Jesus' answer to the problem of history posed by the prophets, ac-cording to Niebuhr, was to reinterpret Messianism in the words "The Son of man must suffer," combining the "son of man" motif of Jewish apoc-alypse and the "suffering servant" idea of second Isaiah in his role as the representative of God. Through vicarious suffering for the sins of the world, God makes his mercy known in history, so that all may become aware of their guilt and redemption. Thus God achieves his purpose "not by destruction of the evil-doers but by his own bearing of the evil." Jesus' affirmation that the kingdom of God "has come" and "will come," Nie-buhr held, implied a historical interim between the disclosure and the full establishment of divine sovereignty: "In thus conceiving history after Christ as an interim . . . a continued element of inner contradiction in history is accepted as its perennial characteristic." The meaning of God's revelation in Christ as judgment and mercy, he went on to say, "can be mediated to the individual only if the truth of the Atonement is appro-priated inwardly" in contrition and faith and in newness of life, or as Kierkegaard put it in his *Concluding Unscientific Postscript,* "subjectively." The truth revealed on the cross, defined by Saint Paul as "the foolishness of God" which "is wiser than men" (I Cor. 1:25), could not have been anticipated by human culture, Niebuhr held, for it cannot be deduced from experience, though it illuminates and is verified by experience in the community of faith. God's revelation in Christ expresses his freedom in mercy beyond judgment through an act of sacrificial love *(agapē),* which according to Niebuhr is both a norm of concern for others, without which human mutualities would degenerate into calculated self-interest, and a divine perfection contradicting false human pretensions of virtue in his-tory.[22]

Niebuhr focused, in the next two chapters, on the doctrine of grace through Christian ages. Saint Paul, he held, expounded grace in its two aspects "as power in, and mercy toward, man," describing it as love and joy flowing from repentance and faith through the power of the Holy Spirit, and as forgiveness of sin mediated by Christ. "There are texts in the Pauline epistles which lean to the one or the other side of the interpretation of grace," Niebuhr pointed out, but taken together they reflect "a profound understanding of the complexities of the spiritual life of man with its possibilities of genuine newness of life . . . and yet . . . the possibility of sin even on this new level." While the truth necessary for such an experience of grace is mediated only through the revelation in Christ, Niebuhr remarked, there is a "hidden Christ" who operates in history among "those who do not know the historical revelation" but "may achieve a more genuine repentance and humility than those who do." Paul's doctrine of grace, Niebuhr went on to say, was obscured in early Christian centuries by perfectionist illusions among the Eastern church fathers. Augustine, however, recovered the biblical understanding of sin and guarded it, together with the importance of grace, against Pelagian moralism; but his doctrine of grace as infused through the church did "not fully recognize the persistent power of self-love in the new life." Augustine's emphasis on grace as power rather than pardon became "definitive for the whole Catholic conception of life and history." As formulated by Aquinas, Catholic doctrine merged "the self-esteem of classical man and the Biblical sense of the contradiction between man and God." The result was a qualified optimism, subordinating justification to sanctification. The medieval church, Niebuhr continued, attempted a synthesis of Christian and classical elements in a system of doctrine and authority that blunted biblical insights and cultural potencies. The Renaissance challenged that synthesis by dispensing with grace and asserting the autonomy of reason in the pursuit of culture and the fulfillment of life, while the Reformation did so by affirming the authority of Scripture and particularly its Pauline emphasis on grace as forgiveness of sin.[23]

Niebuhr then turned, in chapters six and seven, to consideration of what was valid and what false in the Renaissance and the Reformation as movements that ushered in the modern era, for it was his thesis that each represented important truths, prematurely checked or obscured by the medieval synthesis, needed for a profound understanding of life and history:

> Our analysis of the human situation in the light of Christian faith has brought us to the conviction that both the Renaissance and the Reformation embody insights which must enter into an adequate redefinition of the possibilities and limits of man's historical existence.

The Renaissance, as he used the term, designated not only the cultural movement that began in Italy and spread northward in early modern times, but also related philosophical, religious, and social movements that shared its spirit "as a tremendous affirmation of the limitless possibilities of human existence, and as a rediscovery of the sense of a meaningful history." Early Italian humanism, Niebuhr noted, was not merely a return to classical values but an effort to renew society, partly inspired by the historical perfectionism of Franciscan spirituality; but it transmuted the latter into a worldly optimism without the infusion of grace. The eighteenth-century Enlightenment developed Renaissance hopes into the utopian rationalism of the idea of progress, expressed by Condorcet and others, and nineteenth-century variants followed. A similar impulse to perfectionism, in individual or social life, appeared in such Protestant sects as the Quakers, with their idea of an "inner light," and the Diggers and Levelers of Cromwellian England, with their dream of realizing the kingdom of God on earth. Whether in its sectarian or more typically secular forms, the Renaissance, observed Niebuhr, overwhelmed the Reformation as the advance of science, the discovery and settlement of new continents, the growth of democracy and industry, and the expansion of commerce seemed to support the hope of fulfilling the meaning of life in history. Yet, he added, contemporary experience refuted such optimism as nations harnessed modern technology to purely destructive and tyrannical ends.[24]

The Reformation, as defined by Niebuhr, was "the historical locus where the Christian conscience became most fully aware of the persistence of sin in the life of the redeemed," an insight resulting in "appreciation of that part of the gospel which found the final completion of life in the divine mercy." Luther, he pointed out, emphasized grace as pardon without excluding good works, sublimely stating in his *Treatise on Christian Liberty* that love of neighbor flows from gratitude to God for forgiveness in Christ. Unfortunately, Niebuhr continued, he erred in sharply separating gospel and law in his doctrine of "two realms," in which the experience of grace was severed from concern for justice in the civil order by undue emphasis on Romans 13: "the powers that be are ordained of God." Yet it was Luther's achievement to illuminate Paul's doctrine of grace and the primacy of the love commandment. Calvin, on the other hand, Niebuhr pointed out, while expounding in his *Institutes* the same doctrine of salvation by grace and of works as its fruit, saw more vividly than Luther the need for law because of sin even in lives sanctified by grace. But, lacking Luther's freer approach to the Bible as "the cradle of

Christ," he tended to a biblicism that sought in relative historical standards answers to every moral and social problem. Yet Calvin, Niebuhr noted, expressed reservations about political authority that became seeds of later democratic justice. Basically, however, Luther's social ethic was defeatist and Calvin's obscurantist, the one contributing to German authoritarianism and the other to Puritan legalism. The Reformation's failure helpfully to relate its insights, particularly the paradox of grace in its doctrine that the Christian is both "sinner and righteous" *(justus et peccator)*, to social and cultural problems, Niebuhr claimed, contributed to its defeat as the Renaissance triumphed in the modern era of optimism.[25]

As recent tragic experience refuted expectations of progress, Niebuhr emphasized, it became important to discriminate between truth and error in both the Renaissance and the Reformation, lest the vicissitudes of history merely prompt alternate moods of optimism and pessimism, of illusory hope and unjustified despair:

> The course of modern history has . . . justified the dynamic, and refuted the optimistic, interpretation contained in the various modern religious and cultural movements, all of which are internally related to each other in what we have defined broadly as "Renaissance." It has by the same token validated the basic truth of the Reformation but challenged its obscurantism and defeatism on all immediate and intermediate issues of life.

A new synthesis was needed, he went on to say, in which creative possibilities and inevitable corruptions of human existence are recognized:

> It must be a synthesis which incorporates the twofold aspects of grace of Biblical religion, and adds the light which modern history, and the Renaissance and Reformation interpretations of history, have thrown upon the paradox of grace. Briefly this means that on the one hand life in history must be recognized as filled with indeterminate possibilities. There is no individual or interior spiritual situation, no cultural or scientific task, and no social or political problem in which men do not face new possibilities of the good and the obligation to realize them. It means on the other hand that every effort and pretension to complete life, whether in collective or individual terms . . . or to eliminate the final corruptions of history must be disavowed.

Such a synthesis will differ from the medieval one in permitting a freer play between Christian faith and cultural pursuits, in declining to confine grace as God's possibilities to any ecclesiastical institution, and in recognizing more fully the heights and depths of human existence. It will, Niebuhr concluded, apprehend in the paradox of grace "that history is a meaningful process but is incapable of fulfilling itself and therefore points beyond itself to the judgment and mercy of God for its fulfillment."[26]

The two aspects of grace as renewal and forgiveness, illuminated by the Renaissance and the Reformation as human possibilities and limits, provide a perspective on culture and politics elaborated by Niebuhr in the next two chapters as "the paradox of our having, and yet not having, the truth or justice in history." If this paradox is understood and recognized in practice, he pointed out, the quest for truth and the struggle for justice can achieve higher approximations. Applied to the quest for truth, this means tolerance for other views and convictions while holding to our own, for "rational apprehensions are subject not merely to the limits of a finite mind but to the play of passion and interest which human vitalities introduce into the process." Neither Catholicism nor the Reformation had a good record of toleration, for the one (Niebuhr wrote decades before Vatican II altered Catholic attitudes) derived its attempt at suppression of religious liberty from its claim of unconditioned possession of truth, while the other avoided such a claim but practiced intolerance. Nor have secularists always done better, he added, for intolerance is a peril inhering in the whole human enterprise. On the whole, Niebuhr went on to say, "the chief source of toleration in modern history has been in the various forces of the Renaissance movement, both sectarian and secular." Inherent in the sense of history developed by Renaissance scholars was an appreciation of variety in human perspectives which, he observed, prompted Montaigne and Voltaire, Locke and Mill, to advocate toleration; and the same awareness, united with a biblical sense of human limitations, led to eloquent defense of toleration by such English sectarians as Milton. As one of the latter, John Saltmarsh, quoted by Niebuhr, put it in 1646: "Another's evidence is as dark to me as mine to him . . . till the Lord enlighten us both."[27]

The struggle for justice, Niebuhr held, like the quest for truth, engages humankind in the possibilities and limits of historical existence, for no attainment of just relations in society "is secure from criticism from a higher historical perspective or safe from corruption on each new level of achievement." All realizations of justice may rise indeterminately to approximate the love of the kingdom of God, but contradict it in structures determined not simply by conscience or reason but by power:

> All communities are more or less stable or precarious harmonies of human vital capacities. They are governed by power. The power which determines the quality of the order and harmony is not merely the coercive and organizing power of government. That is only one of the two aspects of social

power. The other is the balance of vitalities and forces in any given social
situation. These two elements . . . are essential and perennial aspects of
community organization; and no moral or social advance can redeem society
from its dependence upon these two principles.

The organizing power may degenerate into tyranny, or the balance of
forces may fall into anarchy; those perils "represent the Scylla and the
Charybdis between which the frail bark of social justice must sail." Western nations have tortuously achieved a measure of democratic justice in
an era when social power is chiefly economic and political:

> The history of modern democratic-capitalistic societies is, on the whole,
> determined by the tension between these two forms of power. In this history
> the economic oligarchy has sought to bend political power to its purposes,
> but has never done so with complete success. On the other hand, the political
> power of the common man has been an instrument of . . . justice; but it has
> also not succeeded completely in eliminating flagrant forms of economic
> injustice. This tension is unresolved, and may never be completely re-
> solved.[28]

Moral ambiguities, Niebuhr continued, inhere in all government and
every social equilibrium; power is necessary in achieving order and justice,
but may be used by one class or group to dominate another, or by rulers
to destroy the freedom of the community. The biblical attitude toward
government regards it as divinely ordained but subject to prophetic criticism. Plato and Aristotle were less realistic about the relation of power
to the problem of order and justice, seeking social harmony through
constitutional devices and rule by the wise and virtuous. Augustine, on
the other hand, saw human society as held in tension between contending
forces and threatened by tyranny; his view, though colored by conditions
in the declining Roman Empire, "gives a much truer picture of both the
dynamic and anarchic elements of political life than classical political
theories." After him, medieval theorists tended to obscure historical vitalities and interests in a static concept of natural law, and conceived
inadequate restraints upon unjust rulers. While Lutheranism was uncritical of government and radical sectarianism too critical, Calvinist constitutional theorists wisely comprehended both the necessity of government
as a providential creation of history and the importance of justice as the
criterion for any government momentarily in power. Modern democratic
politics, Niebuhr emphasized, involve us in the moral ambiguity of pressures and counterpressures which cannot be avoided "without also disavowing responsibility for the creative possibilities of justice."[29]

The final chapter of Niebuhr's work concerns the end of history, as understood by Christian faith. All human life and history, he observed, moves toward both fulfillment and dissolution, but the end as fulfillment is not only threatened by death but corrupted by sin in human pretensions of completing the meaning of life. History culminates only through divine completion of what is fragmentary and divine purging of what is evil in human life, which the New Testament expresses symbolically in the "second coming" of Christ, the last judgment, and the resurrection. The symbol of Christ's triumphant return as judge and redeemer, Niebuhr emphasized, is not to be taken literally in the hope of a millennial age, but points to God's final sovereignty in the consummation of history beyond the temporal process, a fulfillment that is neither utopian nor an otherworldly negation of history. The last judgment is an inescapable one in which Christ confronts and purifies all partial human achievements and corruptions. The resurrection of the body is a biblical symbol implying that "eternity will fulfill and not annul the richness and variety which the temporal process has elaborated" and that such transformation of life and history "depends on the mercy and power of God" and is not a human possibility or union with the divine, as in the idea of the immortality of the soul. In the resurrection, Niebuhr stated, human individuality will participate and historic endeavors will have abiding significance, but beyond this we cannot claim to know "the furniture of heaven or the temperature of hell, or to be too certain about any details of the kingdom of God in which history is consummated."[30]

Eternity, Niebuhr continued, stands over time as the source and power of all existence, and at the end of time in outlasting it. Its dimension "above" time gives each individual a direct relation to eternity apart from the continuum of history, but its dimension at the "end" of time means that life has a social and historical meaning in which each person has an indirect relation to eternity. The diverse configurations of history, Niebuhr observed, include civilizations, governments, cultural traditions, and social groups that survive the life span of individuals but eventually decline and fall:

> Sometimes they perish because pride of power prompts them to extend themselves beyond the limits of human possibilities. Sometimes the oligarchy which has been instrumental in organizing a society becomes purely repressive and destroys what it has created. Sometimes the strategies and techniques of yesterday are falsely applied to new situations and problems to which they are not relevant.

Modern Western civilization, Niebuhr commented, "may perish because it falsely worshipped technical advance as a final good." The causes of social and historical decay are, in the final analysis, sins of sensuality and of pride, the former a flight from freedom into the irresponsibility of nature and the latter a pretension of finality in the contingent and finite character of a culture or civilization. The divine long-suffering may allow a declining society to extend its life in possibilities of renewal, but every civilization finally disintegrates in its own faults, vindicating the divine majesty. Cumulations of culture and technique pass from one civilization to another, but such growth is not moral progress, Niebuhr emphasized; evil appears on every new level of achievement as defiance or corruption of the good, symbolized in the New Testament as the Antichrist, and is finally overcome only by God in eternity. Human destiny, Niebuhr affirmed in concluding his magnum opus, is truly found not in efforts to escape the flux of nature and history or to find premature fulfillment within it, but in acceptance of historical striving as meaningful because of God's suffering involvement in it, in trust that neither life nor death nor anything else can separate us from the love of God in Christ, and in a humble wisdom whereby "contrition mitigates our pride without destroying our hope."[31]

ASSESSMENTS OF A GREAT WORK

Niebuhr dedicated *The Nature and Destiny of Man* "to my wife, Ursula, who helped, and to my children, Christopher and Elisabeth, who frequently interrupted me in the writing of these pages." When volume one appeared in the spring of 1941, Bernard Iddings Bell, the redoubtable Episcopal clergyman and author who had reviewed Niebuhr's first book years earlier, described it in the *New York Times Book Review* as a "work of painstaking scholarship and penetrating thought." In these published Gifford Lectures, he declared, Niebuhr "takes his place as the outstanding moral theologian among Protestants today." The work, Bell predicted, would meet resistance in a sector of American Protestantism: "Certainly the 'Liberals' will be inclined toward excommunication. Not for a long time has such a downright and competent attack been made on their position." Paul Tillich, reviewing the volume in the quarterly founded and edited by Niebuhr, proclaimed it "a masterpiece." He expressed reservations about "direct comparisons of philosophical and religious doctrines" in the historical section, but found himself in "very large agreement with the later parts." Tillich valued especially chapters six to nine, where "the difference between finiteness and sin is emphasized against all dualist attempts to derive sin from finiteness" and where is found "the most mature and most elaborated doctrine of sin . . . in present American theology." There followed a review in the *New Republic* by W. H. Auden, who had recently moved from England to New York and became a friend of the Niebuhrs. *The Nature and Destiny of Man,* he wrote, "is the most lucid and balanced statement of orthodox Protestantism that we are likely to see for a long time."[32]

The high opinion of Niebuhr's work held by most reviewers was not shared by Robert Calhoun, known for his erudite lectures in the history of philosophy and Christian doctrine at Yale. He devoted most of a pedantic review of volume one in the *Journal of Religion* to pointing out minor flaws in its account of ancient and modern thought. Niebuhr, alleged Calhoun, made "loose generalizations" about classical philosophy and modern culture; his book "cannot be taken seriously" except as expressing insights growing out of his own spiritual struggle. Mistakes were inevitable in a book of such broad historical scope, but others were more impressed by its blend of scholarship and original thought. John Bennett described the volume as "an extraordinarily acute and profound examination of . . . conceptions of human nature both in theology and in secular thought" and predicted that, when completed in the second volume, Niebuhr's work "will be one of the great syntheses in the history of modern theology." When volume two appeared early in 1943, it was well received; even Calhoun gave it a favorable review. Joseph Haroutunian, who taught at what is now McCormick Theological Seminary in Chicago, concluded his review in the pages of Niebuhr's quarterly in these words: "If this book, together with the preceding volume on human nature, receives the attention it deserves, it will revitalize Christian thought and life in our time; it will give the church a persuasive message for our day; it will exert a powerful and beneficent influence upon those whose task it is to guide us toward justice and peace among the nations. . . . It is up to responsible Christians to mediate its message to a world which is being torn to pieces between pride and despair."[33]

In recognition of Reinhold Niebuhr's achievement, Oxford University bestowed upon him an honorary Doctor of Divinity degree in 1943. He had already been so honored by Eden Theological Seminary in 1928 and by other institutions, including Yale University in 1942. In conferring that degree, Yale recognized him for "uniting the learning of the scholar with the zeal of the prophet," citing his Gifford Lectures, his editorials in *Christianity and Crisis,* and his preaching to college students. Harvard bestowed the same degree in 1944 and Princeton in 1946; others followed, until by 1961 Niebuhr had twenty-one honorary doctorates, the later ones reflecting esteem for his Gifford Lectures among other achievements.[34] *The Nature and Destiny of Man*, his most systematic and widely regarded theological work, had much impact on the rising generation among students and professors at Protestant seminaries and among historians, political scientists, and scholars in other disciplines. It has remained in print for half a century since the early 1940s, and has appeared in Dutch, German, French, Japanese, and Chinese translations.

Niebuhr's magnum opus has been a subject of so many essays, dissertations, panel discussions, and symposia that a full account of assessments would be interminable. Five general observations, however, may be made concerning its qualities and limitations. First, the work is not without flaws in its treatment of great thinkers and movements of the past, but for a study so broad it is impressively accurate and nuanced in dealing with the history of ideas. Scholars in various historical specialties can detect blind spots and mistakes here and there in Niebuhr's treatise, but his main themes are not thereby invalidated. His treatment of the Renaissance has been misunderstood as an instance of rather too sweeping historical generalization. Niebuhr's thesis required a term to designate not only the Renaissance as a distinct and multifaceted movement arising in Italy during the fourteenth and fifteenth centuries and spreading to northern Europe in the sixteenth and early seventeenth centuries, but subsequent movements growing out of it as well, including the eighteenth-century Enlightenment and subsequent social and philosophical developments. All of these were, each in its own way, historically creative but tended to undue optimism about human nature and society. In calling for a synthesis of their creative aspects with the biblical insights of the Reformation, he used "Renaissance" as a broad term to express their inclusive essence at its best. Since the Renaissance contained within it the seeds of modern scholarship and science and social improvement as well as of modern utopian illusions, it is hard to imagine a better term for the context in which Niebuhr used it. His treatments of the historic Renaissance and the ensuing Enlightenment are carefully nuanced, and his rendering of Greco-Roman classicism is also impressive in noting diversity and development within it while pointing out its characteristic tendency, in Platonism and Stoicism, to seek meaning in rational virtues and the soul's ascent to a timeless realm of union with the divine. Niebuhr's two-volume Gifford Lectures, though tracing ideas in historical contexts on the basis of some of the best scholarship available, was essentially a theological treatise and not meant as a full and precise account of any period of intellectual or religious history.[35]

Second, in such an original work Niebuhr should not be expected to cite the source of every idea that had entered the stream of Western culture and shaped his mind, but he acknowledged conscious use of others' books in a scholarly manner. A mistaken impression that he neglected to do that arose from a comment made in later years by Emil Brunner, in his contribution to a published symposium on Niebuhr's thought, that his published Gifford Lectures lacked any reference to *Man in Revolt*, the book about which Niebuhr had written him appreciatively while preparing his lectures. Brunner in his essay emphasized his admiration for Niebuhr's work, even stating that German students of theology should learn English in order to read it. He raised the point about Niebuhr's use of his book only for the record, but, in Japan at the time without Niebuhr's volumes at hand, Brunner was unaware that volume one actually has two footnotes referring to his book (pages 237 and 272). Those references were omitted from the index, however, and Niebuhr, assuming that he had not cited the book, not only apologized in a reply published in the symposium but went on to make amends by overstating his indebtedness to Brunner. Niebuhr's reply, however, truly stated that "Brunner's whole theological position is close to mine." Both held virtually the same doctrines of sin and grace, though Brunner stated them in more personal terms and Niebuhr related them more to social contexts. Niebuhr's treatise was, in fact, rich in footnote references, not only to various books of Brunner but to a vast range of theological and philosophical works of the ages.[36]

Third, Niebuhr's prose, in this as in earlier books, was flawed by occasional awkwardness of sentence structure and the transference of an effective pulpit style to a written manuscript, resulting in undue repetition of words and points and in rough spots. Henry Sloane Coffin once commented that Niebuhr, at least at this stage of his career, was "less clear on the printed page than in moving speech." Ursula, who had a fine sense of style, had helped him make *Beyond Tragedy* more lucid than his previous books and worked with him to improve the style of some of his later books, but her care of two young children and, beginning in 1941, teaching responsibilities at Barnard College prevented her from giving his manuscript fuller attention. In terms of readability, volume two was an improvement over volume one, though both volumes contain many passages memorable for their eloquence as well as insight. Niebuhr's subsequent books show continued improvement in clarity and compactness of style, in part the result of Ursula's labors.[37]

Fourth, Niebuhr's work was conceived as a whole, and his two volumes, though appearing two years apart because of his involvement in the mounting world crisis of 1941, were meant to be read as a whole. His central theme of a synthesis of Renaissance values and Reformation insights, explicitly developed in relation to the paradox of grace in volume two, required—especially in view of modern denial of sin as a problem of human existence—a prior elaboration of the doctrine of sin in volume one. The mind of modernity had been so shaped by confidence in human capacities, and in the historical process itself as fulfilling the meaning of life, that a genuine synthesis of what was valuable in the Renaissance and true in the Reformation depended on a new appreciation of biblical insights about human nature. It was perhaps inevitable that Niebuhr's emphasis on sin in volume one would be misread by some as a tendency on his part to despair, and that his critique of modern optimism in that volume would be misconstrued by his secular and religious critics as opposition to the creative contributions of science and humanism. Each volume of Niebuhr's Gifford Lectures required the other for full understanding. For that reason Niebuhr in 1946 wrote William Savage, his editor at Scribner's, publisher of most of his books over the decades:

> I do not want to press the point about a single volume . . . but if it should be a saving in costs it would be a great advantage to put the two volumes together. From my standpoint, there would also be an advantage in having the two books in one volume.[38]

In 1949 Scribner's published a one-volume clothbound edition of *The Nature and Destiny of Man*, which remained in print first in a brown and then in a handsome green cover until 1964, when the publisher commenced to make it available as a quality paperback in two volumes.

Fifth, Niebuhr's published Gifford Lectures, though incorporating insights from his earlier books and comprehensively elaborating the substructure of his mature thought, were not his final word on all questions addressed in that work. He was only forty-seven years old when he gave those famous lectures and fifty when completing revisions for publication—a relatively young age for Gifford lecturers, who on the average have been a decade older. *The Nature and Destiny of Man* remained definitive as his systematic examination of sin and exposition of grace, but he later found certain points inadequately expressed. Among these was his use of the phrase "the equality of sin and the inequality of guilt" to describe the need for discriminate judgments between good and evil in history while preserving the biblical affirmation that all humans fall short in God's judgment. Another was his statement that, through Christ, sin in human life "is overcome in principle but not in fact"—a paradox for which he never found an adequate formulation.[39] In the years ahead Niebuhr brilliantly developed some themes of volume two in his next two major books, *The Children of Light and the Children of Darkness,* on democratic justice and toleration, and *Faith and History,* on meaning and mystery in and beyond the vicissitudes of human existence. Later, in *The Self and the Dramas of History,* he more richly compared Hellenic and Hebraic approaches to life. *Man's Nature and His Communities* added final refinements in his old age. Yet *The Nature and Destiny of Man* remained Reinhold Niebuhr's greatest work—a masterful, if imperfect and incomplete, statement of his fundamental themes.

CHAPTER FIVE

Defending the West against the Nazi Menace

જી

Niebuhr's role in American life and thought from 1938 to 1945 was significant not only for his Gifford Lectures but for his activities in other areas. He led in countering pacifism in the face of the Nazi threat to Western civilization, articulated Christian conscience on issues of the war after American intervention, emerged as an apologist of the New Deal as an alternative to socialism or laissez-faire capitalism, and related democracy to insights of Christian realism in a notable book.

THE DRIFT TO WAR FROM MUNICH TO THE FALL OF FRANCE

As the international situation grew worse in the late 1930s, Niebuhr followed developments with dismay, for he had no illusions about Nazi tyranny or about Hitler's designs on Europe at a time when British opinion favored appeasement and most Americans wished to remain neutral. After the Third Reich forcibly annexed Austria early in 1938, he wrote in the quarterly he edited:

> With the entrance of the Nazis into Vienna their anti-Semitic fury has reached new proportions. Here was a city in which Jewish intelligence had played a significant role in the cultural achievements of the nation, particularly in medicine and music. The Nazis swooped down upon the city and wreaked havoc with indescribable terror. The Jews have been spared no indignity. . . . The tragic events since the taking of Austria allow us to see the racial fanaticism inherent in the Nazi creed in boldest outline. This is really the final destruction of every concept of universal values upon which Western civilization has been built.

In September of that year, while Chamberlain met Hitler at Munich, Niebuhr wrote William Scarlett: "Isn't the world situation terrible? I'm afraid no good will come of the Chamberlain visit." Late in 1938, after French and British leaders had acquiesced to Hitler's demand for Czech territory, he stated editorially:

> None of us, who feared the consequences of Chamberlain's capitulation at Munich and predicted that it would result in Nazi domination of the continent, had any idea that matters would move quite as rapidly as they have. Czecho-Slovakia is already a Nazi vassal.

He pointed out that the *London Times*, organ of Britain's ruling Tories, had called for incorporating the Sudeten Germans of Czechoslovakia into Germany without weighing strategic considerations of such a partition, which left the Czechs defenseless against German power and enabled Hitler to overrun other lands:

> The fact that Munich represented a tremendous shift in the balance of power in Europe, that it reduced France to impotence, that it opened the gates to a German expansion in the whole of Europe, that it isolated Russia and changed the whole course of European history is not suggested in any of the *Times* editorials after the crisis.[1]

Hitler's seizure of Czechoslovakia was complete when Niebuhr, shortly after arriving in Britain for his Gifford Lectures, met with Dietrich Bonhoeffer early in April 1939 at a cottage in Cooden Beach, a coastal village in Sussex where the Niebuhrs stayed briefly before going to Edinburgh. Bonhoeffer, who as a young visiting scholar from Germany had studied with Niebuhr at Union Seminary in 1930–31, was then teaching at "underground" seminaries of the Confessing Church of his homeland. Predicting the coming war and declaring that he could not support the German side, he sought Niebuhr's help in obtaining invitations to America. Niebuhr cabled Henry Sloane Coffin, who arranged for Bonhoeffer to teach at Union that summer, but after arriving there in mid-June the German theologian changed his mind and wrote Niebuhr a letter in early July about his decision. The letter does not survive, but Niebuhr paraphrased it (in words often mistakenly quoted as Bonhoeffer's own) when news of his execution in a Nazi prison came at the end of the war: "I have come to the conclusion that I have made a mistake in coming to America. I must live through this difficult period of our national history with the Christian people of Germany." From that summer until April 1943, when the Gestapo arrested Bonhoeffer for his role in the plot on Hitler's life, Niebuhr corresponded with him. After his martyrdom, Niebuhr introduced Bonhoeffer to English-speaking readers in a preface to one of his most significant books, translated from the German edition of 1937 as *The Cost of Discipleship:*

Dietrich Bonhoeffer was one of the truly creative spirits in the church. . . . This book reveals with what simplicity and profundity he grasped the real imperatives of the Christian life. His life revealed with what fidelity he adhered to them.[2]

As for the Germany to which Bonhoeffer returned in the summer of 1939, Niebuhr wrote:

Here in the center of Europe, a nation has been subjected to a mad leadership, which subordinates all the energies of a once cultured people to the terrible task of military destruction. The nation is one tremendous armed camp. No bordering nation feels safe.

Writing from London in August of that year, he noted that Hitler's entry into Prague months earlier had "shocked the amazed and incredulous Britishers into a complete reversal of their foreign policy." The ominous Hitler-Stalin pact signed late in the summer prompted Niebuhr, toward the end of his stay in Britain for the Gifford Lectures, to keep a diary published serially as a *Christian Century* feature. On August 23 he wrote: "The announcement of the German-Russian pact has stunned every one." On August 27: "Listening to the German radio I am more and more convinced that Hitler wants war." On September 1, when the Nazi blitzkrieg struck Poland: "War has begun. . . . As one who has been certain for years that this would be the consequence of 'appeasement,' I am no less shaken than those who had more hopes than I." On September 18: "Whatever may be wrong with the British empire or with American imperialism or French nationalism, it is still obvious that these nations preserve certain values of civilization, and that the terror which is sweeping over Europe is not civilization. A moralism which dulls the conscience against this kind of evil is perverse." On October 17: "Quite obviously the issue on the sea is going to be sharply drawn, and the attacks on the British navy from U-boat and bomber will be terrific."[3] Such attacks, sporadic in the fall while Niebuhr was in Edinburgh, became intensive after Denmark, Norway, the Low Countries, and France fell to the sudden thrust of Nazi aggression in April and May of 1940 and Britain stood alone, its navy and its links to friendly nations imperiled by German submarines in the North Atlantic.

The Western Cause in the Age of Churchill

Winston Churchill's accession to power on May 10, 1940, was a historic moment described in retrospect by Niebuhr: "Rarely has a man so gifted with every art and wisdom of statesmanship found his hour so providentially as when Churchill was called to the helm in Britain's and the world's darkest hour." He possessed "eloquence and courage, as well as strategic wisdom, which enabled a very hard pressed nation to survive the bitter days of defeat which preceded the final victory over a very dangerous foe." Shortly after Churchill moved into 10 Downing Street, Niebuhr was one of several prominent Americans who promptly responded to telegrams from William Allen White, the well-known Kansas newspaperman, by joining the Committee to Defend America by Aiding the Allies, organized to mobilize American public opinion in favor of aid to Britain short of war.[4]

While the White Committee began in the summer of 1940 to counter isolationist opinion in the United States, Niebuhr put together a volume of essays, published in the fall as *Christianity and Power Politics*, directed in part against another source of opposition to the war against Hitler's Germany: the pacifism then widely shared by American Protestants. The revulsion against war that began in the aftermath of Versailles during the 1920s crested in the mid-1930s, when a majority of the Protestant clergy and a substantial number of laity declared, in pledges and polls and denominational resolutions, that they would not participate in another war. After Munich, the ranks of pacifism shrank as many concluded, with Niebuhr, that Hitler must be stopped by force, and others turned to the isolationism of Charles Clayton Morrison, who as editor of the *Christian Century* opposed aid to Britain after the fall of France, hoping to negotiate a settlement with Hitler. Yet pacifists remained numerous, led by such prominent clergy as Harry Emerson Fosdick and Ernest Fremont Tittle.[5]

It was in a climate of heated debate, splitting many a local congregation, that Niebuhr, shortly before Nazi planes began to bomb London in August, wrote a booklet published by the SCM Press in England and then included in his book as the opening essay, "Why the Christian Church Is Not Pacifist." A pacifism that recognizes the mystery of evil and disavows the political task, he held, serves as a reminder that coercion and resistance as necessities of justice are not final norms, but most modern forms of pacifism are heretical:

> Presumably inspired by the Christian gospel, they have really absorbed the Renaissance faith in the goodness of man, have rejected the Christian doctrine of original sin as an outmoded bit of pessimism, have reinterpreted the Cross so that it is made to stand for the absurd idea that perfect love is guaranteed a simple victory over the world, and have rejected all other profound elements of the Christian gospel as "Pauline" accretions which

must be stripped from the "simple gospel of Jesus." This form of pacifism ... is equally heretical when judged by the facts of human existence. There are no historical realities which remotely conform to it.

Richard Gregg's *The Power of Non-Violence*, he went on to say, was the standard text for such pacifism, commending nonviolent resistance as the best method of defeating a foe. A wise statesmanship will seek to avoid violence, but undue power grows inordinate if unchecked by power, and the stubborn evil of Nazism could not be defeated by a pacifism preferring tyranny to war, Niebuhr maintained. The churches, he added, nevertheless do well to appreciate the testimony of conscientious objectors.[6]

In another essay of the volume, on the war and the American churches, Niebuhr attacked the *Christian Century* for criticizing Roosevelt's departure from absolute neutrality. The journal, he held, unwittingly condoned "a tyranny which has destroyed freedom, is seeking to extinguish the Christian religion, debases its subjects to robots who have no opinion and judgment of their own, threatens the Jews of Europe with complete annihilation and all the nations of Europe with subordination under ... a 'master race.' " A further essay, on Germany and the Western world, analyzed the Nazi creed as compounded of Hegelian state worship, Nietzschean glorification of power, and romantic emphasis on race in Herder and Fichte. It attributed Chamberlain's appeasement to a weakening of the British genius for political shrewdness during an era of security and stability. It called for renewal in America of the realism of Madison and ancestral Calvinism to replace the fatuous optimism of a culture in which currents of the Enlightenment combined with sectarian Protestantism. In a passage reflecting a new accent in his own maturing thought, Niebuhr wrote:

> There are, or at least there were, some elements of wholesome realism in American life. The political philosophy of James Madison and the concept of checks and balances which entered into our American constitution were based upon a recognition ... of the character of politics as a contest of power, and of the necessity of balancing various centers of power in government against one another in order to prevent tyranny.[7]

Christianity and Power Politics, well received in Niebuhr's growing circle, was denounced in the pages of the *Christian Century* by Harold Bosley, a leading Methodist clergyman and educator, as "a theological green light for the William Allen White Committee." It was, as W. H. Auden remarked in his review, "a tract for the times," but its moral and theological insights have outlasted the crisis that prompted its publication. The volume included his address to the Oxford Conference in 1937 and a memorable lecture, "Optimism, Pessimism, and Religious Faith," delivered to the American Unitarian Association in 1934.[8]

During these years Niebuhr often met in New York with his friends Lewis Mumford and Waldo Frank, authors who shared his interventionist convictions. The three agreed on the need for renewal in the West of an older religious and humanist culture that had grown soft and naive toward the Nazi menace. Niebuhr, who had contributed frequently since 1938 to the *Nation*—edited by Freda Kirchwey, a staunch interventionist in the national debate on foreign policy—commended books by Frank and Mumford on the current crisis. In June of 1940 he announced in the pages of that weekly that, upon being informed by the Socialist Party that his views on foreign affairs did not conform to its platform, he had resigned from the party.[9] The Socialist platform of 1940 reflected the pacifism of Norman Thomas, again the party's candidate for President, who saw no issues at stake in the war and took a stand that drove many away from an already weak party.

Endorsing FDR as the presidential election approached, Niebuhr wrote in the journal he had edited for five years, recently renamed *Christianity and Society*: "Roosevelt must be supported on grounds of both his foreign and domestic policies." The President "has anticipated the perils in which we now stand more clearly than anyone else. In fact there are few among us who did not make unjustified criticisms of his preparedness program." While Wendell Willkie, the Republican candidate, supported social policies established by Roosevelt, he continued, "The crowd behind him are doing everything possible to destroy the Wagner Act and the wages and hours bill. . . . It is significant that most of the people who are fulminating against the third term were opposed to all that the New Deal stands for before there was a third term issue." Although foreign policy issues had prompted Niebuhr's break with the Socialist Party, his appreciation of the New Deal's achievements was more vivid than before, and whatever socialist views he still held vanished in the early 1940s. Recent successes in industrial unionization under the aegis of the Wagner Act especially impressed Niebuhr, who commented when Philip Murray succeeded John L. Lewis as president of the C.I.O. late in 1940 that "the cause for which Lewis stood transcended the defects of his personality. That cause was the organization of the unskilled workers in our mass production industries, a cause which was a *sine qua non* in the attainment of social justice in a technical society."[10]

The months before and after Roosevelt's reelection were critical, as the British heroically resisted Nazi air raids that reduced parts of London to rubble—a drama reported to America from the scene by Edward R. Murrow, who became one of Niebuhr's favorite news broadcasters. Material aid improvised by Roosevelt helped, but Britain needed more to survive, as Niebuhr explained editorially that winter:

> The fact is that Britain is in the gravest peril. We know the stuff of which this nation is made well enough to know that there will be no sudden collapse. However, the ability of the Germans to continue night bombings on city after city and the increasing toll taken by submarine and bomber of the British merchant fleet warrants anxiety with regard to the future. . . . It is obvious that we will have to increase our aid measurably, if Britain is to carry the burden of this battle.[11]

While a majority of Americans, since mid-1940, favored aiding Britain, strong opposition persisted among pacifists and isolationists, the latter spurred by the newly organized America First Committee. In a break with Morrison's *Christian Century*, Reinhold Niebuhr, Union Seminary's president Henry Sloane Coffin, and their colleague Henry P. Van Dusen—all three members of the White Committee—joined in founding *Christianity and Crisis*, a biweekly journal devoted to addressing world events from the standpoint of a sturdy Christian realism, and to the immediate task of halting Nazi aggression.

The new journal, planned as an eight-page fortnightly, was launched in February 1941, with Niebuhr as chairman of the editorial board. Coffin became chairman of the board of sponsors, which included prominent Episcopal, Presbyterian, and other Protestant church leaders. Niebuhr met regularly with editorial advisers in a lounge of the southwest corner of the seminary's quadrangle. The first number of *Christianity and Crisis* included an article by him setting forth convictions that united the journal's founders:

> Where there is sin and selfishness there must also be a struggle for justice; and this justice is always partially an achievement of our love for the other, and partially a result of our yielding to his demands and pressures. The intermediate norm of justice is particularly important in the institutional and collective relationships of mankind. . . . On this level the first consideration is not that life should be related to life through the disinterested concern of each for the other, but that life should be prevented from exploiting, enslaving, or taking advantage of other life. Sometimes this struggle takes very tragic forms.

Nazism, he continued, was a monstrous evil intending "to annul the liberties and legal standards which are the priceless heritage of ages of Christian and humanistic culture, to make truth the prostitute of political power, to seek world dominion through its satraps and allies, and generally to destroy the very fabric of our Western civilization." Nonpacifist Christians "believe that there are historic situations in which refusal to defend the inheritance of a civilization, however imperfect, against tyranny and aggression may result in consequences even worse than war."[12]

Christianity and Crisis differed from the quarterly *Christianity and Society*, which Niebuhr as editor continued to write for, in reaching a larger public—it soon had seven thousand subscribers, while the latter peaked at roughly two thousand—and in addressing itself to pressing events every other week. When the new journal published its first number, it carried an editorial by Niebuhr urging passage of Roosevelt's Lend-Lease bill for massive aid to Britain and other allies, recently proposed by the President in a fireside chat but vigorously opposed by the America First Committee and a bloc of isolationist senators. It was, Niebuhr argued, the best way of helping to defeat Hitler while staying out of war—"a practicable and effective plan for national action." Delaying Lend-Lease, he warned, would give the Nazis a chance to push for victory before American aid became effective: "The importance of early and decisive action on this measure can hardly be exaggerated." Niebuhr also testified before the Senate Foreign Relations Committee in favor of Lend-Lease.[13] The bill, giving the President authority to lend or lease military supplies to any nation whose defense he deemed vital to U.S. security, was enacted weeks later, in March of 1941, with help from Wendell Willkie and the White Committee as well as publicists like Niebuhr.

In May of that year Niebuhr joined a group of disaffected socialists and interventionist liberals in founding the Union for Democratic Action, committed to defending democracy against fascism and to promoting progressive domestic goals. The new organization originated in New York, with support from Freda Kirchwey of the *Nation*, officers of the International Ladies' Garment Workers' Union, and other labor leaders and journalists. Niebuhr became chairman of UDA, which he described in his quarterly as "formed to unite all those on the center and left in American life who believe that democratic civilization must defend itself against external peril, but must not allow this task of defense to beguile it from maintaining and extending social gains in the domestic economy." It "will resist isolationism in the ranks of labor and reaction in the ranks of interventionists." Unlike some other organized liberals and labor groups of the time, it excluded Communists from membership. It was financially weak and had only a few local chapters, mostly in East Coast cities; it hired as executive secretary James Loeb, a teacher of Romance languages whose experience in Spain made him staunchly anti-fascist and equally opposed to Communism. A precursor of Americans for Democratic Action, UDA pioneered in assessing the voting records of members of Congress and rating them in charts published in the *New Republic*. At the time of its founding, UDA called for all-out aid to Britain, including American convoys to defend sea lanes threatened by sinkings.[14]

Not only did enemy sinking of British shipping in the Atlantic increase during the spring of 1941, Nazi forces overran the Balkans and the British suffered reverses in North Africa. As Niebuhr wrote editorially in May: "The hour is dark. It is by no means desperate. . . . So long as the British Isles stand unsubdued, Hitler cannot win his coveted victory." Britain's defense depended on keeping the lifeline from North America open: "The only adequate means envisaged is American naval escorts for shipping convoys. It is true that new risks of war are involved in this necessary next step." When the war took a new turn as Hitler's armies invaded Russia in June, Niebuhr responded to complaints on the right that the Allied cause had become sullied with Communist partners:

> Not only in military but in every conceivable kind of moral and political strategy we make use of allies who do not share our dominant purpose but who, for purposes of their own, serve our ends. We shall scorn such help only if we mistake mathematical-moral abstractions for the real world.

Hitler, he observed, would be even more formidable if he acquired the grain of the Ukraine and the oil of the Caucasus. While supporting the common cause of Russia and the West, Niebuhr pointed out as he had before that Marxist ideologues were as tainted with self-interest as capitalists, and that the Soviet regime possessed an odious combination of political and economic power:

> Stalin may pretend that his interests are identical with those of the workers; but that is an old pretense. We are fools if we are able to puncture the pretenses only of economic oligarchs and are completely naive toward the pretenses of political oligarchs.

Meanwhile, as German armies entered Russia, Japan completed its conquest of Indochina, and the United States applied economic sanctions in the hope of averting further Japanese expansion in Southeast Asia. Niebuhr commented editorially that the sanctions "will either strangle Japan's economic life and bring her to terms, or they will tempt that unhappy nation into a desperate and violent effort to defeat the purposes of the sanctions." Supporting them, he replied to critics who wanted a disavowal of violence added to those pressures that such a declaration would render them futile, as Japan would need only to threaten a violent reaction to end them. In the struggle for justice among nations, "it is not possible to draw an absolute line between violence and non-violence."[15]

The interventionist debate shifted in the fall of 1941 from supplying the Allies to transporting supplies, for sinkings of British ships threatened delivery of Lend-Lease aid and the Neutrality Act of 1939 banned carrying of cargo by American vessels to belligerent ports. Niebuhr pressed, in the pages of *Christianity and Crisis*, for repeal of the law, holding that such neutrality was an escape from moral responsibility. Charles Clayton Morrison, opposed to repealing the Neutrality Act, attacked Niebuhr in the *Christian Century*, accusing him of warped judgment that would "poison the national conscience" by readiness to plunge into any war. When Congress in mid-November, by a vote of 212 to 194 in the House, revised the law by authorizing the arming of American merchant vessels and allowing them to cross the Atlantic, Niebuhr commented on the close vote by which such a weighty decision was made:

> Does no amount of violence not only to the ships but to the lives and liberties of one defenseless nation after another overcome our sense of physical remoteness and relative security? . . . The vote, many of us believe, narrow as it was, will be overwhelmingly ratified by history. But the business we are in is too momentous for any but clear-cut decisions that have a nation behind them.

The national resolve for which Niebuhr called came a week after his words went to press, after the Japanese attack on Pearl Harbor. In the wake of that December day, he wrote: "The swift and furious blow, which brought us into the conflict, found us unprepared, both technically and spiritually, though we ought to have anticipated it." Niebuhr further reflected:

> We could not agree upon the peril in which we stood as a national community until the peril was upon us; that is the stupidity of collective man. And we could not agree upon our responsibilities to the victims of aggression until we had been joined to them, not by moral act but by historical fate.[16]

During the years immediately before and after American entry into World War II, Niebuhr continued to read and review a wide range of books, most of them concerned with the moral and religious foundations of a civil social order threatened by Hitler's spreading tyranny. It was his custom to donate the modest remuneration he received for reviews to various causes, among which in those years the resettlement of refugees from Nazi-occupied countries ranked high. When T. S. Eliot's *The Idea of a Christian Society* appeared in 1939, Niebuhr described it as "a noble utterance, not only because a lofty Christian spirit is expressed in it but because he is able to express his sentiments in a style . . . which is the despair of lesser men." Paying tribute to Eliot's achievement in the world of letters and particularly his ability to search the sense of guilt and need for grace in the individual soul, he concurred with the poet's diagnosis of social ills but questioned his cure. Eliot, in Niebuhr's view, rightly saw that modern Western society "is a spiritual vacuum into which the winds of paganism rush if it is not filled with more positive content," but he relied too much on an "elite who will define the Christian ideal of the society and will implement the ideal in social programs," and did not recognize the extent to which just social relations are achieved through "political pressure and counter-pressure." Reviewing Benedetto Croce's *History as the Story of Liberty* in 1941, Niebuhr wrote that its most obvious significance "lies in the fact that this impassioned plea for liberty as the basic value of history has come out of Mussolini's Italy." The book's lasting significance was that "it represents a probably final word by a great philosopher on . . . the philosophy of history." He found Croce's work especially illuminating in its criticism of various philosophies of history, including "eighteenth-century and later utopianism, which finds the meaning of history in the culmination of certain social values." Marxism was rightly criticized "because it seeks to realize perfect equality in history, a purpose which betrays it into the destruction of liberty." It was the Italian philosopher's thesis that history "is not the story of increasing liberty but the record of the fight for liberty under ever-changing circumstances." Inasmuch as human nature requires "community as well as liberty," Niebuhr held, history "could be more adequately described as the interaction between these two."[17]

Late in 1941 Niebuhr reviewed Pitirim Sorokin's *The Crisis of Our Age*, in which the Harvard sociologist defined three types of culture oscillating through the ages—religious, metaphysical, and "sensate." Sorokin erred, he pointed out, in treating the first "as if all religion were contemptuous of the temporal," and in identifying the third with the last four centuries: "There is not a word in the whole book to suggest that the Reformation also began in the sixteenth century," and the scheme "forces him to regard Bach, Shakespeare, Tolstoi, and Dostoevski as exemplars of the 'sensate' culture" without suggesting any inner relation between their art and its superficialities. Kant was listed with Hume, and Hegel with Comte, as representatives of such a culture. Sorokin added graphs to prove his thesis. The book, Niebuhr concluded, "comes very close to being unmitigated bosh." Bishop Scarlett, reading the review in the *Nation* after sending the Niebuhrs a copy of the book as a Christmas present, sent them a telegram saying that he had just seen the review and asking them to ignore his gift in the mail and buy roses and cigarettes instead at his expense. Reinhold and Ursula kept the wrapped book in their living room as a symbol that friendship transcends difference of opinion.[18]

A year later Thomas Mann, who had left Hitler's Germany to reside in America, published his collected essays in defense of democracy in a volume entitled *Order of the Day*—a repudiation of his youthful indifference to politics. Reviewing it, Niebuhr noted that the German novelist, who had "tried so nobly and futilely to avert" the Nazi tyranny, had earlier typified the mistake of German burghers informed by romantic traditions "which scorned the plodding, discriminating social and political disciplines which bore the fruit of political justice." He pointed out that "Mann's arguments since his conversion to the importance of politics are a plea to the artist and the philosopher to deal with proximate as well as with ultimate issues of existence, lest failure at this point wipe out the ground upon which men stand when they concern themselves with the ultimate." Niebuhr also reviewed a volume of lectures by the nineteenth-century Swiss historian Jakob Burckhardt, posthumously edited and published in 1942 as *Force and Freedom: Reflections on History*. Burckhardt, he wrote, was a humanist who feared democracy partly because of the French experience from the Revolution to Napoleon but also because of "reflection on the necessity of a delicate balance between traditional cultural factors and emerging forces which he thought the rise of democracy had disturbed." Though history refuted some of his apprehensions about democracy, Niebuhr continued, "he must be credited with the most precise kind of prescience in regard to the twentieth century":

> No one predicted the modern totalitarian state more accurately. He was certain that its secularized power would be more vexatious than the sacred power of ancient states. He foresaw that peculiar relation between the industrial workshop and the battlefield . . . which characterizes modern militarism. He believed that modern tyrants would use methods which even the most terrible despots of the past would not have had the heart to use. "My mental picture of the *terribles simplificateurs* who will overrun Europe is not a pleasant one," he wrote a friend.

Burckhardt, concluded Niebuhr, "was one of the most profound historical minds of the last century, and he provides a quite unique illumination of our present difficulties."[19]

"In the Battle and Above It"

By the middle of 1942 the Nazis and their allies imposed a hideous misrule extending from Norway to Libya and from France to much of Russia, while imperial Japan had advanced its sway through almost all of Southeast Asia and the western Pacific. As the Russians desperately defended Stalingrad in the fall of that year, Niebuhr wrote: "Germany will evidently not be completely victorious in Russia, but she will also not be defeated there. The defeat of Germany must probably wait upon a continental invasion." Asked as a radio guest of NBC's "Town Meeting of the Air," broadcast from Lake Chautauqua in upstate New York, whether the churches should declare themselves in favor of an Allied victory, Niebuhr replied in the affirmative, drawing applause from a large audience in the lakeshore amphitheater. Elaborating on this in the pages of *Christianity and Society* in the fall of 1942, he held that Christians engaged in the struggle against the Axis powers must be "in the battle and above it":

> To be in a battle means to defend a cause against its peril, to protect a nation against its enemies, to strive for truth against error, to defend justice against injustice. To be above the battle means that we understand how imperfect the cause is which we defend, that we contritely acknowledge the sins of our own nations, that we recognize the common humanity which binds us to even the most terrible foes, and that we know also of our common need of grace and forgiveness. To be above the battle must also mean some reverent and pitying comprehension of the vastness of the catastrophe which has engulfed us all, friend and foe, and some sense of pity for the victims of the struggle, whether ally or enemy.[20]

Besides the victims of the war itself were those in Nazi-occupied Europe, including the Jews, harassed in Germany after Hitler's rise to power long before reports of extermination camps reached the West in December of 1942. Long sympathetic to the cause of establishing a Jewish homeland in Palestine, Niebuhr had belonged to the pro-Zionist American Palestine Committee in the 1930s. Addressing a national convention of Hadassah, a women's Zionist organization, in the summer of 1938, he supported a haven in the Mideast for Jewish refugees streaming there under League-mandated British rule:

> The Jews of the world have sunk untold treasures into Palestine. What is more, thousands of lives have been devoted to the task of making a wilderness blossom again. . . . This work must go on. The gates to distressed Jewish people from Europe must be kept open.

He acknowledged the difficulties of a Jewish state on land claimed by
Arabs:

> There is no part of the world so unoccupied that a heavy migration and
> the creation of a new state would not create some friction with those already
> settled there. . . . Nothing in the realm of politics can be done without fric-
> tion. Yet Palestine must not be abandoned, not only because there is no
> alternative locale for a similar necessary venture, but because the years of
> expenditure of energy, life and treasure . . . must not be sacrificed.[21]

A few years later, after Nazi persecution of Jews had intensified and
British restrictions on the flow of refugees to Palestine cast doubt on its
future, Niebuhr pressed in print and on the speaker's platform for a Jewish
national home. At the annual convention of the Zionist Organization of
America at Cincinnati in September of 1941, he declared in an address
that drew much applause:

> I may be terribly unorthodox in a Zionist convention when I say that I
> believe thoroughly in Zionism as far as I understand it, if it is understood
> that Zionism must be one foot of Jewry: that is, there is no possibility of
> completely expressing the unique genius of the Jewish spirit by Zionism
> alone for the reason . . . that there is no possibility of gathering all the Jews
> of the world in Palestine. There will always be the problem of how to relate
> the unique genius of this people to . . . various nations all over the world
> . . . but there will also be the problem that finally—and this is where the
> justice of Zionism comes in—there is no spirit without a body, and there is
> no body without geography.

He addressed a wider public in a two-part article, "Jews After the War,"
published in the *Nation* in February 1942. "The problem of what is to
become of the Jews in the postwar world," he began, "ought to engage
all of us, not only because a suffering people has a claim upon our compassion but because the very quality of our civilization is involved in the
solution." He went on to say:

> The assimilability of the Jews and their right to be assimilated are not in
> question; this conviction must prompt one half of the program of the dem-
> ocratic world, the half that consists in maintaining and extending the stan-
> dards of tolerance and cultural pluralism achieved in a liberal era. But there
> is another aspect of the Jewish problem that is not met by this strategy.
> That is the simple right of the Jews to survive as a people.

He invoked the conviction of the late Justice Louis Brandeis, a Zionist as
well as a great American, who held that nationalities or peoples have a

right to develop that ought not be denied by a misguided internationalism. Niebuhr declared:

> We must . . . support more generously than in the past the legitimate as-
> piration of Jews for a "homeland" in which they will not be simply tolerated
> but which they will possess. . . . The Jews require a homeland, if for no
> other reason, because even the most generous immigration laws of the
> Western democracies will not permit all the dispossessed Jews of Europe to
> find a haven in which they may look forward to a tolerable future.

Felix Frankfurter, himself a supporter of the Zionist cause and a friend of Niebuhr during his long tenure on the Supreme Court, read the article and wrote Niebuhr that "I know of nothing in print that faces the Jewish problem more trenchantly and more candidly." The article was widely circulated by Zionist groups in the months ahead.[22]

Soon Niebuhr joined others, including William Foxwell Albright, John Haynes Holmes, and Paul Tillich, in founding the Christian Council on Palestine to focus interest in the churches on the role of Palestine in saving Jewish refugees. Henry Atkinson, a Social Gospeler who became a Zionist after visits to the Holy Land during the interwar years, became chairman of the organization; Carl Hermann Voss, a Congregational clergyman and Zionist, executive secretary; and Niebuhr treasurer. Speaking at the found- ing meeting in New York in December of 1942, Niebuhr called for Amer- ican influence "to help in granting justice to a people who have been the first, and the most cruelly used, of Hitler's victims." The new organization, supported by a growing number of Protestant clergy, worked through local forums to promote action by American Christians to open Palestine to hosts of Jewish refugees during and after the war.[23]

Closer to home, the persistence of Jim Crow drew Niebuhr's comments during the war. In 1941, he saw in a Supreme Court decision requiring equal, though segregated, interstate passenger trains in the South, a small step toward equity through the rule of law when democratic processes fail. After Roosevelt, prodded by A. Philip Randolph, set up a wartime Fair Employment Practices Committee, he called for public support of its efforts to enlarge job opportunities for blacks. "Our nation," he wrote, "must awake to the seriousness of our policy of race discrimination in the armed forces and in industry." His concern also extended to Japanese- Americans on the West Coast evacuated from their homes by the U.S. government in 1942 and interned in camps from southern California to Arkansas. In the spring of that year he replied in *Christianity and Crisis* to mail critical of an editorial published in the journal which attacked the action as a blot on the national record. The internment of citizens of Japanese ancestry, he held, was compounded of war hysteria and racial prejudice. Undoubtedly there were disloyal elements among them, but the Department of Justice was "perfectly capable of singling them out and rendering them innocuous." In wartime many liberties must be circumscribed, Niebuhr held, but it was important to distinguish between essential ones and more peripheral freedoms that must be restricted in an emergency: "The mass evacuation of American citizens without due process of law must certainly be regarded as the abrogation of an essential right." The injustice, he added, was aggravated by economic losses among those interned.[24]

In 1943, as the tide turned against Hitler on the Russian front and Allied planes increased their raids on German industrial centers, Niebuhr commented: "Once bombing has been developed as an instrument of warfare, it is not possible to disavow its use without capitulating to the foe who refuses to disavow it. . . . Yet it is possible to . . . do these things without rancor or self-righteousness." Meanwhile, he maintained ties with the resistance movement inside Germany itself, having the confidence not only of Dietrich Bonhoeffer but of others. One was Adam von Tropp, a young aristocrat of East Prussian ancestry who used his position in the German diplomatic service to advise Western leaders of conspiracies against Hitler. Carrying a letter of introduction from Stafford Cripps, he spoke, as Niebuhr recalled, "feelingly of the shame of the Nazi regime and of the necessity of organizing a revolt against it." Von Tropp was later executed. Niebuhr himself was chairman of the American Friends of German Freedom, organized earlier with exile Karl Frank (alias Paul Hagan) as research director; its task, he stated, was to help those inside Germany to fight Hitler's regime and to "prepare the way for a peace which will give German democracy a new opportunity." Other anti-Nazi Germans with whom he kept in touch were George Eliasberg and Barnard Tauer, who published pseudonymously in 1943 *The Silent War*, for which Niebuhr wrote a foreword:

> Their story is valuable for many reasons. It refutes the rising prejudice of those who profess to believe that all Germans are Nazis. It proves with what heroism and resourcefulness many Germans have resisted Hitler's tyranny and still resist it. It gives an intelligent account of the complex social forces at work in Germany and . . . must certainly convince all but the politically stupid that the reconstruction of German life cannot be achieved without a political program which will allow the forces of residual health in Germany freedom to achieve the rebirth of Germany from within.[25]

As wartime collaboration between Russia and the West became firm, Niebuhr early in 1943 noted Stalin's recognition of "the logic of facts," a tacit admission that history had not conformed to the Communist dialectic. He went on to reflect:

> Americans who imagine that they can establish a world order upon the basis of American conceptions of "free enterprise" will be as certainly frustrated by the complexities of history as Communists, because of those same complexities, will be disappointed in their hope of a world revolution.

Communism differed from Nazism, he pointed out, in that it did not worship race or war, and "is never morally nihilistic, as the Nazis are." Instead it was utopian, believing "in the possibility of banishing force from social life by one final rigorous application of it in the class struggle." Then, when Stalin in May of that year dissolved the Comintern, set up under Lenin to direct revolutionary efforts in all countries, Niebuhr noted that Russian patriotism had superseded the slogan "Workers of the world, unite." He went on to reiterate and develop his earlier critique of Marxism as partly true in its theory of a social struggle accentuated by modern industrialism, but wrong in its failure to anticipate the role of democratic states in redressing imbalances in the economic process—and fundamentally wrong in identifying the economic motive with all self-regarding impulses, an error leading to illusions in dealing with political realities:

> Perhaps the most grievous of these . . . is the illusion that egotism is purely a fruit of the capitalistic system and that it will disappear with the overthrow of capitalism. This utopian illusion is in turn the root of Marxist fanaticism: for any means would seem to be justified if a revolution could really usher in a frictionless society in which all conflicts of interest would cease and in which the State . . . would "wither away."[26]

In early May of 1943 Niebuhr sailed to Britain for two months of lecturing, preaching, and visiting. Reporting his impressions to American readers, he wrote from London that "one sees pictures of Churchill everywhere," posted in gratitude for his expression of British courage and determination to carry on after Dunkirk. He found that people there took satisfaction in a rationing scheme that secured essentials of life for rich and poor, an attitude that seemed to him "a direct result of the strong communal sense developed in the country during the 'blitz' when bombs were no respecters of persons." Once during an air raid Niebuhr himself sat under a table in London with Edward R. Murrow and Harold Laski. He spent a weekend as guest of the Archbishop of Canterbury, William Temple, and another weekend with a group known as The Moot, begun by J. H. Oldham after the Oxford Conference of 1937, which for ten years met periodically to discuss social problems from a Christian perspective. The group's members included, among others, T. S. Eliot, R. H. Tawney, Christopher Dawson, Alec Vidler, Karl Mannheim, and, when in England, Niebuhr. As a British edition of his Gifford Lectures had been published by Nisbet, he was the more in demand as preacher and speaker. Oxford at this time honored him with the degree of Doctor of Divinity, its dons noting that "he seems to have wished to be ours by some link, as he even chose for his wife a most distinguished lady from the alumnae of our own St. Hugh's College." Niebuhr's itinerary also included a tour of British army bases, where he observed the high caliber of educational programs for soldiers. Among British citizens, he found, the Beveridge Report, proposing comprehensive government social insurance, was accepted with a degree of unanimity unknown for such a program in America. Indeed, he observed:

> "Manchester" liberalism is practically dead in the land of its birth, but in our own country . . . reactionaries regard the political restraints upon economic life made necessary by a technical civilization in general, and by war-time requirements in particular, as a New Deal conspiracy against business.

Britain, he explained, "represents a remarkable mixture of feudal and bourgeois traditions," in which the former contributed a sense of community and concern for the commonweal that tempered the claims of the latter: "It is the one nation of the Western world which was able to give effect to the democratic protest against feudalism without sacrificing some of the virtues of the older order." Many Americans, Niebuhr continued, misunderstood the creative aspects of British imperialism, tending to regard it "as merely a system of exploitation—a judgment which not only disregards the very great democratic achievement embodied in the 'Commonwealth' side of the British Empire, but also obscures some very real accomplishments in British colonial administration."[27]

Returning home, Niebuhr joined his family in Heath, the village in western Massachusetts where they had stayed in summers past and where by then they owned a stone cottage. It was probably during that summer, in 1943, that he composed and used a prayer—since known to millions— at a village church where he occasionally preached:

> O God, give us the serenity to accept what cannot be changed, the courage to change what should be changed, and the wisdom to distinguish one from the other.

His friend Howard Chandler Robbins, formerly dean of the Cathedral of St. John the Divine and a professor at General Theological Seminary in Manhattan, who also summered at Heath and from whom the Niebuhrs acquired their cottage, asked for the prayer and had it published by the Worship Commission of the Federal Council of Churches. Soon it was distributed through the armed services. Harold Wilke, who had been a student of Niebuhr a few years earlier, has written: "I first saw this prayer sticky-taped to the bed of a young Marine in a hospital where I was currently chaplain, during the Second World War, at Chelsea Naval Hospital outside Boston." The prayer subsequently has been adopted by Alcoholics Anonymous, and has appeared on plaques and mugs in many a gift shop, with or without Niebuhr's name on it, often adapted for personal use: "O God, grant me the serenity . . ." Niebuhr, though author of the prayer, never claimed copyright, and it has entered the public domain sometimes corrupted and Americanized so that the second line reads, "Give us the courage to change what can be changed"—as if anything that can be altered should be. Commonly called the "Serenity Prayer," it asks for courage and wisdom as well as serenity in social or personal perplexities.[28]

Union Seminary, meanwhile, adapted to wartime conditions; many of its graduates became chaplains in the armed services and others were drafted. New faculty appointments during those years included such notable scholars as Samuel Terrien in Old Testament, John Knox in New Testament, John T. McNeill in church history, and Richard Kroner—like Tillich, a refugee from Germany—in theology. Others equally notable, who had joined the faculty before the war, were Cyril Richardson in church history and David E. Roberts in philosophy of religion. In 1943 Niebuhr gained a close colleague when John C. Bennett arrived from the Pacific School of Religion to become professor of theology and ethics. Bennett long worked with Niebuhr as an adviser and contributor to *Christianity and Crisis*. Ursula Niebuhr, meanwhile, had begun a teaching career at Barnard College of Columbia University, across the street to the south of Union Seminary, first as lecturer and later as associate professor in the religion department. In 1942 Harvard's president James B. Conant had offered to create a special interdisciplinary chair for Reinhold Niebuhr at that institution, but Niebuhr eventually turned it down. Explaining his reluctance to leave Union for Harvard in a letter to Bishop Scarlett, he wrote that "the present job stands on a specifically Christian foundation, while in so great a university one has to a certain extent the position of being a slightly queer exponent of the Christian faith among (to use Schleiermacher's phrase) 'its cultured despisers.' "[29]

As the war continued, Niebuhr had much to say about the relevance of Christian faith and a biblical understanding of history to the struggle. By the fall of 1943, after Anglo-American forces had driven German armies out of North Africa and Sicily and begun preparations in Britain for the massive cross-Channel invasion, the partnership of English-speaking peoples in winning the war and organizing the peace was obvious. Two years earlier Niebuhr had been critical of the notion of "an American century" set forth in a *Life* editorial by Henry R. Luce. The real meaning of the role of the United States and Great Britain, he now wrote, lay in a humble recognition that "various nations and classes, various social groups and races are at various times placed in such a position that a special measure of divine mission falls upon them." Anglo-Saxon peoples held their position "partly by reason of factors and forces in the complex pattern of history that we did not create. . . . If we apprehend this religiously, the sense of destiny ceases to be a vehicle of pride and becomes the occasion for a new sense of responsibility." It was a function of the churches in Britain and America to speak "as the prophets spoke to Israel," that these nations might fulfill their appointed role without regarding their own achievements too highly. Amidst the burdens of the war against Hitler's demonic fury, Niebuhr wrote in *Christianity and Society:*

> It ought to be the task of Christian faith to help our generation to assess the possibilities and limits of history in a deeper dimension so that we will be strong enough to maintain our responsibility toward our historic tasks, whatever may be the disappointments in achieving the desired ends.
>
> It is at this point that the much despised Christian "other-worldliness" becomes a resource for historic striving. We strive for the Kingdom of God in history, but we do not expect its realization there. . . . Even the highest historic achievement points beyond itself to a more final consummation; even as every historic judgment points beyond itself to a more ultimate judgment. To know this is to have a final security beyond the securities of history, and a final hope beyond the achievements of history.
>
> Such "other-worldliness" is not an escape from history. It gives us a fulcrum from which we can operate in history. It gives us a faith by which we can seek to fulfill our historic tasks without illusions and without despair.[30]

DEMOCRACY VINDICATED

In 1944, while millions risked or lost their lives in the war against Nazi Germany and imperial Japan, Reinhold Niebuhr wrote one of his best-known books, *The Children of Light and the Children of Darkness*, significantly subtitled *A Vindication of Democracy and a Critique of Its Traditional Defense*. Delivered in substance as the West Foundation Lectures at Stanford University in January of that year and expanded for publication in the summer, the volume appeared in late fall, after Allied forces had liberated France and gained control of the Central Pacific. In it Niebuhr developed themes on democratic justice and toleration set forth in the penultimate chapters of volume two of his Gifford Lectures. The book's central thesis is that democracy, possessing a validity deeper than the optimistic sentiments commonly invoked to justify it, flourishes best when human nature is understood in both its impulse to pride, aggrandizement, and undue power and its potential for adjustment to the claims of others and the common good. In its pages is Niebuhr's most quoted aphorism: "Man's capacity for justice makes democracy possible; but man's inclination to injustice makes democracy necessary."[31]

Modern democratic civilization, Niebuhr maintained, "required a more realistic philosophical and religious basis" than its underlying confidence "in the possibility of achieving an easy resolution of the tension and conflict between self interest and the general interest." Such a basis, avoiding sentimentality as well as cynicism, would give it more persuasive justification than its theorists of the past few centuries provided. Its contemporary advocates were, in New Testament metaphor, "children of light," whose social conscience needed a better understanding of the power of self-interest in all human life. The evil "children of darkness" knew that side of life well but failed to recognize a law beyond themselves. The human survival impulse, he held, is spiritually transmuted not only into self-giving relations to others but into desire for "power and glory." Seeing perils in nature and history, humans seek security by enhancing their power; seeing their smallness, they seek compensation by pretensions of power. Human freedom subtly compounds natural needs into inordinate desires, so that dining, clothing, and houses become expressions of status, satisfied by seeking more property and social power. Thus, according to Niebuhr, most historical conflicts are between rival ambitions beyond the level of survival. The dominant social philosophies of early modern times—whether Locke's "social contract" theory, Adam Smith's idea of an "invisible hand" producing harmonies in a free market, or Rousseau's notion of a "general will"—assumed there were adequate checks on human ambitions in "reason" or "nature," and so envisaged schemes with minimal social restraints. Bourgeois theories, he added, viewed community and government as instruments of atomic individuals, obscuring their historical character.[32]

If bourgeois social theories erred in regarding human desires as temperate and failed to anticipate injustices of modern industrial capitalism, Niebuhr continued, Marxism made the same error and offered no better solution to the problem of community and property. While the former "regard the world of competitive economic life as essentially tame," the latter expects tameness "on the other side of the revolution." The one has no safeguard against the power of property owners, the other none against that of commissars. Adam Smith and Karl Marx were idealists whose creeds became instruments of ruthless industrialists on the one hand or Russian oligarchs on the other. History, Niebuhr held, may well discredit the views both of those who regard property as an inalienable right and of those who regard it as the root of all evil. Indeed, he observed, modern democratic societies, prompted by the needs of the entire community and the voting power of the workers, have redressed economic inequalities through political power and subjected the economic process to increasing control, thus overcoming capitalist dogmas and invalidating the Marxist claim that the state is run by a capitalist elite. Such control of economic life, however, should not be complete, for the erroneous idea of automatic balances in a free market contains a seed of truth: "We must be careful to preserve whatever self-regulating forces exist in the economic process," lest "the organs of control achieve proportions which endanger our liberty." Social ownership of the means of production also poses a hazard: "A community which preserved its democratic institutions . . . while it socialized its large-scale industrial property, would have the advantage of preserving a democratic check upon the power of economic managers," but "their power might be so great that they could . . . establish control over the political institutions." In the United States, however, a socialist experiment was less likely than an attempted return to laissez-faire economics: "America is probably the only nation in which a serious effort will be made to restore the purer individualism of the past."[33]

Turning to the problem of democratic toleration of diverse religiocultural, ethnic, and economic groups, Niebuhr emphasized the need to integrate them "in such a way that the richness and harmony of the whole community will be enhanced and not destroyed by them." Religious diversity may be accepted by secularists out of indifference, but a religious solution of the problem demands that each religion or version thereof "seek to proclaim its highest insights while yet pursuing an hum-

ble and contrite recognition of the fact that all actual expressions of religious faith are subject to historical contingency and relativity." Ethnic
and racial prejudice, Niebuhr held, is rooted more in pride than in ignorance of divergent groups, and is a deep problem for a heterogeneous
nation such as America. Democratic societies "must use every strategem
of education and every resource of religion to generate appreciation of
the virtues . . . of minority groups . . . and to prompt humility and charity
in the life of the majority." Economic groups engaged in debate over the
degree of freedom or political control of industry and commerce—a necessary and continuing debate—should recognize that their own theories
are colored by class interest. Thus "the preservation of democratic mu-
tuality between class groups finally depends upon the same quality of
religious humility which is a prerequisite of ethnic and cultural pluralism
in a democracy."[34]

The book closed with reflections on the world community within which
democratic nations must strive for a tolerable peace and justice. The sense
of moral universalism, first apprehended by the prophet Amos as God's
sovereignty over all nations, was developed in the Christian proclamation
of a fellowship transcending Jew and Greek, and merged with Stoic conceptions in the rise of Western culture, Niebuhr observed. Such universalism, he continued, gained new urgency with the global interdepend-
ence of a technical age, and yet throughout history national particularities
have remained rooted in geography, an ethnic core, and shared experience
and traditions. Children of light disregarded these cohesive elements of
political authority in projecting schemes for world government after the
war. Realists, on the other hand, were too confident in a balance of power
that did not take into account novel factors in the world situation. The
wartime unity of the great powers, Niebuhr held, was unlikely to outlast
defeat of a common foe; the world faced the prospect of an uneasy peace
maintained by the preponderant power of America, Russia, and Britain,
in which fear of anarchy would be potent and the need for agreements
with smaller nations would restrain their power. The postwar task would
be difficult:

> Since all political and moral striving results in frustration as well as fulfill-
> ment, the task of building a world community requires a faith which is not
> too easily destroyed by frustration. Such a faith must understand the moral
> ambiguities of history and know them not merely as accidents or as the
> consequence of the malevolence of this man or that nation; it must under-
> stand them as permanent characteristics of man's historic existence.[35]

The Children of Light and the Children of Darkness, dedicated "to my friend, colleague and chief, Henry Sloane Coffin," was a concise and comprehensive statement of Reinhold Niebuhr's political philosophy as it had matured since the 1930s. Its influence cannot be measured merely by reviews following publication, for it impressed kindred minds among the rising generation too engaged in the war effort to comment on the book when it first appeared. Reading it in the mid-1940s, Arthur Schlesinger, Jr., wrote a few years later that it "demonstrated that the Christian conception of human nature with its complexity and ambiguity provided a far more solid foundation for democracy than the simple optimism about man with which democracy has been conventionally associated." Appreciation of Niebuhr's volume has included conservative as well as liberal thinkers, among them Russell Kirk, who found it "suffused with Christian sagacity." James Loeb, long associated with Niebuhr through UDA and its postwar transformation as ADA, wrote a quarter century after its publication: "It has always seemed to me that the core of Reinie's political doctrine is contained in a little book called *The Children of Light and the Children of Darkness.*"[36] A compact and lucid treatise, it was not Niebuhr's last word on democracy; the role of the news media in shaping public opinion, and democracy's vulnerability in foreign relations, were among his subsequent concerns. The American edition of the book has remained in print continuously since 1944, and translations have appeared in German, Dutch, Czech, and Japanese.

ROOSEVELT AND THE CLIMAX OF THE WAR

While preparations were made for the long-awaited cross-Channel invasion of Nazi-occupied France, Allied bombers continued to pound German cities—an act Niebuhr regarded as a tragic necessity, though he questioned the change from "precision" to "obliteration" bombing. Days before the great amphibious operation, in early June of 1944, he wrote:

> The invasion of Europe is the climax of a gigantic conflict. It is for this climax that millions of men have been trained and billions of our resources have been expended. The result is, in a sense, a foregone conclusion; for the superiority in men and engines of war on the side of the Allies is so heavy, that victory is certain, however unknown the price of it may be.

Four months later, as Eisenhower's forces advanced toward Germany, he commented that "both Germans and the despoiled peoples of Europe and the great armies of the dominant powers must probably fight to the bitter conclusion, thus giving our generation a tragic lesson in the power and persistence with which evil can defy, for a time, its ultimate undoing."[37]

When pressures of war and problems of party unity led Roosevelt to run for a fourth term, Niebuhr again supported him, as much for domestic as for international reasons. His break with the Socialist Party four years earlier had been prompted by foreign policy issues, but during the intervening years his appreciation of the New Deal grew and his doubts about the socialist alternative became explicit. "For eight years now," he wrote in 1941, "the democratic will of the Administration has shown more strength than . . . forces in the country as a whole." Its record was "a blow in the face of the easy theory that government is a committee of the ruling class for keeping down the ruled." The New Deal, he continued, "carried through a law which made collective bargaining obligatory at a time when there was no labor partner to such a bargaining. It thus implored labor to organize and take advantage of its rights." Shortly after he wrote those words, Henry Ford surrendered to the United Automobile Workers on terms ending conditions Niebuhr had deplored in the 1920s—a development made possible by the Wagner Act, which FDR had signed into law. Although regretting Roosevelt's retreat on many issues in the interest of wartime unity, Niebuhr observed in 1943 that "he has gone further in progressive domestic policy than any previous president." The administration, he noted that year, "has been able to prevent the enactment of various forms of grossly unfair fiscal legislation and has kept its social legislation intact." He understood the elements of the Roosevelt coalition, explaining them to British readers:

> The Democratic party consists of southern conservatives, whose political outlook is still dominated by issues derived from the Civil War; of northern municipal political machines of the type of Tammany in New York and the Kelley-Nash outfit in Chicago; and of the farmers and workers who had never before owed political allegiance to the Democratic party and whom Roosevelt's programme of social legislation recruited for the party.

In September of 1944 Niebuhr—whose Union for Democratic Action endorsed Roosevelt for reelection—replied to an open letter from Norman Thomas calling upon his group to rejoin the Socialist fold:

> Let me say at once the members of the Union for Democratic Action long ago abandoned the "Utopia or bust" position in politics. . . . I remind you once again that the battles ahead will not be contests between unmitigated evil and absolute good, and that a true perspective of the struggles of our

time cannot be had from the Olympian heights of Socialist dogma. . . . Americans cannot afford the luxury of a gesture toward a perfect program, while real issues are being decided on a much more modest level.

The realistic choice, Niebuhr concluded, "is a continuation of the present Administration in office, with a determination to push it forward along the paths of domestic reform and of genuine international organization." He had expressed doubt about the desirability of democratic socialism in the second volume of *The Nature and Destiny of Man*, completed in 1942, pointing out the measure of justice achieved through tension between political and economic power in "democratic-capitalistic" societies. Niebuhr's conversion to the mixed economy of the New Deal was his supreme expression of the Jamesian pragmatism—testing ideas by experience—that had impressed him while a student at Yale Divinity School.[38]

During the early 1940s, then, Reinhold Niebuhr moved away from socialism to support of the New Deal legacy. By the fall of 1944 he became vice-president of the Liberal Party, formed in New York as an alternative to the state's Communist-friendly American Labor Party. The new party, in whose birth David Dubinsky of the International Ladies' Garment Workers' Union played a leading role, supported the Democrats in national politics, and so helped put New York in Roosevelt's column over Thomas Dewey in the presidential election of that year. After FDR won, Niebuhr noted the important part played by the C.I.O.: "In this election labor took over the direction of the campaign to a larger degree than ever before. It is silly to talk of the danger of pressure groups. Labor has merely fashioned its own political power inside the Democratic party."[39]

During the same fall William Temple, Archbishop of Canterbury since 1942, whom Niebuhr had last seen during his visit to Britain of the previous year, died. In a tribute to Temple in the pages of *Christianity and Crisis*, Niebuhr wrote:

The great strength of his theology lay in his ability to harmonize diverse and sometimes conflicting strains of theological thought into a living and creative unity. Thus the traditional medial position of his church between Catholic and Protestant thought achieved a new dimension in his thought, which made him not only the most important theologian of his own church but also the most influential thinker of the rising movement of ecumenical Protestantism. . . . His position as the leader of advanced social thought in Britain and in the Western world was prompted by both religious impulse and a shrewd understanding of the mechanics as well as of the standards of social justice.[40]

During the climactic phase of the war in Europe, three widely read books appeared which Niebuhr reviewed. One was Gunnar Myrdal's *An American Dilemma*, a massive study of the racial problem in the United States by a Swedish social scientist. Niebuhr found it "a really comprehensive analysis of the most vexing problem in our democratic life," shedding light on interrelated factors producing "a vicious circle, which can be effectively cut at a dozen different points and must be attacked from every angle, educational and political, economic and religious." He commended the work to parsons, church study groups, and "every thoughtful student of our American life." Another book he reviewed was Friedrich Hayek's *The Road to Serfdom*, a scholarly but controversial volume by an Austrian economist in Britain, who claimed that any state planning would lead to dictatorship. Niebuhr found it one-sided, almost a laissez-faire reaction to collectivism: "Dr. Hayek sees the perils of political power clearly enough; but there is nothing in his book to indicate the slightest awareness of the perils of inordinate economic power." A third book was Denis de Rougemont's *The Devil's Share*, a study of evil in human existence by a French-Swiss writer. Niebuhr was impressed:

> Some modern readers will fail to profit by the author's profound analysis of the general sources of evil in human history and of the multifarious forms which it may take, because they will be affronted by the poetic and mythical symbols which he uses. . . . If evil is thought of merely as cultural lag or natural inertia, these symbols are not necessary. But if we recognize historical evil as a corruption of human freedom . . . it will become apparent that the "devil" is a meaningful symbol. The devil is a fallen angel, a corruption of something good; and the corruption is caused by an excess rather than a defect of some particular vitality of life.[41]

The reality of historical evil was terribly vivid as both sides in the war suffered heavy losses, especially in Belgium and later on Iwo Jima during the winter of 1944–45. One of Niebuhr's recent students, Roger Shinn, who had entered the army after completing his divinity degree, became commander of an armored infantry company and was reported missing in action in the Battle of the Bulge. In early winter Niebuhr devoted a sermon to Shinn in a memorial service at Union Seminary's James Chapel. Then one day in June he received a telephone call from Boston—it was Shinn, who had been liberated after five harrowing months as a POW and would return for doctoral studies after the war in Union Seminary's joint program with Columbia University.[42]

While Shinn and some fifteen hundred other prisoners were forced on long marches in northeastern Germany and Allied armies pushed into

Poland and the Rhineland, Churchill, Roosevelt, and Stalin met in February at Yalta in a climate of tension over the shape of postwar settlements. Niebuhr commented in *Christianity and Crisis:* "The conference of the 'Big Three', meeting in secret in the Crimea, has had the hopes and fears of the world centered upon it for some weeks." Its greatest achievement, in his view, was the calling of a meeting to establish the United Nations, and another achievement was an agreement to reorganize the Polish government under supervision of the great powers, albeit with concessions to Russia. The Yalta accords contained some possibility of postwar cooperation:

> "If hopes are dupes, fears may be liars," declares the poet. We are not yet in a situation in which we may not be duped by our hopes. But some of our fears have already proved to be liars. We have more justification for moderate hopes than we have had in years.

Shortly before the United Nations conference convened at San Francisco in the spring to implement plans envisaged at Dumbarton Oaks several months earlier and agreed upon at Yalta, Niebuhr supported creation of the new international organization as more realistic than a world government: "It is safer to try to extend the core of world community created by the war partnership . . . than to attempt the constitution of a world authority above and beyond the sovereignty of the great powers." The latter approach, contrived by American idealists after World War I, had failed because strong nations are not inclined to abridge their authority, he held; the structure of the U.N. was more congruent with the currents of history.[43]

President Roosevelt's death in April occasioned a tribute to him from Niebuhr:

> Our sense of grief is naturally mingled with gratitude for the providential emergence of this man in our national life at just such a time as this. . . . While it is much too early to assess his place in American history adequately, one may hazard the guess that future historians will regard his administration as a new level of maturity in domestic policy. Here the nation became aware of the depth of the problems of justice in an industrial society and of the necessity of dealing with it politically. . . . Roosevelt was able to secure the passage of the Lend-Lease Act from a divided nation, a policy which made it possible for us to prevent the collapse of the anti-Nazi cause. . . . As the war finally drew to a triumphant conclusion, Roosevelt, seeking to avoid Wilson's mistakes, developed an international policy . . . derived from a shrewd understanding of the limits of the will of a nation in creating international authority above its own sovereignty.[44]

After Germany's surrender in early May, Niebuhr reflected on the sober public mood arising from the magnitude of the conflict, the high price of victory, and reports from Germany: "As the victorious armies liberated one concentration camp after another and unearthed the hideous cruelties which were practiced in them, they gave us some hint of what the dimensions of total slavery are like, from which we escaped by a total war." Yet the war was not over until President Truman's decision to use the atomic bomb resulted in Japan's defeat three months later. Niebuhr commented: "There is naturally a very great apprehension about the introduction of this frightful instrument into the science of warfare, and an uneasiness of conscience about its immediate use in this war, in order to hasten its end." Some time after the shock of Hiroshima and Nagasaki, he expressed his considered view: "It is a simple matter to condemn the statesmen who made the decision to use the bomb. The question is whether they were not driven by historic forces more powerful than any human decision." The American government, he continued, developed the bomb "in competition with the Germans and under the lash of the fear that they might perfect it before we did," and then found it "difficult to withhold it when its use held out the prospect of a quicker end to the war." But, he added, American statesmen could be criticized for not taking the step of "impressing the enemy with the power of the bomb without the wholesale loss of life" in Japanese cities: "Suppose we had announced the perfection of the bomb to the enemy, threatened its ultimate use, and given some vivid demonstrations of its power in places where the loss of life would have been minimal. The moral advantage of such imagination would have been tremendous." What Niebuhr did not know, and could not have known then, is that the United States government had only two bombs after one test, and could not be sure that either would work. Despite his questioning or criticism of some Allied bombing, Niebuhr maintained at the war's end that the cause against Nazi Germany and imperial Japan was just:

> We were indeed the executors of God's judgment yesterday. But we might remember the prophetic warnings to the nations of old, that nations which become proud because they were divine instruments must in turn stand under the divine judgment and be destroyed.... If ever a nation needed to be reminded of the perils of vainglory, we are that nation in the pride of our power and our victory.[45]

CHAPTER SIX

Politics and Theology
in the Postwar Years

❧

During the early postwar period, from 1945 to 1952, Niebuhr helped promote European recovery, engaged in issues of the developing Cold War between Russia and the West, and backed establishment of the state of Israel. Meanwhile, he continued to teach and preach, addressed the founding assembly of the World Council of Churches, published a sequel to his Gifford Lectures, gave various guest lectures on theological themes, and wrote a widely read book of reflections on American history.

EUROPE DIVIDED: RUSSIA AND THE WEST

In the aftermath of Hitler's defeat, Niebuhr took a lively interest in the problems of war-torn Europe and called for patience and firmness in American relations with Stalinist Russia. As early as the summer of 1945 he had noted that the Russians were making an accord with the West difficult by "their refusal to abide by the Yalta agreement in constituting the Polish government" and "their implicit support of Marshal Tito's high-handed actions" in Yugoslavia. Aware that Soviet troop movements in the war strengthened Moscow's influence in those and other countries, he added: "We will have to be prepared to be outraged by many things which Russia does in eastern Europe." Within the next six months Russian-backed Communist regimes consolidated their control of Poland, Romania, and Yugoslavia, while Hungary and Czechoslovakia stood under the shadow of Soviet dominance of neighboring lands. "The Russians," Niebuhr wrote in the winter of 1945–46, "do not really want war as the Nazis did," but "act as if they did want war," for they mistrusted the Western world—and "this mistrust is partly rooted in Marxist dogmatism," with its notion of an "irreconcilable conflict" between communism and capitalism.[1]

While America could not prevent the expansion of Stalinist Russia in eastern Europe, it could help to alleviate chronic hunger in occupied Germany, Niebuhr wrote in early 1946. "The army reports that the diet of Germans in the American zone now averages 1354 calories," he pointed out in the pages of *Christianity and Crisis*, urging support of religious and international relief agencies. Members of the Fellowship of Socialist Christians, on Niebuhr's initiative, sent food packages to families in Europe, first buying and packaging items themselves and later sending CARE packages—an example of the personal approach he favored as a supplement to public policy. While the war ended in Allied occupation and widespread ruin and misery in Germany, its end brought austerity and a change in government to Britain, where the Labour party under Attlee's leadership won a victory over Churchill's Tories. "The British public," Niebuhr commented editorially, "had the good sense not to allow gratitude to a great war leader to determine its peace-time and domestic policy." Though no longer himself a socialist, he retained an appreciation of the religious roots, social vision, and non-Marxist character of the British Labor Party. While the Attlee government began to expand the nation's welfare state, Britain itself was economically so weakened by the war that it sought a loan from the United States—finally approved by Congress in 1946 with such a burdensome interest rate that Niebuhr cited the experience as "one proof of the necessity of a higher degree of imagination in wielding American power."[2]

While Congress debated the British loan, Stalin early in 1946 broke a wartime agreement by refusing to evacuate Soviet tanks from northern Iran, finally doing so only after Truman "got tough" by sending naval forces to the eastern Mediterranean and threatening further action. Churchill, meanwhile, in the spring of that year warned of the expansion of Soviet power and doctrine in his "Iron Curtain" speech at Fulton, Missouri. In the summer Niebuhr wrote:

> The rift between the Western world and Russia is growing. Again it is a conflict between justice and injustice, or at least between freedom and totalitarianism. On the level of politico-moral judgments, I do not see how it can be denied that the distinctions between the Russian morality and our own are valid. The Russian tyranny is pretty vexatious. . . . Sin is always trying to be strong at the expense of someone else. The Russians want to make themselves strong by dominating eastern Europe, and as much more

beside as they can. They would probably swallow both Turkey and Iran if they thought they could get away with it.

In the same piece he brought the perspective of biblical faith to bear on American attitudes as tensions with Soviet Russia increased:

> The Bible never denies that there are significant conflicts between good and evil forces in history, between just and unjust nations, and between righteous and unrighteous men. The prophets of Israel had no doubt about the special mission and virtue of Israel as compared with the gentiles; and they saw the meaning of history as partly derived from this conflict. . . . But these distinctions did not prevent the prophets from understanding that there was a profounder conflict between all nations and God, and all men and God.[3]

As the Cold War developed, Niebuhr repeatedly affirmed the justice of the Western cause, while pointing to a divine judgment under which all civilized achievements stand. Surveying the dislocations of the recent war and the uncertainties of the emerging postwar world, he reflected:

> We have lived so long in a culture which drew the meaning of our moral responsibilities from the hope of their actual fulfillment in history, that Christians, as well as non-Christians, are poorly prepared for the insecurities of our present existence. "Be not anxious for tomorrow," declared Jesus, "for tomorrow will be anxious for the things of itself; sufficient unto the day are the evils thereof." This warning suggests that our tasks and responsibilities have an intrinsic and absolute validity in God's sight in the present moment without too much regard for their historic fulfillment and justification.[4]

Late in the summer of 1946 Niebuhr joined a State Department educational mission on a month of travel through the American zone of Germany—in Bavaria, Württemberg, and Hesse—and to Berlin. Everywhere he found "decent Germans" who had been separated by Nazism from the outside world and were eager for books and contacts with philosophers and scientists of other countries. The Germans, he also discovered, were attached to a system that determined at an early age who would prepare for a university in a *Gymnasium* and who would pursue a trade, and their university communities seemed not to take much interest in public affairs. The experience confirmed his impression of "the cultural refinement and political ineptitude of the German people." Yet he met Germans, notably Theodor Heuss, whose appreciation of democratic politics was undiminished by the scars of the Weimar and Nazi periods. The scholarly Heuss, from southwestern Germany, who became an architect of the Federal Republic of Germany three years later and its first president, later recalled meeting the U.S. mission in 1946: "I have a particularly vivid memory of the striking personality of Reinhold Niebuhr, the theologian, who was a member of the group." While attending services in a crowded church of Stuttgart—the only one intact in that bombed city—Niebuhr heard Helmut Thielicke of Tübingen University preach, and described him to readers of *Christianity and Crisis* as a "brilliant young theologian" who gave the gospel "precise and helpful relevance to the daily life of a harassed and sorely tried people."[5]

In Stuttgart he also heard Secretary of State James Byrnes deliver in that city on September 8 a major address assuring the Germans, uneasy about Soviet ambitions, that American occupation troops would stay in Germany as long as any other nation's. Six days later Henry Wallace, then a member of Truman's cabinet, criticized Byrnes's firm commitment in a speech at Madison Square Garden that minimized the Soviet threat. In the ensuing controversy Truman fired Wallace, and Niebuhr wrote an article that reached a huge national audience in *Life* magazine. Entitling it "The Fight for Germany," he began:

> I should like to challenge Wallace's foreign politics, as expressed in his recent attack of Secretary Byrnes's policy. . . . I had the advantage of recognizing its errors with particular vividness because I was in Berlin when it was made. I saw the uses which Soviet propaganda made of it and the disappointment and dismay it spread among democratic forces in Europe and Germany. They had just been tremendously heartened by Secretary Byrnes's address in Stuttgart, which I had the pleasure of hearing.

He went on to describe conditions in Germany and to recommend policy. The Russians, he noted, had "pulled up all double railroad tracks between Berlin and our zone to make our occupation of Berlin as difficult as possible through the inconvenience of a single-track road." Nearly all Germans in the western zones, he pointed out, were opposed to Communism, but their economy was in shambles. "As divided Germany sinks into economic misery," he warned, "Russia hopes to conquer her ideologically by attributing this misery to capitalistic exploitation." To its policy of "strategic firmness" America should join one of "affirmative economic reconstruction" by first opening trade between Germany and the West. That "might well be supplemented by a policy toward the present Russian sphere which recognizes where the limits of our power are." War, he concluded, "is neither imminent nor inevitable if we have a creative policy. Let us therefore avoid hysteria even while we abjure sentimental illusions."[6]

Henry Wallace's naivete toward Stalinist Russia, which Niebuhr also attacked in the pages of his own biweekly, was shared by members of the American Communist Party and by far more numerous "fellow travellers" in the American labor movement and various Popular Front groups, especially the Independent Citizens Committee of the Arts, Sciences, and Professions (ICCASP). It was a rally of the latter that Wallace had addressed in September and thereby had, as Niebuhr put it in the fall, "blown himself out of the whole political picture." The once-popular New Deal figure began to make a comeback, however, late in 1946 when the ICCASP merged with other groups to form the Progressive Citizens of America (PCA), a sizable and well-funded Popular Front organization led by Wallace himself. Niebuhr's Union for Democratic Action, meanwhile, opposed to pro-Sovietism, launched plans for expansion to increase its impact on the emerging issues of postwar American politics, especially to counteract the Communist threat to Europe but also to revitalize New Deal liberalism, challenged by the election of the first Republican Congress in years. Niebuhr, as president of UDA, was a moving spirit in expanding the organization, but planning was the work of UDA's executive secretary James Loeb, journalist James Wechsler, attorney Joseph Rauh, and historian Arthur Schlesinger, Jr. Their efforts resulted in the founding of Americans for Democratic Action at a meeting in Washington early in January 1947, attended by 130 liberals opposed to Communism and committed to extending the New Deal. The gathering was held at the Willard Hotel, with Niebuhr and Elmer Davis—a news commentator who had served in Roosevelt's administration—presiding. Participants included, besides the planning circle, labor leaders such as Walter Reuther and David Dubinsky, rising politicians like Hubert Humphrey, government administrators such as Leon Henderson, academics and journalists like Marquis Childs and John Kenneth Galbraith, and Eleanor Roosevelt. After ringing addresses by others, Niebuhr spoke; as Langdon Gilkey, then one of his students who was present at the time has recalled, he "completely transfixed the audience with the brilliance of his analysis of the economic, political, and world situations and the role of the new ADA within that context." When Niebuhr finished, "everyone stood up and cheered."[7]

The ADA absorbed the old UDA, and Loeb continued as executive secretary. Its membership soon rose to eighteen thousand, twice that of the parent organization, and extended beyond a few big cities of the Northeast to others in the Midwest and on the West Coast. ADA took stands on current policy issues, published materials, and endorsed candidates for public office. Niebuhr commented in the quarterly he edited on its significance and its differences with Progressive Citizens of America:

> The new organization has the power and scope we always wanted our original group to have; but the time was not propitious until the present moment. . . . The Progressive Citizens has a large number of Communists and fellow-travelers and beyond them liberals who follow Henry Wallace's line in foreign policy. That line is very critical of our present foreign policy on the ground that it would be in the interest of peace to yield to the Russians on quite a few points. . . . There is room for criticism of our foreign policy which I hope liberals will press. On the whole, however, Americans for Democratic Action agrees with the Administration policy of "patience and firmness" toward Russia.

The onset of the Cold War, he concluded, required an effort to shape and sustain "a middle ground" between the right and the left:

> The situation in the whole Western world would be improved if the fear of Communism did not drive some people into the arms of reaction, and the fear of reaction did not drive others into the arms of Communism. Both fears must be overcome by the development of a healthy democratic program, embracing both foreign and domestic policy and both economic and political problems.

At ADA's first national convention, in March of 1947, Niebuhr was appointed to its national board, which was to meet four times a year as the governing body between conventions.[8]

Niebuhr's growing prominence and his keen interest in world affairs, meanwhile, led the Council on Foreign Relations late in 1946 to invite him to become a member of that influential body. For years thereafter he regularly attended the Council's roundtable meetings and dinners in Manhattan, where important American and foreign guests raised problems for discussion. Speakers and discussions at its meetings engaged his interest, especially when postwar Europe and Germany was the subject. It was the Council's journal *Foreign Affairs* that, in July of 1947, published George Kennan's famous "Mr. X" article calling for containment of the Soviet Union's expansionism until internal stresses and external failures undermined its basis in Communist ideology. Such a policy—striving to avoid war with Russia while standing firm in western Europe—was taking shape in Washington, its outlines much the same as the approach advocated by Niebuhr. During the early postwar years, however, a movement for world federation diverted some, including the famous chemist Harold Urey and Norman Cousins of *Saturday Review*, from the search for proximate solutions of international problems. Niebuhr punctured their illusions in the pages of *Foreign Affairs:*

> It was probably inevitable that the desperate plight of our age should persuade some well-meaning men that the gap between a technically-integrated and politically divided community could be closed by the simple expedient of establishing a world government. . . . It is this hope which adds a touch of pathos to already tragic experiences.

Any such scheme, he continued, fails to take account of the fact that government does not create community but can only perfect its "social tissue" rooted in ethnic kinship, a common language, a shared history, and a common culture—or at least some kind of homogeneity—without which laws and force cannot integrate diverse groups. Social tissue grows slowly and does not exist on a global scale:

> The coalescence of communities from city-states to empires in the ancient world, and from feudal entities to nations in the modern period, was frequently accomplished only by the imposition of preponderant power. The fact is particularly significant, since all these communities could rely upon all sorts of "organic" factors for their force of cohesion which the rudimentary world community lacks.

The notion of setting up a world federation "is the final and most absurd form of the 'social contract' conception of government," Niebuhr declared. As he maintained in a later piece on the same subject, "even if we eliminate the Communist-democratic chasm there is little 'social tissue' to bind up the so-called free world together."[9]

As always, Niebuhr found time, in a varied life of public involvement and religious concerns, for reflective reading. Among books that appeared shortly after the war, one that especially impressed him was Carl Becker's posthumously published *Freedom and Responsibility in the American Way of Life*, which he reviewed:

> The late Carl L. Becker was one of the truly wise men of our generation. He was historian, philosopher of history, and political philosopher, whose special interest it was to find a firmer foundation for democratic life. . . . The eighteenth century had equated democracy with the assertion of inalienable rights. Becker shows that the rights and liberties must be exercised with a higher sense of responsibility for the common good.

Becker, Niebuhr pointed out, perceived that freedom and democracy depend more on the character of a people than on their precise constitution and laws, but he did not seek to solve public problems by moral means only: "He is constantly looking for the best possible instruments for the preservation of both justice and liberty" and "understands that collectivism finally destroys freedom, but is also certain that there must be increasing control of the economic process in the interest of justice." Democracy, according to Carl Becker, "is a living process which requires constant readjustments to new situations." His wisdom was needed "in a day when interested dogmatists speak unctuously of the 'American way of life,' while they seek to preserve some special privilege or evade some obvious responsibility of their power."[10]

Another book that Niebuhr deemed important was Hans Morgenthau's *Scientific Man versus Power Politics,* appearing in 1946 and developing in part certain themes that had been, in the author's words, "most illuminatingly treated in the books of Reinhold Niebuhr." The German émigré scholar, Niebuhr declared in reviewing it, "gives an authoritative, and it seems to me a final, refutation of the school of thought which assumed that all the vexing problems of man's social existence could be solved if only we could extend the 'methods of science' from the field of nature to the realm of history and society." Such scientism erroneously imagined that "events in history follow as necessarily from previous causes as do occurrences in nature." It failed to see that, though there are regularities that a valid social science can illumine, "a purely scientific attitude toward social reality is impossible . . . because the scientist is never a distinterested observer, as in the field of the natural sciences, but always . . . an interested participant."[11]

IN THE CLASSROOM AND ON THE ROAD

A change of leadership occurred at Union Theological Seminary shortly after the Allied victory in Europe, for in May of 1945 Henry Sloane Coffin retired as president of the institution he had led for almost two decades. He had previously been pastor of Madison Avenue Presbyterian Church in Manhattan, and as Union's chief had recruited an outstanding faculty during difficult years of depression and war. At a farewell luncheon Niebuhr, personally close to Coffin, presented him with a festschrift he had edited, entitled *This Ministry,* which included a summary essay by him. "Of all religious leaders of our day," he stated in the volume, "Dr. Coffin was more thoroughly rooted in the work of the parish and most consistently aware of the strategic importance of the local congregation." He "never wavered in his certainty of the uniqueness and profundity of the Christian revelation; and was for that reason not tempted to maintain its authority by obscurantist, legalistic, or authoritarian means. . . . His long years as head of an interdenominational theological seminary, the historical roots of which were in Presbyterianism, were in a sense the perfect vehicle for a man whose spiritual life was also deeply rooted in the Presbyterian tradition but . . . always flowered in an ecumenical faith." Coffin's successor was Henry P. Van Dusen, long a teacher and administrator at Union, who as president continued his predecessor's commitment to preparing men for the ministry but, seeing increased need for teachers of religion in colleges and seminaries, expanded the enrollment of graduate students in Union Seminary's joint program with Columbia University. Two early additions to the faculty after the war were James Muilenberg, who in 1945 became professor of Old Testament, and Paul Scherer, who in the same year began to teach homiletics, the art of preaching.[12]

Reinhold Niebuhr as a preacher had some peculiarities, among them a habit of scratching his left ear with his right hand. Despite such distractions, his message came through. Invited as he was to pulpits of college and university chapels, he was frequently away on weekend train journeys for such engagements. In 1946 he published a second volume of sermonic essays, *Discerning the Signs of the Times*, with such themes as serenely accepting the tasks of today while preparing for fulfillments of unknown tomorrows; carrying into the contests of life a wisdom that is not so much an achievement of the mind as the fruit of prayerful humility; and realizing "the peace of God," dimly sensed in the quiet symphonies of nature, not in calm detachment but in the caring, pain, and forgiveness of lives that find themselves in community and finally in God. Taking I Corinthians 13:12 as text for one theme, Niebuhr stated:

> Faith in God is faith in some ultimate unity of life, in some final comprehensive purpose which holds all the various, and frequently contradictory, realms of coherence and meaning together. . . . The Christian faith . . . believes that God has made Himself known. It believes that He has spoken through the prophets and finally in His Son. It accepts the revelation in Christ as the ultimate clue to the mystery of God's nature and purpose in the world. . . . But . . . God remains *deus absconditus*.

Human sin, he continued, is a mystery that science cannot eradicate. A faith that acknowledges mystery while apprehending meaning amidst the perplexities of life will perceive that "we see through a glass, darkly." Among reviewers was Arthur Schlesinger, Jr., who as a student six years earlier had heard Niebuhr preach at Harvard's Memorial Church. "Niebuhr," he wrote, "doggedly makes certain elemental points which anyone who writes about politics had better absorb: that the world is complicated; that man—all men, not just your political enemies—can be devious and destructive in their motivation; and that these two facts prescribe a certain humility before the problems of the day."[13]

Reinhold Niebuhr then was so well known that callers from near and far came to his office on the seventh floor of Union Seminary's tower. He had access to the secretarial services of Nola Meade, but she was on another floor and so could not protect him from the public. The Niebuhr family had moved on D day, when Allied troops landed in Normandy, from their place across the street into an apartment on the sixth floor of Knox Hall, a faculty residence area in the north side of the Union quadrangle. There Ursula and Reinhold continued to open their home to students on certain nights, and on the next day the whole seminary community was likely to hear about conversations "up at the Niebuhrs last night." Roger Shinn, back from the war for graduate studies, described Niebuhr in the classroom: "Arriving a few minutes before class time, he stood at the lecturer's table like an eagle poised to swoop. . . . As his international reputation increased . . . his classes became more crowded, sometimes in the summer session straining the capacity of the seminary's largest lecture hall. . . . No matter how many times he might have covered the same subject through the years, he approached it with the spontaneity of something new." Shinn continued: "With all the rush of his life, he made himself available to his students. He kept office hours faithfully, rarely accepting engagements which took him away from classes, and was always ready to consult with students."[14]

As a professor, Niebuhr was involved in directing advanced studies in Union Seminary's joint doctoral program with Columbia University—its gray buildings visible from the window of his office at the corner of Broadway and 120th Street. Columbia, in cooperation with Union, gave a doctorate in religion under a special committee chaired by the dean of its graduate school; it was a sizable program with four fields, including one in ethics, religion, and society chaired by Niebuhr, who guided many dissertations. He was also long a member of Columbia's graduate faculty of political science, an appointment that meant that his courses at Union were available to graduate students at Columbia and that he sat on dissertation committees. Later he taught occasionally at the New School for Social Research in Manhattan, a center of European émigré scholars. Another source of Niebuhr's contact with the academic world outside the seminary was the Philosophy Club, a group of eastern university professors who invited him to membership in 1944, soon after publication of his Gifford Lectures. Founded at the beginning of the century and meeting, during Niebuhr's time, usually at the Men's Faculty Club of Columbia University, the group included such diverse academics as John Dewey—long a central figure in the club—Sidney Hook, Horace Friess, Ernest Nagel, William Hocking, John Randall, Herbert Schneider, Robert Oppenheimer, and Paul Tillich. Most of its twenty-five members met monthly for the reading and discussion of a paper, followed by dinner. Niebuhr remained active for many years, exchanging ideas with philosophers, psychologists, historians, and scientists from institutions ranging from Harvard to Johns Hopkins, as well as those in New York City. Niebuhr's attitude toward the various disciplines of higher learning was expressed in an address at Ohio State University's celebration of its seventy-fifth anniversary in 1948:

> It is their business to elaborate every technique of knowledge by which man comes into effective control of the processes of nature and by which he learns to understand the destiny of nations and cultures, the rise and fall of civilizations, the intricacies of the human psyche and the complexities of human relations in the economic, political, and other forms of togetherness. . . . But it is important whether the educational task is pursued with an understanding of the mysteries and perplexities of human character and human destiny . . . or whether it is believed, as the past century tended to believe, that these mysteries are no more than the residual ignorance of a more primitive culture which the ever broader road of learning will overcome.

Concluding that address, he declared:

> Our whole educational enterprise must be sensitive to those larger issues of the spiritual life as they express themselves in the fate of our age. Whether it is philosophy or history or literature or any of the humanities which is the subject of our study, we face the task of interpreting life to confused generations in an age of great perplexity. It will not be sufficient to give them only the tools for vocational proficiency or the sum total of all scientific disciplines.[15]

Beginning in 1946 Niebuhr wrote until 1957 a column distributed by Religious News Service to magazines of various denominations. By the later 1940s his influence was widely felt in American Protestant churches not only directly on those who read or heard him, but indirectly through a new generation of clergy, whether former students of his or those who had attended other theological schools. William Scarlett recalled, in a talk to seminarians in Cambridge, Massachusetts, after his retirement in 1952 as Episcopal bishop of Missouri: "The many young men who came into my diocese while I was bishop, whether they came from Union or from one of our own seminaries, were all deeply influenced by his thought. I must confess that some of them were better at imitating his pulpit mannerisms than in expounding his theology." After ensuing laughter, he continued: "Nevertheless, all had caught something of his vision, something of his fire, and something of his sense of God's justice, and they brought into the diocese an intellectual and social ferment which to me was quite thrilling." In 1948 Scarlett edited and published, under the title *To Will One Thing,* a collection of prayers from the past and present that he had used for clergy conferences and lay classes. It included this prayer composed by Niebuhr:

> O God of grace and truth, Whom the heavens cannot contain, but Who loves to dwell with those who are of contrite heart, look mercifully upon us as we seek Thy face. . . . Help us to escape the tyranny of self by finding our brothers and living in them, by finding Thee and losing ourselves.
>
> Give us the grace to overcome the world's injustice, to hear the cries of the oppressed, to succor the fallen and to heal the victims of man's inhumanity to man.
>
> Grant that as we worship Thee we may come to a truer knowledge of ourselves. May we, for knowing ourselves more honestly, seek Thee more sincerely that Thy grace may make us whole and Thy strength may be made perfect in our weakness and Thy will may make our wills Thy tool; through Jesus Christ our Lord. Amen.

Thanking Scarlett for a gift copy of the prayer book, Niebuhr wrote, "You have chosen and used material of many types most discriminately. It will be our daily companion as it will be in many a home."[16]

Two new books in Niebuhr's own field of Christian social ethics appeared soon after the war, both of which he reviewed favorably. One was Emil Brunner's *Justice and the Social Order,* translated from the German-Swiss edition of 1943, which he judged "in every respect rewarding and illuminating," an improvement over his earlier book *The Divine Imperative.* Niebuhr admired the latter but had criticized its emphasis on the state's function of preventing anarchy; the newer book focused more on the promotion of justice as a complement of love. "One of the great advances of the present volume," he wrote, "is Brunner's treatment of equality as the regulative principle of justice," which it related to historic realities "with greater wisdom than any purely rationalistic political philosophy." The book pointed to resources in Christian faith for an adequate social ethic: "Brunner," unlike Barth, "does not strain to eliminate any possible insight which might come . . . from other than purely Biblical sources, while he proves at the same time that the whole human situation can only be understood from the standpoint of a Biblical faith." The other book, published in 1946, was John C. Bennett's *Christian Ethics and Social Policy,* a lucid statement of convictions by Niebuhr's friend and colleague at Union Seminary. Bennett's strategy, he pointed out, differed from other Catholic and Protestant options by emphasizing both the relevance and the transcendence of the Christian ethic and taking into account the seriousness of sin and autonomous technical elements in politics and society. Such an approach, Niebuhr continued, employs "middle axioms"—neither ultimate principles nor concrete programs—which "are pragmatically conceived and are fluid, requiring periodic adjustment to the moving historical situation." Bennett, he added, also recognized the validity of moral norms supported by Christian faith and yet known outside it, which formed the basis for "a truly ecumenical position in Christian social theory." The book, in fact, stated in systematic fashion and crystalline prose perspectives on economic, racial, and foreign policy shared by Niebuhr himself.[17]

In 1947 Niebuhr took a semester's leave, from February to April, for a lecture tour through several European countries, and reported on their social and religious life to American readers. "The most vivid impression of an American traveler in Europe today," he wrote from Britain, "is of the marked contrast between American abundance and European poverty." In Holland, suffering economic woes from the war, he observed "how conscious the people are that the future depends upon America." He saw "some creative impulses in the church life of Europe, particularly in the ecumenical movement." Its leader in those years, the Dutch churchman W. A. Visser 't Hooft, arranged for Niebuhr to spend an afternoon with Karl Barth in Basel early in April. He and the Swiss theologian, he wrote home to Ursula, argued about the relation of faith to philosophy and to politics. "Barth," he added, "told me several times that he recognized that Brunner and I were closer together than I to him or than Brunner to him and I acknowledged this." Then, Niebuhr related to his wife, he went on to Zurich and spent "two most delightful days" with Emil Brunner and his family, attending a performance of Goethe's *Iphigenie* and dining at a hotel in the Alps. With the Brunners he felt "completely at home." Traveling on from Reformed centers in the Netherlands and Switzerland to the Lutheran lands of Denmark and Sweden, he commented that "continental Calvinism is liturgically bare beyond belief, while the Lutheran churches have a beautiful liturgical service." His week in the northern nations prompted further notes to readers back home:

> A visit to Scandinavia reminds one that the well known faults of German Lutheranism, its uncritical attitude toward government, and its tendency to a transcendentalism which lives above the realm of man's social problems, may well be more German than Lutheran. For these Scandinavian countries have the same kind of political wisdom . . . which we in the Anglo-Saxon world have long associated with British genius.

Niebuhr's trip gave him insights about parts of Europe he had seen before only briefly or not at all, and impressed upon him the severity of postwar economic crisis in Britain and on the Continent.[18]

THE MARSHALL PLAN, ISRAEL, AND AMSTERDAM

In March of 1947, several weeks before Niebuhr's return from Europe, President Truman asked Congress for economic and military aid to strengthen Turkey against Soviet ambitions in the Dardanelles and, more urgently, to enable war-shattered Greece—which Britain could no longer assist as she had—to avoid collapse while struggling against Communist internal forces. ADA promptly backed Truman's request and Wallace's PCA denounced it. As Congress moved to approve it in the spring, Niebuhr wrote that he was "just as certain as most Europeans that the strategic measures which we are taking, in Greece and Turkey for instance, are absolutely necessary." Meanwhile, during the early spring before his arrival home, high officials in the U.S. State Department became aware that most of western Europe was on the verge of economic collapse, barely able to pay for food and fuel and incapable of rebuilding productive capacity and commercial life without outside aid. Deteriorating conditions in France and Italy might soon result in election victories of Communist parties loyal to Moscow's newly founded Cominform. Walter Lippmann called American public attention to the urgent need for a new aid program. Niebuhr, back from his trip, also called for American assistance. "The whole of Europe is sinking in an economic morass," he wrote. "If there is no economic convalescence in Europe there can be no restored political health." Then, after General George Marshall, Truman's Secretary of State, unveiled in June a proposal for a massive, four-year aid program for European economic recovery, Niebuhr commented editorially:

> It is now quite clear that the Marshall Plan, initiated by Secretary Marshall in his Harvard commencement address, has become a kind of turning point

in postwar history. The enthusiasm of the response of western Europe to it proves that it contained something previously lacking in our relations to Europe. We were intent upon strategic problems and Europe knew that democracy could not be saved merely by military strategy. Our offer to help in a comprehensive scheme of European rehabilitation proved a nexus between European and American interests.

The Russians, he noted, declined Marshall's invitation to participate in the plan because they knew its success "would enhance Western and American prestige and make Communism less attractive."[19]

While several European governments consulted on details of the proposal, Congress debated its funding. "An impoverished world," Niebuhr wrote in the fall, "must wait upon the decisions of the American economic Colossus, not because it trusts our wisdom but because it depends upon our economic resources." Noting stupid opposition, he remarked, "We will be accused of playing Santa Claus to the world." Summarizing reasons for American funding, he wrote in *Christianity and Crisis*:

> Our aid need not . . . be prompted purely by either humanitarian concern for the starving or by concern for the preservation of political liberty in Europe, though it is to be hoped that these motives will be operative. We must furnish aid also in the interest of our own economic health. We are exporting 12 billion dollars worth of goods in excess of imports. . . . It is obvious, however, that an impoverished world must stop buying from a wealthy nation, no matter how desperate its needs, if we do not exercise the greatest possible generosity in the terms of payment. . . . It is because motives of national self-interest converge upon motives of generosity, that we have a right to hope that the Marshall Plan will be accepted, no matter how the isolationists may rage.

While the issue was still pending, a Communist coup in Czechoslovakia in February of 1948, following a Soviet takeover in Hungary a year earlier, tightened the "Iron Curtain" over eastern Europe and spread alarm in America. The event, Niebuhr observed, "revealed the relentlessness of the Communist will-to-power." Yet it "did not change the power realities in Europe," since it was already a fact that "Czechoslovakia was in the Russian orbit." While Western strategic precautions were justified, he maintained, "the primary danger is ideological and political." In early April, Congress enacted and funded the Marshall Plan, and two weeks later the pro-Western party of De Gasperi won a victory over the Communists in Italy. "Everyone waited with bated breath for the results of the Italian elections," Niebuhr commented. "Sighs of relief greeted the results." Yet, he noted, while the Communists lost heavily in industrial areas where workers were afraid of losing Marshall aid, they gained support among debt-ridden peasants in rural areas because the ruling party neglected land reforms. In France, meanwhile, the M.R.P., a new Catholic party led by Schuman and Bidault, had formed a governing coalition with socialists, known as the "Third Force," regarded by Niebuhr as a model for postwar European politics. "The 'third force,' " he wrote, "is the middle ground of democracy against communism on the left and reaction on the right." He saw hope for the future in the socially enlightened Catholicism of France and the German Rhineland, as well as in democratic socialism, in a Europe reviving with American aid.[20]

While the peoples of western Europe struggled toward postwar recovery, a quarter of a million Jews were stranded in "displaced persons" camps, prompting renewed efforts to allow them to settle in Palestine, still governed by Britain. Meanwhile, evidence that six million Jews had died in Nazi gas chambers at Auschwitz and elsewhere gave new impetus to the Zionist cause among Christians as well as among Jews themselves, especially in America. Niebuhr remained constant in support of a Jewish national homeland. In an introduction to Waldo Frank's *The Jew in Our Day*, toward the end of the war, he emphasized world Jewry's "purely mundane problem of existing as a people" who were "in the exposed position of trying to express a collective survival impulse under the hazards of a Diaspora." The historical process could not be trusted to eliminate anti-Semitism: "That is why the demand for a Jewish homeland is justified, though we must not for that reason give up the battle for tolerance in the democratic world." Reviewing in 1945 a volume of essays on Chaim Weizmann, the outstanding Zionist leader of the age, Niebuhr described his career as "the embodiment of one of the great political ideas of our time, of an idea which had been dwarfed by the magnitude of the world crisis but which is yet relevant to it." In January of 1946 he testified on behalf of the Christian Council on Palestine at hearings in Washington of the Anglo-American Committee of Inquiry, set up by the governments of Britain and the United States to gather facts and opinions on the problem of Jewish refugees and to recommend policy. Admitting that there was no perfect solution to conflicting rights of Arabs and Jews in Palestine, he stated: "The fact however that the Arabs have a vast hinderland in the Middle East, and the fact that the Jews have nowhere to go, establishes the relative justice of their claims and of their cause." Questioned on the need for a Jewish state as opposed to immigration, he observed that the Jews as a people, a minority wherever they remain, "were almost liquidated."[21]

While the Anglo-American Committee focused attention on the problem, its advice a few months later that a hundred thousand European Jews be admitted to Palestine was rejected by Britain, concerned lest Arab reaction endanger its lifeline to oil. The Committee itself rejected the idea of a Jewish state, and public debate on the issue resumed in the summer of 1946. While Niebuhr was a prominent churchman engaged in the Zionist cause, other Christians opposed it, among them missionaries in the Levant and editors of the *Christian Century*. The editorial board of *Christianity and Crisis*, divided on the issue, allowed both sides to make their case in its pages. The pro-Zionist Christian Council on Palestine, organized during the war, merged in 1946 with another such group to form the American Christian Palestine Committee, of which Carl Hermann Voss was executive chairman. The organization sponsored Niebuhr as a speaker in New York, Philadelphia, and Chicago, at Princeton, and elsewhere. In civic forums and in various American and British journals, Niebuhr pressed for reopening Palestine to Jewish refugees and espoused the Zionist cause. Support of a Jewish homeland, he emphasized, should be accompanied by American subsidy of agricultural development for neighboring Arabs:

> Any solution of the Palestinian issue must be of such a nature that it will finally appeal to the Arab world as just, though it may have to be imposed by force at the beginning. This means that we must help in the economic reconstruction of this part of the world, particularly in terms of soil conservation and irrigation and river development.

The Arabs, he held, "can be given an adequate *quid pro quo* only if there is a large-scale economic development of the whole region." Among Jewish Americans Stephen Wise—"a leonine figure" in Niebuhr's words—led the Zionist cause as he had for decades. Eleanor Roosevelt, then a member of the U.S. delegation to the United Nations, became a staunch supporter of a Jewish state after the Nazi holocaust.[22]

Early in 1947 the British government referred the Palestine question to the U.N., which after months of deliberation passed a resolution in November calling for partition of the land into Jewish and Arab states, and British evacuation in May of 1948. Niebuhr commented editorially:

> The decision of the United Nations Assembly to partition Palestine and to create a Jewish and an Arab state brings several interesting and perplexing chapters of contemporary history to a conclusion. On the purely political level it represents the first real achievement of the United Nations. . . . The "right" of the Jews to Palestine is established partly by the urgency of the

problem of their collective survival and partly by ancient claims and hopes which found their classical expression before the Jewish dispersion. . . . The right of the Arabs is quite simply . . . the right of holding what one has and has had for over a thousand years.

The latter, he added, were so backward that "this whole Near Eastern world has fallen from the glory when the same lands, which now maintain only a miserable pastoral economy, supported the great empires in which civilization arose." While it was right to restore Jews in part of the area, Niebuhr held, America should open its own gates to "survivors of Hitlerism, now in DP camps"—a step eventually taken. Early in 1948 *Christianity and Crisis* published criticism of the U.N.'s partition plan by Bayard Dodge, president of Beirut University, who argued for an Arab-Jewish federation as the best way to peace in the area. In an editorial note following the article, Niebuhr, acknowledging that "many men of good will take completely contradictory views of the situation," pointed out that "the bi-national state was found unacceptable by the United Nations, primarily because the Arabs were unwilling to grant the Jews any freedom of immigration in such a bi-national state."[23]

After Ben-Gurion in mid-May of 1948 proclaimed the creation of a Jewish state, which held its own against a prompt but uncoordinated attack of surrounding nations, Niebuhr wrote:

> It now seems probable that the new state of Israel will be able to establish itself the hard way, by an armed defense of its existence against Arab attacks. . . . The Arabs were, of course, intent upon preventing this new political force from challenging their sovereignty, and also their pastoral-feudal social organization. . . . One cannot speak of this victory as a morally unambiguous one. No political victory can be so described.

As thousands upon thousands of Jews streamed into Israel, before and after the U.N. armistice of 1949 that defined its borders for years to come, he commented in *Christianity and Society:* "How can any one see the DP camps of Europe emptying their sorely tried population into this new state without a sense of moral approbation? . . . Nor can one withhold one's admiration for the actions of the more favored Jews of the world, who raise millions upon millions of dollars to finance the immigrants." In the same piece, however, he expressed concern about an "uncritical religious nationalism which . . . tempts the Jews to be callous in regard to the plight of Arab refugees." If the Jews in Israel "are finally to establish viable economic and political relations with the Arab world," they "must not be quite so certain that justice to the Jews is inevitably just to the

Arabs also, however great may be the opportunities for raising Arab living standards through the technology of a Jewish state." In 1951 Niebuhr endorsed a proposal—subsequently resisted by Arab leaders—to settle Palestinian Arab refugees in surrounding areas under U.N. auspices and to develop, with funds provided by U.N. members including Israel, waterways and other resources in Arab countries that would absorb the refugees.[24]

While the statehood of Israel and the European recovery program were reaching fruition, *Time* magazine on March 8, 1948, featured a pensive Reinhold Niebuhr on its cover, with an article on some highlights of his life and thought. The cover story, which colorfully, but inaccurately, described his theology as "the oldtime religion put through the intellectual wringer," reflected his great influence in American religious and public life. Well known on both sides of the Atlantic, he continued to take part in the ecumenical movement as he had at the Oxford Conference before the war. In late summer of 1947 Niebuhr journeyed to Oslo, Norway, to participate in the World Conference of Christian Youth, a vast gathering from all continents; there he met such leaders of the rising generation as John Karefa-Smart of West Africa and M. M. Thomas of India, who later came to study with him at Union Seminary, and also Bishop Berggrav of Oslo, who took him to a mountain cottage where the Nazis had held the Norwegian church leader prisoner for years. What most impressed him at Oslo was that "the usual differences between American and European Christians were not nearly as wide as in previous years," recent tragic experience having taught many Europeans to engage in politics despite its moral ambiguities and many Americans, once purists in politics, a lesson in those ambiguities.[25]

Meanwhile, Niebuhr prepared for a historic occasion, the founding assembly of the World Council of Churches, held in Amsterdam from August 22 to September 4, 1948. Long anticipated, the event was a milestone in the growing cooperation of Protestant, Anglican, and Eastern Orthodox churches—a convergence of the "Life and Work" and "Faith and Order" movements that had met separately at Oxford and Edinburgh in 1937 and taken steps toward uniting doctrinal and churchly with social and political concerns in a common organ representing many churches throughout the world. Plans for such an ecumenical council, slowed by the war, moved ahead under the leadership of W. A. Visser 't Hooft, who headed a provisional agency in Geneva. Niebuhr was one of many who contributed to a four-volume study series on the theme of the Amsterdam assembly, *Man's Disorder and God's Design*. Besides that, he was asked by

Visser 't Hooft, who held him in high esteem, to address the World Council of Churches in the Dutch capital. During the summer of 1948 Niebuhr was writing his next book, *Faith and History*, and preferred not to make yet another trip abroad. " 't Hooft insisted," he wrote Bishop Scarlett from the cottage in Heath, "that if I came I could take it easy . . . but that I ought to come." In mid-August he sailed for Amsterdam.[26]

Crowds gathered to watch as several hundred delegates and visitors of 147 denominations in forty-four countries—many in black robes, others in colorful national costumes—assembled in procession outside the stately Niewe Kerk in Amsterdam and entered it for the opening service of prayer and hymns. Those present included—to name only some of the better known—Martin Niemöller of Germany, Jacques Ellul of France, Anders Nygren of Sweden, Emil Brunner of Switzerland, J. H. Oldham and G. K. A. Bell and C. H. Dodd of Britain, Lesslie Newbigin of India, and Henry Van Dusen, John R. Mott, Samuel McCrea Cavert, and Charles P. Taft of the United States. The assemblage convened for addresses and discussion in the main hall of the Concertgebouw, each member using earphones to hear speakers in translation or in whatever language was spoken.[27]

Karl Barth gave the first address, raising his voice and shaking his finger as he affirmed the sovereignty of God in a way that seemed almost to exclude human responsibility for the world. "We ought," he declared, "to give up, even on this first day of our deliberations, every thought that the care of the church, the care of the world, is *our* care." Days later Niebuhr, speaking forcefully, delivered a quite different message on "The Christian Witness in the Social and National Order." He was, as Visser 't Hooft later remarked in his memoirs, "not the kind of speaker who reads a prepared text, but the inspired orator for whom his own text is only the point of departure for a spontaneous outburst of ideas." Accordingly, his oral address differed somewhat from the version circulated at the assembly and later published. Surveying the confused and parlous condition of the postwar world, Niebuhr held that it was the church's task to mediate divine judgment and grace to nations, classes, and cultures as well as to individuals. It was wrong, he declared, to preach the gospel *"sub specie aeternitatis,* as if there were no history with its time and seasons." The church must speak to particular nations on particular occasions, "preaching judgment here and hope there," according to whether the sin is complacency or despair. It should speak to the privileged and the oppressed in different accents. It should rebuke those who exalt freedom without community and those who make the state sacrosanct. Toward the climax of his address, Niebuhr stated:

> The final victory over man's disorder is God's and not ours; but we do have responsibility for proximate victories. Christian life without a high sense of responsibility for the health of our communities, our nations, and our cultures degenerates into an intolerable other-worldliness. We can neither renounce this earthly home of ours nor yet claim that its victories and defeats give the final meaning to our existence.

In conclusion, he declared:

> We must work while it is day, and we will work the more diligently if we are not harassed by fears of the perils of the night, since we worship a Lord who is Lord of day and night, having conquered darkness night and day in the Cross and the Resurrection.[28]

In a respite from meetings, the assembly's hosts conducted visitors on an excursion through Amsterdam's canals and harbors and into its Rijksmuseum to view Rembrandt's *Night Watch* and other paintings. Most delegates participated in a Dutch Reformed Communion service at the Niewe Kerk, in which successive groups were seated at a long table and passed the cup around—a special liturgical form described by Niebuhr to readers of *Christianity and Crisis* as a "vivid reminder of the historical Last Supper." Discussions of the assembly, he further reported, "revealed how much of what divides the church represents facets of the truth which belong in a total unity," and also exposed the need for "a little more appreciation of the contingent and conditioned character of particular theological, liturgical, and ecclesiastical traditions." Niebuhr also drew American readers' attention to a report, prepared by a committee of which John Bennett was secretary and commended by the assembly, on "The Church and the Disorder of Society." It criticized, he pointed out, Communist ideology for its false promise of freedom after revolution, and laissez-faire capitalism for its false promise of justice as a by-product of free enterprise. Later he defended the report against American libertarians who criticized it as a "collectivist" rejection of "the free market." He also noted the strong Marxist sympathies of many Asiatic and African Christians at the assembly who, reacting against Western imperialism, "know little and care less about what Communism does in Europe." Concluding his report on the first assembly of the World Council of Churches, Niebuhr stated his impression that participating Christian bodies were "more certainly in a process of renewal than in a process of reunion."[29]

After the Amsterdam assembly, the *Christian Century*, publishing Niebuhr for the first time since his break with it eight years earlier, carried his comments on Barth's address. The theology of Barth, he wrote, emphasizing the coming of God's kingdom through Christ, "outlines the final pinnacle of the Christian faith and hope with fidelity to the Scriptures" but "requires correction, because it has obscured the foothills where human life must be lived." It did not take sufficient account of "the trials and perplexities, the duties and tragic choices, which are the condition of our common humanity." The same journal then published Barth's response to Niebuhr's criticism and Niebuhr's reply. The controversy illuminated long-standing differences in their attitudes toward politics and the authority of the Bible. Barth felt he had been misunderstood, claiming that he sought to view social problems in a biblical dimension, and expressed his own misgivings about selective use of Scripture and lack of exegetical rigor on the part of theologians like Niebuhr. In reply, Niebuhr held that there are "very good reasons for preferring some texts of Scripture to others," and expressed regret that Barth "seeks to establish Biblical authority over the mind and conscience of the Christian with as little recourse as possible to any norms of truth or right which may come to us out of the broad sweep of a classical, European, or modern cultural history." He also paid tribute to Barth's "creative relationship to the resistance movement in Europe" during the war, but held that he "tends to support an attitude of irresponsibility toward the immediate and pressing decisions which Christians must make," as in his notion that differences between the Communist and Western worlds were ultimately insignificant.[30]

TRUMAN AND THE POLICY OF CONTAINMENT

Several weeks before the Amsterdam assembly, the Soviet government imposed a blockade on land routes between Berlin and the Western zones of Germany, prompting American authorities to begin a long and costly airlift of supplies to the free sector of that city, deep inside the Russian zone of Germany. Niebuhr, supporting the U.S. airlift in a *Life* article, reported that he had found European delegates at Amsterdam virtually unanimous in wanting the West to stay in Berlin, even at the risk of war. While hundreds of planes daily delivered food and other necessities to the Berliners, he wrote editorially in the fall of 1948:

> The situation is that the Russians, defeated by the economic revival of western Europe through the European recovery program, are still able to

maintain their prestige by spreading the view that we will yield to them in the end, if they apply enough pressure.

When four-power control of Germany broke down soon after the war, he continued, the West did not abandon Berlin "partly because we did not want to expose the heroic anti-Communist Germans of the city to reprisals, and partly because even then our withdrawal would have meant a serious loss of prestige" with "repercussions in the political life of the Western world." The stakes in Berlin, he observed, were high, calling for measured firmness: "The slightest miscalculation on either side might mean war."[31]

President Truman, meanwhile, faced an uphill campaign for election. Though disappointed in Truman's early performance, Niebuhr had opposed ADA's effort in 1948 to replace him with General Eisenhower as head of the Democratic ticket. As the 1948 presidential campaign drew to a close, he shared the expectation of almost everyone that the Republican candidate, Thomas Dewey, would win. Having voted without enthusiasm for Truman, Niebuhr gave his postelection analysis of Truman's winning the election:

> The laboring masses supported the Democratic ticket more vigorously than anyone had believed possible. A Democratic candidate won the election even though the Wallace rebellion cost him New York's electoral vote and the Dixiecrat rebellion subtracted four Southern states from the Democratic total.

A strong civil rights plank in the party's platform, promoted by ADA, had provoked a revolt among Southerners and won black votes for Truman, who subsequently proposed to Congress attacks on racial discrimination as well as social-welfare measures. Commenting on his "Fair Deal" message in early 1949, Niebuhr wrote:

> The Truman administration may not achieve all of the objectives which the President outlined in his program. But there was a sense of direction in his message and a feeling of confidence among his followers which accurately symbolizes the new mood of the nation. . . . This rejoicing may be a little premature. We do not have an adequate housing program. . . . Our civil rights program has not yet been enacted, and we may expect some pretty hysterical opposition before it is.[32]

During the early postwar period Niebuhr continued to raise the issue of racial discrimination in American life, pointing to the potential of religion, education, and law to mitigate injustices to black citizens. A Southern filibuster in Congress did, as he expected, defeat Truman's proposal for a permanent FEPC to enforce fair employment practices. He saw more hope at the time in antilynching and anti-poll-tax legislation, supported by "the best people of the South" as well as by "the conscience of the nation." Fair employment practice, he held, could be enacted and enforced only in states where consensus for it existed: "Politics is still the art of the possible." Noting strides in sports that began with integration in major baseball leagues and recent Supreme Court decisions forcing Southern states to end discrimination in higher education, Niebuhr wrote in 1950: "Progress in race relations is still too slow in both North and South. But there is real progress." He saw more progress toward justice in the distribution of income under New Deal policies, noting that "the highest paid 5% of our population received 34% of the national income in 1929 but only 18% in 1946," while "the per capita income of the whole working population rose" considerably. There are, Niebuhr wrote in defense of Truman's Fair Deal, limits to any indeterminate," but "one way in which the sovereign power of a government ought to be used" is "to provide health insurance for all of its citizens."[33]

Although Congress in 1949 enacted a public housing program, favored by Niebuhr and ADA, international developments continued to dominate the Truman years. In the spring of 1949 the United States joined several nations of western Europe and Canada in signing the North Atlantic defense pact (NATO), a treaty of mutual assistance occasioned by fear of Soviet expansion. While the treaty awaited ratification by the U.S. Senate, ADA endorsed NATO at its national convention in Chicago after Niebuhr and Arthur Schlesinger, Jr., led discussion in favor of it. Opposition came partly from isolationists, but mostly from those who looked on the U.N. as the world's peacekeeper. Addressing the issue in *Christianity and Crisis,* Niebuhr wrote:

> The present reality is that the United Nations presupposes the unanimity of the great powers, which does not in fact exist. This great organization has therefore been reduced to the status of a minimal bridge between East and West. This function is important; but it is not the function originally intended. The peace of the world does in fact depend upon the maintenance of preponderant power in the West.

NATO, he continued, was necessary:

> It is required primarily because the European nations desire it. . . . Perhaps they ought to have trusted us to come to their assistance without spelling out our obligations so exactly. Yet we must understand why they did desire it. One reason is that Europe, remembering our isolationism of previous

decades, is not yet quite certain that we are committed to a policy of continued, rather than fitful, responsibility.

Senate consent in July made NATO a reality. Niebuhr, meanwhile, became for a while in 1949, with Hans Morgenthau and Arnold Wolfers, a consultant to George Kennan's Policy Planning Staff at the State Department, set up two years earlier to advise on long-range problems. In the early fall of that year he also served on the U.S. delegation to the annual conference of the United Nations Educational, Scientific, and Cultural Organization (UNESCO) in Paris. He found worthwhile UNESCO's promotion of literacy, cultural exchanges, and freer flow of ideas, but regarded as illusory its notion that such undertakings ensure peace. Niebuhr's real public impact, however, was not as an occasional government consultant or participant in some international conference, but in shaping thought and opinion chiefly through publications addressed to a well-educated public. One who read him was Dean Acheson, Secretary of State during Truman's second term. In his memoirs Acheson quoted these lines from an essay by Niebuhr in the *Virginia Quarterly Review:* "There is always an element of moral ambiguity in historic responsibilities. Our survival as a civilization depends upon our ability to do what seems right from day to day without alternative moments of illusion and despair."[34]

Acheson evidently found wisdom in those words during the troubled period that followed the achievement of a measure of stability in western Europe by mid-1949. Late in that year the Communist forces of Mao Tse-tung completed their conquest of mainland China. During the previous winter, as the regime of Chiang Kai-shek retreated south of the Yangtze, Niebuhr had written:

> The Chinese government is slowly disintegrating; and we face the cheerless prospect of a triumphant Communism in China. There are those who think this . . . has taken place because we did not come to the aid of China early enough or with sufficient generosity. But even those who criticize our policy must admit that the Chinese government is corrupt and that it has steadily lost moral prestige in recent years. . . . The . . . ruling clique in it makes it quite impossible for the government to promise or carry through a land reform which would gain the genuine respect and loyalty of the vast masses of Chinese peasants.

In such circumstances, Niebuhr held, "we may have to learn to fold our hands." After Chiang's government had fled to Taiwan and the State Department issued its "White Paper" on the debacle, he editorialized:

> The line against communism in Europe must be rigorously held. But no line can be held in China. Communist victory is a reality. Furthermore, it

offers no foreseeable strategic threat as in Europe. What is more to the point, however, is that communism in the whole of Asia is created by two great forces, the hopes and fears of the abjectly poor and the resentment of "colored" peoples who are in revolt either against their colonial status or against the moral arrogance of the white man.

Indeed, as early as 1932 Niebuhr had stated presciently, "There is a much greater probability that communism will gain its victories in the agrarian Orient than in the industrial Occident."[35]

When in late 1949 events in China were followed by news that Russia had its own atomic bomb, Niebuhr pointed out that chances of armed conflict between Russia and the West were much reduced by the improved condition of Western Europe. Early in 1950 he approved the American government's decision to develop the deadlier hydrogen bomb as a deterrent, on the assumption that Russia would also develop it: "A nation does not have the power to say that it would rather be annihilated than to produce a certain weapon." Niebuhr saw merit in proposed U.S. disavowal of intent to be the first to use the dreaded bomb, and cautioned against developing defenses that placed "undue reliance" on it.[36]

By 1950 the world scene had changed significantly from that of a few years earlier: Stalinist Russia was the homeland of a Communist empire stretching from eastern Europe to China, though Tito since 1948 had led Yugoslavia on its own path of communism; western Europe was shielded by NATO and stronger economically, tied to a quasi-sovereign West German republic; Israel was a state; India had gained independence from Britain in 1947 and Indonesia from the Netherlands in 1949, while France held on to Indochina; and Truman had recently focused on the less-developed nations in proposing a "Point Four" program of technical aid. Niebuhr supported those policymakers in Washington who sought to contain Soviet expansion by means partly military but primarily economic and political, as opposed to others who wanted to prepare for a war they supposed inevitable and still others who would solve problems through a scheme of world government. "Communism," he wrote early in 1950, "must be contained; but the strategy of containment cannot be primarily military. . . . We must not relax our military defenses. But they must remain subordinate to our main purpose." It was during the spring of that year that a skillful demagogue emerged on the American scene who blamed recent advances of Communism on traitors in the U.S. government. "It is rather sad," Niebuhr commented then, "that the tumult and distraction occasioned by Senator McCarthy's irresponsible charges against the State Department should have diverted the mind and conscience of the nation and the government from a much more serious problem in Asia." That problem was whether or not containment should apply to Indochina, where France was pressing for U.S. aid in a local war against native Communists. Opposing initial American support of "the French puppet government" in that land, Niebuhr wrote: "Of course, the alternative in Indo-China is also a communist government, though one which has more impulses toward Titoism in it than the Mao government of China."[37]

In the summer of 1950 the Cold War became hot in Korea, as the Communist regime in the north of the peninsular nation invaded, with Russian approval, U.S.-occupied southern Korea, and America rushed to its defense. Niebuhr commented editorially:

> The outbreak of hostilities in Korea has clarified an aspect of our international situation which we should have known even without this costly illumination. It is now quite clear that the Russians do not want a general war with us. They want rather to test the strength of the non-communist world, politically and militarily, wherever they detect weak points. . . . The peril which we confront is a long-drawn-out struggle, lasting decade upon decade and requiring every possible moral and political resource of the so-called "free" world.

He sensed in mid-1950 an "increasing anti-communist hysteria in this country," reflected in passage of the Internal Security Act, which "imperils more than one constitutional liberty and abounds in such silly provisions as the registration of all members of the Communist party." By December of that year the Korean War entered a new phase, as forces led by General MacArthur overcame early setbacks and not only regained all of southern Korea but swept north to the Manchurian border, where Chinese Communist armies intervened and routed American troops. What had begun as a commitment to containing Communism had expanded into a drive well into Communist territory—a development, Niebuhr pointed out, arising from differences within the American government symbolized by Acheson and MacArthur. He shared Acheson's "insistence that Europe is the strategic center of the fight against Communism" and opposed MacArthur's readiness "to venture into vast and problematic operations in Asia which might end in disaster in both Europe and Asia." The general's desire to bomb Manchuria and carry the war deep into Asia, supported by many Americans, prompted Niebuhr to write in early 1951:

> Great nations are too strong to be destroyed by their foes. But they can easily be overcome by their own pride. One has the uneasy feeling that our

own country is greatly tempted in this critical age to that pride, in which the prophets of old recognized the portent of Babylon's doom.

After MacArthur's insubordination in pursuit of his goals led Truman to dismiss him, and the old soldier had begun to "fade away," Niebuhr expressed relief that the American public accepted "a foreign policy which does not strive simply for victory." Defining wise limits of America's military role in Asia, he wrote:

> We have the right and the duty to protect lands (the island littoral for instance) which are strategically necessary and the defense of which is morally acceptable. Fortunately our relations to both Japan and the Philippines does make their defense morally acceptable to them. But we cannot go much further.[38]

America's relation to most of Asia, Niebuhr held, should be guided by understanding of the poverty of its peoples and willingness to help them raise their living standards. "Our much too modest program of economic assistance," he wrote in 1951, "must be expanded." The poverty of India and Indonesia was, despite Communist propaganda, caused essentially not by Western imperial exploitation but by landlordism and low agricultural productivity, he contended, and experience would dispel illusions that independence would bring prosperity. When a few years earlier India and Pakistan had become independent within the British Commonwealth, Niebuhr commented on Britain's creative role in that event as evidence of the importance of moral as well as coercive factors in relations between nations. Reflecting on Gandhi's significance in an appreciative review of Louis Fischer's *The Life of Mahatma Gandhi*, which appeared after the saintly leader's assassination in 1948, he wrote that "this curious little man . . . had elicited religious veneration in his own nation and something very like it in the Western world." India's independence "crowned his labors with success, while the partition of India and the frightful internecine strife between Moslems and Hindus revealed how little his doctrine of non-violence had really mastered the spirit of the people." That doctrine, Niebuhr went on to say, "has validity insofar as it is always important to make human conflicts of interest non-violent if possible. It has no validity insofar as it is offered either as a certain way of achieving a morally acceptable goal or as an escape from the moral ambiguities of political life."[39]

Among other books that impressed Niebuhr in the early 1950s—when most Westerners had become aware of Stalinist evils—was *The God That Failed*, a symposium by ex-Communists and former fellow travelers, edited by Richard Crossman. Reviewing it, he noted that its six authors, among them Arthur Koestler and Ignazio Silone, all were drawn to Communism by their abhorrence of capitalist injustices and were finally repelled by the greater evils of Communist tyranny. "Most of the confessions," he observed, "reveal not only the inhumanity which is derived from uncontrolled and uncriticized power but the cruelty which is the fruit of a fanatic and absolute creed." Niebuhr continued:

> The editor having been discerning, only essentially healthy ex-Communists are included in this group of penitents. Those . . . who have turned to reaction or to another form of totalitarianism or have become cynical are rightly not heard from. The six remain devoted to the cause of social justice, but they have found that freedom is a more important component of justice than they had realized in their pilgrimage to Moscow.

What Koestler called "the gravitational force which keeps civilization in its orbit" derived, Niebuhr suggested, "from a humility that recognizes the incomplete and fragmentary character of every scheme of justice, so that the highest form of perfection in history is incompatible with any claim that we have the final form of perfection in our keeping." Niebuhr's review, appearing in 1950, was one of the last pieces he published in the *Nation*, the old and respected weekly to which he had frequently contributed for more than a decade. Its editor, Freda Kirchwey, though staunchly anti-Nazi earlier, had allowed a pro-Soviet bias on its pages after the war, especially in the regular articles of its foreign editor, J. A. del Vayo. After she refused to publish certain letters critical of del Vayo and of her editorial policy, Niebuhr in May of 1951 had his name removed from the journal's masthead.[40]

By 1951 Cold War tensions had led to a Western defense buildup and the institutionalization of NATO, with General Eisenhower as supreme commander in Paris. After a brief trip to Europe in the summer of that year, for a conference of theologians near Geneva preparing for the theme of the next septennial assembly of the World Council of Churches, Niebuhr commented to American readers on the climate of opinion he found on the Continent. Europeans, he wrote, were grateful for U.S. economic and military support and yet critical of American culture:

> French resentments epitomize and exaggerate the resentments of a "cultured" parent civilization against its uncouth son. All over Europe "Americanization" has become synonymous with the threat of "technics" against the organic and traditional elements of culture. . . . Perhaps we ought to admit that a civilization as preoccupied with technics as our own unavoidably exhibits vulgarities which mellow cultures find difficult to bear.

He saw less validity in European stereotypes of American society based on old Marxist dogmatisms, and expressed hope that Continental socialists would discard those dogmas:

> European socialism is ideologically weak because it cannot bring itself to realization of the disquieting truth that Communism is not so much a corruption of orthodox Marxism as the inevitable consequence of its most basic presuppositions. To be sure, Marx did not intend the corruptions of power which Communism practices. They nevertheless follow inevitably from . . . the naive belief that property is the only source both of economic power and of the corruption of self-interest in the use of power.

British socialism, though not Marxist, also had a lesson to learn, Niebuhr had recently observed, for its new program of "socialized medicine" went too far: "The British health service will have to find some way of placing a check upon claims that individuals make upon it."[41]

As the postwar world took the shape that it would hold for decades to come, its features owing much to decisions made by the man in the White House, Niebuhr commented in 1951 that Truman "has managed to achieve a fairly consistent foreign policy that does some justice to the vast responsibilities which our power implies and is cognizant of the hazards of the age." Some years later he stated, "In retrospect, I would say that Truman was one of the great presidents." Looking ahead in the grim Cold War year of 1951, he wrote in *Christianity and Crisis:* "We do not know how the Communist tyranny will disintegrate or when; nor how it might lose it virulence. We do know that the consequences of an atomic conflict are so terrible that no one has a right to prefer its calculable destruction to an incalculable future."[42]

THEOLOGICAL INSIGHTS ON LIFE AND HISTORY

The tragic experience of two world wars and the possibility of worse to come raised deep questions about the meaning of history among thoughtful spirits on both sides of the Atlantic, prompting renewed interest in the thought of Saint Augustine, who had faced such questions during the crisis of the late Roman Empire. One result was the publication in 1948 of a new two-volume edition of selected works of the great father of the Western church, entitled *Basic Writings of Saint Augustine,* edited by the Princeton classicist Whitney Oates. Niebuhr acquired a copy and used it heavily.[43] Before the Oates edition appeared, he had nearly completed a book, based partly on his Beecher Lectures at Yale Divinity School three years earlier, which sought to do for his age what Augustine had done long ago in *The City of God.* Summarizing and elaborating themes presented earlier in *Beyond Tragedy* and toward the end of his Gifford Lectures, he published *Faith and History* in 1949.

"The history of mankind, " Niebuhr observed in the opening pages, "exhibits no more ironic experience than the contrast between the sanguine hopes of recent centuries and the bitter experience of contemporary man." Modern technology, he continued, was regarded as a harbinger of redemption of humanity from its difficulties, but became the occasion for new dimensions of ancient perplexities. Evolutionary optimism typically assumed that growing rationality would resolve all social problems, whether through universal education as envisaged by Condorcet or through the application of scientific method as proposed by Comte. A recent expression of such hope, Niebuhr noted, was H. G. Wells's *Outline of History*, projecting growth toward a democratic world community. The Christian faith, he went on to say, with its biblical idea of a good creation and of history as moving in it toward a goal, prepared the soil for modern consciousness of history as dynamic. But, he pointed out, modern culture is so preoccupied with detailed analyses of things as to give shallow answers to ultimate questions, finding a false fulfillment of life in history itself, while a more profound interpretation of life takes evil seriously as a persistent force arising in human freedom, and views history as pointing beyond itself to a more ultimate source of meaning. The modern creed was "a very clever contrivance of human pride to obscure the weakness and the insecurity of man . . . and of human sloth to evade responsibility."[44]

History, like the human self, is a complex unity of the natural and the spiritual, Niebuhr emphasized, its eventful character distinguished from the recurrences of nature by "the unique freedom, which enables man to transcend the flux of time, holding past moments in present memory and envisaging future ends of actions which are not dictated by natural necessity." The Athenian dramatists, he perceived, saw human life as a unity of finiteness and freedom, tragically involved in exceeding its bounds, but their insights became submerged in the rise of Greek philosophy, which equated history with nature in an inferior realm of change and sought emancipation in virtuous conformity to the rational principles of an eternal order. While Plato and Aristotle took an interest in politics, and the Roman Stoics did so more actively, all aspired to a contemplative ideal looking toward the soul's participation in a timeless eternity. It remained, he pointed out, for Saint Augustine in his magisterial work to ridicule the classical view of life and history as drearily cyclical, affirming instead the biblical interpretation of it as meaningfully linear under God. The modern view of history, unlike the classical, understood that cultural achievements and social institutions are capable of indeterminate development but, he held, erred in discounting the self-seeking tendencies and destructive potential of human freedom and in proudly supposing that human mastery can supplant divine providence in the processes of history.[45]

Biblical faith, Niebuhr emphasized, must be distinguished not only from cultures that negate the meaning of history but also those which conceive themselves as the center of historical meaning. The most sublime of the prophets, Second Isaiah, he noted, reminds us of a source and end of existence too transcendent to be humanly comprehended or manipulated: "My thoughts are not your thoughts, neither are your ways my ways, says the Lord" (Isa. 55:8), and he also spoke of a God before whom "the nations are as a drop of a bucket" (Isa. 40:15). All the prophets, Niebuhr pointed out, "believe that God's judgments are executed in history" and yet "sense a divine judgment above and beyond the rough and inexact historical judgments." Thus Amos predicted in specific terms the coming doom of a corrupt and complacent nation, while Second Isaiah in quite different circumstances affirmed God's hidden sovereignty over history. In the course of history, Niebuhr observed, at least extravagant forms of injustice are destroyed, but innocent individuals often suffer. While the life and death of Christ is apprehended by faith as the disclosure of a divine power and mercy that will ultimately purge the evil of history, and promises indeterminate renewals of life in history, the Christian faith recognizes that "history remains morally ambiguous to the end." It "insists upon the potential meaningfulness of man's fragmentary life in history and its final completion by a power and love not his own." The church, according to Niebuhr, is a community of believers "persuaded that the whole of life and all historical vicissitudes stand under the sovereignty of a holy, yet merciful God"—a community where the grace of Christ is known through sacraments and preaching, and pride is pierced in transformed lives. Finally, Niebuhr stated, Christianity insists on the last judgment and the resurrection as symbols of a final divine judgment upon the sin of history, and of the hope for "an eternity which transfigures, but does not annul, the temporal process."[46]

Faith and History was dedicated "to my colleagues on the faculty and to the students of Union Theological Seminary," in whose fellowship "the sun and rain is provided, without which no fruit of mind and spirit can ripen." Lynn Harold Hough, Niebuhr's friend from Detroit days who had recently retired as dean of Drew Theological Seminary, quoted the book repeatedly in an appreciative review. "Dr. Niebuhr," he wrote, "subjects modern conceptions of history to the most searching analysis. . . . The possible fulfillments in history and the fulfillment of history itself in that which is above and beyond history, with the relation of the church to the final goal, bring a full round to the whole discussion." Demurring on certain points, Hough felt that Niebuhr was too influenced by Cochrane's critique of classicism to appreciate the Greek genius at its best. Another friendly reviewer, Perry Miller, wrote: "For the general reader *Faith and History* is possibly the most convenient approach to Niebuhr's theology." Daniel Jenkins, a prominent British Congregationalist, found that the book treated moral aspects of the biblical view of history "in such a way as to lead its readers to understand anew what the power of the Lord of history over the false gods of this world means." Arthur Schlesinger, Jr., reviewing Niebuhr's latest volume, wrote that "the distinction of his analysis is his success in restating Christian insights with such irresistible relevance to contemporary experience that even those who have no decisive faith in the supernatural find their own reading of experience and of history given new and significant dimensions." It was, he added, "a critique of modern culture and not a rejection of it."[47] In the book Niebuhr criticized not science and education, but a pretentious rationalism and scientism; a biblical and Augustinian sense of mystery and meaning within and beyond the human drama suffuses its pages. Other such works appeared in the early postwar years, including the Cambridge historian Herbert Butterfield's *Christianity and History*, also published in 1949, with a strikingly similar Augustinian theme. *Faith and History*, one of Niebuhr's best-written books, was a clear summation of his theological perspective on history.

Saint Augustine's thought, continuing to fascinate Niebuhr, underlay the theme of a guest lecture, "The Foolishness of the Gospel in Relation to the Wisdom of the World," which he gave early in 1950 at Union Theological Seminary in Virginia, a Presbyterian institution (which later issued it as a tape entitled "How Faith and Reason Are Related"). Starting with a text of Saint Paul (I Cor. 1:20–21), he took up anew, as before in his Gifford Lectures, the relation of Christian faith to the disciplines of culture. The latter, he observed, have since the Greeks made a rational effort, philosophically and scientifically, to understand the natural world and human life; the wisdom thus achieved establishes causalities and coherences, seeing the harmony of things. However, he pointed out, it knows nothing of the deep irrationality of human sin or the mystery of the grace of a just and loving God disclosed in Christ, for "the human mind, however great its achievements, is not an adequate instrument to deal with the ultimate issues of life." Christian faith, on the other hand, "is a response of the total person toward the total problem of the meaning of existence," and "always involves repentance" as the self becomes aware of its sin and grasps that "God so loved the world, that he gave his only begotten Son" in the sacrifice of the atonement. Niebuhr went on to cite three inadequate ways of relating this faith to the disciplines of culture: that of Thomism, by which "faith becomes a kind of cupola on top of the great temple of knowledge"; that of the Protestant Reformation, which "tends to cultural obscurantism"; and that of liberal Christianity, which saw "no essential difference" between faith and reason and reduced the God of the Bible to "a kind of grandfatherly God who is kind to birdies and little children." Then, outlining his own approach, he told the gathered seminarians:

> I become more and more impressed with a man who was both the father of Catholicism and of the Reformation, as he dealt with this problem, St. Augustine, and I am unashamed to call myself an Augustinian as I deal with this issue, for it seems to me that Augustine, who came out of a neo-Platonic tradition and was highly schooled in philosophy and recognized the limits of philosophy, showed us how these things must be related to each other better than most of the theologians of the classical age and our own.

Augustine, for example, Niebuhr continued, drew upon philosophical and psychological insights of Neoplatonism regarding human consciousness; yet, in meditating on the significance of memory, he moved beyond the self to the rim of God, by whom all finite human selves are known and by whom life in its fragments and contradictions is given final meaning. Such a dialectic of faith and reason, Niebuhr held, can be applied to modern culture in the realms of psychiatry and social theory. It was Freud's achievement to explore "labyrinths of complexity in the subconscious"; pastors "have to send some people to psychiatrists" for treatment, but such therapy has limits because it is based on a science that "misses the ultimate mystery of selfhood." Similarly, political and social science contribute to "proximate salvations," coming out of "a shrewd analysis of the way people live," but when a social theory, like Marxism in its pure form, presumes to solve the problem of life on the ultimate level, it turns into "the damnedest nonsense." A modern Augustinian dialectic will "take every discipline of culture seriously but understand its limits," Niebuhr concluded:

This means . . . that the Christian must be involved constantly in the world of culture, practically and theoretically, and accept such truth as he can find there that leads to any concept of meaning and coherence as the world by its wisdom gives, and yet finally, of course, understand how inadequate the wisdom of the world is from the standpoint of the foolishness of the Gospel, and how provisional and tentative all redemptions are as against the redemption in Christ.[48]

Later, in July of 1950 at the Aspen Institute, situated in the snow-capped mountains of Colorado, Niebuhr developed a related theme in another memorable lecture, "Augustine's Conception of Selfhood" (also audio-recorded). More than any previous theologian, he began, Augustine "understood what was unique in the faith of the Bible," and upon that understanding expounded an interpretation of history and selfhood that recognized history as meaningful but not self-fulfilling and the self as a unity of body and soul, its sin found not in the body but in the self itself and overcome not by an act of willing but in strength given by grace. Indebted also to Plotinus's insight on the self's capacity as subject to make itself object, Augustine marveled at its self-transcending use of the inner chamber of memory and perceived its freedom over natural necessity: "His understanding of history as a unique realm belonging to neither nature nor eternity is derived from his understanding of the self as being in time and transcending time." Augustine, Niebuhr continued, set forth his conception of "an integral self operating in mind, memory, and will" as an analogy of the triune God—a mysterious human self that is more than any of its functions:

It refutes every naturalistic interpretation of selfhood, according to which the individuation of the self is derived purely from the particularity of the physical organism. Augustine recognizes that the spiritual mystery of self-consciousness is the real seat of selfhood. His conception also refutes all forms of idealism which seem first to establish and then lose the self in the mind. This is Kierkegaard's protest against Hegel.

According to Augustine, he went on to say, the self truly becomes itself in love of God and neighbor; its sin consists in anxiously exalting itself by seeking absolute security through its power or by claiming absolute validity for its knowledge or absolute perfection for its virtue. Unlike Pelagius, who held that the human will is essentially good, Augustine recognized the self's inevitable tendency to prefer its own good to that of others, and its inability to escape self-centeredness in action and attitude without the gift of grace. Accenting the last point, Niebuhr declared:

> The Christian faith is the discovery of a power great enough to complete the incompleteness of our mortal and fragmentary existence, mysteriously related to a love which overcomes the aberrations which come out of our efforts to complete ourselves prematurely within ourselves. In this ultimate security our frantic efforts for false security can be overcome. This is the grace, the mercy, the forgiveness which heals our will.

It was a moving lecture, laced with apt quotations from Augustine's works and packed with references to philosophical alternatives from Plato to the twentieth century. "The Augustinian interpretation of human self-hood," Niebuhr said in conclusion, "is not some anachronistic doctrine invalidated by modern knowledge; I think it contains wisdom by which some of the foolishness of modern knowledge can be overcome."[49]

Another facet of Augustinian thought was the subject of a lecture Niebuhr gave at Columbia University within several months of his Aspen lecture, under auspices of the Francis Carroll Memorial Foundation, later elaborated in an essay published as "Augustine's Political Realism." Saint Augustine, he began, "was, by general consent, the first great 'realist' in Western history" and "deserves this distinction because the picture of social reality in his *De civitate Dei* gives an adequate account of the social factions, tensions, and competition which we know to be well-nigh universal on every level of community." His conception of social evil was "a corollary" of his doctrine of selfhood:

> "Self-love" is the source of evil rather than some residual natural impulse which mind has not yet completely mastered. This excessive love of self, sometimes defined as pride or *superbia*, is explained as the consequence of the self's abandonment of God as its true end and of making itself "a kind of end." It is this . . . which sows confusion into every human community.

Conflict was worse on a world scale, in Augustine's words, "as the greater sea is more dangerous." Regarding earthly peace as good, Augustine saw that, again in his words, "they will not have it long for they used it not well while they had it." That is, Niebuhr pointed out, "unless some larger love or loyalty qualifies the self-interest of the various groups, this collective self-interest will expose the community to either an overt conflict of competing groups or to the injustice of a dominant group." Augustine, he continued, erred in drawing too sharp a distinction between the "two cities," one loving God and the other self, "because the conflict between love and self-love is in every soul"—a fact important to recognize in political analyses. Despite defects in his approach to politics, Niebuhr concluded, a perplexed generation "might well take counsel of Augustine."[50]

Niebuhr's continued theological interest and viewpoint are also seen in reviews of two books that appeared at this time, one of them Perry Miller's *Jonathan Edwards*. This biography, he wrote, improved on others in giving "a fuller appreciation of the significance of this backwoods genius," whom historians had either "condemned as a fire-and-brimstone revivalist" or "praised as a profound philosophical mind, without elucidation." Miller's "sophisticated analysis" of Edwards's achievement "reveals how the new wine of the thought of Locke and Newton in the old wineskin of New England Calvinism produced a quite remarkable system of thought." The other book was Karl Barth's *Dogmatics in Outline*, a translation of lectures he had given at the University of Bonn after the war. "The main emphasis, as always in Barth," wrote Niebuhr, "is upon the Bible. . . . The Biblical revelation is essential; faith, not reason, is the basis of Christian knowledge." With that Niebuhr agreed; however, he continued, "the rigorous rejection of every commerce between theology and the disciplines of culture drives Mr. Barth further and further into literalism." The volume, providing "a good general view of Barth's system of thought," revealed why he was "so effective an antidote to sentimental versions of the Christian faith—and also why the antidote has not been very effective in the Anglo-Saxon world."[51]

During these years of Reinhold Niebuhr's prominence in American life and thought, his brother continued on his own distinguished path at Yale Divinity School, becoming in 1954 Sterling Professor of Theology and Christian Ethics. A more polished writer than Reinhold, and less public in his interests, H. Richard Niebuhr produced some notable books, including *Christ and Culture*—his best-known work—published in 1951 and dedicated "To Reinie." As one respected scholar who studied under both of them has put it, "Helmut Richard never failed to refer to his brother in the most gentlemanly and irenic terms, and vice versa for Reinhold with reference to Helmut Richard. Mutual respect and genuine brotherly love were the hallmarks of their relationship in both public and private circumstances." Meanwhile, their sister, Hulda Niebuhr, had left Madison Avenue Presbyterian Church in 1946 to become professor of Christian education at McCormick Theological Seminary in Chicago, where her mother continued to live with her. In 1949 she published her masterpiece, *The One Story*, an account of the Bible in its unity from Abraham to Paul—long widely used in American Sunday schools. Reinhold's reputation was international, but each of the three Niebuhrs contributed importantly to the recovery of a vital biblical faith in the American Protestant churches.[52]

AMERICA'S PRECARIOUS EMINENCE

Theological perspectives remained implicit, if not always stated explicitly, in Reinhold Niebuhr's view of the contemporary scene and of American experience. Events of the past decade had thrust the United States suddenly into a role of world leadership to which it was not accustomed. "Rome in the ancient world and Britain in the modern era," Niebuhr wrote in the late 1940s, "both served a long apprenticeship of a slow accretion of power before they were called upon to bear responsibilities comparable to those which now engage us." Germany's defeat and Britain's decline, he observed while Americans fought in Korea, "have lifted us up to a precarious eminence in the community of nations." Saint Paul's warning, "Let any one who thinks that he stands take heed lest he fall" (I Cor. 10:12, RSV), applies not only to individuals, he wrote in 1951: "Any nation which is too certain of either its power or its virtue hastens its fall by its very complacency." These thoughts were on Niebuhr's mind in the summer and fall of that year as he wrote *The Irony of American History*, one of his shorter and most widely read books. It was developed largely from lectures on the theme "This Nation under God," which he gave at Westminster College in Fulton, Missouri, in 1949 under auspices of the John Findley Green Foundation (the same series in which Churchill had recently delivered his "Iron Curtain" speech), and from others at Northwestern University in 1951 under auspices of the Shaffer Lectureship. Although he had compensated for a deficiency in his formal education by reading such works as Merle Curti's *The Growth of American Thought* and Henry Bamford Parkes's *The American Experience*, he disclaimed expert competence in the field of American history, presenting instead his somber reflections on certain ironies or contradictions between present realities and a youthful nation's claims to virtue, wisdom, and power.[53]

The book—which Niebuhr dedicated to his son, Christopher, who had a keen interest in history—began by tracing certain characteristics of American society to its Puritan and Jeffersonian past. Noting that every nation has its own peculiar form of self-appreciation, Niebuhr stated, "Our version is that our nation turned its back upon the vices of Europe and made a new beginning." A fusion of strains in early American culture, he continued, produced a strongly bourgeois ethos which correlated virtue and prosperity—a social condition and attitude expressing, as Tocqueville observed, an assumption of innocence and a certain worldliness. More than a century later most Americans still attributed their high living standards to superior diligence, or to their skills and freedom:

We have forgotten to what degree the wealth of our natural resources and the fortuitous circumstance that we conquered a continent just when the advancement of technics made it possible to organize that continent into a single political and economic unit, lay at the foundation of our prosperity.

These elements in national success, Niebuhr held, refuted pretensions that American ways and values are valid for the rest of the world. Indeed, he pointed out, America's fluid class structure rested on those conditions, and the nation eventually would face difficult issues of justice when its economy ceased to expand. Against the backdrop of an optimistic culture, Niebuhr went on to say, American political institutions were based on a realistic awareness of potential conflicts of power and passion: James Madison, chief of the founding fathers, not only understood human egoism but anticipated Marx in recognizing economic factors in social friction. The government established in 1787 eventually became, through movements culminating in the New Deal, an instrument of pragmatic social policies which are "closer to the truth than either Marxist or bourgeois ideology."[54]

Niebuhr found irony not only in the contradiction between cherished dogmas and actual practices in American life but also in the frustrations of America's position in the contemporary world. The same forces that had made the United States prosperous, he observed, had also made it a global power—involved in "a vaster and vaster entanglement with other wills and purposes"—and the custodian of the ultimate weapon which . . . symbolizes the moral ambiguity of physical warfare." As the Marxist-Leninist creed spread from Russia into Asia and other impoverished areas of the world, America became "the residuary legatee" of resentments against a fading European imperialism, because "the difference between our wealth and the poverty of the technically undeveloped world is interpreted by communist propaganda as irrefutable evidence of the exploitative character of our economy." Thus Communism became an attractive option on continents where indigenous problems were blamed on American capitalism, and ancient Oriental or primitive African cultures lacked the socioeconomic, educational, and spiritual foundations for democracy. In those lands "legitimate desires for greater well-being are so inextricably intertwined with illusory hopes that decades upon decades will be required to bring order out of this chaos." In the conflict with Communism, Niebuhr concluded, Lincoln's awareness of an overarching providence while engaged in the Civil War was a model for the task of "remaining loyal and responsible toward the moral treasures of a free civilization on the one hand, while yet having some religious vantage

The parsonage and St. John's Church in Lincoln, Illinois, where Reinhold Niebuhr grew up while his father was pastor there early in the twentieth century. *Courtesy of the Library of Congress*

The old Elmhurst campus, west of Chicago, as it appeared when Niebuhr was a student there from 1907 to 1910. *Courtesy of Elmhurst College*

Reinhold Niebuhr in his senior year at Elmhurst. *Courtesy of Elmhurst College*

Samuel D. Press, professor at Eden Theological Seminary near St. Louis, who was Niebuhr's teacher there from 1910 to 1913. *Courtesy of Eden Theological Seminary*

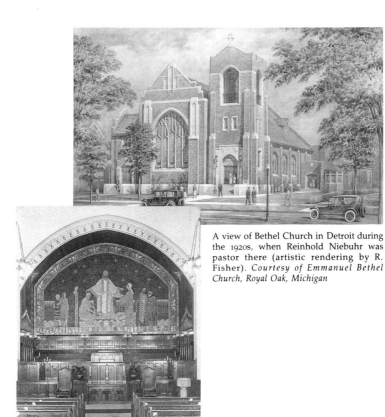

A view of Bethel Church in Detroit during the 1920s, when Reinhold Niebuhr was pastor there (artistic rendering by R. Fisher). *Courtesy of Emmanuel Bethel Church, Royal Oak, Michigan*

Bethel Church's center-front pulpit, choir loft, and reredos depicting Jesus attended by Mary and Martha. *Courtesy of Emmanuel Bethel Church, Royal Oak, Michigan*

Reinhold Niebuhr ca. 1930, in the customary dress of clergy of his denomination at the time. *Courtesy of Union Theological Seminary Archives, New York City*

Union Theological Seminary in New York, as seen from the corner of Broadway and 120th Street in Niebuhr's time. *Courtesy of Union Theological Seminary Archives, New York City*

Portrait of Henry Sloane Coffin, president of Union Theological Seminary in New York, 1926–45, who recruited most of its renowned faculty of the mid-twentieth century (painted by Gordan Aymar). *Courtesy of Union Theological Seminary Archives, New York City*

The Niebuhr family—Reinhold, Ursula, Christopher, and Elisabeth—at their summer cottage in Heath, Massachusetts, ca. 1945, with friend Helga Marville in the background. *Courtesy of Ursula M. Niebuhr*

Portrait of William Scarlett, Episcopal bishop of Missouri, 1930–45, a close life-long friend of Niebuhr (painted by Annie Ware Sabine Siebert). *Courtesy of Christ Church Cathedral*

Niebuhr (center) in a boat on the Rhine during an educational mission to Germany for the U.S. State Department in 1946.

The cover of *Time's* twenty-fifth anniversary issue, March 8, 1948. *Courtesy of Time magazine*

Niebuhr with Hubert Humphrey at an ADA meeting in 1949, soon after Humphrey's election to the U.S. Senate. *Courtesy of Union Theological Seminary Archives, New York City*

Reinhold Niebuhr lecturing to a class at Union Seminary, ca. 1950. *Courtesy of Union Theological Seminary Archives, New York City*

Niebuhr with a student. *Courtesy of Union Theological Seminary Archives, New York City*

Niebuhr preaching in James Chapel of Union Seminary, 1954. *Courtesy of Union Theological Seminary Archives, New York City*

Reinhold Niebuhr talking with friends while walking poodles, Vicky and Winnie, on the west side of the Union Seminary quadrangle, ca. 1960. *Courtesy of Union Theological Seminary Archives, New York City*

Reinhold Niebuhr, ca. 1960. *Courtesy of Union Theological Seminary Archives, New York City*

Niebuhr in his seventies with Arthur Schlesinger, Jr.'s *A Thousand Days*, on the Kennedy presidency, beside him. *Courtesy of Ronald H. Stone*

Niebuhr with John C. Bennett in 1966, after many years as colleagues on the Union faculty and as partners in editing *Christianity and Crisis. Courtesy of Union Theological Seminary Archives, New York City*

point over the struggle." Americans must learn to temper urgencies of the Cold War with "a sense of awe before the vastness of the historical drama in which we are jointly involved" and "a sense of contrition about the common human frailties which lie at the foundation of both the enemy's demonry and our vanities."[55]

When *The Irony of American History* appeared in the spring of 1952, Peter Viereck quoted those last words on the front page of the *New York Times Book Review*. "I predict," he wrote, "that before the end of the decade, Niebuhr will be our most influential social thinker." Yet, Viereck added, many of his followers, whether in ADA or in pews, would fail to grasp his way of relating a deep Christian faith to "the vital center" of public life. Another reviewer was the Princeton scholar E. Harris Harbison, who found the book rather sketchy in historical treatment and yet "a searching and disturbing essay, brilliant in its insights, unusually lucid in expression, and as moving in its closing pages as anything the author has written." Among other reviewers, Anthony West, William Leuchtenburg, and Morton White objected to Niebuhr's theological presuppositions, each setting reason against faith. Arthur Schlesinger, Jr., however, was more appreciative, and defended Niebuhr against such critics by pointing out that, unlike some religionists and some pragmatists, he drew "a firm line . . . designed to keep the absolute out of the relative, and at the same time to prevent the relative from confusing itself with the absolute." Crane Brinton was also impressed by the book, drawing special attention to the relevance of Niebuhr's chapter on America's resented position among impoverished peoples of emerging nations. In Britain, Herbert Agar, finding Niebuhr a timely guide to America in its new world role, acclaimed the book as "primarily a long and eloquent sermon." A decade and a half later Henry F. May recalled the deep impression Niebuhr's book had made on many historians when it was first published. He mentioned, however, a flaw, also noticed by others, in the book's silence on the irony of racial discrimination in a nation professing inclusive ideals—an unfortunate omission that is puzzling in view of Niebuhr's sensitivity to that blot on American practice, to which he turned time and again over the decades. Despite that defect, May declared in 1968 that the book still "contains a message that we badly need." A third of a century after its publication, George Kennan alluded to "the brilliant insights of Reinhold Niebuhr's *The Irony of American History.*"[56]

Weeks before the book appeared, Niebuhr in his sixtieth year suffered a serious stroke on February 15, 1952. During weeks of hospitalization and a slow convalescence at home, where Ursula cared for him, Robert

E. Fitch took over his classes during the spring semester at Union Seminary. As word of his illness spread, expressions of concern and sympathy flooded his mail. One friend, William Turner Levy, professor of literature at a branch of the City University of New York, sent him selections from T. S. Eliot's *Old Possum's Book of Practical Cats* for light reading. Thanking Levy for the poems, Niebuhr wrote in May, "They represent a side of his genius that I had not been acquainted with before, and I am delighted to find him so frolicsome." Arthur Schlesinger, Jr., meanwhile, with James Loeb, organized a collection of contributions from his friends in ADA for a television set to enable him to follow news and watch political events he could not attend. "I have been deeply touched," he wrote Schlesinger, "by the loyalty of my friends during my illness—I may say particularly by yours and Jim's." By late spring it was clear that the stroke had so lamed his left arm that he could no longer type as before. That moved John Bennett to bring together the faculty and trustees of Union Seminary in giving Reinhold Niebuhr on his sixtieth birthday an IBM electric typewriter adapted for use with one hand, including a foot pedal for controlling capitals. "This present," he wrote them all in a letter of thanks, "is particularly valuable to me because I have found that I cannot compose articles or anything more than letters on a dictaphone, as my mental processes seem to require that I look at the page before me."[57]

Eventually Niebuhr regained sufficient strength to resume teaching and writing, but thereafter he worked on a restricted schedule and rarely traveled for engagements outside New York. The stroke slowed his pace, causing him to limp and taking the fire out of his speech, but his mind remained clear and lively. Much of his best work lay ahead.

CHAPTER SEVEN

The World and Union Seminary at Mid-Century

 è‰

Turning to the emerging issues of a more placid era after the crises of recent decades, Reinhold Niebuhr commented perceptively on changes in Russia after Stalin's death in 1953, on cultural and religious and social problems in a diverse and affluent America, and on Cold War tensions in an age of nuclear weapons and of rapid change in Asia and Africa. During these years he continued to teach at Union Theological Seminary, then in its greatest period as a center of Protestant thought and scholarship, until 1960.

THE ADVENT OF THE EISENHOWER ERA

The year 1952 was a time of transition and drama in American presidential politics. After nearly two full terms ending in an unpopular and stalemated war in Korea, President Truman was about to retire. It seemed likely that twenty years of Democratic leadership would end, especially after General Dwight Eisenhower—widely respected and liked as a hero of World War II and more recently as NATO commander in Europe—entered the contest and became the Republican candidate for President. Niebuhr, meanwhile, joined many Democrats in urging Governor Adlai Stevenson of Illinois, an articulate man of broad experience, to make himself available for their party's presidential nomination. When illness forced him to cancel plans for a talk with the governor in Springfield, he wrote Stevenson in March: "It would be presumptuous on my part to press my views upon you, so I will merely express the hope that you will not resist the pressures upon you unduly, and allow your name to become a rallying point for the liberal opinion of America." Stevenson, drafted as the Democratic candidate, occasionally turned to Niebuhr for advice on public issues in coming years. Asked about Niebuhr's influence on him, he later remarked, "Has he had any effect on me? I don't know, but I hope so."[1]

As Americans prepared for the 1952 election campaign, Niebuhr reminded them of the distinction between faith and politics:

> While it is certainly true that the Christian life and faith include political responsibility, it is nevertheless dangerous to derive political decisions too simply from our Christian faith. Every political decision requires dozens of subordinate and relative judgments which cannot be derived from, or sanctioned by, our faith.

Elaborating further, he stated:

> Christians must make these hazardous political decisions with full recognition that others equally devoted to the common good may arrive at contrary conclusions. They will be less affronted and baffled by the different conclusions if they have some humble recognition of the taint of individual and collective self-interest which colors even our purest political and moral ideals.

After Eisenhower won the election, sweeping his party to control of Congress, Niebuhr commented that "one of the real gains of a Republican victory is that it makes the party of the dominant business group of the nation thoroughly responsible for foreign policy," for the GOP out of office "was developing some dangerous tendencies toward hysteria." The general's road to the presidency was, in his words, "engineered by eminent proconsuls of the budding American imperium," whose experience abroad prompted them to turn to him for leadership. A moderate, opposed in Congress by the right wing, Eisenhower would need "Democratic votes to overcome defections in his own party." Stevenson, meanwhile, became "a new and authentic voice in the counsels of the nation."[2]

Within two years of the onset of the Eisenhower era, a new calm and equilibrium replaced the tense Cold War conditions of the early 1950s. Stalin's death in March of 1953 was followed by a truce in Korea a few months later, possible because, as Niebuhr noted, "both sides wanted to stop the blood-letting." In the reshuffling of power that took place in the Kremlin after the legendary dictator died, he pointed out, Malenkov emerged as the tentative leader in an alliance of the party with the army; the latter's influence, which only Stalin was strong enough to suppress, was hopeful, "for modern armies are hardly ever intent upon war." While Communist tyranny remained a fact and a threat, Niebuhr wrote in 1953, the prospect for peace had improved:

It is becoming increasingly clear that the death of Stalin resulted in a radical shift of policy in the Soviet Union, and that the immediate effect . . . is a relaxation of the almost intolerable tension of the "cold war" in every part of the world. . . . These developments are what Christians mean when they talk about a providence in the events of history which is beyond human foreknowledge or contriving.[3]

The world, meanwhile, watched in June of 1953 as Queen Elizabeth II rode in a horse-drawn coach through London to her coronation at Westminster Abbey. Commenting on the occasion as an expression of "poetry in politics," Niebuhr reflected on the British monarchy as "symbolic of the fact that the authority by which a community orders its life is not merely a conscious contrivance" but a "slow accretion" of institutional arrangements historically transmitted:

It may be significant that the nation which produced Edmund Burke's *Reflections on the Revolution in France* . . . should have a more stable government and no less liberty and justice than the home of the French Revolution. Britain is not the only nation which reformed, rather than abolished, the institution of monarchy; but it is eminently fitting that a nation which gave us the common law, in which justice is defined by historic rather than abstract concepts, should also exemplify this historic wisdom so excellently in its monarchical institution.

The royal family, he added, symbolized not only historic continuities but also the unity of a people beyond particular elected governments. Britain's prime minister then was Churchill, returned to power in 1951. Britain's Tories, he commented, had no intention of undoing the basic welfare program enacted by Labour: "They were schooled in an older and wiser tradition than our own conservatism." Later in 1953 Niebuhr took satisfaction in Adenauer's resounding election victory in West Germany, for the old statesman, opposed to German unification on Soviet terms, was guiding his country in the path of democracy and integration with Europe. This achievement showed that "Rhineland Catholicism, the basis of Adenauer's strength, is the most creative Catholicism in the world." Noting increased dislike of America in France, Niebuhr saw its roots in U.S. involvement in Germany's economic revival and in more recent proposals for its rearmament, in distorted Marxist images among French intellectuals, and in resentment of American criticism of France's stubborn imperialism.[4]

The Atlantic community, Niebuhr wrote in 1954, was anchored in the common culture and historical exigencies of western Europe and its North

American offshoots. Its underlying unities included religions "derived from Biblical faith," a secularism which "does not seriously challenge the main ethical affirmations of that faith," and "a long history of gradually achieved toleration" together with "delicate balances of social forces to preserve justice." Though some nations sharing this heritage declined to join NATO and strategic necessity involved others who only partly shared it, a remarkable degree of common culture and purpose existed among the members of the pact. It was the duty of NATO nations, Niebuhr insisted, not only to protect the cherished values of their civilization against a foe but to relate this achievement to a global community by striving to dissipate historic resentments so that Western countries would not be seen as desiring for themselves what they were not ready to share with others. Meanwhile, the Atlantic nations were "so placed that, by defending their own liberties, they also contribute to the liberties of others not in their community of destiny."[5]

In America, meanwhile, the anti-Communist hysteria of the late Truman period did not suddenly abate under the new Administration. McCarthy, the Wisconsin demagogue, gained new prominence as a Senate investigator of alleged traitors in government. His aberrations, Niebuhr wrote, "are not due to an excess of patriotic zeal so much as to his discovery that the fears of the nation represent a resource which he can exploit for political and personal advantage." Early in 1954, in the first of regular articles for many years in the *New Leader*, a respected journal of liberal anti-Communist persuasion, he attacked McCarthy's practice of "indiscriminate accusation." Challenged by a well-known McCarthy backer in a letter-to-the-editor, Niebuhr replied:

> Four years ago, McCarthy burst into public view with the charge that umpity number of "card-carrying Communists" were employed in the State Department. The number was changed from time to time, but the charge always remained outrageous and unsubstantiated. . . . In his recent television performance, McCarthy insinuated that all the victories gained by the Communists in recent years were due to treason in the "Acheson-Hiss" State Department.

McCarthyism, also practiced by the House Un-American Activities Committee and appeased by the Republican administration, peaked in the spring of that year. Deploring official mistreatment of J. Robert Oppenheimer, the physicist who had fathered the atomic bomb, in the climate of suspicion created by McCarthy, Niebuhr advised the nation's leaders to heed the words of Scripture, "Resist the devil and he will flee from you." Some did so, and after McCarthy discredited himself in televised hearings, the Senate censured him late in 1954.[6]

The Supreme Court's ruling, in May of that year, against racial segregation of schools received Niebuhr's prompt support. The older "separate but equal" doctrine, he commented, had helped "to close the hiatus between law and custom" in transportation and professional education, but the Court "wisely decided that the time was ripe for another step forward." The differences between the two races involved were "due to historical rather than to natural causes" and were accentuated by "a sinful pride" in "the mores of the ex–slave states." The Court rightly declared that separate schools carried "the implication of inferiority for the colored group," but in calling for desegregation it "wisely postpones application of the principle for most of the affected states until they have time to adjust themselves." The nation, Niebuhr held, was prepared to move toward implementation of the new standard: "The Negroes have most obviously excelled in the arts and in sports; but they have shown the validity of the doctrine of equal worth in every department of life."[7]

The year of McCarthy's downfall and the Court's call for school desegregation was also a time of crisis and decision in U.S. foreign policy. In a speech early in 1954, John Foster Dulles, Eisenhower's Secretary of State, discussing the new administration's emphasis on air power, stirred confusion and worry by declaring that the cornerstone of American defense in unspecified local situations was "massive retaliation." Niebuhr, joining Dulles's critics, pointed out that a policy of such threat caused dismay among allies, who saw in it "the peril of enlarging a local war into a global atomic one." Then in the spring, as Dulles and other officials proposed American military intervention in Indochina to avert imminent French defeat by Communist-led insurgents, he wrote:

The tardiness of the French in granting independence to Indo-China served to fan the flames of resentment against the West throughout Asia, and deprived the anti-Communist cause of the moral basis without which mere military power is always futile.

Those who urged such action there, Niebuhr went on to say, erred in measuring the non-Communist cause only in terms of land and population:

Thus the fact is obscured that we are bound to Europe as we are not bound to Asia by two basic facts. One is that Europe is as passionately devoted as we are to the conditions of freedom and justice which have slowly evolved in our common civilization. The other is that Europe's technical efficiency and power is a richer prize than all the square miles of Asia.

After Eisenhower refused to intervene militarily, and the war-weary French negotiated in July a settlement with native Communists and pulled out of Indochina, he commented that "this dismal result is better than our involvement in another Asian war."[8]

Early in the same summer Churchill, in Washington for talks with Eisenhower, spoke publicly of the need for "co-existence" with Soviet Russia, inasmuch as victory could only be won "on a heap of ruins." Churchill's statement, Niebuhr observed, was needed to counter a certain heedlessness toward the risks of global war in an age of hydrogen bombs: "The world may yet heed the advice of a man who has added the display of prudence to his previous reputation for courage." As Niebuhr wrote in a symposium of the *New Leader*:

> We are forced to share this narrow world with a ruthless and unscrupulous foe, who has corrupted every human sanctity. . . . Yet to get rid of this foe requires policies which contain the risk of universal annihilation. Since that is an unthinkable alternative, we are forced to opt for "co-existence," however grim the prospects of such a condition may be. . . . It implies only one moral preference, and that is that survival is preferable to annihilation.

In taking this position, Churchill was prompted by an understanding that "wise statesmanship requires a combination of resolution in meeting present dangers and prudence in measuring ultimate consequences." Furthermore, Niebuhr observed in the fall of that year, British statecraft so sensed the need for adjustments within an alliance of nations that it succeeded, where American diplomacy had failed, in working out European defense arrangements which overcame historic French fears of German rearmament.[9]

Early in 1955 Niebuhr, after watching Edward R. Murrow's review of the past year on television, concluded that anti-Americanism abroad was ebbing, replaced by a new prestige resulting chiefly from "the Supreme Court decision on segregation, the Senate's censure of Senator McCarthy, and increased confidence in President Eisenhower's fervent desire for peace, particularly after he vetoed war measures in the Indo-China crisis." Eisenhower had prevailed over the right-wing hysteria of recent years: "His long experience with European defense and his intimate contact with the statesmen of Europe give him a wholesome perspective on the issues." Yet Dulles took a somewhat different view of the world, fostering policies against which Niebuhr warned as "preoccupied with our 'defense perimeter' in Asia." In August of 1955—the most quiescent year in American experience since the outbreak of World War II—Eisenhower met in Geneva with Bulganin and Khrushchev, the current Soviet leaders, in the first "summit" conference of the Cold War. "The Russian face now wears a smile rather than a scowl," Niebuhr commented. The meeting was important because it "prompted the mutual acknowledgment of both sides that neither side desired or plotted war in an atomic age." The new Russian leadership, he pointed out, clearly dropped the Stalinist line picturing Americans as "capitalist warmongers," allowing facts to replace doctrinal rigidities: "As the complexities of the political scene begin to penetrate through the dogmatic preconceptions, empirical reality is bound to dissolve the fanaticism which gave the Communist world its cohesion and its striking power." While this development improved the prospect for peace, Niebuhr added, Communism's "tactical flexibility" presented new challenges as the Soviets used aid or infiltration to influence neutral nations from Egypt to Indonesia. Yet the international climate had basically improved: "The prospects for the future are so much better than any of us dared to hope that the popularity of Eisenhower is quite understandable."[10]

During these years Niebuhr also commented on the varied facets of a revived interest in religion among Americans that had begun after the war. By 1955 almost half the population attended services on a typical Sunday, and new churches were being built everywhere. Discussing the development in that year, he wrote: "It may be viewed with contradictory emotions of satisfaction or alarm by those who rather too simply regard religion *per se* either good or bad. But about the evidences of this revival there can be no doubt." One facet was reflected "in the phenomenal sale of the books by Norman Vincent Peale" that were "pious guides to personal success."

> There is nothing in this religion of Biblical faith, of man's encounter with a just and merciful God, of the judgment which he feels upon himself in such an encounter, of the forgiveness and new life which is available to those who "truly repent." Nor is there anything which might have a sobering influence upon a nation as great, as powerful, and as fortunate as the United States, which is tempted to pride and arrogance.

Such religiosity, as Jeremiah saw in warning against the "false prophets" of Judah, "induced complacency rather than repentance." Billy Graham, on the other hand, expounded a version of Christian faith rooted in "the traditions of our old frontier evangelical piety." Such evangelism was "certainly superior to the success cults"; it "converts drunkards and adulterers from their evil ways" and "convicts all of us who regard ourselves as 'normal' of really being quite self-centered." Graham, however, had politically irrelevant "individualistic and perfectionist illusions," as when "he suggested that conversion to Christianity could solve the problem of the hydrogen bomb." Yet, Niebuhr went on to say, there were more significant, if less visible, facets of religious revival. One was "the increased interest in religious courses in our colleges and universities and the increased sympathy for religious faith among 'intellectuals.'" Another was renewed vitality among the traditional churches "ready to mediate the age-old answer to the human problem which is given in Biblical faith." Indeed, Niebuhr himself was by then a pervasive influence in the American Protestant mainstream, read and quoted by thousands of clergy. While the deeper occasion for renewed interest in religion was the discrediting of alternative secular schemes of redemption, Niebuhr commented, another factor was identified by Will Herberg in his new book *Protestant, Catholic, Jew*: "the ability of the religious communities to build integral local communities in the anonymity of our technical civilization and to give people a 'sense of belonging' in the impersonal relationships of our culture." He agreed with Herberg, a sociologist and Jewish lay theologian, that public recognition of Protestant, Catholic, and Jewish faiths tended to confuse them with reverence for American civic and economic values.[11]

The American economy, meanwhile, was booming to new levels of prosperity for most of the population. Niebuhr wrote in 1955:

> The question is whether the preoccupation of American culture with the comforts of this life, with ever higher standards of living, with automobiles and refrigerators, vacuum cleaners and television, and all the other gadgets of the "American way of life"—whether this is not a real peril to our soul. . . . We enjoy a standard of living beyond the dreams of avarice of the rest of the world. . . . This problem is undoubtedly one of the chief spiritual issues confronting our nation. It cannot be solved by mere strictures against riches but also not by a glorification of creature comforts. The question is where each of us will draw the line.

As he put it elsewhere, "fatness, ease, and complacency are greater perils to our faith than lean years."[12]

By the end of 1955 the Supreme Court's school desegregation decision began to meet opposition, particularly in Southern states or counties in which the ratio of blacks to whites was high. Whole communities, including churches, Niebuhr noted sadly, were being intimidated by newly organized "white citizens councils" similar to the old Ku Klux Klan. "If the South does not become too hysterical," he wrote, "the adjustments which have begun in those Southern regions where the Negro population is smaller will gradually spread to the hard core of resistance and recalcitrance." When national attention turned early in 1956 to tensions in Montgomery, Alabama, where Martin Luther King led black opposition to segregated buses, Niebuhr commented: "Their boycott must appeal to sensitive men everywhere as another assertion of the dignity of man." Northern critics of Jim Crow, meanwhile, should refrain from self-righteous judgments, he maintained, for racial prejudice "is not a Southern sin but a general human shortcoming."[13]

Such, as seen by Niebuhr, was the national and world scene during the early years of the Eisenhower era.

UNION SEMINARY IN THE 1950S

During Niebuhr's final decade of teaching, Union Theological Seminary—which for decades had been preeminent among the divinity schools of American Protestantism—reached the peak of its influence, with a constellation of renowned faculty, a rich curriculum, and the largest student body in its long history. The core of the faculty had been recruited during Henry Sloane Coffin's presidency: Reinhold Niebuhr, Paul Tillich, Cyril Richardson, David E. Roberts, Samuel Terrien, John C. Bennett, John Knox, John T. McNeill, James Muilenburg, and Paul Scherer, among others. Under Van Dusen's leadership, new faculty were appointed to augment the range of course offerings and replace retiring professors—among them Robert T. Handy in 1950 and Wilhelm Pauck (succeeding John T. McNeill) in 1953, both in church history; and Robert McAfee Brown, who began teaching systematic theology in 1954. For ten years until 1955 George Buttrick, the most eminent preacher of the day, taught homiletics part-time, thereafter giving all his time to editing *The Interpreter's Bible*, to which many scholars teaching or educated at Union contributed. In 1955 Union lost Paul Tillich, who reached its retirement age and moved on to Harvard University, although he often returned as guest preacher or lecturer. By 1956 student enrollment swelled to a high of 677, predominantly from the American Protestant mainstream: Presbyterians and Methodists were most numerous, followed by Anglicans, Lutherans, Congregationalists, Evangelical and Reformed, and Baptists. One fourth were women. Nearly a hundred came from many foreign lands.[14]

After resting through the spring and summer of 1952, following his stroke, Niebuhr gradually resumed teaching, moving then from his office in the seminary's tower to Room 409, on the fourth floor of the south side of the building. From 1950 to 1955 he was dean of the faculty, a position involving occasional supportive responsibility for special projects; and from 1955 to 1960 he was vice-president of the seminary, a largely honorary position. Niebuhr's presence was felt throughout the seminary community. One of his students of the early 1950s later recalled his warm, personal manner: "What I remember most about his informal relations with students was his genuine, spontaneous interest in them. Even in a casual encounter in the Union quadrangle he would stop to speak, would know who you were, and would be interested in what you were doing or had to say. Real meeting was possible, despite the difference in status and the student's natural awe of Niebuhr." Because of his need to slow down after the stroke, the Niebuhrs discontinued the evening open-house gatherings that had become legendary, but instead occasionally invited students over for coffee or tea in the afternoon. As before, Niebuhr often joined students and colleagues in the seminary's refectory during the noon hour, sometimes moving later to the upper refectory for extended conversations.[15]

Union Theological Seminary was then a truly great ecumenical center of Protestant theological scholarship and ministerial training. Its library had the largest collection of theological volumes in the United States, and its faculty wrote books used in the seminaries and local churches of all the major denominations. Among the varied practical opportunities available to its students was experience in the East Harlem Protestant Parish, an ecumenical undertaking in a nearby slum, founded in 1948 with help from Niebuhr's circle in the Frontier Fellowship. Meanwhile, *Christianity and Crisis*, informally related to Union, continued to reach fortnightly several thousand readers from coast to coast. In the early 1950s it rented an office on Broadway, across the street from the seminary, and in 1956 Wayne H. Cowan became managing editor of the journal. A professionally trained journalist with competence in theology, he worked with its editorial board, cochaired by Niebuhr and John Bennett, to produce issues of quality to which many distinguished writers contributed. Niebuhr, in whose office the board met during these years, remained "amazingly productive," Cowan later recalled, adding that he patiently accepted heavy editing of his work required because of his typing difficulties after the stroke and his tendency to write "lead sentences half a page in length and heavily Germanic in form." The journal's format and masthead were rather plain, but its substance commanded respect. One reader, Felix Frankfurter, wrote Niebuhr to express "exhilarating assent" to an article on "Winston Churchill and Great Britain," which appeared at the time of Churchill's retirement in 1955. "You proved once more," declared Frankfurter, "as you frequently do, in the slim pages of *Christianity and Crisis*, how much can be said in how little. I am carrying myself with the thought of sending your piece to the great man himself."[16]

Although Niebuhr made a two-thirds recovery from his stroke, he was a semi-invalid, dependent on his wife for many things. "I am conscious," he wrote William Scarlett in 1956, "of the great sacrifices which Ursula has made for me since my illness." The summer of that year was the last the Niebuhrs spent at their cottage in Heath; thereafter they acquired in its stead an old, rambling house in Stockbridge, situated in the Berkshires of western Massachusetts. Ursula, as Reinhold explained to Scarlett, named the place Yale Hill in keeping with English custom for rural addresses, for the house was on a hill originally owned by a Yale family. Their son, Christopher, meanwhile, had graduated from Harvard, and their daughter, Elisabeth, entered Radcliffe. Ursula continued to teach in the department of religion at Barnard College, holding the position of associate professor. The Niebuhrs during these years had two poodles, Vicky and Winnie—named after Queen Victoria and Winston Churchill— the latter christened by their friend W. H. Auden. Reinhold often walked them outside the gray stone walls of the seminary. With his family and among friends he enjoyed hearing or telling an occasional joke, as when he wrote William Scarlett's wife, Leah, late in 1957:

> Let me tell you one I just heard from Wystan Auden: A pious Catholic lady went to heaven and after having been there a couple million years she said to the Angel Gabriel, "Couldn't I see the Virgin Mary? I patterned my whole life after her." The Angel told her this could be arranged. When she saw the Virgin she said how much she had patterned her life after Mary, fidelity, love, devotion, etc., "and then too you were the Mother of that great son of yours," said the pious lady. Mary, an old Jewish lady sitting in a rocker, said, "Me, I always wanted a girl."[17]

At Union Seminary Niebuhr, besides teaching courses and preaching in the chapel, sometimes spoke on special occasions to students or guests. In January of 1952, a month before his stroke, he gave the first in an annual series of lectures under auspices of the Women's Committee of the seminary, a lay group from churches throughout the New York metropolitan area. Delivered in James Chapel, it was taped and distributed under the title "Christian Faith and Humanism." In it Niebuhr developed the theme that Christianity shares with the best Western humanism, derived from Plato and Aristotle and the Stoics and transmuted by the Renaissance, a sense of human dignity and historical responsibility, as opposed to extravagant forms of mysticism or of naturalism; but that it differs from such humanism in its understanding of human self-transcendence, of the uniqueness of the individual self, and of "the movement of the self in its self-love against the law of love." It was a lecture rich in allusions, for instance, to T. S. Eliot's *The Cocktail Party*, which had recently played on Broadway. Before moving on to the "saving grace" of Christ which transforms the will from without, Niebuhr here recalled the neglected theological doctrine of "common grace," defining it as "every security of the natural life that saves us from undue anxiety, every love and brotherhood that extends our life beyond itself, and every responsibility which draws us beyond ourselves." The doctrine, derived from Calvin, included the realms of parenthood and citizenship as he expounded it in this lecture and in certain of his later works.[18]

In March of 1953 Niebuhr addressed a conference on the ministry at Union Seminary. Touching on many points, he described the pastor's vocation as "confronting people with Christ, and being oneself confronted." Christian life involves "dying to live"; it is "a perpetual Lent and Easter," in which sin is stubborn but grace is available as renewal and forgiveness. The triune God is known in meditation "as Holy Spirit." In worship and pastoring, the preacher "is the mediator of God's judgment and also of his mercy" to strong and weak alike. While sermons are part of the ministry, he said, "I am impressed by good pastors who do not necessarily specialize in the word of God from the pulpit." In September of 1955, Niebuhr gave a talk to Union Seminary students on theological education, which he likened to going up one side of a mountain and down the other. The ascent, he said, includes historical study of the Bible in its original languages, which "opens facets of meaning," but it also includes prayer, for scholarship does not induce faith, which "is possible only by the kind of prayer that Kierkegaard calls 'passionate subjectivity.'" Thus seminary education combines scholarship and prayer: "A theological institution," Niebuhr stated, "is a very curious place which is on the one hand a school, and on the other hand a church." On the downward side, he went on to say, seminary work includes the task of establishing relevance by validating the Christian faith and relating it to such aspects of professional training as homiletics and counseling. Observing that Protestant worship is dependent on the sermon, he emphasized his hope that everyone who is going to preach will be "forced to take courses in the homiletical art."[19]

Niebuhr's semi-invalidism after 1952 prevented his crossing the Atlantic, as in years past, for visits to Britain and ecumenical gatherings. Among those whom he used to see abroad, Emil Brunner was one of the first to write after his stroke, closing a warm letter by saying, "We need you so much!" In 1953 he received a letter, composed by Lesslie Newbigin on behalf of old friends and acquaintances meeting near Geneva to prepare for the next assembly of the World Council of Churches. Expressing their "affectionate greeting" and stating that "we miss you very much," it was signed by W. A. Visser 't Hooft, C. H. Dodd, Karl Barth, and John Baillie, among others. In the spring of 1955, T. S. Eliot, visiting in America, stopped to have tea with the Niebuhrs at their Union Seminary apartment. "It was so nice to have you bring Mr. Eliot over," Niebuhr wrote William Levy, who arranged the occasion, "and we appreciated the visit very much."[20]

In a rare out-of-town engagement during these years, Niebuhr in November of 1955 participated in a seminar at Kent School in Connecticut on its jubilee, joining such distinguished panelists as John Courtney Murray, William G. Pollard, Jacques Maritain, E. Harris Harbison, Georges Florovsky, and Massey Shepherd, Jr. Another was Alan Paton of South Africa, whose novel *Cry, the Beloved Country* Niebuhr had read and appreciated. Paton later recalled that Niebuhr, reading an impressive paper on "The Two Sources of Western Culture" sitting down, momentarily stopped to elaborate spontaneously on a point, remarking that freedom in the United States allowed choices of good and evil, so that high endeavor lived alongside vice and decadence. Somberly he remarked, "It's a mess," pausing while the audience gloomily pondered his words. Then he added, "But I like it!" Those words, Paton recalled, "brought down the house, and we felt that there was hope for the world after all."[21]

It was a measure of Niebuhr's stature that in 1956 his thought was the subject of a volume of twenty essays by eminent contemporaries in various fields. Entitled *Reinhold Niebuhr: His Religious, Social, and Political Thought*, it was edited by Charles Kegley and Robert Bretall—the second in a series treating certain leading theologians of the age. The contributors included Emil Brunner and Paul Tillich among Protestant theologians, the Jesuit Gustav Weigel, the Jewish scholar and theologian Abraham Joshua Heschel, historian Arthur Schlesinger, Jr., political scientist Kenneth Thompson, John C. Bennett and Paul Ramsey in the field of Christian ethics, and others friendly or not to Niebuhr's positions. The volume opened with a brief account by Niebuhr of his own development and concluded with his reply to the interpretation and criticism of contributors. The Kegley-Bretall symposium was, as one reviewer noted, "of uniformly high quality." It has long remained a stimulating source of insight on the mind of Reinhold Niebuhr. Two years after its publication he was elected to the American Academy of Arts and Letters as one of its fifty distinguished members.[22]

Earlier in the decade Niebuhr himself had contributed to a volume in the same series on the thought of Paul Tillich, who had risen to fame in America with the publication of *The Protestant Era* in 1948 and *The Courage to Be* in 1952. As an immigrant in mid-life, Tillich felt lost in the politics of his adopted country and devoted himself instead to artistic and therapeutic concerns and to his *Systematic Theology*, publishing the first of its three volumes in 1951. That work confirmed the uneasiness some had felt that he tended to insinuate Greek ideas into Christian theology. Niebuhr, who appreciated his esteemed colleague at Union Seminary, expressed this concern in his essay for the symposium on Tillich. The Bible, he wrote, conceives of life as a divine-human drama for which there are "ontological presuppositions," but is concerned primarily with "events in history through which and in which the ultimate power which bears history reveals its mystery" rather than with "the structures of being." Tillich's "ontological speculations," in his view, obscured the historical context in which human sin is known and divine grace is apprehended by faith. Reviewing a few years later Tillich's *Biblical Religion and the Search for Ultimate Reality*, Niebuhr wrote that he "states the issue between Biblical faith and the metaphysical search for 'ultimate reality' fairly" and "tries to do justice to the peculiar insights of Biblical religion" but "somewhat dubiously equates the question of meaning with the question of being and non-being."[23]

Like Tillich, Abraham Heschel came to America to escape Nazism. A Polish Jew in the Hasidic tradition, he eventually became a professor at the Jewish Theological Seminary on the corner northeast of Union, and often joined Niebuhr for walks in the neighborhood. Heschel's *God in Search of Man*, wrote Niebuhr in a review of 1956, "shows what is unique in Biblical thought," particularly its awe before the divine mystery and response of trust to the disclosure of meaning in the mystery. Heschel makes clear that biblical faith "does not merely cling to irrational theophanies which a better science and philosophy may dissolve" but sees in events such as those culminating at Sinai "a revelatory power which gives meaning to the flux of events in history." The book was partly an exposition of Judaism but "has equal relevance for Christians as well as Jews."[24]

For some three decades Reinhold Niebuhr always taught, whatever his other courses on topical and contemporary subjects, a two-semester course listed in the seminary catalog during these years usually as "The History of Ethics." It focused first on the pre-Christian ethics of the ancient Near East and the Greco-Roman world and then, during the second semester, on Christian ethics from New Testament to early modern times. Over the years he developed it into a solid, well-organized course, with three lectures per week before his stroke and two per week after it, and a required paper. One student, who took it in 1959, recalled an office visit with Niebuhr to discuss his paper topic on Calvin and law: "I brought my outline and bibliography. He made a few suggestions and, dispensing with formalities, spent most of the time asking about my background, interests, and plans. Later the paper was returned to me with an 'A' and Dr. Niebuhr's comments." Another student, who took the course in 1959–60, remembered his classroom presence: "He might start his lecture seated at a table in front of us; but he was soon on his feet striding around in front of us and he raced our minds across the centuries." Although the stroke had impeded his speech, Niebuhr was as mentally alert as ever, thinking as he spoke, infusing his lectures with humor, and answering students' questions toward the end of each hour. Troeltsch's *The Social Teachings of the Christian Churches* had helped him shape much of the course, but he also drew on many more recent scholarly works and his own extensive reading of the Christian classics. The core was the second semester, consisting of twenty-two lectures, which were taped as delivered in the spring of 1960 just before his retirement. In them he traced Christian ethics through the ages, pointing to the tension between "the impulse toward perfection and the impulse toward responsibility." A brief overview, noting some points of interest, must suffice here.[25]

First, Niebuhr took up New Testament ethics. The double commandment to love God and neighbor, he pointed out, was derived by Jesus from the Old Testament as "the anchor against all heresies that make the love of neighbor simple without the transcendent reference, and against all mysticism that subordinates love of neighbor to love of God." The rigorous love ethic (*agapé*) enjoined in the Sermon on the Mount—radically universal, sacrificial, and forgiving—is an ultimate perspective relevant to human life but not immediately applicable, Niebuhr held, citing the view of C. H. Dodd, "the greatest New Testament theologian of our day." Paul, making explicit the universality of sin attested by the prophets and Jesus, expounded—as did the Johannine evangelist in his distinctive way—an ethic "on the other side of the Cross," where the human situation is understood in light of Christ as "the bearer of grace as forgiveness and as power." Second, Niebuhr traced the ethics of the early church through its initial critical attitude toward property and government, surveyed the moral climate of Constantinian Christianity, and discussed the theological framework of Augustine's ethics and the political responsibility implied in his idea of the "commingling" of the godly and worldly cities. Third, he focused on medieval Christianity, culminating in the sway of the papacy, ascetic ferment, a social structure bounded by natural law, and the philosophy of Aquinas. This scheme of things, Niebuhr held, was too neatly conceived, providing in monasticism a vent for the impulse to perfection, while defining political and economic justice in static, rational Aristotelian terms; a sense of sin and grace had no place except as something added to the system. The result was a certain complacency in which, as Troeltsch observed (in Niebuhr's translation from the German edition), "the church idealized the actual circumstances of medieval life, regarded as true to the concepts of revelation and reason." Fourth, he moved on to the Protestant Reformation, making this point:

> Luther's conception of the realm of grace is rather purer than Calvin's is. As a matter of fact, one could say (though I have some difficulties with my esteemed colleague Professor Pauck on this because he's more Lutheran than I am) that on the ultimate pinnacles of the spiritual life Luther is the best guide, but he isn't very good when you're dealing with all the proximate things. If you think of an architect being both an artist and an engineer— you have to be an artist to put the pinnacles on the building, an engineer to take care of the plumbing—well, Luther didn't take care of the plumbing very well.

While Luther viewed the state as an instrument of order with absolute authority, Niebuhr went on to say, Calvin's political theory contained the seeds of resistance to tyranny developed by John Knox and Calvinist constitutionalists of the seventeenth century. Calvin, furthermore, saw that law is necessary because sin persists even in Christian communities, and his emphasis on this-worldly discipline became fruitful in middle-class life. Finally, Niebuhr turned to sectarian Protestantism, expressing the medieval monastic impulse toward perfection in a different form. Its types included the Levelers and Diggers of Cromwellian England, whose utopian dreams of liberty and equality interested Niebuhr as a counter to the Reformation's social complacency; the pacifist Quakers and Mennonites; and the evangelical sects of the American frontier, whose sanctificationist conception of grace combined with the Enlightenment to shape the optimism of the Social Gospel. Discussing Wesley's doctrine of radical stewardship, he drew a laugh by recalling his visit to Southern Methodist University (where he had lectured early in 1952) and his meeting there Texas millionaires who followed Wesley by handsomely endowing the university and were quite humble about it: "I thought to myself, 'Hurrah for Methodism: it saved Texas!' " At the close of the last lecture of Niebuhr's teaching career, the class broke into sustained applause.[26]

As Niebuhr looked back on the milieu of Union in relation to the world of the 1950s, he wrote in the seminary's newsletter:

> Domestic problems, with the exception of the issue of racial justice, proved more or less soluble, and the problem of peace for a world living under the Damocles sword of nuclear catastrophe proved, if not insoluble, then at least more stubborn than anything anticipated in the twenties and thirties. I will forbear to describe the period theologically, except to observe that the insecurities of our age strongly tempt this generation, not to the utopianism of yesterday, but to flight into any kind of storm cellar of religious security. . . . Fortunately, there are also many ways of reacting creatively to the insecurities of the age, and Union students have done so, discovering in the process that the insecurities of the age are but the enlargements of the insecurities of life itself, about which a mature faith has always known and which have always provided an ultimate test of the vitality and honesty of such a faith.[27]

THE UNEASY PEACE OF A NUCLEAR AGE

The relative calm in the world of the mid-1950s gave way later in the decade to rising tensions as Soviet Russia, under the ebullient leadership of Nikita Khrushchev, developed the first intercontinental missiles with nuclear warheads and gained influence among nations of Asia and Africa with large grants of technical aid. Anti-Americanism swept the neutral bloc from Egypt to Indonesia, diplomatic crises mounted in the Cold War, and the possibility of nuclear war by miscalculation in Moscow or Washington was real, even though neither side wanted it. America, as Niebuhr put it in 1957, was a "gadget-filled paradise in a hell of international insecurity."[28]

In 1956 Niebuhr again supported Stevenson for President, and Eisenhower again won by a landslide. In October of that year, just before the election, two international crises occurred in quick succession, prompting his comments. The first was the Soviets' brutal suppression of revolt in Hungary spurred by Poland's recent success in gaining limited freedom as a Russian satellite. Soviet tanks, wrote Niebuhr, "made a shambles of Budapest and annulled the dearly bought liberty of a few days," proving that "the big thaw after Stalin's death had "not melted the core of tyranny, which is pure force." Meanwhile, the Poles' achievement of semi-freedom under the Gomulka government, backed by an alliance of Roman Catholicism and Polish nationalism, "proved the first crack in the monolithic structure of the Russian empire since Tito's defection."[29]

The second crisis of October 1956 centered on the Suez Canal, recently seized from Britain by Egypt's Nasser, who had also concluded an arms deal with the Soviet bloc and threatened to drive Israel into the sea. An Anglo-French-Israeli attack on Egypt was aborted under United Nations pressure initiated by the U.S. and Soviet governments. Critical of the Eisenhower administration's intervention, Niebuhr deplored "our failure to recognize the seriousness of either the Israeli-Egyptian crisis or the peril of the Nasser dictatorship to the economic life-line of Europe." The debacle caused a temporary rift in the Western alliance, boosted Nasser's standing in the Arab world, and weakened British prestige, while strengthening Soviet influence in the Mideast. There and elsewhere in the non-Western world, Niebuhr pointed out, post-Stalinist Soviet policy "consists in subordinating Communism's primary dogma, according to which capitalism is the root of all evil and a Communist order the beginning of utopia, to its secondary dogma, which asserts that capitalism is the cause of imperialism and colonialism." While the first dogma was discredited in the West, the second, though largely false, seemed plausible among peoples who knew Western dominance but nothing of Communist imperialism, the chief instances of which "occurred in Europe rather than Asia and Africa, and were therefore not vivid in the consciousness of the colored continents."[30]

While the Soviets exploited anti-Western sentiments in the Mideast and gained influence through aid to Arab dictators, Nasser's radio propaganda set Arabs from Cairo to Baghdad aflame with a transnationalism rooted in their history, Niebuhr observed. The Egyptian leader, he wrote, "thinks of himself as a new Saladin." Aware that the forces championed by Nasser threatened Israel, he published a major article discussing the significance and problems of the Jewish state since its founding nearly a decade earlier. Originating in the Zionist dreams of Theodore Herzl and Chaim Weizmann and established on a wave of sympathy after the Nazi atrocities, he wrote, the new state had since "opened its doors to Jews from all over the world." It "brought the most advanced techniques into the service of the new community, irrigated the deserts in order to create orange groves, and built a healthy industrial life through the skills of its people." Its experience, Niebuhr continued, "is thrilling in many respects," including the cooperation of Orthodox Jews "informed by an archaic piety" and others "informed by a rather self-conscious secular enlightenment" in building a nation led by "the robust prime minister of today, Ben-Gurion," a Polish Jew. Yet its future was problematic:

> The question for us is how we can save the state from annihilation, for it is still the sworn intent not only of Nasser but of the whole Arab world to destroy it. . . . For Israel is an offense to the Arab world for three reasons:
>
> 1. It has claimed by conquest what the Arabs regard as their soil. . . .
> 2. This enmity has been increased by the problem of the refugees whom the Arab states will not resettle and whom the Jews cannot absorb except in small numbers without imperiling the security of their nation, because the refugees are sworn enemies of the new state.
> 3. The third cause is even more potent. The state of Israel is, by its very technical efficiency and democratic justice, a source of danger to the moribund feudal or pastoral economics and monarchical political forms of the Islamic world and a threat to the rich overlords of desperately poor peasants of the Middle East.

In promoting the state of Israel, the West "did not reckon with the depth of the Arab spirit of vengeance." Its survival "may require detailed economic strategies for the whole region and policies for the resettlement of the Arab refugees."[31]

More surprising and portentous than developments in the Mideast or Hungary was the Russian launching of *Sputnik*, the first earth satellite, into orbit in the fall of 1957. The achievement, as Niebuhr observed, "proved that Moscow had the intercontinental ballistic missile and that, therefore, we were in a position of inferiority . . . which makes us desperately dependent on advanced bases and placement sites for our missiles." It "also proved that technical achievement is not incompatible with tyranny." As Russia and the West competed for the loyalty of the nascent nations of Asia and Africa, the latter were "tremendously impressed" by the Soviet feat, seeing in it the promise of technical progress without the democratic ways of Western civilization. Khrushchev, he warned, was wooing their rulers with offers of large-scale technical and capital aid, "while Secretary Dulles is still lecturing them on the immorality of neutralism." This, added to anti-Western nationalism, gave the Soviets short-term advantages in that part of the world:

We must expect to suffer many defeats in Asia and Africa before they become fully aware that the Communist oligarchy is a new form of imperialism more dangerous to their freedom than the old.

Niebuhr called for a more sympathetic American attitude toward such neutral and less capitalistic nations as India, and readiness to help them overcome their poverty through economic aid and reciprocal trade arrangements.[32]

As U.S.-Soviet tensions rose in the late 1950s, each side competing in guided missiles and nuclear testing, Niebuhr wrote in the *New Leader:*

I would like to hazard one observation and one admonition concerning this long, tortuous dialogue between the two power blocs. The observation is that the possibilities of disarmament are very slim. The admonition is that we ought to seek to reduce the hazards of the arms race by recognizing that, whatever weighty differences in political principles between us and the Russians, both sides are involved in a common predicament. At least we should admit that the Russians, like us, do not want to start the ultimate conflict and that, if it does start, it will be by some miscalculation.

He continued:

Recognition of this common predicament . . . can contribute to our moral health in two ways. First, it will tend to mitigate the sharpness of the anxiety about a surprise attack, and consequently the clamor for ever greater military power. We need to preserve the military equilibrium; but a tolerable equilibrium will be enough to guarantee an uneasy peace. Second, such recognition will prepare us to live for decades in a continuation of responsibility, anxiety, tension and frustration, an experience which our young nation has never before faced.

The prospects for arms reduction were dismal, for the evidence of history was that "disarmament has always been consequent upon, not requisite to, relaxed tensions."[33]

It was as a journalist rather than as a platform speaker that Niebuhr engaged in foreign and domestic policy issues after his stroke. Unable to attend political meetings as before, he was asked by the national chairman of Americans for Democratic Action to write a message of greeting for the organization's tenth anniversary convention in March of 1957, and sent these words:

The ADA has had a decade of honorable history in revitalizing American democratic life. It started with two presuppositions which I hope will always guide it. They are both embodied in the achievements of Franklin Delano Roosevelt. The one was that liberalism must be "realistic" in foreign policy, and must not overlook the power factors in the international struggle. The second was that liberalism must be constantly intent on perfecting the balances of a democratic society whereby justice is achieved.

The ADA, distributing Niebuhr's message widely, passed a resolution honoring him: "The delegates to this 10th Anniversary Convention of Americans for Democratic Action send their warmest greetings to Reinhold Niebuhr and regret that his health has not permitted him to attend the Convention. We look upon him as the spiritual father of ADA. The greatness of his spirit has been a source of strength and inspiration to us. Through his writing and counsel, he has guided us even when illness has kept him from our midst."[34]

The ADA had reason to be pleased by the 1958 elections, which produced, as Niebuhr observed, "the largest Democratic majorities in both houses of Congress since the days of the New Deal," proving that the nation was still "committed to the social and political standards that Roosevelt initiated." As Niebuhr himself had become an eloquent apologist for those standards, it was fitting that his friend Arthur Schlesinger, Jr., two years earlier had dedicated the first volume of his work *The Age of Roosevelt* "for Reinhold Niebuhr." It was the New Deal's legitimation of industrial unionism that had most impressed him, and when the C.I.O. merged with the A.F.L. in 1955 he had this to say:

> The organization of the total union strength in one camp will raise the specter of "bigness" for the enemies of the union movement. But the danger, if any, of such a large organization to the democratic balance can be considered only in the context of the larger problem of the bigness of the social and economic units in our society generally. There is certainly less danger in balanced bigness than in unbalanced bigness.

By 1957 seventeen states had passed "right to work" laws banning compulsory union membership. The real purpose of such laws, Niebuhr wrote, was the "weakening of labor under the guise of preserving or restoring the 'individual liberties' of our democratic society." The union shop, which they outlawed, allowed anyone to work or seek employment anywhere, but prevented workers "from benefiting from a collective contract which they refuse to support," he pointed out. Another danger was that the corrupt Teamsters Union would tarnish the public image of the entire union movement: "The enemies of labor will try to make the Teamsters' picture appear typical for unionism as a whole, and that would obscure the virtues, the honesty, and the devotion to the general welfare which characterizes union leadership as a whole."[35]

The success of industrial unions and of social-welfare measures, Niebuhr often emphasized, had rendered Western democracies immune to the Communist virus, while in Russia Lenin and his heirs had built a despotism on Marxist utopian illusions about human nature. In 1957 he reviewed Milovan Djilas's *The New Class*, a stark analysis of the Communist system—as practiced in Yugoslavia on the Soviet model—by a former exponent then imprisoned by Tito. It consisted of total control of ideas and public enterprise:

> The "new class" is the class of oligarchs and bureaucrats who have seized the monopoly of power in the Communist state. They are the "owners" because they alone have the right to manage and manipulate the collective power of the Communist state.

The Soviet regime, though oppressive, showed some signs of change for the better, Niebuhr held, for Khrushchev, consolidating his power as the new boss of the Kremlin, had in 1956 denounced Stalin for executing army officers and colleagues suspected of disloyalty to him:

> It is one of the achievements of the post-Stalin era that Khrushchev has gained his triumph over his foes without terror. He has merely banished them to Outer Mongolia or to equally remote places. This represents a real gain.

If the system ever evolves into a democracy, he wrote, "the vehicle of change will be the Central Committee of the party," but "we had better wait upon developments before we become too sanguine in our hopes."[36] The danger of nuclear war by miscalculation arose partly from the dated picture which Russians and Americans had of each other, Niebuhr wrote in 1959. Noting that Khrushchev saw the U.S. through Marxist spectacles, apparently believing that America's "working masses" were about to revolt against a "ruling clique," Niebuhr supported Eisenhower's project for an exchange of visits with the Soviet leader. A Khrushchev visit to America, he held against its right-wing critics, might help to correct some misconceptions. After the event, in September of that year, Niebuhr concluded that if the jovial oligarch had not learned much, perhaps Americans realized that the man who once was "Stalin's 'hatchet man' in the Ukraine" presided over a Russia subject to change and a system not purely evil. He pointed out that creative elements in Soviet society included "an educational system that offers a fair equality of opportunity to talented youth in a technically advancing civilization." Late in 1959 Niebuhr wrote:

We require the best possible journalism and academic disciplines to keep us in contact with the rapid developments in Russia. Such disciplines are not supplied by any religious institution. But religious discipline could play a role in softening the animosities which years of cold war have created.[37]

While an uneasy peace prevailed in U.S.-Soviet relations during the late 1950s, the winds of change began to sweep through areas of Africa governed by Europeans since the nineteenth century. Though health problems prevented his traveling there, Niebuhr read such books as John Gunther's *Inside Africa*. "France has done fairly well in tutoring both Tunisia and Morocco for self-government," he wrote in 1957, "but she is bogged down in Algeria." There one tenth of the population were French settlers, favored by "a system of weighted voting" and defended by the French army against rebels who "want the right to govern Algeria." France's futile effort to preserve its rule over resentful Algerians, he pointed out, embarrassed the West and played into Communist hands. When in May 1958 an army coup in Algeria prompted the floundering government of the French Fourth Republic to dissolve itself by summoning General Charles de Gaulle to power, Niebuhr, who weeks earlier had noted that de Gaulle was waiting in the wings for such a moment, observed that Paris had to call upon him "because he had an authority over the army which the government did not have." France, moreover, needed "the strong executive which de Gaulle promises to make the *sine qua non* of the constitution." As the prestigious French leader took steps toward eventual Algerian independence, Niebuhr wrote:

One can only be thankful that, if the unity of the nation depends upon one man, that man should be of the stature of General de Gaulle, who had the courage to defy the Right which brought him to power, because he saw no hope of solving the Algerian problem except by proposing the formula of "self-determination." . . . The sympathetic world will have to regard his rather extravagant nationalism and egotism as a price which must be paid for such a boon.[38]

South of the Sahara, meanwhile, Ghana achieved independence in 1957 and Nigeria and the Congo in 1960. The Belgians, Niebuhr noted, had given the Congolese the highest living standards in Africa but failed to educate them professionally or to give them experience in self-government. As a result, the new nation promptly fell into tribal and regional strife, mitigated only because "the astute Dag Hammarskjöld used all the powers of the United Nations to arrest the chaos in the Congo." The prospects were better where British tutelage, as under Lord Lugard in

Nigeria, had prepared the way for independence, Niebuhr wrote. Britain was "the greatest midwife of new nations," and Nigeria, though its Islamic north and Christian or primitive regions in the south were "not thoroughly cemented," was "the potentially greatest nation of Africa." But even such well-prepared nations as Nigeria faced problems of stability, justice, and unity: "Their history is not likely to be less dramatic, confused, and complex than was the history of the European nations from the sixteenth to the nineteenth centuries." Still different was the case of South Africa, where a Boer-dominated white minority during the 1950s instituted an increasingly repressive policy of *apartheid*, by which the Bantu majority was held, as Niebuhr commented, "in a status as close to slavery as anything known in modern life." While the regime's "hated pass system" was "heaping indignities on the black population," he lamented, the churches in league with the South African government piously proclaimed their "mystic unity" with them.[39]

It was the government of Harold Macmillan, British prime minister from 1957 to 1963, that launched most of Britain's African dependencies on the course of independence, and it was he who adjusted his homeland to participation in an American-led alliance. Thus Niebuhr wrote in 1959 of the man who led Britain with an air of wearied nonchalance:

Macmillan has become the rather impressive voice of a nation which knows how to transmute the natural resentments of a once mighty nation, forced by a new constellation of power to second place in the prestige of the democratic world, into the assertion of a quiet dignity and self-respect. In Macmillan's phrase, "It will be a loyal ally but not a satellite."

The British, he added, helped by infusing American diplomacy with "their traditional empirical approach." Macmillan had worked hard, he noted, to prepare the way for a mid-1960 summit conference, wrecked by Khrushchev when an ill-timed U.S. reconnaissance flight was caught over Soviet territory. That development, also leading to cancellation of Eisenhower's visit to Russia, "has shaken the whole world," Niebuhr wrote at the time. "The disaster is the more serious in a nuclear age when the world is at the edge of the abyss of a nuclear holocaust."[40]

CHAPTER EIGHT

Christian Faith and the Social Order

ર્જી

During the Eisenhower years Reinhold Niebuhr not only commented regularly on current affairs but, in books and essays, further elaborated the mature Christian realism he had set forth during the 1940s. Despite his stroke in 1952, he wrote a major new work of theological and social reflection and a timely and durable treatise on international relations. Having earlier become increasingly critical of Marx, he expressed continued and growing appreciation of Burke and Madison as bearers of Christian political wisdom. Niebuhr turned his attention also to such other concerns as the mass media, sexual morality, higher education, and Christian-Jewish relations.

POLITICS AND CULTURE IN A TECHNICAL SOCIETY

Niebuhr's political theory—his approach to the problem of achieving a tolerably just order within and among nations—had matured in the early 1940s and thereafter remained constant, rooted in a Christian view of human nature and informed by American pragmatism. It was stated most systematically in two books, *The Children of Light and the Children of Darkness,* which had appeared in 1944 (and has been discussed in an earlier chapter) and *The Structure of Nations and Empires,* which was published in 1959 (and will be treated later in this chapter). In the meantime, he developed some themes of his social philosophy in other books and occasional writings. Among the latter was an essay for a symposium planned by members of the group once known as the Fellowship of Socialist Christians, which in 1948 tardily changed its name to the Frontier Fellowship as more accurately descriptive of their views—for most of them had, like Niebuhr, come to accept the New Deal as much better than either socialism or laissez-faire capitalism. Reconstituted in 1951 as Christian Action, the group continued to publish the quarterly *Christianity and Society*, edited by Niebuhr, until 1956, when it folded because of financial problems. The symposium, published in 1953 as *Christian Faith and Social Action*, was edited by John A. Hutchison and dedicated to Niebuhr, the editor and other authors conspiring to do so without his prior knowledge. In his own essay for the volume, Niebuhr wrote:

> If the libertarian creed failed to anticipate the disproportions of power in modern economic society, the collectivist creed failed to anticipate the moral perils in a system which compounded political and economic power in a single oligarchy. It also failed to provide for sufficient local and immediate centers of initiative in both the economic and political life of the community.

An "empirical and pragmatic approach" was needed instead: "It will not assume that all government interference in economic process is either good or bad; but it will study the effect of each type of interference." Such an undogmatic approach, he insisted, is an essential element of an adequate Christian social ethic, and to it must be joined a religious understanding of "the law of love as a final imperative" and "the persistence of the power of self-love in all of life but particularly in the collective relations of mankind."[1]

In 1953 Niebuhr, endeavoring to correct some current illusions, published *Christian Realism and Political Problems*, a volume of essays addressing various public issues and presenting the philosophical and theological substratum of his perspective on them. In one essay, critical of the behavioral approach to the study of politics then in vogue, he pointed out the limitations of scientific method in resolving social conflict, since even the most impartial observer of the human scene views it from some locus and as an interested self rather than as pure mind. In another essay Niebuhr called for an approach to politics combining "the spirit of liberalism," defined as free criticism of the status quo, with "that part of the conservative creed" which emphasized historical experience, recognized the persistence of sin, and was "cautious not to fall into worse forms of injustice in the effort to eliminate old ones"—a conservatism "expounded in Edmund Burke's *Reflections on the Revolution in France*." Elsewhere in the volume he described Communism as a dangerous system in which "ruthless power operates behind a screen of pretended ideal ends," and criticized the socialist parties of Europe for retaining "an excess baggage of Marxist dogma." Also included was the text of Niebuhr's Amsterdam address to the World Council of Churches, his Francis Carroll lecture at Columbia University on Augustine's political realism, and an earlier essay puncturing schemes for world government (all three discussed earlier, in chapter VI). The volume concluded with an essay on theological methodology, developing the theme of faith and reason treated earlier in his lecture at Union Theological Seminary in Virginia.[2]

Niebuhr dedicated *Christian Realism and Political Problems* "to my friend, comrade, and colleague, John C. Bennett, with gratitude." Among reviewers was political scientist Ludwig Freund, who wrote: "Through it all shines more clearly than through any previous book of the author the mature judgment of a mind which accomplished the rare feat of balancing liberal elements of thought and true conservatism." Harry R. Davis, who later collaborated with Robert C. Good in editing a volume of Niebuhr's writings on political philosophy, stated in his review that, while Niebuhr "remains a forceful 'liberal' in terms of current American politics," he was "laying some deep intellectual foundations for the development of the authentic, decent conservatism we so urgently require." Impressed also by Niebuhr's treatment of Augustine's political realism and by his final essay on faith and reason, he wrote that the book "bursts with implications in countless directions." T. S. Eliot, arranging for a British edition of the book as an editorial director of Faber and Faber, wrote to Niebuhr from London that "it is a great pleasure to me to find myself in such close sympathy with your political wisdom, especially in view of the fact that we must have set out from very different starting points." Soon after the volume became available to British readers, Eliot, lecturing in London, described Niebuhr as one of the few writers on politics "preoccupied in penetrating to the core of the matter, in trying to arrive at the truth and to set it forth . . . without being downcast or defeated when nothing appears to ensue."[3]

Elaborating during these years his social philosophy as it had matured in the early 1940s, Niebuhr expressed a growing affinity for the thought of Burke, whose *Reflections* he read in the edition of the Everyman Library. He had mentioned Burke favorably more than a decade earlier, but invoked his social wisdom repeatedly during the 1950s. A revived interest in Burke developed early in the decade among thoughtful Americans, facing in Soviet Russia an ideological challenge similar to that of Britain in the era of the French Revolution. Burke's defense of the British civil social heritage against the abstract rationalism of the French *philosophes*, his empirical method in politics, his openness to timely reform, and his grasp of human nature and historical complexities—all this appealed to Niebuhr, whose own development had led to a similar philosophy. In

The Irony of American History he had written that "America has developed a pragmatic approach to political and economic questions which would do credit to Edmund Burke." Niebuhr's thought converged with Burke's philosophy on other points as he affirmed that prudence is "the final virtue of statesmanship" and declared that democracy "requires an aristocracy of knowledgeable and wise leaders in every realm of policy." While explicitly incorporating themes of Burkean conservatism into his thought, he made clear his continued loyalty to liberalism as understood in contemporary American political parlance—a strategy "which sought to bring economic enterprise under political control for the sake of establishing minimal standards of security and welfare"—and his opposition to conservatism in its parochial American sense, "as a combination of nationalistic preferences and a passion for the economics of laissez-faire." In correspondence with Ludwig Freund, published in 1957, Niebuhr expressed himself succinctly: "You said exactly the true word in regard to my attitude toward conservatism and liberalism. . . . I am conservative only in wanting to recognize the 'organic' aspects of community and the elements of interest and power. But I want to remain a liberal, even though I abhor the creed of liberalism which proceeded from the French Enlightenment."[4]

Niebuhr's commitment to the legacy of the New Deal was evident in his review of James MacGregor Burns's *Roosevelt: The Lion and the Fox*, which appeared in 1956. Burns, he wrote, "gives us a clear portrait of the greatest political figure of the past generation" and "an instructive account of the political and social history of a revolutionary and creative age." FDR "beguiled an isolationist nation from its isolationism and a conservative nation, dominated by the business creed of laissez-faire, to a pragmatic revolution" in which government was used "for the purpose of assuring the general welfare and guaranteeing at least minimal securities to the people most exposed to the hazards of the complex machinery of a technical age." While finding the book for the most part superb, Niebuhr disagreed with Burns's judgment that Roosevelt was to a large degree a captive, rather than the shaper, of political forces:

> That judgment seems erroneous when one considers the achievement of remolding a rather moribund, Southern-based party into an instrument of Northern liberalism. On the other hand, Burns shows that Roosevelt did not consciously initiate the new dynamism of the labor movement, was rather ignorant of its importance, and only tardily came to the support of Senator Wagner in the passage of the Labor Relations Act. Since the rise of labor power is one of the most enduring consequences in the reshaping of

the American economy and in the achievement of a more adequate equilibrium of social power in a technical age, this must be regarded as a curious irony of history.

Noting the Eisenhower administration's acceptance of FDR's domestic policies, he observed that "the gains won in the Roosevelt era have been made secure through their unchallenged adoption by the opposition."[5]

During the 1950s Niebuhr commented now and again on the American cultural scene, especially the impact of the mass media on popular taste and opinion, and the pursuit of technical affluence, and other concerns ranging from sexual conduct to women's rights. Aware that the rich and deep cultural tradition of Britain and the European continent survived in the United States as a thin layer among a people whose dominant values were utilitarian, he wrote in *Partisan Review*:

> American sanity is threatened not only by the combination of power and insecurity which has become our fate. Our culture is also threatened from within by the preoccupation of our nation with technology. The resulting crudities are much more serious than those of which our fathers were ashamed. The cultural and spiritual crudities of a civilization preoccupied with technics compare with the pastoral and rustic crudities of a frontier civilization as a neon-lighted movie palace compares with a cow-barn. Our problem is not merely the synthetic and sentimentalized art of Hollywood or the even lower depths to which television has reduced this art. It is also the problem of cheap technocratic approaches to the tragic historic drama in which we are all involved.

Responding to European critics of American cultural shortcomings in a symposium published at Harvard in 1952, he wrote: "It is fairly obvious that the relation of America to the culture of Europe is roughly analogous to the relation of Rome to Greek culture." European culture, like the Greek, was more highly developed, he observed, yet it was American power that provided security for the West, as the Romans did for the ancient Mediterranean world, maintaining peace with a sense of justice. This task was no less important than art, philosophy, and literature: "The plight of modern man is too serious to be met by the expedient of establishing a few islands of 'culture' in a social chaos."[6]

Niebuhr's concern about the mass media in American life had been stimulated while serving from 1944 to 1946 on a distinguished panel, chaired by Robert Hutchins, that published *A Free and Responsible Press*—a memorable report surveying the various media and recommending standards of quality and a pattern of diversity in publishing, broadcasting, and filmmaking. In 1950 he delivered a lecture at the University of Minnesota, in an annual series on the press later published as a book. Taking as his theme the role of newspapers in America's function as a world power, he stressed that the nation's press shared responsibility with other organs of cultural life for enabling people "to understand both their friends and their foes" in other parts of the world. The reporting of foreign affairs involves interpretation: "The problem is that our nation, like every nation, needs not so much isolated facts to inform its mind as the understanding of facts in their setting." He urged American newspapers to emulate Europeans in giving more emphasis to "the quasi-editorial interpretive article on the editorial page." Good journalism, he added, should also "supply the material through which a healthy national self-criticism is possible." Several years later, in a volume of essays honoring Walter Lippmann, Niebuhr wrote that "foreign policy has proved to be the Achilles heel of democracy," for most voters can only judge policies directly affecting their lives, but without aid cannot make informed and wise judgments on international affairs. An adequate American foreign policy, therefore, requires "various aristocracies or elite groups," including elected officials and specialists in foreign affairs, journalistic as well as academic educators—including newspaper columnists like Lippmann—and members of the general public who are competent on issues of foreign policy. The latter "may be devoted readers of one of the wise columnists, or of a newspaper that gives more than ordinary attention to foreign affairs."[7]

As television began to have its pervasive influence on American society in the early 1950s, Niebuhr observed that quality suffered because it "strives for a maximum audience for each program." It "affords an even more serious threat to culture in terms of the communication of ideas than it does in the projection of artistic images," because "discussion topics seem to be chosen not because they are important but because they lend themselves to visual elaboration." Television and other mass media, he insisted, had a deleterious effect:

> Pretending to serve hypothetical mass tastes, they actually contaminate them. Furthermore, the mass media of the present day tend to destroy the inner core of a cultural discipline by their too frantic efforts at popularization. Even a democratic culture cannot afford an equalitarianism which threatens the sources of discipline of the mind and heart by trying to bring them *down* to the lowest common denominator.

Niebuhr discussed the problem further in an introductory essay in Wilbur Schramm's *Social Responsibility in Mass Communication*, a study commissioned by the National Council of Churches and published in 1957. While the newer medium had broadened appreciation of good music and made science interesting with graphic material, he held, it had lowered the level of drama and of public discussion and allowed advertising to become obtrusive. Standards could be improved in America without resorting to regulation or banning advertising, Niebuhr advised, by creating alongside the commercial networks "a quasi-governmental agency such as the British Broadcasting Company," which would cultivate more specialized audiences. The mass media, especially television, produced images that endangered national culture by "a soft conformity in which the community, rather than the state, becomes the arbiter of opinion, and in which nonconformity is made difficult by the weight of standardized opinions—not only in politics but in all manner of taste and standards of living." It presented the churches, he declared, with a challenge to maintain the validity of the scriptural injunction: "And be not conformed to this world: but be ye transformed by the renewing of your mind" (Rom. 12:2).[8]

Another issue engaged Niebuhr as interest focused on what became known as the Kinsey Report, completed in 1953 when *Sexual Behavior in the Human Female* followed *Sexual Behavior in the Human Male* five years earlier—a massive presentation of data collected by Alfred Kinsey, a professor of biology. When the earlier volume appeared, Niebuhr had expressed distress not only at the promiscuous habits of many Americans statistically documented but at the disregard for moral and religious norms in Kinsey's approach to the subject. After the second volume appeared, he found disturbing "this further evidence of the decay of the family" and, more disturbing, Kinsey's presupposition "that men and women face a rather purely physiological problem in their sex life." Deploring his disregard for traditional restraints, Niebuhr wrote:

> The fact that human beings are persons in whom a whole hierarchy of values and ends can be related to, and superimposed upon, the natural basis of their life . . . is obscured or denied in Kinsey's consistent naturalism and its logical fruit of a crude hedonism, in terms of which the achievement of sexual pleasure becomes the *summum bonum* of his value scheme.

Kinsey also "obscures the universality of the prohibition of adultery, equalling the prohibition of murder and theft, by calling attention to peripheral relativities in sexual codes." Despite these strictures, Niebuhr found interesting the Report's finding that devout Catholics, Protestants, and Jews were highly disciplined in sexual conduct: "The religious heightening of the sense of personal responsibility for covenants in which one is engaged, of mutual respect and fidelity between persons and the religious accentuation of personal self-respect, must certainly be operative in the lives which yield these impressive statistics."[9]

Disdainful of Kinsey's hedonistic naturalism, Niebuhr respected Freud's achievements despite the naturalistic framework of his theory. Contributing to a symposium on the father of modern psychoanalysis, he wrote:

> The position of Sigmund Freud as one of the great scientific innovators of our era is now generally acknowledged. The therapeutic efficacy of his disciplines and discoveries has been amply proved. By laying bare the intricate mechanism of the self's inner debate with itself, and its labyrinthian depths below the level of consciousness, he enlarged or indeed created new methods of healing "mental" diseases.

Freudian theory, he went on to say, though adding insights for treating maladjustments of the self, lacked the political relevance some Freudians claimed for it: "Its lack of relevance is due to the fact that it pictures an ego which is bedeviled, not by organized and coherent ambitions in conflict with other interests and ambitions, but with the anarchy of passions within and below the level of selfhood." Freud's *ego* is too closely identified with the *id*, Niebuhr held, and his *superego* is not an integral part of the self; thus his system does not comprehend the self's transcendent freedom and the corrupt or noble exercise of it in history. He concluded:

> The self is of course always rooted in nature and does not escape any of the impulses and needs which Freud describes. But all of these impulses are subject to historical elaborations, individually and collectively. . . . Therefore, a realism which ascribes the expression of particular interest and vitality to a nature which is too non-historical is bound to be oblivious to all the complexities of creativity and self-concern which historical development constantly elaborates.[10]

Another question which Niebuhr addressed over the years, by way of occasional comment rather than sustained argument, was the role of women in the family and in society. In 1949 he had written:

> A technical society has indeed given women various forms of freedom, once enjoyed only by men. . . . But the more rationalistic forms of feminism have drawn some extravagant and unwarranted conclusions from this historic development. They have forgotten that the difference between fatherhood as a kind of avocation and motherhood as a vocation has a biological basis which can never be completely overcome. The mother bears the child in her body; and even when she no longer suckles it, the bond between the

two is of a special order. . . . Women may choose another vocation beside that of motherhood or they may exchange the vocation of motherhood for another vocation. But biological facts make these choices more difficult than those which a mere male faces.

Rejecting in those words a radical feminism, he also made a case for women's rights in this passage ten years later:

In the relation between husband and wife, the modern family stands under the obvious necessity of constantly re-assessing the position of the woman in the home and in the community because many factors in technical civilization have given her a potential freedom and equality which were not granted in agrarian civilizations and which cannot be denied now.[11]

Those two passages, and others like them in books and articles, expressed his moderate and sensible views on a subject much debated after his lifetime.

So Niebuhr ruminated, in the milieu of the 1950s, as a political thinker and cultural critic. He had more to say in other books of those years.

Hebraic and Hellenic Sources of the Western Heritage

Niebuhr's next book, which he began to write while recovering from his stroke, was *The Self and the Dramas of History*, published in 1955. Its main theme was that the Hebraic component of the Western heritage is superior to the Hellenic in appreciating the freedom of the self and the dramatic character of history, while the Hellenic component comprehends, as the Hebraic does not, the structures that underlie the flow of events. In the first of the book's three parts, he commenced with meditations on the self "in constant dialogue with itself, with its neighbors, and with God," expressing indebtedness to Martin Buber's *I and Thou* for insights on these aspects of selfhood. According to the biblical view, Niebuhr stated, human selves are unique as creatures involved in these dialogues, in which they possess freedom over their rational faculties, regarded by Aristotle as the defining characteristic of humanity. Freud, he continued, discovered intricacies of the psyche which disproved the "mind-body" dualism of classical philosophy, but his naturalistic psychology, though therapeutically helpful, obscured the self in its exercise of will and conscience. The self, Niebuhr went on to say, not only looks at itself in internal dialogue but engages in unique dialogic relationships with others, and also coalesces in communities formed by natural cohesion and historical experience. As both creature and creator in the dramas of history, the self is partly determined and partly free, he held; it is also too involved to view past events with complete detachment, and unable to predict or master the future. Its search for meaning takes one of four forms, according to Niebuhr: idolatrous devotion to some collective self, as in primitive polytheism and modern totalitarianism; quasi-idolatrous assertion of the meaning of one's life as self-created, as in the existentialism of Sartre and Heidegger; an effort to transcend particularity in some universal realm, as in oriental mysticism; or the biblical way of dialogue with God in terms set by a historical revelation. Only the last "asserts a discontinuity between the self and God" and thus "prevents the self either from usurping the place of the divine for itself or from imagining itself merged with the divine."[12]

In the second part of the book Niebuhr, focusing on the Hebraic and Hellenic strains in Western culture, pointed to "the peculiar virtues and defects of each part of our heritage." The Hellenic side laid the foundations of philosophy and science but erred in identifying the self with its mind and in regarding history as part of nature, while the Hebraic side saw more deeply into the self and the dramas of history but mistakenly viewed nature as part of history:

> Thus the one culture misunderstands human selves and their history, where freedom is more apparent than laws. The other misunderstands nature because it is primarily to be understood in terms of analyzable laws.

Contemporary life and thought, Niebuhr maintained, needed what was best in each component of the Western heritage to correct the deficiency of the other for an adequate understanding of both the self in its historical dramas and the world in its causalities and coherences. Christianity, he continued, is essentially Hebraic, a version of the covenant faith of Moses and the prophets in which the Christ event has unique meaning in the experience of the church—a meaning blunted by some interpreters. Rudolf Bultmann's enterprise of cleansing its message of prescientific attitudes was, in his view, laudable but obscured historic New Testament faith in existentialism:

> That "God was in Christ reconciling the world unto Himself" is verifiable in the experience of everyone who experiences the mercy and new life which flows from true repentance in the encounter with God. . . . Thus there is a significant distinction between the "myths" with which a pre-scientific world describes natural phenomena and the symbol which is central to . . . Christian faith, namely, the assertion that a Jesus of Nazareth was the "Son of the living God."

The content of Christian faith, Niebuhr went on to say, has sometimes been shifted by efforts to interpret it in terms of Greek ontological modes in which God is conceived as "being" and finitude rather than sin is regarded is the primary human problem; thus "the achievement of the 'eternal' under conditions of time becomes the *summum bonum*, whereas the Biblical message is of forgiveness by God toward man and the corresponding forgiveness which men must practice toward one another and will practice the more successfully if they realize the fragmentary character of their own virtues and achievements." Augustine, and later the Reformation, restored the biblical understanding of the divine-human encounter, he maintained. In modern times, Niebuhr asserted, the self and the dramas of history are better understood by jurists, novelists and playwrights, historians, and the best political scientists than by a naturalistic philosopher like John Dewey, who aspired to transform society by scientific method, or a behavioral psychologist like B. F. Skinner, who envisaged a community conditioned without freedom or dignity.[13]

In the third part of the book, Niebuhr chiefly reflected on the development of community as "organism and artifact," in which the self participates as creature and creator of history. Human communities, in his terms, are "organic" insofar as they are formed by loyalties, cohesive factors, and social hierarchies that have grown unconsciously or with a minimum of conscious contrivance. They are "artifacts" insofar as their cohesion and integration have been consciously contrived. The Hebraic part of our heritage was more aware of the organic aspects of community and had a sense of divine providence ruling over the historical process, Niebuhr noted, while the Hellenic saw more vividly the elements of artifact contrived by rational discrimination—an approach which the Renaissance transmitted to the modern West, adding a new sense of history and optimism. It was, he continued, the Anglican thinker Richard Hooker and seventeenth-century Calvinism that first appreciated both organism and artifact as essential aspects of a just and rooted social polity:

> Thus a balance was reached between proper reverence for the ordinance of government and affirmation of the principle of consent by which particular governments are made and unmade; between the conception of the community as an organism and as an artifact; between the factors which are beyond the power, and those within the power of a given generation. This balance is also creative of a government with a maximum of stability and a maximum of justice.

Britain, he held, combined the two approaches well in a wisdom, passing through Burke to the present, that recognizes the self as both creature and creator in the dramas of history. It is, declared Niebuhr, important both "to justify the inheritance of good laws from previous generations" and "to exercise discriminate judgment in rearranging or reconstructing any scheme of togetherness which has been faulty in providing justice." In closing, he turned to the destinies of individuals and of the whole drama of history, finding them related and yet distinguished in the New Testament hope of "the resurrection of the body" and a "general resurrection"—a climax in which variegated human dramas, partly fulfilled in historical communities, receive a lasting significance "grounded in a power and purpose beyond our comprehension, though not irrelevant to all our fragmentary meanings."[14]

Niebuhr dedicated *The Self and the Dramas of History* to Ursula, acknowledging her "rigorous criticism" which "frequently resulted in changes in both form and content"—indeed, this and each of his subsequent books benefited from her stylistic improvements. In a long and friendly review, Will Herberg wrote that its theme was the perennial debate between Athens and Jerusalem: "The fresh and profound treatment of this theme, developed on a variety of levels, in a multitude of variations, makes this work perhaps the most significant Niebuhr has written since *The Nature and Destiny of Man*." It was "essentially a presentation and critical defense of the biblical way of thinking in contrast to 'Hellenism.' " Niebuhr "develops his argument on many fronts—with Catholic scholastics, Protestant fundamentalists, and religious liberals; with rationalists, mystics, and positivist devotees of scientism," among others. Paul Tillich, Herberg continued, was not mentioned but implicitly criticized, for "ontological thinking" that obscured the human encounter with God in biblical faith. James Luther Adams in his review also noted that Niebuhr's critique of ontology was directed at Tillich: "This issue— the dramatic-historical versus the ontological, as Niebuhr puts it—promises to become more acute as readers of both men take sides." The work, wrote Adams, "in certain ways reminds one of the Augustinian vision of life." In it the truths of Hebraism and Hellenism are "maintained in dialectical tension." The book, he concluded, "will stand high in that notable corpus of writings through which Niebuhr has increased both the stature and the prophetic relevance of American theology." Reviewing *The Self and the Dramas of History*, J. Harry Cotton, a prominent Presbyterian clergyman, seminary president, and professor of philosophy in the Midwest, found it a penetrating study of selfhood and its relation to history and community. The book, he declared, "will surely rank high among Niebuhr's works, perhaps next to *The Nature and Destiny of Man*."

John Baillie, reading the British edition, wrote Niebuhr from Edinburgh, "It is all first-class stuff, up to your very best."[15]

A PIOUS AND SECULAR NATION

Since his Gifford Lectures, Reinhold Niebuhr had explored the polarity of faith and reason as developed in the movements initiated by the Renaissance and the Reformation. At their best, he maintained, both entered the stream of modern Western culture creatively. "In our own nation," he wrote in 1953, "the equal contributions which were made to our political thought by New England Calvinism and Jeffersonian deism are symbolic of this confluence of Christianity and secularism in our democracy." Those who condemn all "secularism" as bad, or who think all evil comes from "religious superstition and fanaticism," are extremists on either side of the controversy between Christian faith and secular humanism, Niebuhr declared a year later: "Meanwhile, such decency and charity as we are able to preserve in an evil world is maintained by those Christians and Jews who have learned humility and charity in the worship of God, and by those secularists who understand the limits of human reason and therefore practice toleration and 'reasonableness.' "[16]

Niebuhr gathered some of his best materials of the mid-1950s into a volume published early in 1958 as *Pious and Secular America*, which took its title from an essay appearing in the one-hundredth anniversary issue of the *Atlantic Monthly*. America, he began in that essay, was "at once the most religious and the most secular of Western nations": its religious communities enjoyed the devotion and active loyalty of more lay people than in any European nation, while the nation as a whole was so preoccupied with technology that its culture was in danger of being subordinated to its economy. Its secularism was of two kinds: "a theoretic secularism which dismisses ultimate questions about the meaning of existence, partly because it believes that science has answered these questions and partly because it regards the questions as unanswerable or uninteresting" and "a practical secularism, which expresses itself in the pursuit of the immediate goals of life." Since enlightened philosophy and technical success could not solve ultimate human problems, the historic faiths of biblical origin had become more relevant than once supposed, Niebuhr held. In America, he pointed out, traditional piety and modern secularism had common virtues enabling them to cooperate democratically, and each possessed unique virtues that prevented the other from degenerating into pious obscurantism or secular utopianism. Piety became deeper insofar as it recaptured religious accents that "knew that the meanings of life were surrounded by a penumbra of mystery and that life's joys and sorrows are curiously mingled."[17]

In another significant essay, Niebuhr discussed American higher education in terms of its role in cultivating discernment as to what is valid in the different strands of cultural and political tradition, and in guarding the humanities and sciences against utilitarian pressures and the influence of mass media. He noted the vital function of four-year liberal arts colleges, many of them with departments of religion and campus ministries that helped to prevent American education from becoming too consistently secular. In surveying the scene, he commented that American education was especially deficient in language studies, that the nation's equalitarian ethos resulted in the inundation of many institutions by youths who were not interested in learning, and that its culture was "too intent upon the immediate to cultivate those resources of the educational enterprise which require patience and which defer hopes for the sake of some long-range achievement or some competence which can gain only limited popular acclaim."[18]

Perhaps the most memorable essay in *Pious and Secular America* was on Christian-Jewish relations, delivered a year earlier as an address before a joint meeting of the faculties of the Jewish Theological Seminary and Union Theological Seminary. At a well-attended event held in Union's Social Hall on February 12, 1957, Niebuhr spoke on "The Relations of Christians and Jews in Western Civilization." Two years earlier the neighboring Jewish Theological Seminary had honored Niebuhr with a citation stating: "Through precept and example, you have taught all of us how we can draw nearer the goals set before us by the Prophets of old." He had served many causes, it continued, including "your championship of those of the Jewish fold who have been exposed to persecution." In his address and essay, Niebuhr reviewed the sorry history of anti-Semitism in the Western world, rooted in prejudice against an ethnically and religiously divergent minority; and pointed out that the Jews' capacity for civic virtue and the spirit of justice, derived from the prophets of Israel, often exceeded that of Christians, for whom the ideal of love applied to individual situations more than to community life. He went on to observe that Judaism and Christianity share a common faith in the creator God as sovereign of history and a common attitude toward historic responsibilities, but accept different revelatory events as the ultimate disclosure of God and thus differ as covenant faiths, the one adhering to Mosaic law and the other rooted in grace as mediated in the Christ drama. However true and more adequate the insights of Christian faith are from a Christian standpoint, Niebuhr argued, it is wrong for Christians to carry on missionary activity among Jews, "because the two faiths are sufficiently alike for the Jew to find God more easily in terms of his own religious heritage than by subjecting himself to the hazards of guilt feeling involved in a conversion to a faith which, whatever its excellencies, must appear to him as a symbol of an oppressive majority culture." Christians, he held, must understand that the symbol of their faith, though bearing an unconditioned message, is to Jews "defaced by historic taints."[19]

The volume closed with an essay, based on sermons preached at Union Seminary and Harvard University, recapitulating certain motifs of the Gifford Lectures in terms of mystery and meaning—a theme to which Niebuhr returned now and again in his later years. Human life, he began, "is full of contradictions and incongruities, not to speak of its tragic dissonances"; it is lived "in various realms of meaning," which "are surrounded by a penumbra of mystery." First, there is the mystery of creation, for "all contingent existence points beyond itself" to ultimate and unconditioned being, which reason cannot penetrate. Second, there is the mystery of human freedom "established introspectively" as a sense of responsibility transcending the determining conditions of life. Third, there is the mystery of sin, a corruption of that freedom which "is not derived from finiteness or ignorance but is rather the consequence of man's futile effort to escape or to obscure the fact of his finiteness"—commonly made by grasping after wealth or power or by asserting ultimacy for some relative truth. Biblical faith, Niebuhr continued, not only recognizes these human and divine mysteries but asserts that human existence has "some meaning in the realm of mystery" and, in the New Testament, affirms "that the most definitive revelation of meaning occurred in the Christ event." The Pauline affirmation that "God was in Christ reconciling the world unto himself" succinctly expresses the ultimate claims of the Christian faith. The revelation of God in a crucified Savior "relates the mystery of creation to the meaning of history" by answering the human predicament of sin with an assurance of mercy, matching the rigor of divine judgment, that can bring forth fruits of repentance in lives of humility, tolerance, and charity.[20]

The essays in *Pious and Secular America*, which Niebuhr dedicated to his daughter, Elisabeth, were diverse. As Robert Fitch remarked in a friendly review, the volume's contents "cannot really be brought under one rubric." The published address on Christian-Jewish relations, reprinted in the *Journal of the Central Conference of American Rabbis*, was gratefully received by the Jewish community for its fresh approach to the problem and its sensitivity to centuries of suffering among Jews in a civilization predominantly Christian. Among American Protestants reactions were mixed, some feeling that Niebuhr's approach weakened the basis for Christian missions, others welcoming it as a constructive initiative toward better relations with Jews while upholding the uniqueness of the Christian revelation. The address, as published in this volume, became a historic document in Christian-Jewish relations, for its declaration against Christian efforts to convert Jews—then an unusual position among Christians—later became the dominant position among most American Protestant denominations. It reflected not only Niebuhr's concern to eradicate anti-Semitism but also his appreciation of the common prophetic heritage of Jews and Christians. "I have, as a Christian theologian," Niebuhr had written in 1944, "sought to strengthen the Hebraic-prophetic content of the Christian tradition." A passion for justice, he wrote in 1959, "is vividly expressed in the Old Testament and particularly in the Prophets. The Old Testament witness is necessary because it deals with collective relations more explicitly than the New Testament."[21]

America, wrote Niebuhr in the late 1950s, differed from Europe not only in its unique mixture of pious and secular aspects but in its greater religious pluralism:

> Our own nation is distinguished from Western European nations both by the degree of the pluralism found among us and the assurance that pluralism will be preserved which is guaranteed by our Constitution. The degree of the pluralism is due to the multiplicity of the Protestant sects in America and the very strong influence of both Judaism and Catholicism in our national life.

These unique conditions, he continued, resulted in a more complete separation of church and state than found in European countries, and complicated the problem of integrating religious instruction in American schools. When the Supreme Court ruled a decade earlier against a plan for "released time" religious education in the public schools of Champaign, Illinois, he criticized Protestant merging with secular forces to create a climate of opinion giving rise to such a Court decision, based on an erroneous notion that the First Amendment called for a "wall of separation" between church and state. Since the prevailing pattern secularized public schools and Sunday schools lacked time to do an adequate job, Niebuhr proposed that the nation's major religious groups press the case for using public school classrooms for educational programs under their separate auspices:

After all, the Constitution, which prohibits "the establishment of religion or the suppression thereof," cannot in the long run be tortured to mean such a rigorous separation of church and state that no public school buildings may be put at the disposal of the churches, if this is done on a fair and equal basis.

He envisaged an expansion of "released time" that would enable Protestant churches to develop joint programs and allow Catholics and Jews to maintain their own programs. It would fill a vacuum in the schools and contribute "to our culture and to the forming of character among our young people." Though opposed to tax support of Roman Catholic parochial schools, or tax exemption of parents whose children attended them, as measures that would disturb unity in support of public schools, Niebuhr favored some compensation to Catholic parents paying tuition to parochial schools as well as taxes for public schools, arguing that "any 'fringe' benefits to Catholic children and parents, such as free lunches and common rides on school buses, would be advisable forms of relief." His friend and colleague John Bennett reached similar conclusions in *Christians and the State*, published in 1958—a major work on the basis and function of the state, political ethics, and church-state relations in America, making the same case for "fringe" benefits to Catholics and expanded "released time" programs. "I am sure," Niebuhr wrote Bennett, "your book will have a very salutary influence on Protestant opinion in America."[22]

In the encounter between Christian faith and the world, Niebuhr wrote in his monthly column for church magazines, witness rather than argument is required:

One has the uneasy feeling that Christians, living in a secular society, are too intent upon arguing with their secular friends and opponents about the problem of whether God exists or whether the biblical accounts are credible and in what sense credible. The problem about the "existence" of God is an old conundrum; his existence cannot be proved or disproved for the very simple reason that God, if he is God, must be the very ground of existence, the end and fulfillment of life. His existence, therefore, cannot be established as we establish finite existences.

In all of these intellectual arguments, the Christian is liable to forget that the Bible calls upon him not to prove anything but to "bear witness" to the revelation of God in Christ. That revelation is the "light that shines in the darkness," and it illumines both the mystery of the divine and the mystery of sin and grace in human life. When there is a genuine confrontation of the divine and the human in our experience, the result must be the shattering of human pride and emancipation from self. "The fruit of the Spirit is love, joy, peace," declares St. Paul. And Jesus insists that "you will know them by their fruits."

Those words appeared in a 1956 issue of the *Messenger,* then the journal of his own denomination, which by a merging of the German Evangelical Synod with the German Reformed Church in 1934 had become the Evangelical and Reformed Church. In a historic gathering at Cleveland in June, 1957, that denomination merged again with the Congregational Christian Churches to form the United Church of Christ. The German Evangelical side, Niebuhr commented on the eve of that event, entered as "poor relations" in the merger, for the Congregationalists were bearers of a richer cultural and educational tradition rooted in New England. Declaring the union "a landmark," he wrote that it was "a particularly vivid example of the kind of mutual invigoration which is proceeding in the whole range of American Protestant pluralism."[23]

NATIONS AND EMPIRES IN THE CONFIGURATIONS OF HISTORY

By the late 1950s the grim possibility of an eventual nuclear war cast a shadow over all other problems of the social order. U.S.-Soviet competition in developing arsenals of the dreaded weapons and guided missiles capable of delivering them was a novel situation in human history, prompting demands for negotiated nuclear disarmament on the one hand or for construction of bomb shelters on the other. Regarding such approaches as futile, Niebuhr addressed the problem in a new book drawing on the experience of the ages, *The Structure of Nations and Empires,* published in 1959 and bearing the subtitle *A Study of the Recurring Patterns and Problems of the Political Order in Relation to the Unique Problems of the Nuclear Age.* He wrote it during the previous year on sabbatical at Princeton's Institute for Advanced Study. He was supported with a grant from the Rockefeller Foundation and was accompanied by Ursula, who took a leave from Barnard and helped by improving the lucidity of his prose. In part, Niebuhr drew on his own considerable knowledge of ancient civilizations, acquired during years of teaching the first semester of his course in the history of ethics at Union Seminary, but he also did fresh research for this panoramic study of nations and empires. While the project was in progress, he discussed its theme with George Kennan and Hans Morgenthau, among others, whose expertise in history and international affairs he valued. "Morgenthau and Kennan have both studied my manuscript," he wrote William Scarlett from Princeton, "and Ursula and I are now embodying their suggestions into the text. Their good opinion did much to revive my spirits."[24] The published work, offering guidance for a critical period in the long Cold War, was more than a tract for the times; it was Niebuhr's most systematic and rigorous treatment of international relations.

"It is important," Niebuhr began, "for us to gain some historical perspective on our contemporary problems lest we regard a new manifestation of an old imperial configuration, as we have it in Communism, as a completely new and unheard-of display of imperial power projected by evil men." For such perspective he examined ancient and medieval empires, autonomous nations in the modern world, and national empires from the sixteenth to the nineteenth centuries. The authority of all these political orders, he stated, can be shown historically to rest on both "prestige," by which uncoerced consent to national or imperial authority is induced, and "force," the capacity to coerce, always minimal in a well-established state and usually drawing its authority from prestige. The source of prestige, Niebuhr continued, has been, in empires through the ages, a religious or ideological claim to serve some universal purpose or, in modern democratic nations, a presumed ability to extend justice as well as to preserve order. In the ancient Near East, for example, the rulers of Egypt and Mesopotamia, and their Persian successors, gained prestige by giving their realms stability and invoking the idea that they represented the cosmic order of the gods. The Hellenistic monarchs, in lands conquered by Alexander, used Stoicism as a bond between Greeks and Near Eastern peoples. If order was the basic achievement of early empires, Niebuhr went on to say, justice was emphasized later where, as in England, emerging classes were able to insist on rights within a traditional order and to assert their interests in a changing society. Thus Burke saw that the authority of British government arose in implicit consent derived both from tradition and from its ability to harmonize varied interests, adjusting the new to the old, while in America Madison similarly envisaged the prestige of a wide federal union through inclusion of interests so varied as to prevent any of them from becoming oppressive.[25]

Since the dawn of civilization, Niebuhr pointed out, imperial dominion of one city-state or nation over others has either annulled or abridged their sovereignty, resulting in "the enlargement of community, but usually only on the level of the expansion of trade." Only Rome established a more cohesive community, its rule imbued from the younger Scipio to Marcus Aurelius by Stoic ethical standards; indeed, "the Roman Empire increasingly availed itself of Stoic universalism as an ideological cement of cohesion, to supplement the force which was the final source of its unity." Later Constantine used Christianity as such a cement, he observed, and Rome's medieval heirs—the empire of Charlemagne and his successors, the Byzantine empire, and the Islamic empire—based their dominion on religion, though Western Christendom was unique in distinguishing between church and state as Augustine had done in his concept of the "two cities." In short, the imperial impetus "is able to use the most varied and contradictory religious impulses and philosophies as instruments of its purposes."[26]

Niebuhr then turned to integral nations in world history, finding in their formation constant and variable factors of ethnic, linguistic, or geographical unity, enhanced by common history, economic mutualities, and modern communications. He surveyed the rise of England and France, the development of the United States, the belated emergence of Germany and Italy, the establishment of the Latin American states where Spain and Portugal had ruled, and the experience of Ireland and Israel. He extended the survey to nations never under imperial rule—to the Scandinavian countries, Japan, and Thailand; to nations emerging from the Hapsburg empire—Holland, Belgium, Czechoslovakia, Hungary, and Yugoslavia; to those once in the Ottoman empire—Turkey, Saudi Arabia, and others; to offspring of Britain in the Commonwealth of Nations—chiefly Canada and Australia; to newly emerging nations once ruled by Britain—notably India, Pakistan, and Nigeria—and by Holland—Indonesia—and France—Vietnam, Tunisia, Morocco. From all of these, Niebuhr concluded: "One or another of the linguistic, ethnic, and geographic factors may be deficient, but they cannot all be deficient." Racial and religious pluralism, he also noted, is a peril to national unity if the differences are regional. He added that "autonomous nationality is so universal that it will finally prove a great hazard to the Communist imperialism."[27]

America, Niebuhr went on to assert, tended to view the world in terms of a vague universalism, expressed by the United Nations, as the chief alternative to the sovereignty of nation-states, without sufficiently appreciating forms of community "above the level of the nation and below the level of the community of mankind." These intermediate structures included alliances such as NATO, trading communities like the prospective European Common Market, and the British Empire-Commonwealth. American leaders, he held, while exercising power of imperial proportions as the hegemonic nation of the West, expressed "anti-imperial" attitudes that failed to acknowledge the creative aspects of European imperialism, especially as practiced by the British, whose rule was more beneficial than exploitative in Asia and Africa, though resented because of white racial arrogance.[28]

Turning to Soviet imperialism, Niebuhr observed that it rested on a combination of force and the prestige of a utopian ideology, rooted in the doctrines of Marx as amended by Lenin and his heirs, which promised an international classless society for which the Russian Communist Party was the revolutionary vanguard. Thus, while it resembled the ancient empires in some ways, it differed in projecting a scheme of universal social redemption even as it transmuted that dream into a harsh despotism. In the tension between the Soviet and Western blocs, Niebuhr continued, "bombs are piled on bombs and guided missiles will be piled on guided missiles in an armory of such frightfulness that man's technical progress throughout the ages has taken on a new dimension." Yet the prospect of avoiding catastrophe, he insisted, depended not on idealistic proposals for abolition of nuclear weapons but on the willingness of both sides to refrain from directly challenging the survival of the other and also to accept the other's commitment to strategic points in Europe. A precedent for such coexistence was the Peace of Westphalia, ending Protestant-Catholic wars following the Reformation, "when it became apparent that neither side could eliminate the power of the other." The task in the decades ahead, he went on to say, "must include, on our part, a less rigid and self-righteous attitude toward the power realities of the world and a more hopeful attitude toward the possibilities of internal development in the Russian despotism." The Central Committee of the party to which Khrushchev owed his power, Niebuhr noted, was analogous to the Whig aristocracy of Britain which eventually evolved into an open society. Such a change might occur in Russia "as the revolutionary enthusiasm abates and the oligarchy acquires a sense of responsibility for the preservation of order and the adjustment of interests within the growing system." America, meanwhile, must patiently cope with the moral ambiguities of the Cold War in a nuclear age:

> Only a religious faith and a humanism more profound than many extant varieties can make sense out of these terrifying facts of modern history, particularly those facts which prove that all historic responsibilities must be borne without the certainty that meeting them will lead to any ultimate solution of the problem, but with only the certainty that there are immediate dangers which may be avoided and immediate injustices which may be eliminated. Thus modern men of whatever persuasion of faith must learn the modesty of acting on the principle, "Sufficient unto the day is the evil thereof."[29]

The Structure of Nations and Empires, which Niebuhr dedicated to Charles C. Burlingham, a longtime friend who was a prominent New York attorney and a member of the editorial board of Christianity and Crisis, received mostly quite favorable reviews. Arnold Toynbee, writing in the New York Times Book Review, found in it Niebuhr's "usual acumen and realism" and cited as "encouraging" his suggestion that the Cold War could be settled along lines of "the sequel to the Catholic-Protestant wars of religion" in seventeenth-century Europe. The historian Hans Kohn wrote: "With the true sense of a historian Niebuhr has tried to teach the American people, who face the seemingly novel perplexities of the nuclear age and of their encounter with Communism, not to forget the lessons of the past." Among specialists in international relations, Arnold Wolfers found the book "an invaluable source of insight and stimulation," commenting that "the history of ideas and political philosophy" were "fields in which he is anything but an amateur as he modestly claims." Samuel P. Huntington wrote: "The material is always interesting, the discussion original and the judgments sound"; inasmuch as pundits were prone to emphasize the unprecedented nature of contemporary challenges, he held, Niebuhr's stress on recurring patterns and problems provided needed perspective. Another foreign policy expert, Robert Strausz-Hupé, considered the work "important," but thought Niebuhr took "too sunny" a view of prospects for reduced Cold War tensions. Kenneth W. Thompson, on the other hand, did not think Niebuhr's work too optimistic: "It is firmly and unequivocally realistic while searching unremittingly for signs of hope in the future. It is, in a word, a book that has about it the marks of a classic by a sovereign mind who in Western society has few equals." Nearly three decades later Thompson, eminent as a scholar in the field of world politics, stated that "in Structure, Niebuhr anticipated the slow but perceptible changes within the Soviet Union that culminate in Gorbachev," and added that "teachers of contemporary foreign policy and international politics assign this work as much or more than any of his writings."[30]

Hans Morgenthau paid tribute to Niebuhr's book for demonstrating perennial patterns in history as a guide for the present: "The articulation of both the similarities and dissimilarities—but particularly the former—between the great empires of the past and the imperial structures and claims of communism illuminates both the historic and contemporary scene." Morgenthau, whose first major book Niebuhr had earlier praised, was steeped in the realist school of European diplomacy. A German émigré at the University of Chicago, he criticized, as Niebuhr had, idealist and behavioral approaches to politics widely held in America during the first half of the twentieth century, and set forth his influential concept of "the national interest," recognizing the role of power as well as moral restraints in international relations. Influenced by Niebuhr, whose theological premises he did not fully comprehend, Morgenthau pointed out that his genius as a political thinker, like that of Burke and others, developed in dealing with concrete problems of his age. That, and an ability to view society in theological perspective, made him "the greatest living political philosopher of America," Morgenthau stated in a symposium of 1961.[31] By then the Eisenhower era had given way to the ferment of the Kennedy years.

CHAPTER NINE

Advice and Reflections
in a Troubled Decade

❧

During the 1960s Reinhold Niebuhr, retired from regular teaching, continued to comment on public affairs and the religious scene. He supported Kennedy's leadership in a perilous phase of the Cold War, pressed for action on civil rights for black Americans and for programs to reduce poverty in the nation, took a keen interest in Vatican II, and advised against U.S. military involvement in Vietnam as a misguided venture. After writing a final book of theological and social reflections, he spent his last years in Stockbridge, Massachusetts, viewing world developments.

KENNEDY'S ACHIEVEMENT

When Niebuhr retired from the faculty of Union Theological Seminary in May of 1960 and moved with Ursula to a nearby apartment on Riverside Drive, campaigns for the American presidency were under way. His preference for the Democratic nomination was Humphrey, whom he had known since the early days of ADA, or Stevenson, but John F. Kennedy—a bright young senator from Massachusetts, whom Niebuhr's friend Arthur Schlesinger, Jr., supported for President—emerged as the party's candidate at the convention during July in Los Angeles. Niebuhr observed the event close by, for at the invitation of Robert Hutchins he spent the summer as a visiting fellow of the Center for the Study of Democratic Institutions in Santa Barbara. He shared Kennedy's approach to salient foreign and domestic policy issues, but felt uneasy about the use of his family's fortune in the primaries and raised questions about his religious depth and private life. Yet Richard Nixon, the Republican candidate, was the bête noire of most Democrats and ADA liberals like Niebuhr, whose leaders he had long accused of being soft on Communism. By fall, therefore, Niebuhr publicly associated himself with Kennedy, reassuring Protestants that the candidate's Catholicism was fully compatible with American democratic traditions. Supporting the case for new national leadership, he wrote in October: "There is always a chance that we will grow into the wisdom and political resourcefulness demanded by our vast responsibilities, but not guaranteed by our previous rather too comfortable existence." After Kennedy won by a narrow margin, he commented that "the young President-elect grasps the helm in one of the most fateful periods of our history."[1]

When the new President took office in January of 1961, the United States faced serious difficulties in various parts of the world, especially in central Europe, where Khrushchev—truculent after the failed summit—threatened to abrogate Western rights in Berlin in order to stop an embarrassing flow of refugees from East Germany, and in Latin America, where Communism had gained a foothold in Castro's Cuba a year earlier and threatened to spread wherever poverty bred discontent. Conditions elsewhere in the Third World, including areas of Southeast Asia, were favorable to Communist propaganda and insurgency. At the same time, U.S. and Soviet testing of nuclear bombs, though currently suspended, posed the danger of radioactive contamination of the atmosphere. Kennedy, with a talented new team of administrators and diplomats, sought a modus vivendi with the Soviets and constructive relations with Third World countries, through such initiatives as the Peace Corps, sending American volunteers to help developing nations, and the Alliance for Progress, offering funds for economic development and social reform in Latin America.

These promising beginnings were momentarily set back in April by the abortive Bay of Pigs invasion of Cuba by exiles, planned by the CIA and approved by Kennedy—a fiasco widely criticized at home and abroad. Niebuhr commented:

> The criticism involves the question of what business an intelligence agency has in mounting a revolution even if no American soldiers are involved. . . . Perhaps there was an even more serious error—the failure . . . to measure the breadth and depth of the anti-Yankee sentiment both in Cuba and the whole of Latin America. Some of this represents the natural resentment of weakness against strength, some of it represents a justified reaction to our economic imperialism, to our heavy stakes in Latin American economies.

In a *New Leader* piece two weeks later he praised Kennedy's basic, long-term policy toward America's southerly neighbors. Except for Mexico, where democratic reforms had produced a stable regime, and a such a hopeful prospect as Venezuela under Betancourt, he wrote, Latin America did not possess the healthier Western nations' immunity to the Communist virus:

> It is threatened by Communism, not so much because the Russians are building up Cuba militarily, but because social realities in Latin America correspond to the Communist image. . . . In Latin America, the prevailing social pattern is one of agrarian feudalism, aggravated ethnically by the conjoining of a Spanish or Portuguese aristocracy and an Indian peasantry. Most of the nations of South America have constitutions patterned after our own, but these countries have been ruled either by democracies more or less controlled by the landed aristocrats, or dictatorships which usually combined military power with demagogic appeals to the poor.

Niebuhr continued:

> President Kennedy's "Alliance for Progress" program was the first genuine effort to use our nation's economic power to help our hemispheric neighbors to change their social patterns and undertake land reform and a system of universal education—measures designed to mitigate the social inequalities which abstract constitutionalism does not touch.[2]

Meanwhile, tension mounted in Europe as Khrushchev prepared to sign a peace treaty with East Germany that would curb the freedom of West Berlin, which since the earlier blockade and airlift remained a symbol of American resolve to defend western Europe. The crisis posed a grim possibility of nuclear warfare. After Kennedy made it clear that he would protect Western rights in the city and would not interfere with steps the Soviets might take on territory under their control, Khrushchev's East German regime built a wall blocking access to West Berlin, thus stopping the daily stream of refugees that was draining their land of able farmers, technicians, and professional people. Niebuhr, observing that the city's Western sector was "an obvious showcase of the desirability and economic viability of free institutions in the context of European culture," commented that Khrushchev "has shrewdly sealed off East Berlin" and in so doing "has violated the liberties of the East Germans more than our rights." The West, he added, must stand firm: "We must not initiate hostilities; but we can counter force to push us out. This is undoubtedly a war of nerves."[3]

As the Berlin crisis receded, another issue arose in Europe. Britain had applied for membership in the European Common Market, which since 1957 had worked to lower tariff barriers among six continental nations of western Europe, but France under de Gaulle threatened to oppose British entry. Niebuhr regarded the Common Market as a positive development which not only brought prosperity to member nations but locked West Germany into the European community with a strong economic tie and promoted "the political health as well as economic strength of the European core of the non-Communist world." He supported British membership in it, and American partnership through reciprocal tariff reductions. Though crediting de Gaulle for liquidating France's empire in Algeria, he found the French leader's attitude toward British integration in the Common Market disturbing. In 1962 he wrote that "the primary motives of France's reluctance about British inclusion are not economic but political," having to do with "the pride and prestige of France *vis-à-vis* Britain," and more particularly "with France as de Gaulle . . . conceives the 'grandeur of France.' " De Gaulle's policy, "inspired by an archaic and nostalgic patriotism," unrealistically projected a Europe dominated by French power in a contest between Soviet Russia and "the gigantic nephew of the British nation, the U.S., now in the position of the hegemonous power in the loose non-Communist alliance." General de Gaulle was "an impressive boulder" but "a lonely eminence in the modern currents of international politics." Niebuhr deplored his veto early in 1963 of British entry into "one of the most hopeful of all continental supernational institutions," an act that delayed the event for ten years; thus, he commented, did de Gaulle "spurn the creative internationalism of the French center, including Jean Monnet—a man greater than he—the father of the Common Market and of the vision of a united Europe."[4]

Meanwhile, remote from Europe, the newly independent Congo, later renamed Zaire, continued to be torn by civil strife, as its copper-rich Katanga province sought to secede from the central government and tribalism compounded the problem of national unity in the wake of the Belgians' sudden withdrawal. Niebuhr supported the U.S.-backed United Nations policy of forcing the Katanga secessionists to stay in the federation, pointing out that they were in African eyes too identified with Belgian imperialism for the West to support without playing into the hands of Communists. Katanga, he also noted, had long provided one half of the Congo's revenue. Various languages, hundreds of dialects, and a multiplicity of tribal loyalties, he further observed, complicated the achievement of integral nationhood in the Congo. "These are issues," he wrote in 1962, "that vividly display the hazards of regionalism and tribalism that are not unique but common to the budding nations of Africa." In the same year, Niebuhr was impressed by a new book about South Africa,

Chief Albert Luthuli's *Let My People Go,* describing and criticizing the country's rigorous racism, rooted in its past and culminating in the policies of the current Verwoerd government. America, he commented, was farther on the road to racial justice, but stubborn resistance to every step proved that the problem was broadly human and not only a South African one: "On the one hand, we are dealing with the arrogance and fear of the white overlord and, on the other, with the essential humanity of human beings who may once have been weak in their backwardness but who are growing stronger and more capable of expressing their outraged sense of human dignity." White communities were beholding, as Niebuhr put it, "the rising tide of color."[5]

Early in the 1960s, as the Cold War shifted increasingly to the Third World and Kennedy inspired American efforts to help the emerging nations of Africa and Asia as well as Latin America, Niebuhr enlarged upon points he had made during the past decade and sought to define opposition to Communism in terms broader than the defense of Western democratic culture. Military concerns, he insisted, should not obscure basic socioeconomic problems in those vast areas:

> The unappreciated hazards in our contest with Communism have a common root, which can be briefly stated: the nations of the "uncommitted world" have either primitive or feudal-agrarian economies. . . . When technics are introduced into such an economy, they serve to aggravate rather than mitigate the inequalities. . . . We must, indeed, help the new nations to achieve technical competence. But the more difficult problem is to achieve social justice under the dynamic conditions of technical civilization. The Communists simply thrive on the social havoc resulting from failure to achieve a tolerable justice. . . . Of course, we must not neglect our military defenses. Yet if we allow the military task to preoccupy us or to deflect us from the primary problem, Communism will appear to the new nations to be the "wave of the future" that Mr. Khrushchev declares it to be.

Niebuhr further emphasized that Americans, whose cultural heritage and social fabric enabled democratic institutions to become rooted at the founding of their nation, should understand that Western-style democracy is not immediately relevant in most of Asia, Africa, and Latin America but might take centuries to evolve as it is in Britain and other European countries. Its prerequisites, he pointed out, included a core of ethnic and linguistic homogeneity, widespread literacy extending from the upper to the lower classes, a dynamic middle class, and an equilibrium of social forces. Most non-European cultures lacked these conditions for stable democracy, he observed, citing postwar Japan as the principal exception.

Surveying various countries of the Third World, he noted the achievements of one-party democracy in Mexico and Tunisia and the encouraging, if uncertain, prospect for parliamentary government in the huge and diverse nation of India, guided by Nehru, but found more typical the authoritarian regimes of Indonesia, Pakistan, Iraq, Egypt, and Ghana, or the alternation of democracy and dictatorship in nations like Brazil. As Niebuhr put it:

> Democratic self-government is indeed an ultimate ideal of political community. But it is of the greatest importance that we realize that the resources for its effective functioning are not available to many nations.[6]

The non-Communist cause, Niebuhr wrote in 1961, encompassed more than democracy: it was the preservation of (borrowing a phrase from Karl Popper) an "open society." This broadly included not only systems of self-government that dispersed power as far as possible and subjected it to criticism and review but, in a larger sense, a world order of varied political forms in which human life could develop without the constraints of a pretentious ideology demanding total loyalty and promising final fulfillment:

> The more ultimate virtue of an open society is that it does not coerce either the community or the total process of history into a dogmatic mold. . . . It is a method of organizing the human community in terms that are consonant with the basic character of human experience, with its freedom over and limitation by the temporal process, which is at once the ground and the dynamic of the drama of human history.

Such an attitude, accepting divergent human vitalities and refusing to claim omniscience and omnipotence, "conforms to the nature of man as both creature and creator of history." The survival of an open society, by preventing Communism from usurping all centers of power and prestige, was a compelling cause, Niebuhr maintained. It called for patient and prudent resolve in a nuclear age, but the outcome could be hopeful:

> The foe is human and not demonic. He is informed by a creed with demonic pretensions. If not resisted, these unchallenged pretensions will grow. If resisted, the opportunity is given for the common experience of history to dissolve and refute pretentious dogmas that have prematurely dug channels for historic vitalities. . . . Our modern task is to escape the hell of mutual annihilation while exorcizing the false heaven of the utopian creeds. Fortunately, the two tasks are not as incompatible as they seem.[7]

To protect vital interests in the non-Communist world without stumbling into nuclear war with the Soviet adversary was, indeed, the supreme challenge of American statecraft, as both sides in the Cold War developed long-range missiles capable of delivering the dread weapons. Niebuhr, supporting U.S. development of such an arsenal as a deterrent to Soviet use of its own nuclear missiles, continued in the early 1960s to address the dilemma arising from the fact that these weapons were necessary to Western security but potentially a grave peril to humanity. As talk of building civilian nuclear fallout shelters mounted in America, he wrote that he and Ursula "would rather perish than survive such a war." Reviewing *Nuclear Weapons and the Conflict of Conscience*, a collection of essays edited by John Bennett, he commended its presentation of expert opinion informed by a sober realism that rejected unilateral disarmament and called for a strategy of coexistence with Soviet Russia. "We must," stated Niebuhr, "modify our polemical attitudes toward the Russians, cease from ascribing to them all the ills from which we suffer, and come to regard them as partners in saving mankind from catastrophe." In 1962 he wrote in the *Annals of the American Academy* about the contest with Communism:

> World peace requires that the dynamic of this strange political movement be contained, its ambition to control the world be frustrated, and its revolutionary ardors be tamed by firm and patient resistance. Any lack of firmness on our part, and, on the other hand, any lack of soberness, any lapse into hysteria, might well prove fatal to the uneasy peace which stands between us and disaster.[8]

Only a few months after Niebuhr's words just quoted appeared in print, the world faced the most perilous crisis of the Cold War—one of the gravest international crises in all of history—when the Kennedy administration ascertained in October of 1962 that the Russians were installing nuclear missile–launching sites in Cuba, a threatening intrusion into the Western Hemisphere. President Kennedy, rejecting the option of bombing the sites and invading the island—which could easily have escalated into World War III—solemnly announced a blockade of further Soviet shipments, called upon Khrushchev to dismantle the sites and remove the missiles, and warned that the U.S. would respond to any missile attack from Cuba by a nuclear attack on the Soviet Union. Tension rose as the possibility of nuclear war became imminent, until Khrushchev yielded on the condition that the U.S. not invade Cuba. Niebuhr commented afterward in *Christianity and Crisis*:

> During the last week of October the whole world peered into the depth of the abyss, on the edge of which we had known ourselves to be living as a

result of a precarious "balance of terror," namely the equal capacity of both sides to retaliate with nuclear weapons of such destructive power as to make irrelevant the difference between victors and vanquished. . . . The present outcome may have at least laid a minimal bridge across a deep chasm. That bridge is a common sense of the responsibility to avoid the nuclear holocaust.

Kennedy, he wrote, "met the crisis with that combination of firmness and moderation which is the criterion of true statesmanship."[9]

The Cuban missile crisis resulted in increased concern on both sides of the Cold War to cooperate for the sake of peace, and particularly to seek ways to limit the development and proliferation of nuclear weapons. Since the mid-1950s, after radioactive fallout from U.S. nuclear tests in the Pacific caused ghastly illness among Japanese fishermen, international pressures to ban such testing rose; but tests continued off and on, the Soviets conducting nuclear tests of unprecedented proportions in Siberia during 1961 and 1962. Since U.S.-Soviet negotiations for a comprehensive test ban had floundered on the issue of on-site inspection of underground tests, Kennedy proposed, and Khrushchev accepted, a limited ban on atmospheric testing as a first step toward nuclear arms control, and one that would stop hazardous debris from washing to earth in the rain. After the signing of the test ban treaty in Moscow in August of 1963, followed by the U.S. Senate's ratification and eventual signing by one hundred nations, Niebuhr wrote:

> The whole world rejoiced, for the agreement would rid the world and its unborn generations of the perilous radioactive fallout. . . . The real possibility is that it may be the beginning of a Russo-American partnership. . . . Since we cannot predict the future, we must take these hopeful, if uncertain, first steps. Cardinal Newman's hymn "Lead, Kindly Light" has a line that is relevant to our wintry and dark world situation: "I do not ask to see the distant scene; one step enough for me."[10]

While international perils and hopes predominated in the early 1960s, the same years also marked a new phase in the American civil rights movement, as emphasis shifted from court litigation to nonviolent direct action, often by groups of black and white students working together. In 1960 sit-ins began to bring about desegregation at lunch counters in the South, and in 1961 "freedom riders" defied segregated bus travel in Alabama and Mississippi, prompting the Interstate Commerce Commission to set new standards. Noting these developments, Niebuhr commented that such racial ideals "could not be fulfilled without the joint efforts of humane elements in a society who resent injustice without being its victims, and articulate members of the victimized group who express the resentments and the will to justice of the affected class."[11]

Despite successful sit-ins in some Southern cities, racial segregation in places of public accommodation persisted in others, of which Birmingham, Alabama, was a symbol. There, in May of 1963, peaceful demonstrations led by Martin Luther King were disrupted by police dogs and other violence, provoking nationwide dismay and prompting Kennedy to address the nation and call for sweeping civil rights legislation. Niebuhr wrote in *Christianity and Crisis:*

> The next step has been outlined by the President's new legislative program, which is the natural fruit of the increasing tension of what he has defined as our "moral crisis." The legislative program as proposed seeks to outlaw discrimination in all private commercial ventures on the basis of the 14th amendment and the interstate commerce clause of the Constitution. It will not pass without a great political struggle. If successful, it might put the legislative capstone on the emancipation of the race. But the retreating white supremacists are increasingly desperate. Their murders, their police dogs, and their terror have contributed as much to the mounting tension as the impatience of the Negroes.

Then, after a throng of close to a quarter of a million marched to the Lincoln Memorial in late August and heard King deliver his "I Have a Dream" speech, Niebuhr wrote to William Scarlett:

> You are quite right about the March on Washington. It was a splendid triumph for the Negroes. . . . King's address was one of the most eloquent in recent years. It won't influence the hard core of racists, but it will influence the nation.

Weeks later, in a televised dialogue with James Baldwin following the bombing of a black church in Birmingham, he remarked, "From my standpoint Martin Luther King is one of the great Americans of our day." King's doctrine of nonviolent resistance, he added, was not pacifism.[12]

Two months later, when assassination ended the Kennedy presidency and a shocked and mourning nation watched a state funeral attended by heads of state from around the world, Niebuhr paid tribute to the fallen leader. "The untimely death of President Kennedy by an assassin's bullet," he wrote, "has aroused a depth and breadth of grief in the nation and the world that historians may well regard as unprecedented." JFK "had a quick and searching intelligence combined with a rare degree of political shrewdness and personal and political courage." He "proved his mettle in foreign policy" in the Cuban missile crisis "when a nuclear war was threatened—and averted by a combination of boldness and prudence" and also when "he courageously initiated the limited test-ban agreement, which may well go down in history as the beginning of a new era in the Cold War." His name will also be associated, Niebuhr stated, with his "creative thrust in world affairs" and "his stand on civil rights." He hoped that JFK's "otherwise senseless death may become meaningful in the light of history by furnishing the inspiration needed for completing his unfinished tasks."[13]

BELATED JUSTICE FOR BLACK AMERICANS

By 1964 civil rights became the central issue in American public life, as President Lyndon Johnson, succeeding Kennedy, pushed for passage of the bill pending before Congress and a coalition of churches, labor unions, and black organizations lobbied for it on Capitol Hill. Managed on the Senate floor by Hubert Humphrey and enacted in early July, the Civil Rights Act of 1964—meant primarily to secure the rights of blacks in the South—was a landmark, forbidding segregation in places of public accommodation, promoting fair employment practices, outlawing racial barriers to voting, and banning discrimination in federally assisted programs. While Niebuhr strongly supported it, he observed that none of its provisions "seriously affects the status of unemployed Negroes in Northern ghettoes"—victims of deficient education and lack of job training, caused in turn by de facto school segregation and by family incomes too low to pay for college studies or technical education. As Niebuhr had noted a year earlier, American society contained "enclaves of injustice" not only in the deep South but in Northern urban centers to which many Southern blacks had fled; there, though able to vote, they "must live in ghettoes such as Harlem." Observing in the summer of 1964 that the plight and hopelessness of black youths in Northern cities was becoming manifest in violence, he wrote: "The reason for this despair is obvious, but I, for one, was slow to gauge its import." He expressed some apprehension that in their struggle for justice "the Negro minority lacks any economic power comparable to the right of collective bargaining." The consumer boycott, used effectively by Martin Luther King for certain goals and useful in encouraging local employers to hire blacks, was "not a potent economic force." The extension and exercise of the franchise was potentially "the most hopeful" instrument in the hands of the black minority, Niebuhr held.[14]

The nation's focus on civil rights was temporarily diverted by the presidential election of 1964, when the Republicans chose Senator Barry Goldwater to run against President Johnson. Declaring that his aim was not to pass new laws but to repeal old ones, Goldwater voted against the civil rights bill of that year and the nuclear test ban a year earlier; he wanted to dismantle the New Deal and use atomic weapons in Vietnam. His nomination for the presidency, Niebuhr wrote, "will be regarded as a strange phenomenon." It was "an expression of national nostalgia . . . yearning for the good old days of uncomplicated domestic and foreign issues." Although such archaic sentiments found a home in the GOP, he continued, "the Republican party as a whole is not conservative in Goldwater's sense," differing from the Democrats not in seeking to restore the pure individualism of an earlier era, but in its greater reluctance to support government intervention in the economic process. "Even liberals," wrote Niebuhr, "might well long for Senator Taft's conservatism as against Senator Goldwater's." He further noted that "the party of Lincoln made massive contributions to the Civil Rights Bill" and that "without its aid the bill would not have passed either house of Congress." The most dangerous aspect of the Goldwater movement, however, was in the realm of foreign affairs, where "a primitive anti-Communism cuts across all the realities of the international arena, including the tacit partnership that obtains between Russia and the United States for the sake of avoiding a nuclear catastrophe." While campaigning in September, the President paused to confer the nation's highest civilian recognition, the Medal of Freedom, on thirty Americans—among them Reinhold Niebuhr, who was unable to attend the ceremony in the East Room of the White House; others so honored at the time ranged from Dean Acheson, Walt Disney, and T. S. Eliot to Helen Keller, Edward R. Murrow, and A. Philip Randolph. After Johnson won the election in one of the biggest landslides in American history, Niebuhr stated: "The recent Presidential election vindicated the common sense of the majority of the nation's voters."[15]

Johnson's victory swept into Congress the largest Democratic majorities since the mid-1930s, enabling him during 1965 to expand a broad-scoped antipoverty program enacted a year earlier, to initiate federal aid to education partly designed to improve inner-city schools and to help disadvantaged youth finance college studies, and to enlarge an earlier housing program for low-income families. Meanwhile, resistance developed in parts of the South to the voting-rights provision of the recent civil rights legislation. In March of 1965, after thousands of blacks attempting to register in Selma, Alabama, were jailed, King led a march, joined by others from all parts of the country, to the state capital, where police whipped and beat demonstrators, shocking the nation. Niebuhr commented:

A climax has been reached in the State of Alabama, occasioned by the determination of the Negro minority to achieve belatedly their constitutional voting rights. A century has elapsed since the post–Civil War constitutional amendments guaranteed those rights. . . . The brutality by which the demonstrations were suppressed . . . also clarified the hysterical desperation of the white oligarchy in the old slave states in resisting every effort to breach their fortress of special privilege. . . . The march on the capital by citizens of conscience of all persuasions will undoubtedly give great support to the new voting rights bill presented by President Johnson in a matchless address to the Congress and the nation.

While Johnson's bill, authorizing the sending of federal officials where necessary to register black voters, was pending, a nationally distributed *Mississippi Black Paper*, with a foreword by Niebuhr, documented many recent instances of harassment of persons involved in voter registration drives. Introducing this collection of affidavits gathered by civil rights organizations, he wrote:

The crimes described in the following pages, committed either by local officials or with their connivance, include the bombing of homes and churches, the arrests of Negroes on false charges for every type of fanciful law infraction, and—most frightening of all—a brutality by the police that frequently approaches sadistic cruelty and on occasion has resulted in murder. . . . Not all the states of the Southern Confederacy have sunk to the standard of inhumanity described in these documents. . . . Admittedly the national community has its own problems of racial prejudice and injustice . . . but perhaps these affidavits will suggest to the readers that justice in Mississippi is corrupted to such a degree that without aid from the outside it is doomed.[16]

Outside aid came to hundreds of thousands of blacks in Mississippi, Alabama, and five other Southern states, with passage in August of the Voting Rights Act of 1965.

In big cities outside the South, meanwhile, black youths—whom new federal antipoverty efforts were barely beginning to reach—rioted during the summers of the mid-1960s, first in Harlem in 1964. The worst occurred in the Watts area of Los Angeles in 1965 and in Detroit in 1967, on a scale far larger than the riots in 1925 which had led to Niebuhr's chairing a committee on racial relations in that city. As the first signs of these disturbances appeared, Niebuhr wrote that such destructive violence "can never be condoned and authorities can never be criticized for taking proper police measures to reduce them," but he added that "the white majority must stretch its imagination and empathy radically to understand the roots of this unrest." After rioting reached a peak in 1967, he commented that the violence among blacks in the inner cities of America called to mind the frustrated impotence of the Luddites, who had smashed the new machines that displaced them in early nineteenth-century Britain. The absence of an economic weapon like the strike, he added, "makes the Negro so dependent upon government help in achieving his objectives in housing, education, and job training."[17]

In 1968, after Johnson's National Advisory Commission on Civil Disorders made its report, Niebuhr observed: "The riots occurred after the Supreme Court school integration decision of 1954 and the Civil Rights Act of 1964 had corrected the most obvious injustices from which the Negro minority suffered." The commission's report, he noted, pointed to some less obvious facts: the high percentage of illiteracy and of dropouts from high school and college among blacks, the much higher rate of unemployment among them as compared with whites, and the lower median wage among employed blacks. It further established "a natural relation between narcotic addiction and crime and the unemployment of school dropouts" and "the vicious circle of poverty, poor housing, unemployment, and underemployment." The report showed that "our Negro minority is so deeply mired in poverty that it cannot escape without the help of government." It was important, Niebuhr went on to say, to view this problem in historical perspective. After the Civil War "the freed slaves were given no livelihood in land ownership nor opportunity to exercise a craft" but "were reduced to the status of debt-ridden sharecroppers on the former plantations." That legacy, he held, compounded by Jim Crow laws, contributed to the injustice which the nation tardily sought to rectify. Niebuhr suggested, as a further national measure, "a system of scholarships for college students whose parents fall below the minimal poverty line and who show promise of intellectual leadership in the arts, in science, and in public life." In conclusion, he stated that "our debt to our Negro minority is immense and obvious, and its burden lies heavy upon our consciences."[18]

CATHOLICISM AND PROTESTANTISM IN TRANSITION

By the mid-1960s significant changes occurred in the religious communities whose life and thought Niebuhr had long stirred or observed as friendly critic and prophetic spirit. Especially was this so in the Roman Catholic Church in the wake of Vatican II, the council called by Pope John XXIII which opened a new era in Catholic-Protestant relations and in other ways transformed the Tridentine traditions to which Pope Pius XII had held fast through the previous two decades. The relations of Protestants to Roman Catholics in America had for years been strained by Catholic opposition to community funding of birth control clinics, by Protestant opposition to federal aid for parochial schools, by Pius XII's invoking the doctrine of papal infallibility when dogmatizing in 1950 Mary's bodily ascension into heaven, and by the persistence of an official Catholic attitude accepting religious pluralism on grounds of expediency rather than of principle. Niebuhr had addressed those issues, criticizing the Roman Church's tendency to be too sure of its truth and calling for better mutual understanding between Protestants and Catholics. In 1953, he suggested establishing "methods of intercourse through which Protestants might learn to appreciate the Catholic Church as a religious community with a treasure of graces of the spirit, and Catholics might know Protestant Churches as religious communities with a common treasury of faith."[19]

On the eve of Vatican II in 1962, Niebuhr, writing in *Atlantic Monthly*, refuted some misconceptions of Catholicism among those outside it. The Church of Rome, he pointed out, was not alien to the American democratic ethos, even though it maintained its unity through a hierarchy with its apex in the papacy, nor was it socially reactionary, but had promoted standards of justice in modern society since Pope Leo XIII's encyclical *Rerum novarum*. Furthermore, he continued, its transnational character did not involve loyalty to a foreign sovereign, for the papacy's medieval status as the arbiter of European politics had long since been transmuted into the embodiment of authority for a universal religious community, with its temporal dominion confined to Vatican City. The elimination of misconceptions about the Roman Catholic Church, Niebuhr went on to say, will not resolve tensions arising from the ultimacy of its claims as a historical institution, which children of both the Renaissance and the Reformation continued to regard as pretentious, and recent popes had increased the tension by lifting the Virgin Mary virtually into the Godhead. There was another source of tension between Catholicism and modern society:

> Among the causes of friction on moral issues, the Catholic prohibition on contraception is most serious, and bound to become more serious as the weight of our responsibility for raising the living standards of the

undeveloped nations grows and we find ourselves frustrated when rising birth rates threaten to undo all advances in the conquest of nature. Here even the friendliest critic of the Church is bound to observe that the Church is caught with the most naturalistic and inflexible part of its natural-law theory.

In the same piece, Niebuhr reiterated his long support of fringe benefits for parochial schools—buses, lunches, nonreligious textbooks, and low-interest loans—in any program of federal school aid, since "the Catholic minority feels itself aggrieved by the issue of a double taxation," but continued to oppose direct tax support of such schools as inviting in so pluralistic a nation as America "the confusion of a proliferation of tax-supported schools for all the sects of Christendom."[20]

When Pope John XXIII issued his famous encyclical *Pacem in terris* in the spring of 1963, Niebuhr commented that it was "an added evidence of a very creative pontificate already marked by the formidable encyclical *Mater et magistra* and the convening of the Second Vatican Council." The significance of *Pacem in terris* was, in his view, its weaving modern "natural rights" theory together with traditional "natural law" theory, affirming that rights imply duties and duties rights, including those of conscience, emigration, just wage, women in the community, racial minorities, poor nations in need of help from wealthy ones, and political participation. Such a document, he suggested, was valuable to statesmen "as a prod rather than as a guide," for it spoke of the human community somewhat too idealistically without taking into account, as in Augustine's criticism of Cicero's universalism, of the reality that "mankind is divided by a multitude of languages, customs, traditions, and parochial loyalties." In the same spirit, John XXIII advocated disarmament without considering the immediate problems of security on both sides of the Cold War, and tended to overestimate the capacity of the United Nations to safeguard human rights. "The encyclical," Niebuhr stated, "is thoroughly modern in many ways, but particularly in breathing a Pelagian, rather than an Augustinian, spirit." Yet its "eloquent advocacy of natural rights" was a welcome corrective to some tendencies within Catholicism.[21]

As Vatican II progressed from its first session in 1962 to its fourth in 1965, and Pope Paul VI succeeded John XXIII, Niebuhr noted the tensions between those, chiefly the hierarchy of Italy and Spain and the Curia in Rome, who remained medieval in outlook, and the "transalpine" bishops and archbishops of the Western world and of Asia and Africa, who were engaged in dialogue with Christians and others outside the Catholic fold. On the Council's agenda of *aggiornamento*, or bringing up to date of the church, was a proposed declaration on religious liberty, promoted by the respected American Jesuit scholar John Courtney Murray, who often engaged in dialogues with Niebuhr and argued at Vatican II for freedom of conscience on principle in a pluralistic modern world. Amidst mounting concern that the Council might avoid acting on the declaration, opposed by the papal Curia, Niebuhr wrote early in 1965 that "the issue must finally be resolved, and not shelved, in the fourth session, for the whole world will regard this issue as a test of the good faith of Pope and church." Months later Vatican II approved that important declaration. Looking back on the more open, more tolerant, more creative Catholicism that emerged from the historic Council, Niebuhr wrote four years later that "a proper ecumenical approach is to regard the polemics of the sixteenth century as historically instructive, but not as definitive for . . . our century."[22]

On the Protestant scene, meanwhile, the theological milieu variously shaped by Niebuhr, Barth, Brunner, and Tillich, and latterly by Bonhoeffer and Bultmann, persisted until the mid-1960s. Tillich, who spent his final years at the University of Chicago Divinity School until his death in 1965, enjoyed growing eminence in his adopted country. Barth's influence in America, however, remained quite limited, and Niebuhr continued to criticize his expounding biblical themes without offering adequate guidance for political decisions. As he put it in 1960:

> Interpreting everything in terms of the radical newness of the event of Christ and the hope of his Second Coming, Barth disavowed all sources of discriminate judgments not found in Scripture and counseled Christians to make their judgments not in terms of systems or ideologies but by looking at each new event in the light of the revelation in Christ.

The Swiss theologian had initiated "a creative religious movement" enabling the church "to speak a word of judgment to the pretensions of nations, cultures, and civilizations," but in social ethics "has become irrelevant to all Christians in the Western world who believe in accepting common and collective responsibilities without illusions and without despair." A year or so later a former student of Niebuhr, Donald Scruggs, participating in the World Council of Churches' Ecumenical Institute, attended a seminar that Barth held in a coffee place at Céligny on Lake Geneva. Barth, he recalled, sensed that he had studied under Niebuhr, remarking, "Niebuhr's students always ask the same and the best questions. Why do you always ask these questions?" "Because," Scruggs replied, "you don't give good enough answers." Barth laughed and admitted that Niebuhr had made telling criticisms of his ethics.[23]

Niebuhr had more in common with Emil Brunner, as he acknowledged from time to time, stating in 1956 that "Brunner's whole theological position is close to mine." In 1962 he contributed to a symposium on Brunner's thought, by then presented in a three-volume *Systematic Theology*. Brunner's *The Divine Imperative*, he wrote, "was the first, and in my opinion still the best exposition of a social ethic from the standpoint of a Reformation theology which disavows the Biblicist tendencies of some so-called neo-othodoxy to derive all moral and social standards purely from Scripture." It provided "many fresh insights into the intricacies of community life and the life of the Christian by applying Reformation principles to modern problems." By way of criticism, Niebuhr opined that Brunner made too much of the Lutheran concept of *Schöpfungsordnung*, or "order of creation," as the foundation for social life without due emphasis on the need for creative schemes of justice to modify natural inequalities. Declaring that "Brunner has been one of the seminal theologians of our generation," he acknowledged "the debt we all owe to him, particularly the Protestants of the Anglo-Saxon world who have always found his exposition of Reformation theology so much more sympathetic and relevant than any other version of . . . 'neo-orthodoxy.' " Brunner, long a major influence on the American Protestant community, died in Zurich four years later. A year earlier, in 1965, Martin Buber, whose work had long impressed both Brunner and Niebuhr, died at an advanced age in Israel, where he had lived since fleeing Nazi persecution in central Europe. Buber's death occasioned Niebuhr's reflections on such memorable works as *The Prophetic Faith*, his "great book on the prophets of Israel," and *I and Thou*, eloquently expounding "his theory that selves can realize themselves only in dialogue and in relations with other selves." The latter "corrected the individualistic existentialism of Kierkegaard." The great Jewish thinker was, for Niebuhr, a creative spirit who perceived "a dimension of depth in all personal encounters" and thus contributed "to both religious and psychiatric counseling."[24]

Theology, in the American Protestant churches, was then as always a subject of discourse in the seminaries and of pursuit in the pastor's study of local churches, mediated to laity in sermons. There was also a more practical side of church ministry on which Niebuhr commented in 1962:

> Fortunately hundreds of pastors in cities, towns, and villages live their lives and exercise their ministries in a spirit of humility and integrity while serving the people in the ordinary relations of life: visiting the sick and dying, healing animosities between and within families, guiding young life, and comforting declining life. In all these pastoral duties a compassionate heart will show forth the spirit of Christ and save the church from triviality.

In the same year the Supreme Court provoked a furor by ruling against the Regents' Prayer used in the schools of New York State. Niebuhr, pointing out that participation was voluntary and its content was reverent but nonsectarian, criticized the Court's decision as "an instance of using a meat ax for solving a delicate problem." He added, however, that it was "not as important as it seems at the moment because the religious substance of our culture will be preserved not by a Regents' Prayer, but by the creative relation of religious piety to the individual and common problems of our daily life." By 1963 most Protestant churches were deeply involved in the civil rights movement. Robert W. Spike, a pastor of the United Church of Christ who served with Niebuhr on the editorial board of *Christianity and Crisis*, became director of the National Council of Churches' Commission on Religion and Race. Joined by Catholic and Jewish groups, he led Protestant clergy and lay people in the March on Washington in August of that year, and in a gathering on Capitol Hill in support of the pending civil rights bill in May of 1964. "It was necessary and inevitable," Niebuhr wrote, "that this united witness should have been mounted, both to influence the mood and conscience of the nation, and to give testimony to the common moral substance of three divided faiths."[25]

In 1965 statistics gathered by the National Council of Churches showed a slight decline in church membership—from 63.6 to 63.4 percent of the American population—which subsequent years proved to be the beginning of a long trend among the traditional Protestant churches, accompanied by the growth of evangelical and fundamentalist churches and of Eastern cults in the United States. Niebuhr commented that the decline "reveals a break in the formerly ascending curve, which brought religious affiliation up from only 16 percent of the population in 1850 to 49 percent in 1940, with the recent remarkable postwar increase bringing it above 63 percent." Its causes, he suggested, might be any or a combination of four:

> Perhaps some Americans wanted easier solutions than Christianity provides. . . . Perhaps some people touched only the shallows of religion, and found it inadequate, without ever realizing its full dimensions. Perhaps the churches themselves have been superficial, preoccupied with trivia. . . . Perhaps other, substitute forms of integral community have developed—civic associations, neighborhood clubs, action groups.[26]

Meanwhile, some younger theologians began to challenge the Christian realism that Niebuhr had so persuasively expounded—notably

Harvey Cox in his utopian book *The Secular City*. Far more radical a departure was the short-lived "death of God" theology presented in such books as Thomas Altizer's *The Gospel of Christian Atheism*, which an interviewer found on Niebuhr's desk in 1966. "What do you think of the 'death of God' theologians?" Niebuhr was asked. "I think," he replied, "they are stupid." Those radical theologians, he went on to say, "don't realize that all religious convictions and affirmations are symbolic" and "are for doing away with the schemes of meaning" expressed by symbols and "put nothing in their place." Elaborating in an essay of that year, Niebuhr wrote:

> Religious affirmations avail themselves of symbols and myths, which express both trust in the meaning of life and an awareness of the mystery of the unknowable that surrounds every realm of meaning. . . . Religious faith posits not only a mysterious creator God but a mysterious divine providence, which somehow brings unity into the incoherences and incongruities of man's individual and collective history; but only symbolic statements are possible. . . . Such faith is bound to be expressed in symbolic and prescientific terms. . . . Yet such naïve notions as providence and creation . . . derive their permanent relevance because they express a basic trust in the meaningfulness of human existence. The Book of Job is the most striking statement of this trust, which is affirmed despite, and because of, the experience of confusion, cross-purposes, and meaninglessness in human life. Religious faith is permanently valid, despite the discredit it suffers, because of its trust that the incoherences of nature and history are finally overcome in a transcendent order.[27]

DYNAMICS AND ENIGMAS OF HUMAN EXISTENCE

After retiring from the faculty of Union Theological Seminary, Reinhold Niebuhr became a visiting professor at various institutions, including Harvard University during the academic year 1961–62. There, while teaching a course at the Divinity School and lecturing in the Department of Government, he collaborated with Alan Heimert in writing *A Nation So Conceived: Reflections on the History of America from Its Early Visions to Its Present Power*, treating the national quest for identity and unity through social ferment and growing world responsibility. Another book coming out of his year at Harvard was *The Democratic Experience: Past and Prospects*, a discussion of the tortuous rise of democracy in the West and its uncertain future in other parts of the world—a book not published until 1969, with Paul Sigmund as coauthor responsible for its chapters on the politics of Africa, the Mideast, Latin America, and Asia. Though well done and useful, neither of those books caught the interest of reviewers, perhaps because their historical substance did not have enough of Niebuhr in it. From the fall of 1963 through the spring of 1968 Niebuhr taught a series of advanced, wide-ranging seminars as Charles A. Briggs Graduate Professor Emeritus of Ethics and Theology at Union, attended by scholars of neighboring universities as well as of the seminary. He was assisted during most semesters by Ronald H. Stone, a bright young graduate student who had come to his attention. Questions posed by Stone early in those seminars stimulated Niebuhr to write a refined and revised statement of his "realism" as part of the final book in the lasting corpus of his work, published late in 1965 as *Man's Nature and His Communities,* with the subtitle *Essays on the Dynamics and Enigmas of Man's Personal and Social Existence.*[28]

The double purpose of the book, a slender volume, was, in Niebuhr's words, "to summarize and to revise previously held opinions." In its title essay he surveyed political theories over the centuries and found many of them one-sided:

> The most consistent theories, whether realist or idealist, of political behavior fail to observe the intricate relation between the creative and disruptive tendencies of human freedom. The realists are inclined to obscure the residual moral and social sense even in the most self-regarding men and nations. The idealists of both religious and secular persuasion are inclined to obscure the residual individual and collective self-regard either in the "saved" or in the rational individuals and groups.

Thus Cicero's idealistic picture of Roman law missed the elements of power, while Augustine's realism focused too much on contending forces; and Machiavelli cynically championed the interests of Italian city-states, while Locke expressed a rational idealism that failed to take account of traditions and interests in British history. Against the Lockean view, Burke "provided a more adequate analysis both of human nature and of political community." In America, Madison, unlike Jefferson, "was governed by a basic insight of political realism, namely the 'intimate relation' between reason and self-love" and thus "wisely realized that the price of liberty was the free play of interests in collective terms." Christian realism, Niebuhr stated, "holds that human nature contains both self-regarding and social impulses and that the former is stronger than the latter." Its social impulses, however, must receive due recognition in an adequate, moderate realism, for democratic politics involved "not only contests of interest and power, but the rational engagement and enlargement of a native sympathy, a sense of justice, a residual moral integrity, and a sense of the common good in all classes of society." In international politics, such a realism points to a conception of the "national interest" in which not only are power impulses understood but "a web of mutual and universal and general interests is discovered in which the national interests are inextricably related."[29]

Elsewhere in the volume Niebuhr amended a few theological statements and positions he had taken earlier. He regretted that in his Gifford Lectures traditional terminology "prompted me to define the persistence and universality of man's self-regard as 'original sin.' " Though "historically and symbolically correct," that was a "pedagogical error," because moderns associate the term with an ancient legend without understanding the truth expressed in the myth of Adam's fall. Niebuhr also, enlarging upon a subordinate note of his previous thought, placed a bit more emphasis on "common grace"—as distinguished from "saving grace"—in freeing the individual for self-giving in place of undue self-regard. Saving grace had long "meant an ultimate redemption from self-regard by the infusion, sacramental or evangelical or experiential, of divine grace into the dynamics of human selfhood." Common grace, on the other hand, is "mediated through the security of parental affection, or the self-forgetfulness prompted by a crisis, or the pull of the exercise of creative capacities or of responsibilities and loyalties to a cause greater than the self, all of which are the daily experiences of mankind." Impressed by the insights of Erik Erikson, whom he knew through books and personal conversations, Niebuhr wrote that "the community, chiefly the family in the infancy of the self, is the primary source of the self's security which enables the self to love and relate its life to others." Civic and cultural communities, he added, also can make the self secure for fulfillment through self-giving. Saving grace remained an important concept because it contains truth "revealed in genuine evangelical experience in which the self apprehends a larger system of loyalty and meaning than the common loyalties and commitments which are the stuff of common grace."[30]

Niebuhr dedicated the book "To Ursula, for many reasons," explaining in his introduction that it dealt with problems "we have discussed together and in which we have had parallel interests," and that, though published under his name, it was a work of "joint authorship." Among reviewers, Gordon Harlan, who five years earlier had published a book on Niebuhr's thought, wrote that the title essay was "a remarkably packed and perceptive analysis" which "demonstrates again Niebuhr's capacity to penetrate to the core of diverse traditions and movements and to interpret their operative concepts with great clarity." Political scientist René de Visme Williamson, on the other hand, found the book a disappointing "retreat in content and quality" from the heights of *The Nature and Destiny of Man*. In his estimation Niebuhr, in treating the subject of sin, had "downgraded the very thing which has been his life's work's outstanding and distinctive contribution, namely: the theological dimension." Roger Shinn, however, who had joined the faculty of Union Seminary six years earlier, wrote: "He questions his own past use of the symbol of 'original sin.' But—lest anyone think he is getting tame—he quickly reaffirms the reality to which the symbol points." The book, Shinn held, contained "changes of nuance rather than of basic direction and method"; it was "a precious and gallant gift to those who want to understand the human condition."[31]

A MISGUIDED VENTURE IN SOUTHEAST ASIA

The year 1965 marked a fateful turning point in America's engagement in the long civil war between Communist and anti-Communist forces in Vietnam, and the result transformed the hopeful national consensus of the Kennedy and early Johnson years into one of dissension, of bitter disillusionment, and of massive rebellion among draft-age youth on the nation's college and university campuses. Niebuhr had warned repeatedly during the 1950s against U.S. military involvement in that Southeast Asian nation, partitioned since 1954 into a Communist-governed North and a U.S.-aided South. In 1962 he had written:

> The political situation is . . . so serious, indeed, that the question must be raised whether it has not been a mistake to commit our prestige unqualifiedly to the defense of this nation. President Ngo Dinh Diem of South Vietnam had some early success in consolidating the economic life of his half of the nation and in settling refugees from the North. But his government has become increasingly corrupt and repressive.

The Diem regime, he commented a year later, "has not invested its struggle with communism with sufficient moral substance to gain the loyalty of either the peasants or of some of the patriotic officers of the army." After Diem was overthrown in a military coup in the fall of 1963, Niebuhr noted months later that the ruling junta had so far failed to rally the peasants of South Vietnam. In 1964 Niebuhr supported continuation of a limited U.S. commitment to assist, with economic aid and military advisers, the Saigon government's struggle against Communist insurgency, but he opposed carrying the war to North Vietnam. As to the possibility of abandoning all of Indochina to Communism, he wrote: "In the end, we must debate and decide about the conflicting demands of prestige and strategy in a part of the world in which our form of government is not immediately viable and also not obviously imperiled."[32]

It was in February of 1965 that President Johnson, responding to the persisting instability of the Saigon regime and an attack on U.S. personnel, began to escalate American participation in the war by ordering the bombing of targets in North Vietnam. Niebuhr wrote:

> The retaliatory air strikes may indeed have proved our resolution. But in a military sense they showed only that we have superiority in the air—and thus at least a balance against increasing Communist superiority on the ground. In short, we seem clearly bogged down in a war which neither side can win.

As Johnson transformed the U.S. role in Vietnam into an open-ended military commitment, with troop deployments as well as bombing raids, Niebuhr was joined in sharp criticism of his policy by Walter Lippmann among the columnists, J. William Fulbright in the Senate, and Hans Morgenthau at the University of Chicago. Previous Presidents had supported non-Communist forces in Vietnam, but on a quite limited scale. As Niebuhr wrote in the fall of 1965:

> The origins of our dubious Vietnamese venture were not of the present Administration's contriving; but the Marine landings, the bombing of North Vietnam, and the military build-up with attendant high draft recruitment are distinctly Lyndon Johnson's policies. . . . Journalists, academics, and senators have had their doubts about our undeclared Asian war, but the Johnson prestige has either quieted or dulled their outcry.[33]

In an interview for the *New Republic* early in 1966, he stated:

> There is no alternative to making South Vietnam an American colony if we persist in our military escalation. We might, however, choose a different locus for our military might, perhaps Thailand or even the Philippines. If we take our stand there, we will at least be assured of . . . the moral support of other nations who are not impressed by our pretense of the defense of the right of self-determination in military actions which spell physical ruin to a nation which we are claiming to defend.

It was part of Niebuhr's argument that the jungles and rice paddies of Vietnam were not vital to the non-Communist cause, and that Ho Chi Minh's guerilla forces did not pose a menace on the scale of Hitler's

Germany or of Communism in Stalin's time. Dean Rusk, Johnson's Secretary of State, he wrote, "has ignored relevant contemporary facts in his constant reiteration that the only way to ensure peace is to resist aggression"—an argument reinforced by Rusk's "explicit analogies with Nazi aggression, thus equating criticism of the war in Vietnam with appeasement on the order of Munich." It was also misleading, Niebuhr held, to warn of the "international Communist conspiracy" without recognizing "that Russia and China are now mortal enemies and that Russia is, at least implicitly, a partner with us in the precarious nuclear peace."[34]

Christianity and Crisis, founded in support of the war against Nazism, came out against Americanization of the war in Vietnam, Niebuhr himself taking the lead. On February 25, 1966, the journal—which then had over ten thousand subscribers—celebrated its twenty-fifth anniversary with a colloquium at Riverside Church, to which notable panelists and speakers were invited. Walter Lippmann, who read its pages regularly, donated for the occasion a $5,000 Family of Man award he had recently received. In the evening of that snow-blanketed day the church's South Hall was packed as Vice President Hubert Humphrey and Professor Hans Morgenthau paid tribute to the journal and especially to Niebuhr, who did not attend the affair because of ill health. Humphrey, who had just completed a long, global trip, visited the Niebuhrs beforehand. Then, speaking at length, he opened his remarks thus: "We all know that to speak of *Christianity and Crisis* is to speak of Reinhold Niebuhr, our good friend. It is with this deep sense of privilege and humility that I join this very distinguished assemblage tonight in honoring one of America's and, I think, one of the world's most profound political philosophers, scholars, theologians, and prophets." Niebuhr, he went on to say, "showed how to combine decisive action with a sensitive knowledge of the complexity of life, including politics." In books and articles, "Reinie has hammered away at this basic theme: 'Man's capacity for justice makes democracy possible, but man's inclination to injustice makes democracy necessary.' " He "has contributed to American life and thought because he has been a realist without despair, an idealist without illusion." Testifying to Niebuhr's impact on his own generation in the 1940s and 1950s, Humphrey said that his wisdom was needed by young social activists of the 1960s, lest they miss "the vital need for self-criticism" and "picture what ought to be without enough attention to what can be."[35]

Humphrey's speech at the anniversary banquet was politely received even though most of the audience had reservations about his public stand in support of America's role in the Vietnam War. His own views had, in fact, paralleled Niebuhr's through 1965, his first year as Vice President, when he dissented from Johnson's decision to bomb North Vietnam but felt that his office required public acceptance of a policy with which he disagreed. It was, as Humphrey later explained in his memoirs, a trip to Vietnam early in 1966 that persuaded him that the administration's policy was sound, and another late in 1967 that convinced him it was not working. Niebuhr, meanwhile, continued to criticize Johnson's policy, pointing to evidence that most South Vietnamese peasants did not support the Saigon regime of Marshall Ky but were neutral or covert allies of the Vietcong guerillas, and that bombing the North was not achieving its goal of stopping the flow of men and supplies to the South. He joined others in protesting the use of chemical warfare in defoliating forests and spoiling crops of the enemy. American public opinion, Niebuhr observed in the fall of 1966, was beginning to turn against the war, for "its horrendous realities are daily reported on our television screens" and "the casualties are mounting."[36]

The year 1967 was a time of divisive national debate, as the number of American troops sent to Vietnam approached half a million and the bombing was intensified and enlarged to include economic as well as military targets in the North. Niebuhr probed the reasons for such a vast undertaking:

> The most obvious motivating forces must have been the unconscious concern of the people for the pride and prestige of their imperial nation, and the unconfessed identical concern of our political leaders. To these one has to add some vague residual fear of Communism which ignores the recent developments that have disintegrated the Communist monolith.

In a letter of March to the *New York Times*, he concluded that the "only hope of getting out" of the civil war in Vietnam "is a rising reaction in Congress and the public against these abhorrent policies." A month later, in a foreword to a volume of addresses on the war that had been given at Riverside Church by Martin Luther King, John C. Bennett, Henry Steele Commager, and Abraham Heschel, he invoked a phrase of Denis Brogan: "Some of our citizens regard our involvement as an expression of our sense of responsibility, but we are among those who regard it as an example of the 'illusion of American omnipotence.' " In the spring Niebuhr also wrote a dust-jacket blurb for Theodore Draper's *Abuse of Power*, a penetrating account of how America became tangled in the Vietnam conflict: "This documented and responsible indictment of American policy is invaluable for all citizens who are increasingly apprehensive about our tragic involvement in a civil war in an obscure nation in Southeast Asia, which is costing billions of dollars and thousands of American soldiers' lives." When Americans for Democratic Action in April called for a bombing halt, a truce, and a negotiated settlement, he wrote William Scarlett: "I am as glad as you are about the ADA position on Vietnam." Writing Scarlett again in July, Niebuhr stated: "Johnson had a brilliant domestic record, but I think his foreign policy is for the birds."[37]

The massive American involvement in the Vietnam War, meanwhile, drew increasing criticism and demonstrations at home, and passed a turning point early in 1968, when the Vietcong guerilla forces launched their Tet offensive, attacking Saigon, Hue, and other cities with mortars and artillery fire and retreating only after heavy fighting costly in American as well as Vietnamese lives. "The Saigon command was taken by surprise," Niebuhr wrote, "but our surprise was the greater because our military brass had given us to understand that the Communist forces were really spent and would be finished in two years." In the midst of this blow, the total number of American lives lost rose to twenty thousand. Soon thereafter Senator Eugene McCarthy, campaigning against the war, did so well in the New Hampshire primary that Johnson announced he would not seek reelection. McCarthy's strong showing, Niebuhr commented, was "a real ray of hope." After negotiations for peace began in Paris, Niebuhr wrote in the summer of 1968 that "a dwarf nation like Vietnam is so intractable in accommodating a giant nation like the United States with an honorable peace because it shrewdly suspects the November elections will reveal that the giant nation is sick of this costly war, which the dwarf nation, fighting for Communist-inspired 'national liberation,' is quite prepared to continue." It was not McCarthy but Humphrey whom the Democrats nominated to run against Richard Nixon in the fall election. As Humphrey broke with Johnson on terms for peace in Vietnam, Niebuhr wrote William Scarlett in October: "I am afraid that HHH, who is getting better all the time, will not get over the handicap of the LBJ albatross." After Humphrey lost narrowly to Nixon, Niebuhr again wrote Scarlett, finding consolation in Republican responsibility for liquidating a war which could only end on terms favorable to the Vietnamese Communists: "It's just as well that the G.O.P. must accept this peace. If the Democrats had the responsibility for the peace, we would have heard much about their being 'soft on Communism.' " Meanwhile, Niebuhr added, "we are stuck with Nixon."[38]

Early in 1969, after President Nixon's inauguration, Ronald Stone journeyed to Stockbridge—where the Niebuhrs had recently moved from their apartment in Manhattan, to reside in the house where they had summered before—to interview Reinhold for *Christianity and Crisis*. Stone put this to him: "Dr. Niebuhr, a question that many are asking is why some of you scholars who identify yourselves as political realists, such as Hans Morgenthau and yourself, have so vigorously opposed the Vietnam War, while others who consider themselves political realists have in principle supported the Vietnam struggle. Does this mean that political realism is not immediately relevant to policy?" Niebuhr replied:

> I wouldn't say "not immediately relevant to policy," but let us be clear that realism means particularly one thing, that you establish the common good not purely by unselfishness but by the restraint of selfishness. That's realism. Now, on the basis of this realism you have all kinds of contingent facts which one man will see one way and one the other way. . . . Some of the people that believed in the Vietnam War thought this was a matter of world responsibility. Some of the people that did not believe in Vietnam . . . said that it was a futile gesture.
>
> And incidentally, somebody ought to quote Aristotle on the standards of a just war. One of the standards of a just war is that it must have a good prospect of success. This is very cynical, but the Vietnam War failed to meet this test. And second, the means must be proportionate to the ends. Well, the means were *not* proportionate to the ends, either in blood or in money, in Vietnam.[39]

Nixon, meanwhile, began slowly to reduce American troop commitments in Vietnam while equipping the poorly led South Vietnamese army to take over the burden of fighting—a process that prolonged the U.S. military role there for four more years. The nation's continued engagement in a war not declared by Congress prompted Niebuhr to complain in 1970 that "our 'elected monarchs,' our Presidents, have become too powerful." In the spring of that year Nixon ordered attacks on Communist targets in the Cambodian jungle, provoking a furor at home and demonstrations on college and university campuses across America. Niebuhr commented: "Long since alienated by the futile, bloody, and costly conflict that has prevented the nation from addressing its human needs, students were newly incensed when a President ostensibly elected to end the war extended it into Cambodia." While sympathizing with such protests, however, he was critical of those who "engage in violence of every kind, from the occupation of college buildings to arson against ROTC headquarters to battles with policemen." Such behavior, "induced by a combination of self-righteous perfectionism and a sense of impotence," could only "complicate rather than cure the problem which prompted it."[40]

THE WORLD IN THE LATER 1960S

While the Vietnam War dominated the news and public debate in America for some years after the escalation in 1965, important developments occurred elsewhere during the same period, and Niebuhr commented on them. In April of 1965 Johnson ordered the Marines into the Dominican Republic, where reformist and right-wing forces had been contending for power after assassination ended Trujillo's long despotic rule in 1961. His hasty action, based on inaccurate reports of an imminent Communist takeover, provoked a storm of criticism throughout Latin America. "The President," wrote Niebuhr, "thought it so important to prevent the establishment of a new Castroite government in the Caribbean that he did not take the time to consult with the Organization of American States (OAS), which body alone could have invested our force with moral authority." The show of force, he continued, "certainly has not endeared us to our Latin American neighbors" and was especially resented in the Dominican Republic, as seen in the protest of its erstwhile leader Juan Bosch, whom he quoted: "We are not a colony but an independent nation, and you have twice violated our sovereignty." Niebuhr wrote further:

> The combination of pride of power and pride of virtue is a very dangerous one. Most of the errors in the foreign policy of the Johnson administration are derived from its uncritical acceptance of this conjunction of power and virtue. Two examples of current policies—in Southeast Asia and the Dominican Republic—illustrate the point.[41]

In July of the same year Adlai Stevenson, who had served since 1961 as United States ambassador at the United Nations, died suddenly in London. Niebuhr, who had twice supported him for President, wrote in tribute that Stevenson's voice "had given the wings of rare eloquence, spiced with wit, to the spiritual and intellectual endowments of a leader who had meditated long and wisely on the problems raised by America's becoming a hegemonous power in a nuclear age, and on the domestic problems of a technological nation." He continued:

> Adlai Stevenson could not present ultimate answers to the vexing problems of a powerful, but perplexed, nation. In fact, he was modest enough to suggest only proximate solutions. His modesty and his freedom from political clichés and grand slogans were characteristics that endeared him to thoughtful citizens, who had grown cynical about the sweeping promises of politicians. . . . As a candidate he won the solid affection of millions of Americans, and his popularity in Europe was phenomenal. . . . In Stevenson's second career as U.S. ambassador to the United Nations, he made

brilliant use of his endowments as a tribune not only of our nation but also of the hopes and yearnings of all the nations coming to birth.

Worldwide grief over his death indicated an awareness that "we have parted not so much with a wielder of power as with a noble soul who prompted and expressed the highest aspirations of enlightened peoples."[42]

Events of the 1960s confirmed doubts about prospects for democracy in much of Asia and Africa. Niebuhr observed in 1966 that in many nascent nations of those continents the military, above subnational loyalties and skeptical of Communism, had a role to play in the absence of democratic traditions. In Indonesia, for instance, an army coup of that year routed Communist infiltrators and produced administrative reform, replacing Sukarno with Suharto as head of state. "Sukarno's dependence on Chinese Communism," he wrote, "and his fiscal irresponsibility . . . prompted the army to revolt." General Suharto acted shrewdly without challenging Sukarno's "immense prestige as superb demagogue and father of his country." Similarly in the Congo, "General Mobutu took the reins of authority" in a nation "riven with strife among its numerous tribes and regions."[43]

Another development was the six-day war, in June of 1967, between Israel and its Arab neighbors, resulting in the expansion of Israel's borders to include the Sinai, the Gaza Strip, the West Bank of the Jordan, the Golan Heights, and all of Jerusalem. Niebuhr commented:

> No simile better fits the war . . . than the legend of David and Goliath. David, of course, is little Israel, numbering less than 2.5 million souls. . . . Goliath, of course, is the Arab world under Egyptian president Gamal Abdul Nasser's leadership, numbering a population of 20 to 40 million. This Goliath never accepted Israel's existence as a nation or granted it the right of survival.

Nasser, he pointed out, mounted his troops on the border after inducing the U.N. to withdraw its long-standing peacekeeping force from the area, and then blockaded a port on the Gulf of Aqaba vital to Israel's economy. So it was that "Israeli troops, tanks, and aircraft struck the first blow" and "gained astounding victories," for "a nation that knows it is in danger of strangulation will use its fists." Niebuhr added:

> There remains, of course, the awful problem of reconciliation between Jew and Arab and the building of a more viable coexistence between these two peoples. Though "cousins," the one is just emerging from its medieval past while the other, claiming its Middle Eastern homeland only two decades

ago after a diaspora of millenia, brings with it all the arts and technics of modernity.[44]

Two years later the world watched as America, in July of 1969, landed a manned spacecraft on the moon, the fruition of a long and costly program. "With all Americans," Niebuhr wrote, "I have a proper pride in the technical achievement of our first moon landing. It was a triumph of technology, teamwork, and discipline." But, he went on to say, while many had sung paeans to this technological "breakthrough," its high priority as a national goal "represents a defective sense of human values," for America in recent years had "woefully neglected" its urban centers: "They are stinking with air and water pollution. Their inner cities are decaying." A rich nation "which can afford the technical 'breakthrough' cannot offer the impoverished cities tax help to feed the hungry or educate the uneducated." Weeks later Niebuhr pointed out that Nixon drew erroneous conclusions from the feat in space:

> After the successful moon shot, the triumphant President . . . exulted: "Any culture which can put a man on the moon is capable of gathering all the nations of the earth in peace, justice, and concord." He was so persuaded by this conclusion, weighted with error, that he repeated this hope and promise in all the capitals of Asia. The error of the President has persisted in Western culture since the 18th century. Quite simply it is the error of identifying the self with the mind. When the mind considers, studies, and conquers nature, then it is pure mind. . . . But when there is the problem of relating man to man and nation to nation, then the mind becomes the servant of the self's hopes, ambitions, pride, and fears.[45]

Nixon also drew Niebuhr's strictures for initiating religious services in the East Room of the White House with a semiofficial, conformist tone lacking the prophetic quality of biblical faith. Among invited preachers, he noted, was a rabbi who declared that "in a period of great trial and tribulation the finger of God pointed to Richard Milhous Nixon, giving him the vision and wisdom to save the world." Such a practice Niebuhr compared to King Jeroboam's chapel at Bethel in ancient Israel, where the court priest Amaziah told Amos: "O thou seer, go, flee thee away into the land of Judah, and there eat bread, and prophesy there: but prophesy not again any more at Bethel: for it is the king's chapel, and it is the king's court" (Amos 7:12–13). Niebuhr continued:

> If we consult Amos as our classical type of radical nonconformist religion, we find that he, like his contemporary Isaiah, was critical of all religion that was not creative in seeking a just social policy. Their words provide a sharp

contrast with the East Room's current quasi-conformity: Thus Amos declared: "I hate, I despise your feasts, and I take no delight in your solemn assemblies. . . . But let justice roll down like waters, and righteousness like an everflowing stream." (Amos 5:21, 24)[46]

"A Prophet among Us"

Reinhold Niebuhr's stroke in his sixtieth year, from which he recovered sufficiently to work on a restricted schedule, was the first in a series that, combined with other ailments, progressively weakened his health, confining him mostly to the house at Stockbridge in his late seventies. His sister, Hulda, had died in 1959, and his brother H. Richard in 1962. It was remarkable that, suffering since the initial stroke from partial paralysis, vascular spasms, and occasional depression, Reinhold did so much— meeting classes and seminars, preaching in chapel, attending panels, and typing manuscripts with one finger. In his old age, however, his articles became fewer. The last piece published in his lifetime appeared in the *New York Times* late in 1970, after Earth Day of that year had drawn attention to growing environmental problems. Recognizing that a new crisis faced humankind as momentous as others he had addressed in the past, Niebuhr wrote: "Perhaps the most perplexing problem is the ecological one of rendering modern urban, industrial society fit for human beings, not poisoned by polluted air and water."[47]

Once during his final weeks of failing health, Niebuhr used the telephone to encourage the editors of *Christianity and Crisis* in their criticism of American policy in Southeast Asia. As reported in its pages, he spoke "with halting voice but resolute spirit." He died peacefully, in his seventy-ninth year, on June 1, 1971. Many distinguished persons and several close friends, among them William Scarlett, joined the Niebuhr family at the funeral in Stockbridge. The service was held at the town's First Congregational Church, which belonged to the United Church of Christ, the denomination of which Niebuhr's German Evangelical Synod had become a part. It was led by the Rev. T. Guthrie Speers, a friend of Niebuhr and Presbyterian clergyman in New Canaan, Connecticut; Abraham Heschel took part with a prayer, and J. Brooke Mosley, then president of Union Theological Seminary, gave the benediction.[48]

The *New York Times* ran a lengthy half-page obituary and published an editorial tribute stating that "there were few within the Protestant community who did not feel his influence, while many who shared other beliefs or rejected all religion also responded to his arguments," and that in a time of moral confusion and rapid change "he was a frequent source of political wisdom." Afterward George Kennan, calling Kenneth Thompson to ask him to write the memorial for Niebuhr in a professional publication, referred to him in a heartfelt comment as "the father of all of us." The phrase had long been widely attributed to Kennan and implied, Thompson later explained, "an intellectual tradition that Kennan and others have continued." Hubert Humphrey, back in the U.S. Senate, wrote a correspondent days after the funeral that "one of Mr. Niebuhr's greatest contributions was to bring his clear understanding of social ethics to political philosophy and political realities." Another tribute to Niebuhr soon appeared in *Christianity and Crisis*, unsigned but written by Roger Shinn, who had recently succeeded John Bennett as Reinhold Niebuhr Professor of Social Ethics at Union Seminary. It carried a biblical caption: "And whether they hear or refuse to hear . . . they will know that there has been a prophet among them" (Ezekiel 2:5). "As we celebrate the life and mourn the death of Reinhold Niebuhr," Shinn began, "the ancient words ring in our ears. We know that there has been a prophet among us. Not that he claimed the gift of prophecy. He, who knew so well the fallibility of men, brushed off flattery. His style was to risk many a judgment for which he would never claim the rubric, 'Thus saith the Lord.' Often he stated his new insights by criticizing his past errors." Niebuhr, continued Shinn, "united flashing polemic and profound piety, scintillating wit and awed reverence, spectacular intellect and deep feeling. . . . He put theology in the middle of the cultural and political world as it had not been for generations. He taught the meaning of sin and forgiveness for massive institutional behavior as well as for personal life."[49]

A few months later, on November 1, 1971, a memorial service for Reinhold Niebuhr was held at Riverside Church in Manhattan, attended by persons who came from near and far. One of them was Nathan Scott, Jr., then teaching at the University of Chicago Divinity School, who as a young man was so impressed with *Beyond Tragedy* that he went to Union Seminary to study under Niebuhr. Another was Lionel Trilling, the literary critic at Columbia University who, once asked by Scott whether Niebuhr had influenced him, replied, "We must talk about that some time." Also present was Carl Hermann Voss, long an associate of Niebuhr, who had written of "this dynamic man whose multi-faceted personality makes him beloved by many as professor, preacher, editor, author, ecumenical leader, political sage, social critic, religious guide, counselor, and friend." It was those various sides of Niebuhr that accounted for the diversity of the assemblage at Riverside Church. The most memorable address, entitled "Prophet for a Secular Age," was given by Arthur Schlesinger, Jr. "Looking back," he told the gathering, "one cannot but feel that part of Niebuhr's influence on his age was a product of his capacity to show how the most piercing contemporary insights had their precedents in historical Christianity—or, to put it in an opposite way, in his capacity to restate historical Christianity in terms that corresponded to our most searching modern themes and anxieties." Niebuhr, continued Schlesinger, "had to a rare degree the gift of political diagnosis," and "his intuitive grasp of politics and society found coherent expression in the Augustinian approach to history." He also "assimilated so much of the spirit of James—the sense, for example, of the universe as streaming, provisional, unfinished, unpredictable" and "of the relativity of human ideals and perspectives" and "of the mysteries of existence, which distinguished James so sharply from Dewey." Niebuhr, he went on to say, "was a man whose humility was not theoretical but authentic" and who "never mistook his own ideas for absolute judgments." Schlesinger remembered him "above all restlessly pacing the floor, throwing out ideas, jokes, and challenges."[50]

The service closed with a prayer prepared and delivered by John C. Bennett, who had served during the 1960s as president of Union Seminary:

"We thank thee, O God, for the illumination that has come to us from the vision and faith and intellect of our friend, Reinhold Niebuhr, illumination of thy world, of thy ways, and of ourselves. We thank thee . . . for his humility that matched his greatness, for his capacity to turn his criticism of others against himself, for his sense of humor that took a heavy solemnity from his role as prophet and judge, for his wonderful gift of friendship and for his spontaneous delight and laughter which kept his relations with all kinds of people very human.

"We thank thee for his compassion and his self-spending commitment to justice that made him the champion of oppressed people, of all who were struggling for their rights or against poverty, of all who knew the bitterness of racial or religious hostility. . . . We thank thee for the strength of his attacks on the pride and self-serving illusions, on the injustice and the cruelty of the powerful in so many situations from the early days of his ministry in Detroit to his writings in his last months of illness. . . . We thank thee for the honesty and the courage with which he faced new situations and for his refusal to be imprisoned by his own past teaching, for his leadership in new directions when he saw that the times called for them. . . .

"We thank thee for his devoted service to this seminary which was so large a part of his life, for his love of teaching, for his care for his students and for his generosity and openness of spirit among colleagues. We remember his courage and grace and constant thoughtfulness of others and his continuing achievements during many years of pain and weakness.

"We see as a gift to us the light that came from his mind and spirit and pray that it may be widely seen and known in our time of confusion, and may our hearts be sustained by the faith which sustained him and enabled him to say so often to himself and others: 'If we live, we live unto the Lord and if we die, we die unto the Lord; so then, whether we live or whether we die, we are the Lord's.' Amen."[51]

CHAPTER TEN

The Niebuhrian Legacy

At a session of the 1974 meeting of the American Political Science Association, attended by some five hundred scholars in the Grand Ballroom of the Palmer House in Chicago, Arthur Schlesinger, Jr., expressed a consensus in saying of Reinhold Niebuhr: "No one has taken his place or the role he performed from the 1930s to the 1960s." While Niebuhr long a leonine figure—was no longer present on the American religious and public scene, the prophetic and pragmatic Christian realism for which he stood had become rooted among thoughtful spirits who felt his impact during the middle decades of the century. Many were pastors of Protestant churches throughout the land or scholarly educators at denominational or interdenominational seminaries. Others were college or university professors, especially historians and political scientists, reflective writers, and figures in national politics. After Niebuhr's death some of his closest associates united to establish an annual Reinhold Niebuhr Memorial Award, with a cash prize of $5,000 to persons who exemplified his values in public life. Recipients were Willy Brandt of Germany, Theodore Hesburgh of Notre Dame, Cesar Chavez in California, and Beyers Naude, a black South African church leader. After four years, fund-raising difficulties prevented continuation. Later in the 1970s the west end of 120th Street in Manhattan on the south side of Union Theological Seminary was, on the initiative of a city councilman and other community leaders who appreciated Niebuhr's contribution to public life, named Reinhold Niebuhr Place.[1]

Among American leaders who read Niebuhr was President Jimmy Carter. Impressed by *Reinhold Niebuhr on Politics*, a systematic arrangement of his thought by political scientists Harry Davis and Robert Good, he also valued June Bingham's *Courage to Change*, underscoring in his copy of her biography of Niebuhr such quotations as "justice must be the instrument of love" and "we must never confuse our fragmentary apprehension of truth with the truth itself." Speaking at Stephens College in Missouri eleven years after leaving the White House, Carter invoked Niebuhr's ethics in support of his contention that government programs like low-rent public housing—for which funding had sharply declined since the 1960s and 1970s—are as necessary as volunteer efforts like Habitat for Humanity. It is well, he declared, "to remember what Reinhold Niebuhr said: The highest commitment of a government is justice; the highest commitment of a human being is *agapē* love."[2] Most of Niebuhr's books, meanwhile, remained in print. *The Nature and Density of Man*, his masterpiece, had long since become standard reading in many a seminary and graduate school. His thought in one or another of its aspects was the subject of a growing number of dissertations, while for countless souls who have not read his books the "Serenity Prayer" remained a devotional resource in the tribulations of life.

At the same time, however, there were signs that American religious and political life was losing the ballast Niebuhr had done much to impart. As early as the late 1960s radical social activists of the rising generation were attracted to new versions of the soft utopianism he had attacked. By the 1970s a resurgent fundamentalism and a ubiquitous secularism were growing in America at the expense of the Protestant middle he had helped to revitalize. During the 1980s right-wing ideologues successfully popularized a doctrine of economic individualism he had opposed, and treated an erstwhile Soviet adversary with self-righteous rhetoric oblivious to the universality of sin recognized in his theology. As American society careened through the 1970s and 1980s, some observers felt that Niebuhr's wisdom and insights were needed more than ever. His dialectic of Christian faith and modern culture—the synthesis of Renaissance and Reformation called for in his Gifford Lectures—was more profound than either the simple biblicism or the secular humanism prevalent in late twentieth-century America. Church assemblies and television evangelists on either side of the political spectrum often needed to be reminded that, as he had pointed out, specific political decisions usually involve complex pragmatic judgments not derived from faith. Niebuhr's Christian realism offers not a detailed agenda for public policy but certain guiding axioms still valid. One is that love and justice are complementary, implying that both government action and voluntary efforts are needed for human welfare, whether in housing, nutrition, education, or other areas. Another is that organism and artifact, best combined in the British social order, are both essential to healthy democratic communities. Other axioms concern ways of achieving a tolerable world community, including the pursuit of a concurrence of interest among nations, the use of force when necessary to counter threats to legitimate national or international interests, and the importance of meeting present exigencies without the illusion that final solutions are possible.

In the wake of Soviet withdrawal from eastern Europe and the collapse of the Communist system in Russia itself, it appeared in the 1990s that democracy might evolve in some lands long accustomed to quite different forms of government. If so, their peoples might well appropriate the wisdom found in *The Children of Light and the Children of Darkness*, Niebuhr's compact and widely translated treatise on democracy. American citizens themselves, whose republic can be gravely weakened by naive ideas, cynical attitudes, simplistic slogans, and intolerance among diverse groups, could benefit by turning anew to the same book, which impressed some of their wisest leaders of past decades and is still read in political science courses. Indeed, Niebuhr's shorter writings on various problems of American society, ranging from standards in the mass media to poverty among urban blacks, remain relevant long after the occasions of their mid-twentieth century publication.

When addressing a political public wider than the Protestant churches and seminary communities where he lectured and preached, Niebuhr usually allowed his theology to remain more or less implicit. It was most explicit in his sermons, in his two volumes of Gifford Lectures and other books such as *The Self and the Dramas of History*, in the pages of *Christianity and Crisis*, and in other journals or special lectures for a Christian audience or for one which he was asked to address theologically. As noted earlier, his theology was less complete than that of some eminent contemporaries. He elaborated systematically on sin as an existential and social reality and on grace as mediated through Christ, and as he grew older added to those motifs an appreciation of common grace through family and community, and an apprehension of mystery and meaning in the Christian experience of life and history. More biblical than Tillich but less Christocentric than Barth, Niebuhr appropriated the prophetic heritage and Pauline understanding of Christian faith and united these to the insights of modern social philosophers. He did not set forth, in the manner of Brunner or some Anglican theologians, a sustained doctrine of the church and its sacraments or of the Holy Spirit, but he did help many clergy in their vocation by publishing his *Leaves from the Notebook of a Tamed Cynic*, and offered churches his considered advice that their

Sunday worship is best served by combining good preaching with an edifying liturgy.

Reinhold Niebuhr's legacy, so multifaceted and instructive as the twentieth century draws to a close, at the same time has limitations for the era now dawning. "The truths of the Christian faith," he himself acknowledged at mid-century, "must be explicated theologically and related effectively to the problems of each age." His works can hardly be expected to offer guidance for moral issues arising from medical developments after his lifetime. Although late in life he saw air and water pollution looming ahead, he did not address the issue in detail as a problem of Christian ethics. He was critical of extravagant living standards in America at mid-century, but seems not to have anticipated impending depletion of the world's oil reserves or the potential for ecological disaster in the affluent ways of modern technical society. It remained for his successor at Union Theological Seminary, Roger Shinn, who held the Niebuhr chair in social ethics after 1970, to take up problems of the environment and natural resources in his work *Forced Options: Social Decisions for the 21st Century.* In facing these and other perplexities of the post–Cold War world, it is well to recall words that Niebuhr wrote in 1959, after years of exposing the social perils of shallow optimism about human nature and history: "But there is another danger: that, having discovered the delusion of historical progress, we shall slump into the lethargy of despair."[3]

While Niebuhr's achievement has certain limitations for the late twentieth century and after, it also has some flaws, as noted at the outset of this study. The foregoing chapters have frequently quoted him at his best, but his writings tended now and then to be repetitious, to lapse into patches of opaqueness, and to suffer from stylistic infelicities that vitiated their effectiveness on the printed page. Sometimes he used words without clear definition. Often, for example, he castigated or identified with "liberalism" without making clear that he rejected the optimistic assumptions about human nature and history with which the word "liberal" had become associated in the theology of Ritschl and the Social Gospel and in the philosophy of Dewey and other secular thinkers, but stood instead in an older liberal tradition of democratic tolerance, and supported from the 1940s onward a legacy and agenda of moderate social reform dubbed "liberal" in American political parlance. Niebuhr's grasp of the history of ideas and civilizations was remarkable, but his works do contain some generalizations a bit too sweeping and occasional inaccuracies on fine points. J. Harry Cotton, for example, in his generally favorable review of *The Self and the Dramas of History*, noted that he misquoted Kant "as saying that we ought always to treat human personality as an end and 'never' as means"; actually, Cotton pointed out, Kant "did not say 'never as means' but 'not merely as means.' "[4] Such errors seem inevitable in broad works transcending the bounds of one or two disciplines, and Niebuhr—who once called himself a "quasi-scholar"—was aware of them.

Sometimes Niebuhr overlooked merits in the traditions or books or positions he criticized, though his appreciation of them might appear elsewhere in criticism of opposing viewpoints. Like all of us, he had blind spots. In reading books he looked for certain things, at times missing an author's insights on other things. In reviewing T. S. Eliot's *The Idea of a Christian Society,* for example, Niebuhr rightly criticized its neglect of the role of pressures and counterpressures in achieving just social relations, but he overlooked other merits of the book, such as Eliot's prescient observation that unbridled capitalism was leading "to the exhaustion of natural resources," that "a good deal of our material progress is a progress for which succeeding generations may have to pay dearly," that "a wrong attitude towards nature implies, somewhere, a wrong attitude toward God," and that it would be "well for us to face the permanent conditions upon which God allows us to live upon this planet." Niebuhr, his friendliest critics agree, emphasized sin as pride too much, and sin as sloth or apathy too little, as causes of social evil. His analysis of human nature, it is now widely agreed, does not adequately describe some aspects of women's experience, but radical feminists go too far in objecting to his use of language, standard in his and earlier ages, that does not meet a subsequent standard of gender inclusiveness. Whatever shortcomings are found in the works of Reinhold Niebuhr, many will agree with his old friend Lynn Harold Hough, who long after their years together in Detroit, observed: "Certain characteristic faults of Niebuhr are so overshadowed by the genuine quality of his achievement that, like gargoyles on cathedrals, they seem almost a part of the total harmony."[5]

Niebuhrian theology and social philosophy, suffused by a modified Augustinianism and a Jamesian temperament, has at its core certain themes introduced at the beginning of this book and expounded throughout it. Interpreters differ in finding one motif or another especially profound. A tribute to Reinhold Niebuhr after his death, in the minutes of the faculty of Union Seminary, suggested that "interweaving of human activity with trust in God" is the central theme of his legacy, and closed with this passage from one of his books:

> The world community, toward which all historical forces seem to be driving us, is mankind's final possibility and impossibility. The task of achieving it

must be interpreted from the standpoint of a faith which understands the fragmentary and broken character of all historic achievements and yet has confidence in their meaning because it knows their completion to be in the hands of a Divine Power, whose resources are greater than those of men, and whose suffering love can overcome the corruptions of man's achievements, without negating the significance of our striving.[6]

Words like those reverberate from Niebuhr's age to ours and into the distant future.

APPENDIX A

A Reinhold Niebuhr Chronology

1892	Born on June 21 in Wright City, Missouri, the son of Gustav and Lydia Niebuhr
1902	Niebuhrs settled in Lincoln, Illinois, where Gustav became pastor of St. John's Church of the German Evangelical Synod
1907–10	Attended *Evangelische Pro-Seminar*, now Elmhurst College, near Chicago, graduating as valedictorian
1910–13	Attended Eden Seminary, near St. Louis, graduating as valedictorian
1913–15	Attended Yale Divinity School, receiving B.D. in 1914, and Yale University, receiving M.A. in 1915
1915	Began thirteen-year pastorate at Bethel Church in Detroit
1922	Became a regular contributor to the *Christian Century*, until 1940
1923	Traveled to Europe during the summer with a group led by Sherwood Eddy, the first of several trips to Britain and the Continent over the next three decades
1926–27	Criticized Henry Ford's treatment of his workers
1928	Joined the faculty of Union Theological Seminary in New York
1929	Selections from pastoral diary (1915–28) published as *Leaves from the Notebook of a Tamed Cynic*
1928–30	Came to a deepened appreciation of Pauline doctrine
1931	Married Ursula Keppel-Compton at Winchester Cathedral, in England, on December 22
1932	Supported Norman Thomas, the Socialist candidate, for President *Moral Man and Immoral Society*, his first major book, published
1933	Publicly deplored the Nazi regime's anti-Semitic policy
1935	Became founding editor of *Radical Religion*, renamed *Christianity and Society* five years later
1936	Began to read in earnest the works of Saint Augustine
1937	Addressed Oxford Conference on Church, Community, and State in July

	Beyond Tragedy, a volume of "sermonic essays," published
1938	Commenced writing regularly for the Nation, continuing until 1950
1939	Delivered Gifford Lectures at Edinburgh University from April 24 to May 14 and from October 11 to November 1
1940	Joined William Allen White's Committee to Defend America by Aiding the Allies
	Christianity and Power Politics, a volume of essays, published
1941	Led in founding the biweekly Christianity and Crisis
	The Nature and Destiny of Man, volume one (first series of Gifford Lectures) published
1940–43	Moving away from socialism, accepted Roosevelt's New Deal
1942	Honorary D.D. conferred by Yale
1943	The Nature and Destiny of Man, volume two (second series of Gifford Lectures) published
	Honorary D.D. conferred by Oxford
	Composed (probably at this time) "Serenity Prayer" at Heath, Massachusetts, where the Niebuhrs summered from 1932 to 1956
1944	Elected to the Philosophy Club in New York City
	Honorary D.D. conferred by Harvard
	The Children of Light and the Children of Darkness, his treatise on democracy, published
1946	Pressed for a Jewish state in Palestine, realized in 1948
1947	Cochaired founding of Americans for Democratic Action, growing out of the Union for Democratic Action he had led since 1941
	Urged support of the Marshall Plan for European economic recovery
1948	Addressed the founding assembly of the World Council of Churches in Amsterdam
1949	Supported the North Atlantic pact and served as a consultant of Kennan's Policy Planning Staff
	Faith and History published
1950	Lectured on "Augustine's Conception of Selfhood" at the Aspen Institute in July
1952	Lectured on "Christian Faith and Humanism" to guests at Union Theological Seminary in January
	Suffered a stroke in February, remaining quite ill for months
	The Irony of American History published
1953	Denounced McCarthyism
	Christian Realism and Political Problems, a volume of essays, published
1954	Became a regular contributor to the New Leader until 1970
	Called for U.S.-Soviet coexistence in a nuclear age

1955	*The Self and the Dramas of History* published
1955–57	Pointed out changes in post-Stalinist Russia, and urged restraint of American power in Asia
1957	Gave address on "The Relations of Christians and Jews in Western Civilization" at Union Seminary in February
1958	*Pious and Secular America,* a volume of essays, published
	Elected to American Academy of Arts and Letters
1959	*The Structure of Nations and Empires* published
1960	Retired from three decades of teaching at Union Seminary
1963	Pressed for civil rights legislation, enacted in 1964 and 1965
1965	Opposed escalation of U.S. military involvement in Vietnam
	Man's Nature and His Communities, his final book, published
1968	Moved with Ursula to Stockbridge, Massachusetts
1971	Died on June 1 in Stockbridge
1974	*Justice and Mercy,* a volume of sermons and prayers edited by Ursula Niebuhr, published posthumously

APPENDIX B

A Review of Literature on Reinhold Niebuhr's Life and Thought

ેૹ

During the past few decades a vast amount of literature has appeared on the life and thought of Reinhold Niebuhr—volumes of essays, book-length interpretive studies, and essays in journals that have not been gathered into books. Much of it is richly informative and insightful, much else is not, and still more imparts misinformation and misunderstanding even while it illuminates and informs. This essay is appended to the present book as a guide to, and assessment of, selected books and essays on Niebuhr. A more lengthy bibliographical essay, even a book, could and perhaps should be written to help teachers and scholars find their way through the maze of writings on his life and his contributions as theologian, social philosopher, and journalist. None of the secondary literature is a substitute for reading Reinhold Niebuhr's own books and shorter writings and listening to his recorded lectures and sermons, but few persons have time to immerse themselves in more than limited segments of this material. Studies of Niebuhr—whether primarily historical or systematic, integral or topical, introductory or critical-analytic—are indispensable for understanding the man and his thought.

The published symposium edited by Charles Kegley and Robert Bretall, *Reinhold Niebuhr: His Religious, Social, and Political Thought* (1956), briefly discussed in chapter 7, remains a landmark, with essays on varied aspects of Niebuhr's achievement by twenty distinguished contributors, followed by his reply to criticism and interpretation. Its continued value prompted publication in 1984 of a second edition, with afterwords by three of the original contributors and two new essays.[1] Among the more perceptive essays in the original volume was one, perhaps the most read and cited, by Arthur Schlesinger, Jr., "Reinhold Niebuhr's Role in American Political Thought and Life," which later appeared in Schlesinger's *The Politics of Hope* (1963). Here America's best-known historian showed how Niebuhr's "old demand for a social balance of power" in the 1930s, satisfied neither by Marxist prescriptions nor by the fusion of love and reason current in some American circles, "found its objective correlative" in the pragmatic political and economic equilibrations of the New Deal. Some years later historian William Becker, closely examining Niebuhr's half-forgotten journalistic writings of the early 1940s, argued that his conversion from socialism to Roosevelt's legacy, which Schlesinger had dated in the late 1940s, was actually complete by 1943. Since then Schlesinger has written: "I find Becker's argument about the timing of Niebuhr's conversion to the New Deal quite persuasive, so I would amend my own earlier statement on that point."[2] In his afterword for the 1984 edition of the

Kegley-Bretall volume, Schlesinger turned to Niebuhr's perspective on U.S. foreign policy since 1945, finding him essentially sound in opposing Stalinism during the early phase of the Cold War and, in *The Irony of American History* and subsequent writings of the 1950s and 1960s, "a powerful and penetrating critic" of "unnecessary excesses in the wake of a necessary defense of democratic societies."

Another perceptive essay in the same volume was that of John C. Bennett—one of several he wrote on Niebuhr over the decades, notable for their lucid and authoritative treatment. Here he traced the development of Niebuhr's social ethics from his early pacifism and socialism to his mature Christian realism, rooted in deepened theological insights and applicable to changing circumstances. He commended as representative of Niebuhr's mature ethical convictions the chapter on "The Kingdom of God and the Struggle for Justice" in *The Nature and Destiny of Man* (volume 2, chapter 9). Closing his essay with remarks differentiating Niebuhr's affinity for Burke from a typically American kind of conservatism, Bennett cited his differences with Russell Kirk on certain issues but overlooked such an appreciative passage as Niebuhr's comment in a published Harvard symposium: "Dr. Kirk is right when he calls attention to the indiscriminate character of the concept 'the American way of life' as evidence of that lack of discrimination which is so dangerous to a healthy democracy, since democracy depends upon discriminate judgment between competing values and loyalties which may be equally necessary to the community."[3] A third notable essay in the volume was one by Kenneth W. Thompson on Niebuhr as a political thinker who probed the source in human nature of the perennial power struggles in national and world politics, while recognizing love and not power as normative for humankind. Critical of Niebuhr's sometimes confusing use of terms and vagueness on practical problems of adjusting interests among groups and nations, Thompson nevertheless ranked him with Burke as a social philosopher, finding in Burke the perception that prudence is chief among the political virtues and in Niebuhr a theological understanding of politics transcending the prejudices of a scientific age. In his afterword for the 1984 edition, Thompson observed that Niebuhr's grasp of facts distinguished him from many social theorists and moralists, and that his understanding of the tension between competing principles in human affairs led him to resist the "facile slogans" of "those who saw freedom or security or justice as the controlling objective of American foreign policy." Furthermore, he noted, Niebuhr, understanding the tribulations of less-privileged people, "had sympathy for the new nations" and was not sanguine that "the American example had much relevance for the problems of the Third World."

Elsewhere in the Kegley-Bretall volume theologians illuminated other dimensions and characteristics of Niebuhr's thought. Richard Kroner, tracing its roots back through a line of Christian and humanist thinkers to the Bible and Hellenism, commented that he "adopts whatever he deems right or profound even from sources he dislikes" and "rejects whatever seems wrong or weak to him even when it comes from . . . men esteemed by him." William J. Wolf explained that Niebuhr was dialectical, not in the Hegelian sense of fusing opposites but in stating deep truths by relating seemingly contradictory aspects of reality to each other as complements. He questioned Niebuhr's claim that pride is the basic form of sin, observing that escape from the responsibilities of being human is just as common and socially consequential. Noting that Niebuhr, though commenting perceptively on the historic churches, lacked a doctrine of the church as God's redemptive instrument, Wolf cited seeds for such a doctrine in the closing chapter of *Faith and History*. Paul Lehmann pointed out the centrality of the atonement in Niebuhr's doctrine of Christ and the dialectical relation between justification and sanctification, or forgiveness and renewal, in his doctrine of grace. Taking up the question whether Niebuhr's theology was adequately trinitarian, he found it needing development, but noted a suggestive passage on the redemptive power of the Holy Spirit in history as "a radical break-through of the divine spirit through human self-sufficiency" (*Faith and History*, pp. 167–68).

Among other essays in the Kegley-Bretall volume, Emil Brunner's was discussed in chapter 4. It suffices here to mention three more. Paul Scherer, discussing Niebuhr's homiletic art, remarked that to a degree unusual among preachers he identified himself "on the spot" with points made in the pulpit. In his sermons, Scherer wrote, "the Bible comes alive," with illustrations drawn "from art and literature, but most frequently from history, philosophy, and the contemporary scene." Abraham Heschel, in a Jewish evaluation of Niebuhr, concluded: "He reminds us that evil will be conquered by the One, while he stirs us to help conquer evils one by one." Finally, Ronald H. Stone, in an essay for the enlarged edition of 1984, explored Niebuhr's adoption over the years of methods appropriate to varied challenges in racial relations and international affairs, including boycotts, study panels, legislation, use and restraint of military power, and articulate criticism of failed social philosophies. Contributors to the Kegley-Bretall volume, in short, examined Niebuhr's thought from different angles, most of them critically appreciative. Niebuhr's opening autobiographical sketch and his closing responses, accepting or rejecting various criticisms, add value and interest.

Two decades later another published symposium appeared in a volume entitled *The Legacy of Reinhold Niebuhr*, edited by Nathan Scott (1975).[4] An important supplement to Kegley-Bretall, it consisted of seven essays, including a trenchant introduction by Scott emphasizing "the great feat of imagination represented by Niebuhr's analysis of the nature of selfhood." In one of the more valuable essays, Martin Marty, surveying Niebuhr's numerous but scattered references to the American religious experience, found him more interested in transforming the Protestant churches than in reporting on them and "somewhat stereotypical" in his comments on "Protestant individualism." He pointed out that Niebuhr, without denying the special responsibilities of the churches, emerged in later years as a "public theologian" interpreting American history and engaged in the nation's affairs, and as such became a model for which he will be remembered. Niebuhr tended, indeed, to stereotype American Protestant "individualism," as noted by Marty; that faulty generalization apparently arose from his Detroit experience in the 1920s and persisted because he was unaware of the extent of his own impact on a whole generation of clergy and laity in several denominations.

In the same symposium Langdon Gilkey treated Niebuhr's theology of history in a magisterial essay expounding major motifs of his thought, and contrasting them with Pannenberg and Moltmann's future-oriented "theology of hope," which had a following by the 1970s. He showed that, while the latter claimed that God's power would overcome a sinful past in a historical future, Niebuhr "was driven to understand the Christian meaning of history in quite different terms, in terms of reconciliation and the hope of historical renewal rather than the promise of total historical fulfillment." Niebuhr, Gilkey explained, saw history as a realm in which God's providence, and grace mediated through the atonement, intermingled with human freedom to produce endless possibilities of personal and social renewal, subject to taint by the persistence and universality of sin arising, inevitably but not necessarily, in the structure of human nature. Thus for Niebuhr the significant dialectic is not temporal but vertical, between God and humanity in all ages; distinctions between better and worse social orders and causes are politically important; and even the best human achievements are partial, pointing to a transcendent fulfillment beyond history. According to Niebuhr's understanding of Christian faith, Gilkey concluded, "the relative creative renewals of history become the promise of the final Kingdom."

Less substantial and comprehensive than the Kegley-Bretall and Scott volumes but worth consulting are two other published symposia, *Reinhold Niebuhr: A Prophetic Voice in Our Time*, edited by Harold Landon (1962) and *Reinhold Niebuhr and the Issues of Our Time*, edited by Richard Harries (1986).[5] The former, held at the Cathedral of St. John the Divine, involved Hans Morgenthau, Paul Tillich, and John Bennett, with Niebuhr's response to their contributions. The latter, held in London, consisted of essays by several British and North American scholars relating to public debates and theological concerns of the 1980s.

Several broad-scoped, book-length studies of Niebuhr have appeared over the years, contributing in various ways to the body of literature illuminating his life and thought. The first important book, following three earlier ones, was Gordon Harland's *The Thought of Reinhold Niebuhr* (1960), an expository and interpretive presentation of his major theological and political themes, focusing on the relation of love to justice, followed by an account of his views on current events and public issues.[6] Harland's approach was systematic rather than historical, well suited to its major purpose of elucidating constant themes of Niebuhr's mature thought but less satisfactory for presenting his views on events and issues of the 1940s and 1950s. Theologically competent and grounded in the sources, he lucidly expounded Niebuhr's dialectic of love and justice, his insights on selfhood and perspective on history, and his delineation of resources in Christian faith for the social task, incorporating subthemes ranging from Niebuhr's critique of natural law to his rejection of scientism. When this carefully wrought volume appeared, Niebuhr himself wrote to William Scarlett: "That book by Harland on my thought is the best yet." It exhibited, Will Herberg commented in a *Christian Century* review, "a sharp insight into the patterns, complexities, and involutions of Niebuhr's thought."[7] Written before Niebuhr's work was completed, it remains a helpful guide.

June Bingham's *Courage to Change: An Introduction to the Life and Thought of Reinhold Niebuhr* (1961) was a ground-breaking biography.[8] The author, who came to know Niebuhr through ADA and audited his ethics course at Union Seminary, collected old letters, interviewed many contemporaries who knew Niebuhr, and read extensively in his works. Her account, combining in alternate chapters a portrait of the man with an outline of his ideas, preserved irreplaceably vivid memories and anecdotes that capture the texture of Niebuhr's personality, including his restless energy, quick pace, keen intellect, openness to others, and commanding presence in public. It was enhanced by excellent photo illustrations. Somewhat sketchy on Niebuhr's earlier life, it focused mostly on the years of his prime at mid-century. Though without supporting footnotes, Bingham's book was carefully researched. She does seem to have misdated Niebuhr's "Serenity Prayer" as originating in 1934; evidence points to 1943. Her alternation of chapters on Niebuhr's life with chapters on his mature thought was a contrivance criticized in a *Christian Century* review by Robert Lee, who pointed out that often "the thought described is far in advance of his life situation." Martin Marty, in the *New York Times Book Review*, criticized irrelevancies but went on to say that readers will move past them "to the worthier portions of the book." August Heckscher, reviewing Bingham's biography in the *New York Herald Tribune*, found it "a candid and charming picture of the man" going "deeply into his thought."[9] The author later added a brief update for an edition published in 1972. Sympathetic but not hagiographic, this biography conveys a sense of immediacy unique in the books on Niebuhr.

Ronald Stone's *Reinhold Niebuhr: Prophet to Politicians* (1972) was another pioneering work that provided perspective by identifying periods of Niebuhr's evolving thought, with emphasis on its political aspects.[10] This account, by a scholar who knew the elderly Niebuhr well and was steeped in the sources, identified four periods in Niebuhr's intellectual development: his youthful Social Gospel liberalism, his Marxist-influenced socialist phase in the 1930s, his Christian realism in the 1940s, and a final pragmatic-liberal synthesis. The third was marked by an Augustinian rejection of optimistic secular creeds, and the fourth combined Jamesian pragmatism with an older tradition of liberalism more realistic than varieties current early in the twentieth century. Reviewing Stone's account of Niebuhr in the *American Political Science Review*, James Childress found it "a sound and valuable overview, by no means uncritical, of his intellectual odyssey." Franklin Sherman, in *Worldview*, saw it as primarily "an essay in conceptual analysis and clarification" that "deserves to be taken seriously." Roger Shinn, in *Union Seminary Quarterly Review*, esteemed it "the best" yet done, but added that he would "give more emphasis to the dazzling dialectic of Niebuhr." Shinn, Sherman, and other friendly reviewers felt that Stone had accented nuances in Niebuhr's septuagenarian reflections without fully appreciating his classic works, and missed the continuity of his thought from the 1940s through the 1960s.[11] Stone has since come to see that continuity, in which Christian realism and pragmatic liberalism are joined, and has written a new book, *Professor Reinhold Niebuhr* (1992), freshly researched and reflecting the perspective of intervening years since his closeness to Niebuhr in the 1960s. Rich in anecdotal material and impressions gathered from hundreds of Niebuhr's former students, it treats his mature vocation as a teacher at Union Seminary, showing the relation of his thought to long experience there.[12]

Paul Merkley's *Reinhold Niebuhr: A Political Account* (1975) focused heavily on Niebuhr's socialist period in the 1930s, assiduously researched by the author, himself a Canadian leftist.[13] That decade of Niebuhr's development is interestly recounted; Merkley, for instance, quotes a letter from Norman Thomas recalling that Niebuhr "in his socialist days" was "a little to the left of me." Earlier and subsequent periods, however, are treated episodically, with errors and omissions, among them misdating of Niebuhr's period at Eden Seminary and neglect of his long efforts on behalf of a Jewish homeland and of racial justice in America. Merkley's contention that Niebuhr after 1945 sank into "increasing complacency about domestic affairs" and came "perilously close to becoming a Cold War ideologue" is colored by author's socialist prejudices and his blindness to the Soviet threat in postwar Europe. His claim that America's disastrous involvement in the Vietnam War resulted from policies "based upon propositions inherent in Niebuhr's misjudgment" is refuted by Niebuhr's published views on U.S. policy toward Indochina from 1950 onward, including his opposition to Johnson's fateful decisions of 1965. Still very useful for details on an early phase of Niebuhr's evolution, Merkley's book was, as C. F. Stoerker concluded his *Christian Century* review, "unsatisfactory as political history."[14]

Richard W. Fox's *Reinhold Niebuhr: A Biography* (1985) was the first continuous narrative account of Niebuhr's life and thought from his youth to old age, enterprisingly researched and written in smooth journalese.[15] Declared by *Time* "the definitive Reinhold Niebuhr" and unqualifiedly commended by most of the early reviews, it quickly became popular. Yet this book, relating various aspects of the Niebuhr story in interesting detail, has received negative verdicts—for it was seriously flawed, as Langdon Gilkey and others pointed out in later lengthy, more critical reviews. "I found," wrote Gilkey in the *Journal of Religion*, "neither understanding of nor appreciation for the originality, power, and importance of his social theory and especially of his theology; no sensitivity to the integrity both of his person and of his religious faith; and, as a result, utterly no comprehension of why this man whom Fox found so energetically intent on fame and prominence and so haphazardly reflective was acclaimed, admired, followed, and even loved."[16] Fox's biography was the most widely reviewed of all books done thus far on Niebuhr. If *Time* represented an extreme form of its rather uncritical acceptance by most reviewers, Gilkey—in the most thorough and important of all the reviews—expressed the reservations of most persons who had known Niebuhr well and written authoritatively on his thought. A close examination of this book is required to sort out its contributions and fatal flaws as biography.

Fox, a historian, traveled widely for interviews and research, unearthing new materials, especially widely scattered letters not in the Niebuhr Papers, and organized a mass of details into a readable account illuminating some periods, facets, and episodes of Niebuhr's life treated less fully hitherto. He narrates well Niebuhr's emergence from a parochial German-American community into the national mainstream, his role in opening his parish and denomination to broader currents in American life, his growing reputation in Social Gospel circles during the 1920s, developments leading to his appointment to the Union Seminary faculty, his leadership of the Fellowship of Socialist Christians in the 1930s and his role in other organizational and editorial endeavors, several of his trips abroad, and various important speaking engagements over the decades. Among Fox's more interesting discoveries is a sheaf of columns written by Niebuhr for the *Detroit Times* from 1928 to 1931, the fact that in 1936 he voted for FDR though still a socialist, and a letter from Walter Lippmann in 1929 expressing his intention to read Niebuhr in the future after seeing his review of *A Preface to Morals*. His research turned up details of Niebuhr's brief stint with George Kennan's Policy Planning Staff, and of his medical problems in the aftermath of his stroke. The book is also rich in photographs. Fox's most important finding was that a German version of the "Serenity Prayer," attributed to eighteenth-century theologian Friedrich Oetinger, was actually a mid-twentieth-century translation of Niebuhr's prayer into German, thus quashing rumors that Oetinger had written it and leaving no doubt that Niebuhr himself had composed that memorable prayer.

Despite these merits, Fox's biography has serious defects, among them its treatment of Niebuhr's education, his Bethel pastorate, and his teaching years at Union Seminary. Niebuhr's Yale experience receives due attention, but his earlier studies at Elmhurst and Eden are ignored or erroneously described. The former, according to Fox, "offered a stale curriculum of classics and ancient history" that "passed over the sciences, English, and modern history"—an undocumented and totally inaccurate description. Dismissing Niebuhr's studies at Eden with a remark that he "scarcely had to crack a book"—and, after all, how could Fox know?—he makes no mention of his course in the prophet Amos and other studies under Samuel Press, which made a lasting impression. Moving on to Niebuhr's pastoral years in Detroit, Fox accuses him of becoming an itinerant preacher who "showed up for his sermons" on Sundays while an assistant "assumed charge of Bethel six days a week." That, too, is refuted by incontrovertible evidence presented in this book and fails to recognize that out-of-town engagements are not unusual for gifted preachers sought by the larger church. Fox's claim that Niebuhr neglected his parishioners while portraying himself as a "super-shepherd" in *Leaves* has no basis in fact and is most unfair to him. Equally egregious is his almost total neglect of Niebuhr's mature vocation as a professor at Union Seminary for a third of a century, passing over his well-crafted courses in Christian ethics, his close relations to students, and the community of distinguished colleagues with whom he lived and worked for most of his professional life. Taking no account of his long involvement at Columbia University—through its joint doctoral program with Union, membership in the Philosophy Club, and other unique contacts—Fox misperceives him as isolated from the academic world, sinking into "intellectual stagnation." The environment of a great seminary adjacent to a great university is obscured as much as Niebuhr's dedication to the teaching mission of Union.

On a deeper level, Fox fails to grasp Niebuhr's creativity, significance, and impact as a theologian and social philosopher. His account of *The Nature and Destiny of Man*, as Gilkey has pointed out, "is strewn with unrelieved negative comments," including misplaced emphasis on "Calhoun's rather crabbed critique" of volume one.[17] Fox misconstrues letters to Reinhold from his brother Richard in 1933, theologically critical of *Moral Man and Immoral Society*, to mean that Niebuhr's later magnum opus was "the mature flowering of the seed which Richard had planted ten years before." So crediting Richard takes no account of Reinhold's turn a few years earlier to Pauline theology and his interest since the late 1920s in theological currents from Europe, nor of his independence of Richard in subsequent study of Augustine and Kierkegaard. Of Fox's account, John Bennett has written: "I was puzzled about what seemed to me an exaggeration of the influence of Richard on his thought. His own constructive theology had other roots and at the point at which he and Richard differed, they continued to differ. Reinie's great sense of responsibility to do what he could to influence history, which Richard lacked and even rejected, was not changed at all."[18] Fox, moreover, does not do justice to the biblical dimensions of Niebuhr's thought, as when he writes: "His religion, for all its biblical allusions and ethical drive—was more like a philosophy of life than a mystical encounter." Citing those words in his *Times Literary Supplement* review, Richard Harries commented: "But it was neither. It was a religion of prophetic Hebrew tradition, with a sense of awe before the Holy and a fierce sense of divine hostility to the pretensions, vanities and sheer wickedness of so much human life."[19] Carefully analyzing Fox's interpretation of Niebuhr's ideas, Gilkey found that he reduced them to "a secular, empirical naturalism," adding that "it does not seem to have occurred to Fox that it was this view, his own view, still common as it is among American intellectuals" that "Niebuhr was in the process of deeply and successfully challenging."[20] Indeed, Fox misses the Christian dimension and dialectical profundity of Niebuhr's achievement in concluding as he does that "his prime intellectual contribution was to weld together the tragic sense of life with the quest for justice."

Fox attributes Niebuhr's greatness not to his brilliance as a religious and social thinker but to his driving energy, oratorical gifts, and familiarity with public affairs. He draws a caricature of Reinhold as "always on the run, suitcase packed"—a man obsessed with "the political frenzy." It is hard to imagine such a man sitting still to read works like Cochrane's *Christianity and Classical Culture* or Kierkegaard's *Concluding Unscientific Postscript*, or writing the books that impressed many thoughtful spirits of his age. Fox's treatment of Niebuhr's books is cursory and unappreciative of nearly all, expressing his own negative opinion of this one and that and citing unfavorable reviews without mentioning other appreciative reviews by eminent theologians, historians, and political scientists. Thus, for example, *The Children of Light and the Children of Darkness* is found to be merely a "quick spin-off" of the Gifford Lectures and is sharply criticized for ignoring the problem of the influence of advertisers on news—an issue that Fox doubts Niebuhr ever thought about, though in fact he addressed it several years later. Declaring *Faith and History* "a weak book," Fox goes on to say that in it Niebuhr "cavalierly dismissed" psychology as "unworthy of serious attention"; yet on page 167 Niebuhr appreciated "every discipline of psychology and every technique of psychiatry . . . as contributing to the cure of souls." He finds all but two essays in *Christian Realism and Political Problems* "scarcely memorable"; but Robert McAfee Brown chose five from that volume for his anthology *The Essential Reinhold Niebuhr*. He judges *The Structure of Nations and Empires* "an intellectual disappointment" without acknowledging the high opinion of it held by authorities in the field of world politics. Fox, as Richard Neuhaus remarked in his review, "would have us believe that the mature Niebuhr arrived at his political views in a twenty-five-year fit of absentmindedness."[21]

Fox's account of Niebuhr's political journalism is also defective. After suggesting that his gloomy prognostications in the wake of Hitler's rise to power were colored by his wife's having a miscarriage, Fox claims that "his plea for American aid to the Allies was based less on a clear conception of the threat to the U.S. than on a passionate desire to rescue Britain." Fox's attributing Niebuhr's position on such a fateful issue to personal Anglophilism, Gilkey has commented, makes one wonder whether he himself "sees the danger a Nazi Europe would have posed for America and the world."[22] Critical of Niebuhr for not warning against excessive wartime zeal, Fox makes no mention of his speaking out against interment of Japanese-Americans. Again, Fox criticizes Niebuhr for calling for firmness against Soviet designs on Germany, in his *Life* article of 1946, without balancing that with a call for patience as well, but Niebuhr concluded that important piece as follows: "War with Russia is neither imminent nor inevitable if we have a creative policy. Let us therefore avoid hysteria even while we abjure sentimental illusions."[23] Turning to the rise of McCarthyism in the early 1950s, Fox incredibly blames Niebuhr—who denounced McCarthy while meanwhile opposing the Soviets and their fellow travelers—for "his own part in creating the atmosphere of suspicion." On racial relations in America, he acknowledges Niebuhr's support of civil rights in the early 1960s but overlooks his long record in criticism of Jim Crow and his support of federal efforts in the mid-1960s to reduce poverty among urban blacks. Throughout, Fox criticizes passing misjudgments and inconsistencies in Niebuhr's journalism. The reason for mistakes like that, Roger Shinn has responded, "is that such judgments always depend, in part, on empirical data; new information means revised opinions." The better journalists, like Walter Lippmann, have made mistakes: "To maintain a higher consistency would be to allow dogma to triumph over new evidence."[24]

Especially offensive is Fox's treatment of Niebuhr as a person, which is blemished with misconceptions that are at odds with the testimony of those who knew him and the respect of wider circles who esteemed and honored him. Reinhold Niebuhr, he says, was "an uncouth country bumpkin"—this about a professor who received honorary doctorates from Oxford and twenty other institutions and was elected to the American Academy of Art and Letters, facts not mentioned in this biography. He was, Fox says, "the educated Protestant's Billy Sunday"—a statement as inaccurate as it is demeaning. It was Niebuhr's habit, he adds, to "strut" to the pulpit—a claim no one else has made. "Reinhold Niebuhr," Nathan Scott has protested, "did *not* strut." Arthur Schlesinger has written that "to a greater degree than anyone I have ever known, Niebuhr was a man whose humility was not theoretical but authentic."[25] Fox repeatedly says that Niebuhr craved and sought "renown," "visibility," and "influence," adding that in later life he "cherished his position on a pedestal." Such, Gilkey has commented, is "amateur psychology at its worst."[26] Fox's suggestion that Niebuhr married a British woman to compensate for his "sense of displacement" as the son of a German immigrant is absurd. His claim that Niebuhr "always put his friends to a severe test since they could rarely secure his undivided attention" rests merely on Waldo Frank's complaint. Commenting on that, Arthur Schlesinger has stated: "I knew Waldo Frank; he was a very demanding friend." Ursula Niebuhr's correspondence with Lewis Mumford also confirms that Frank made excessive demands on others.[27] Surely there are limits to the time any human being can give to hundreds of people.

This book contains much new information, but so many misstatements and misjudgments that it should be read very cautiously. A few more examples must suffice. *Christianity and Crisis* in 1956 adopted a new masthead, retaining its dignified but plain format, whereupon Niebuhr's daughter, as managing editor Wayne Cowan later recalled, chided her father for being an "aesthetic philistine." Fox takes this out of context as a comment reflecting Niebuhr's "ignorance of art"—a mistaken claim refuted by such insights of Niebuhr as this: "Study a Greek statue and compare it with a portrait of Rembrandt, and you have the difference between a classical depreciation of the individual and the Christian appreciation of the individual."[28] Fox asserts that Niebuhr called Barth a fundamentalist until they met in 1947, but the fact is that he had never done so, pointing out in 1928 that Barth accepted the results of biblical criticism and the findings of modern science. He blames Niebuhr for "frequent failure to acknowledge his intellectual debts," citing as the only evidence the Brunner-Niebuhr exchange of 1956, in which both forgot footnote references in Niebuhr's magnum opus to Brunner's *Man in Revolt*, as pointed out in chapter 4 of this book. His claim that Niebuhr "distrusted the scholars but hoped for their respect" is contradicted by Niebuhr's frequently expressed appreciation of scholarly works in many fields. Pitting H. Richard Niebuhr against Reinhold, Fox strangely asserts that "Helmut's faith was closer to the Gospel" and quotes Richard as having angrily "snapped" when asked why he had published less than his brother: "I think before I write." If indeed Richard—who dedicated *Christ and Culture* "to Reinie"—said that, it is more credible that he did so humorously.

In sum, Fox's biography is uneven in quality, a mixture of factual data with blunders that have the effect of diminishing the man and his achievements. Abounding in off-target criticisms, he does not give Niebuhr himself much of a hearing. As Neuhaus concluded his review in *Commentary*, "the definitive biography, when it is written, will give Reinhold Niebuhr at least equal time." Fox responded to that with a published attack on Neuhaus, to which Neuhaus replied—and then organized a conference to which he invited Fox, with papers and proceedings published in a volume entitled *Reinhold Niebuhr Today*.[29] Fox's book, Gilkey observed, "is by no means a complete disaster"; it is "good on the *external* aspects of Niebuhr's life," but "falls short" with regard "to the inward person and the reflective interpreter." He concluded: "One lesson surely is that a historian who takes on a religious or theological subject, like one who works on a great scientist, must be intellectually (and spiritually) at home in the special field within which his subject lived and worked, lest he have no notion of what his subject did."[30]

Kenneth Durkin's *Reinhold Niebuhr* (1989) is a study of Niebuhr's books, impressively analyzing one after another with special reference to the biblical motifs of Creation, Fall, Atonement, and Parousia that entered his matured perspective on politics and history, as well as theology and ethics.[31] Durkin, a British scholar, treats the books in their historical setting, sketching theological milieus and public events, and is best on those of the 1930s and 1940s, from *Moral Man and Immoral Society* to *Faith and History*. His account is a bit heavy on the theological side of Niebuhr's thought, and is marred by certain errors. Durkin's statement that the raising of a red flag by students at Union Seminary once in 1934 was "inspired" by Niebuhr's writings is false.[32] He is also wrong in attributing to Niebuhr's books of the postwar years an "hysterical anti-Communism." Also, he identifies Gustav Niebuhr too closely with Harnack's theology. On the whole, however, this is a good book which deserves more attention than it has received.

Unique and especially valuable is *Remembering Reinhold Niebuhr: Letters of Reinhold and Ursula M. Niebuhr*, edited by Ursula Niebuhr (1991), a rich selection of correspondence, mostly between them but also of Reinhold with some of his friends, supplemented with Ursula's memoirs of highlights in her past and in their life together.[33] Included in this volume are her reminiscences of growing up in England, of meeting Reinhold, and of joining him on trips to Britain for the Oxford Conference and the Gifford Lectures. Letters tell the story of their engagement and of Reinhold's travels in wartime Britain and in Europe on various occasions after the war. They are filled with comments on people and events, and provide glimpses of him as a devoted husband and caring father. Also included are selections of his correspondence with, among others, Felix Frankfurter, Lewis Mumford, and Arthur Schlesinger, Jr. Well-chosen photographs enhance the book. Reviewing it, Martin Marty remarked that he will "trade 50 pages of *The Nature and Destiny of Man*" for such passages in Reinhold's letters as expressions of "longing" for Ursula and reference to his bringing home "a little wood cart" from Bavaria as a birthday gift for their son. Of the Niebuhrs' marriage as revealed in these pages, Roger Shinn commented in his review: "Theirs was a sharing of life in which each partner kept a stalwart personal identity, yet found completion in the other." The letters, he added, also "show Niebuhr's enormous capacity for friendship." Far from being sentimental about the family, he pointed out, Niebuhr in one of his books "observed that the preservation of peace and integrity in the family is as difficult as in international relations" (*Christian Realism and Political Problems*, pp. 125–6). Those who are curious about Niebuhr's private life as well as those who knew and loved him, Shinn concluded, "can rejoice in this priceless book."[34]

Besides the more lengthy works on Niebuhr, there are three introductions, each done by a well-qualified scholar for a reputable series on twentieth-century theologians or American writers. The first was Nathan Scott's *Reinhold Niebuhr* (1963), concise and eloquent.[35] Discussing a multiplicity of themes as expressed in books from the 1930s to the 1950s, Scott made an impressive case for the fundamental and lasting importance of Niebuhr's doctrine of selfhood, set forth in volume one of his published Gifford Lectures, as a compound of nature and spirit prone to sin in the anxious condition of freedom and finiteness. The next was Gabriel Fackre's *The Promise of Reinhold Niebuhr* (1970), lucid and coherent.[36] Outlining motifs of the Gifford Lectures, Fackre pointed to resources in Niebuhr's legacy for a generation following him, accenting especially themes that sustain vision while tempering it with realism in the social order. The third was Bob E. Patterson's *Reinhold Niebuhr* (1977), the longest and fullest of the introductions.[37] Expounding basic doctrines of Niebuhr with care and clarity, Patterson focused chiefly and systematically on sin and grace as treated in the Gifford Lectures and other works, and then turned to the relation of love and justice in social ethics. Various Niebuhrian terms are helpfully elucidated. Each of these introductions includes pertinent biographical background (though, echoing earlier works, Patterson misdates Niebuhr's conversion to the New Deal and Fackre misdates his "Serenity Prayer"). All three are sound and packed with insights, Scott and Patterson concluding with informed critiques of Niebuhr's work.

Some of the best writing on Niebuhr has appeared not in book form but in periodicals, available in old bound volumes on library shelves. A notable piece of this genre is William Lee Miller's "The Irony of Reinhold Niebuhr," which appeared in the *Reporter* in 1955.[38] It is hard, he observed, to pass on the whole of Niebuhr to "conservatives" who like his theology but not his politics, or to "liberals" who like his politics but not his theology. He is best understood, Miller held, as combining historic Christian doctrine and American democratic pragmatism in such a way as to relate biblical faith to politics without deriving specific policies from theological convictions. Another such piece is John C. Bennett's "The Greatness of Reinhold Niebuhr," appearing in *Union Seminary Quarterly Review* in 1971, the last of a sequence of fine essays he wrote on Niebuhr over the decades.[39] Reflecting on his impact at the seminary and in the world outside it, Bennett recalled many of his contributions as a thinker and doer but emphasized his role as a theological giant engaged as a prophetic interpreter of Christian ethics. Niebuhr, he pointed out, did not have a tight system, but spoke and wrote from an open and yet strong theological center, not fully expounded in a single place, that was inspired by the revelation in Christ. Also memorable is Arthur Schlesinger, Jr.'s "Prophet for a Secular Age," published in the *New Leader* in 1972.[40] It is the text of his memorial address at Riverside Church, quoted in chapter 9 of this book. Among the more impressive topical essays is Vigen Guroian's "The Possibilities and Limits of Politics: A Comparative Study of the Thought of Reinhold Niebuhr and Edmund Burke," which appeared in *Union Seminary Quarterly Review* in 1981.[41] Niebuhr and Burke, he argued persuasively, were profoundly similar in their approaches to politics, representing an Anglo-American tradition in which interests are balanced and issues resolved in a framework of freedom and order. Both, he pointed out, recognized the need for prudence in striving for timely reforms, and, rejecting abstract schemes and libertarian dogmas, viewed statecraft as the art of preserving and improving living historical communities. Also important is Franklin Littell's "Reinhold Niebuhr and the Jewish People," appearing in *Holocaust and Genocide Studies* in 1991 after delivery as the annual Niebuhr Lecture at Elmhurst College.[42] Reviewing Niebuhr's long appreciation of Judaism and his exceptional sensitivity to Jewish identity and survival, Littell explored the roots of his thought and leadership on behalf of a Jewish homeland and healthy Christian-Jewish relations, and appended a bibliography of his numerous writings on Zionism, Jewry, and Judaism. Finally, mention should be made of three excellent encyclopedia articles on Reinhold Niebuhr: by John Bennett in *Encyclopaedia Britannica*, Roger Shinn in *Encyclopedia Americana*, and Robert Handy in *Encyclopedia of American Biography*.[43] Other valuable pieces on Niebuhr are listed, together with the foregoing, in the section on selected secondary literature in the bibliography.

The books and other writings discussed in this essay by no means exhaust the literature on Reinhold Niebuhr's life and thought. More can be found through D. B. Robertson's *Reinhold Niebuhr's Works: A Bibliography* and through periodical and book review indexes. So diverse are the viewpoints and experience of his interpreters, and of their readers, that probably anyone reading anything about him—including this bibliographical essay and the book in which it appears—will find something to disagree with, as in reading Niebuhr himself. Yet some of the literature is more factual and insightful than others, and even rather flawed works may have redeeming worth. Niebuhr's greatness will inspire future studies, and as more letters and other Niebuhriana are discovered or made available fuller and more accurate accounts will be possible.

Notes

Because so much of this book is based directly on Reinhold Niebuhr's published work, references in the notes are to his books, periodical pieces, and other writings, unless other authorship is indicated. In all citations of his books—each of which is listed with full publication data in the Bibliography—the following abbreviations are used:

    DCNR = Does Civilization Need Religion?
    LNTC = Leaves from the Notebook of a Tamed Cynic
    CRSW = The Contribution of Religion to Social Work
    MMIS = Moral Man and Immoral Society
    REE = Reflections on the End of an Era
    ICE = An Interpretation of Christian Ethics
    BT = Beyond Tragedy
    NDM = The Nature and Destiny of Man
    CLCD = The Children of Light and the Children of Darkness
    DST = Discerning the Signs of the Times
    FH = Faith and History
    IAH = The Irony of American History
    SDH = The Self and the Dramas of History
    SNE = The Structure of Nations and Empires
    MNHC = Man's Nature and His Communities

His volumes of collected essays and addresses are cited as follows:

    CPP = Christianity and Power Politics
    CRPP = Christian Realism and Political Problems
    PSA = Pious and Secular America

Anthologies of his writings, addresses, and sermons are cited thus:

    LJ = Love and Justice
    WCAR = The World Crisis and American Responsibility
    EAC = Essays in Applied Christianity
    FP = Faith and Politics
    JM = Justice and Mercy
    YRN = Young Reinhold Niebuhr
    ERN = The Essential Reinhold Niebuhr

RNTPL = *Reinhold Niebuhr: Theologian of Public Life*

Pages of Niebuhr's books, cited in these notes, match those of the first edition. (Scribner's, his chief publisher, always retained the original paging in reprinting his books, but some publishers of later paperback editions have reset type and changed the paging.) Pieces reprinted in anthologies are cited in the original source, with periodical and date, followed by the anthology and page references in it.

The two journals Niebuhr long served as founding editor are so often cited as sources of his writings that each is abbreviated as follows:

C&C = *Christianity and Crisis*
C&S = *Christianity and Society* (previously *Radical Religion*)
RR = *Radical Religion* (later renamed *Christianity and Society*)

The Reinhold Niebuhr Papers, in the Manuscript Division of the Library of Congress, are cited in notes as Niebuhr Papers. The Reinhold Niebuhr Audio Tape Collection of Union Theological Seminary in Virginia is cited as Niebuhr Tape Collection with numbers of particular tapes given in parentheses.

CHAPTER ONE

1. Interview with Arthur M. Schlesinger, Jr., March 25, 1987; Alan Paton, *Journey Continued: An Autobiography* (New York: Charles Scribner's Sons, 1988), 149; John Gunther, "Are We Strong Enough to Live without God?" (article interviewing RN), *McCall's Magazine* 78 (Apr. 1951): 30; interview with Kenneth W. Thompson, June 5, 1991 (on Lippmann's remark); Nathan A. Scott, Jr., to author, Oct. 22, 1991. The conference at which Lippmann heard Niebuhr—held in Washington and attended by Dorothy Fosdick, Hans Morgenthau, Paul Nitze, James Reston, Dean Rusk, and Arnold Wolfers, among others—is described by Thompson in "Toward a Theory of International Politics," *American Political Science Review* 49 (Sept. 1955): 733–46.

2. II Corinthians 4:8.

3. "Faith for a Lenten Age," *Time* 51 (Mar. 8, 1948): 70–79.

4. "Faith and Optimism," *Messenger* 12 (Nov. 11, 1947): 7; "The Case for Humility," *Messenger* 18 (Sept. 8, 1953): 4.

5. The line appears in Arthur Hugh Clough's poem "Say Not the Struggle Naught Availeth" (1849).

6. *To Honor Reinhold Niebuhr*, brochure published by the Reinhold Niebuhr Professorship Fund, Union Theological Seminary in New York, 1960.

7. "Is Social Conflict Inevitable?" *Scribner's Magazine* 98 (Spring 1935): 167; "Can We Avoid Catastrophe?" *Christian Century* 65 (May 26, 1948): 506; "Modern Man and the Unknown Future," *Messenger* 17 (Jan. 15, 1952): 6; "The Gospel in Future America," *Christian Century* 75 (June 18, 1958): 714.

8. Richard H. Rovere, *The American Establishment and Other Reports, Opinions, and Speculations* (New York: Harcourt, Brace & World, 1962), 13.

CHAPTER TWO

1. William G. Chrystal, *A Father's Mantle: The Legacy of Gustav Niebuhr* (New York: Pilgrim Press, 1982), xv.

2. Hans Bahlor, *Deutsches Namenlexikon* (Munich, 1967), 352–53; Chrystal, 3–12, 15–16; Hulda Niebuhr to June Bingham, Apr. 5, 1959, Niebuhr Papers (on Gustav's anti-Prussianism).

3. Carl E. Schneider, *The German Church on the American Frontier* (St. Louis: Eden Publishing House, 1939), 409.

4. "A Landmark in American Religious History," *Messenger* 22 (June 18, 1957): 12.

5. Schneider, 292–94, 314–16, 483.

6. Chrystal, 26, 35–36; June Bingham, *Courage to Change: An Introduction to the Life and Thought of Reinhold Niebuhr* (New York: Charles Scribner's Sons, 1972), 55.

7. Chrystal, 71–72; "Intellectual Autobiography," in *Reinhold Niebuhr: His Religious, Social, and Political Thought*, ed. Charles W. Kegley and Robert W. Bretall (New York: Macmillan Co., 1956), 3, hereafter cited as Kegley and Bretall.

8. Bingham, 58; interview with Ronald Stone, June 18, 1987 (on RN's inheriting Luther's *Werke* from his father, related by him to Stone in 1967); Chrystal, 45–48, 61–62, 75–76, 79–80, 84, 91–94, 102–6.

9. Chrystal, 78; Christopher Niebuhr to author, Oct. 24, 1988 (on RN's confirmation); Fox, 14; RN's report cards from Lincoln High School for 1906–07, Elmhurst College Archives.

10. *Mein Lebenslauf;* RN to Daniel Irion, June 17, 1907. Both translated by Adolf Schroeder, professor of German at the University of Missouri, July 17, 1987, from originals found by Rudolf Schade in the Elmhurst College Archives.

11. *Jahrbuch des Evangelischen Proseminars,* 1910–11, 4–14 (on Elmhurst's history and character); 1909–10, 8 (on its accreditation), Elmhurst College Archives.

12. *Jahrbuch des Evang. Proseminars,* 1907–08, *III. Klasse,* 17; 1908–09, *II. Klasse,* 18–19; 1909–10, *I. Klasse,* 18–20, Elmhurst College Archives.

13. *Jahrbuch des Evang. Proseminars,* 1907–08, 17; 1908–09, 18; 1909–10, 19. These and the preceding sections of Elmhurst's catalogs were translated for the author by Luverne Walton, professor of German at the University of Missouri, July 14, 1987.

14. RN to Samuel Press, Mar. 2, 1914, Niebuhr Papers; "The Keryx and Our Educational Problems," *Keryx,* Feb. 1920, and "Shall a Minister Have an Education?" *Magazin für Evangelische Theologie und Kirche,* May 1921, in *YRN,* 116–23; [John C. Helt] *The Niebuhr Distinguished Chair . . . at Elmhurst College,* brochure published by Elmhurst College in 1984 (on the Niebuhr brothers' later work on behalf of the college); "Reinhold Niebuhr: In Memoriam," *Elmhurst College Magazine* 5 (Summer 1971): 1.

15. William G. Chrystal, "Samuel D. Press: Teacher of the Niebuhrs," *Church History* 53 (Dec. 1984): 505–11, 514–15; Samuel D. Press to June Bingham, June 8, 1954, Niebuhr Papers (on Harnack).

16. Chrystal, "Samuel D. Press," 512–3.

17. "A Landmark in American Religious History," 12; William G. Chrystal, Introduction, *YRN* 29; RN to Elmer Arndt, Dec. 11, 1940, Niebuhr Papers; typescript of address by RN entitled "Dr. Press and Evangelical Theology," 1–4, Eden Theological Seminary Archives.

18. *Keryx,* Feb. 1911, in *YRN,* 41–45; Bingham, 63–65; Chrystal, Introduction, *YRN,* 30–31.

19. Bingham, 79; sermon dated Aug. 17, 1913, Niebuhr Papers; RN to Samuel Press, Oct. 15, 1913, Eden Theological Seminary Archives (on RN's reading of Harnack).

20. RN to Samuel Press, Sept. 28, 1913, and Oct. 15, 1913, Eden Theological Seminary Archives.

21. RN to Samuel Press, Nov. 21, 1913, Eden Theological Seminary Archives. RN later wrote that at Yale "my concern was not with the moral usefulness but

with the metaphysical validity of religious conviction"; see "A Religion Worth Fighting For," *Survey* 58 (Aug. 1, 1927): 444.

22. RN to Samuel Press, Apr. 6, 1914, Niebuhr Papers; author's examination of RN's books at the Niebuhr home in Stockbridge, Mass., Mar. 23, 1987; "The Validity and Certainty of Religious Knowledge," B.D. thesis, Yale Divinity School, 1914, 39 pages, copy in Niebuhr Papers.

23. RN to Samuel Press, Nov. 21, 1913, Eden Theological Seminary Archives; "Yale-Eden," *Keryx*, Dec. 1914, in *YRN*, 57; Bingham, 82; Richard W. Fox, *Reinhold Niebuhr: A Biography* (New York: Pantheon Books, 1985), 35.

24. "The Contribution of Christianity to the Doctrine of Immortality," M.A. thesis, Yale University, 1915, 40 pages, original in Yale University Library; Fox, 27, 34-35.

25. "Intellectual Autobiography," Kegley and Bretall, 4; Bingham, 83; "Yale-Eden" in *YRN*, 57; "Ethics of the Renaissance and Reformation," Apr. 12, 1960, Niebuhr Tape Collection (N47).

26. "Intellectual Autobiography," Kegley and Bretall, 6; Ralph C. Abele, "A Woman Named Lydia," *United Church Herald* 2 (Sept. 17, 1959): 10–12; "Lydia Niebuhr: Queen Bee of American Theology," unpublished paper by John C. Helt for doctoral studies at Garrett-Evangelical Seminary and Northwestern University, 1987; *DCNR*, [v].

27. Chrystal, Introduction to *YRN*, 33; "An Anniversary Sermon" and "That They All May Be One," in *YRN*, 59–68.

28. RN to Samuel Press, Nov. 3, 1915, Niebuhr Papers; "The Failure of German Americanism," *Atlantic Monthly* 118 (July 1916): 13–18.

29. William G. Chrystal, "Reinhold Niebuhr and the First World War," *Journal of Presbyterian History* 55 (Fall 1977): 287–89, 291–92; *LNTC*, 14 (1918), 22 (1919); "A Message from Reinhold Niebuhr, *Keryx*, Oct. 1918, in *YRN*, 96–97; "What the War Did to My Mind," *Christian Century* 45 (Sept. 27, 1928): 1161.

30. *LNTC*, [iii]; "Intellectual Autobiography," Kegley and Bretall, 6–7.

31. Helt, "Lydia Niebuhr" (on Hulda Niebuhr); "An Anniversary Sermon," in *YRN*, 63; "A Modern Sunday School," *Evangelical Teacher* 2 (Oct. 1917), in *YRN*, 86; "Educational Principles in Church Schools," address at a convention in Chicago in July 1919, in *YRN*, 114; Martin E. Marty, "Pastor Niebuhr," *Christian Century* 107 (Jan. 17, 1990): 63.

32. "Dedication to Require Week," *Detroit Free Press*, Feb. 11, 1922, 8; "To Dedicate New Bethel Church and House Sunday," *Detroit Journal*, Feb. 11, 1922, 13; "Intellectual Autobiography," Kegley and Bretall, 5; Bingham, 101–2; *LNTC*, "Preface—1956" (New York: Meridian Books, 1957).

33. "The Church and the Industrial Crisis," *Biblical World* 54 (Nov. 1920): 590–92; Walter Rauschenbusch, *Christianizing the Social Order* (New York: Macmillan Co., 1912), 449.

34. Charles D. Williams, *The Christian Ministry and Social Problems* (New York: Macmillan Co., 1917), passim; Bingham, 113; "A Voice Crying in the Wilderness," *Michigan Churchman* 28 (Apr. 1923): 7; Ursula M. Niebuhr to Franklin H. Littell, Mar. 8, 1984 (on RN's possession of Rauschenbusch's books in editions of 1922 and 1924; copy in author's possession).

35. "The Church and the Middle Class," *Christian Century* 39 (Dec. 7, 1922): 1514; Charles Clayton Morrison to RN, Mar. 22, 1923, Niebuhr Papers.

36. *LNTC*, 46–47 (1923); "The Dawn in Europe," *Evangelical Herald*, Aug. 7, 1924, in *YRN*, 152; "Is Europe on the Way to Peace?" *Evangelical Herald*, Sept. 25, 1924, in *YRN*, 159.

37. "A Trip through the Ruhr," *Evangelical Herald*, Aug. 9, 1923, in *YRN*, 125, 127 (on visits at Krupp works and Cologne Cathedral); "Germany," *Worldview* 16 (June 1973): 14 (on visit at ancestral estate); "Dr. William Temple and His Britain," *Nation* 159 (Nov. 11, 1944): 584 (on meeting Temple); *LNTC*, 55 (1924) (on visit at York Minster); "Germany and Modern Civilization," *Atlantic Monthly* 135 (June 1925): 843–46; "Protestantism in Germany," *Christian Century* 40 (Oct. 4, 1923): 1258–59; "Christianity and Contemporary Politics," *Christian Century* 41 (Apr. 17, 1924): 498–500.

38. Bingham, 113; "The Death of Senator LaFollette," *Christian Century* 42 (July 2, 1925): 847–48; "Jesus as Efficiency Expert" (rev. of Barton's *The Man Nobody Knows*), *Christian Century* 42 (July 2, 1925), 851.

39. *LNTC*, 78 (1925); "How Philanthropic Is Henry Ford?" *Christian Century* 43 (Dec. 9, 1926), in *LJ*, 100; "Ford's Five-Day Week Shrinks," *Christian Century* 44 (June 9, 1927), in *LJ*, 106; RN to Ronald Stone, June 13, 1969, copy in author's possession (on Marquis's book); *LNTC*, 154–55 (1927); Bingham, 129.

40. Donald B. Meyer, *The Protestant Search for Political Realism, 1919–1941* (1960; Westport, Conn.: Greenwood Press, 1973), 83–84; interview with Donald L. Scruggs, a student at Union from 1958 to 1961, Sept. 20, 1985 (on labor speaker at Bethel); "The Battle of Detroit," *Christian Century* 42 (Oct. 21, 1926): 1287–89.

41. John Hope Franklin, *From Slavery to Freedom: A History of Negro Americans*, 3d ed. (New York: Random House, Vintage, 1969), 484; *Report of the Mayor's Committee on Race Relations* (Detroit, 1926), 3–16; Ronald H. Stone, *Reinhold Niebuhr: Prophet to Politicians* (Nashville: Abingdon Press, 1972), 31–34; "Race Prejudice in the North," *Christian Century* 44 (May 12, 1927): 583–84; Christopher Niebuhr to author, Nov. 11, 1986 (on investing in banks that hired blacks); Bingham, 111.

42. Bingham, 112; *LNTC*, 187 (1928); "Is Protestantism Self-Deceived?" *Christian Century* 41 (Dec. 25, 1924): 1662.

43. Introduction to Sherwood Eddy, *Eighty Adventurous Years: An Autobiography* (New York: Harper & Brothers, 1955), 9; Theodore C. Braun, "The Professor as Pastor," *United Church Herald* 14 (Aug. 1971): 43; Viola C. Braun to Martin E. Marty, Mar. 1, 1990 (copy in author's possession); Theodore C. Braun, reminiscences taped by Richard C. Braun, Dec. 1978–Jan. 1979 (copy in author's possession).

44. Sunday bulletins of Bethel Evangelical Church, 1921–28, passim, Archives of Emmanuel Bethel United Church of Christ, Royal Oak, Mich.; "Tyrant Servants," *Preachers and Preaching in Detroit*, ed. Ralph M. Pierce (Old Tappen, N.J.: Fleming H. Revell Co., 1926), in *YRN*, 165–66, 169; *LNTC*, 145 (1927); "The Hazards and Difficulties of the Christian Ministry" (address at Union Theological Seminary, Mar. 26, 1953), in *JM*, 129.

45. *LNTC*, 91 (1925), 95 (1926), 112–13 (1926).

46. "Lynn Harold Hough in Detroit," *Drew Gateway* 18 (Spring 1947): 37; Meyer, 84; Introduction to Lynn Harold Hough, *The University of Experience* (New York: Harper & Brothers, 1932), vii–viii; *LNTC*, 167 (1928); Hough quoted in Carl Hermann Voss, "Niebuhr: 20th Century Prophet," *Advance* 136 (July 1944): 10; *LNTC*, 92 (1926); *DCNR*, 201–2; Ursula M. Niebuhr to author, Dec. 30, 1987 (on RN's use of Dods).

47. Nathan A. Scott, Jr., to author, Dec. 5, 1986 (on RN's reading of Troeltsch in Detroit); "Capitalism—A Protestant Offspring," *Christian Century* 42 (May 7, 1925): 600; "How Civilization Defeated Christianity" (rev. of Tawney's *Religion and the Rise of Capitalism*), *Christian Century* 43 (July 15, 1926): 895; "Another Outline—and a Good One" (rev. of Thorndike's *Short History of Civilization*),

Christian Century 43 (Nov. 25, 1926): 1458; "Is Western Civilization Dying?" (rev. of Spengler's *Decline of the West*), *Christian Century* 43 (May 20, 1926): 651–52 (on Spengler, see also *YRN*, 161); "Science and the Modern World" (rev. of Whitehead's book so titled), *Christian Century* 43 (Apr. 8, 1926): 448–49; *LNTC*, 162 (1928).

48. *DCNR*, 139, 161; 80, 114–15; 31; 234; 207; 47; 60; 238. For further analysis of this book, see Stone, 43–51.

49. "Ten Years That Shook My World," *Christian Century* 56 (Apr. 26, 1939): 542; Bernard Iddings Bell, rev. of *DCNR*, *Saturday Review* 5 (Sept. 29, 1928): 164.

50. Robert T. Handy, *A History of Union Theological Seminary in New York* (New York: Columbia University Press, 1987), 157–62; Introduction to Sherwood Eddy, *Eighty Adventurous Years*, 9; Fox, 105–6; "Specialists and Social Life," *Detroit Times*, May 5, 1928, 18; "Niebuhr Quits Detroit Pulpit: Widely Known Pastor Accepts Call from Union Theological Seminary," *Detroit News*, April 23, 1928, 1; Nancy Manser, "Detroiters Have Memories of Famous Dr. Niebuhr," *Detroit News*, June 5, 1971, 7, sec. A.

51. "Ten Years That Shook My World," 545.

CHAPTER THREE

1. Handy, 4–19, 45, 47–51, 53, 82, 100, 126, 117–18, 177.

2. Handy, 99, 133–34, 147–48; John C. Bennett, "Change and Continuity in the Theological Climate at Union Seminary," *Union Seminary Quarterly Review* 18 (May 1963): 357–61; "On Academic Vagabondage," in *YRN*, 149; "Ethics of the Renaissance and Reformation," Apr. 12, 1960, Niebuhr Tape Collection (N47).

3. "How Adventurous Is Dr. Fosdick?" *Christian Century* 44 (Jan. 6, 1927): 17–18; "The Significance of Dr. Fosdick in American Religious Thought," *Union Seminary Quarterly Review* 8 (May 1953): 5; interview with Victor Obenhaus, a student at Union from 1925 to 1929 and 1936 to 1938, March 23, 1989 (on RN's talk at Riverside Church).

4. Emil Brunner, "Reinhold Niebuhr's Work as a Christian Thinker," Kegley and Bretall, 28; "Barth—Apostle of the Absolute," *Christian Century* 45 (Dec. 13, 1928), in *EAC*, 141, 143–44. RN must have had Brunner's *The Theology of Crisis*—which he later quoted in *NDM*, 2, 124—in mind when referring in 1932 to European neo-orthodoxy's protest against American tendencies to identify the kingdom of God with movements of social reform; see "The Ethic of Jesus and the Social Problem," *Religion in Life* 1 (Spring 1932), in *LJ*, 33.

5. "The Terrible Beauty of the Cross," *Christian Century* 46 (Mar. 21, 1929): 387; "Christianity and Redemption," in *Whither Christianity*, ed. L. H. Hough (New York: Harper & Brothers, 1929), 110, 114, 119–21; "The Sin of Pride," *Detroit Times*, July 6, 1929, 18. Chesterton's "If I Had Only One Sermon to Preach" appeared in the *London Daily Telegraph*, Dec. 31, 1928.

6. "Metropolitan Life," *Detroit Times*, Jan. 12, 1929, 18; "The City Man and Nature," *Detroit Times*, Sept. 28, 1929, 18; "Right Use of Leisure," *Detroit Times*, July 26, 1930, 18.

7. "Labor Day," *Detroit Times*, Sept. 1, 1928, 18; "Protestantism and Prohibition," *New Republic* 56 (Oct. 24, 1928): 265–67.

8. "Governor Smith's Liberalism," *Christian Century* 45 (Sept. 13, 1928): 1107–8; Paul Merkley, *Reinhold Niebuhr: A Political Account* (Montreal: McGill-Queen's University Press, 1975), 54, 243; "Why We Need a New Economic Order," *World Tomorrow* 11 (Oct. 1928): 397; Fox, 122, 124, 135–36.

9. "Glimpses of the Southland," *Christian Century* 47 (July 16, 1930): 893–95; "What Chance Has Gandhi?" *Christian Century* 48 (Oct. 14, 1931): 1274–76.

10. "Awkward Imperialists," *Atlantic Monthly* 145 (May 1930): 670–73; "Political Currents in Germany," *New Leader* 10 (July 26, 1930): 5; "The German Crisis," *Nation* 131 (Oct. 1, 1930): 360; "German Election Prospects," *New Leader* 11 (Aug. 16, 1930): 5; RN to John C. Bennett, July 20, 1930, Niebuhr Papers.

11. "Russian Efficiency," *Christian Century* 47 (Oct. 1, 1930): 1178; "The Land of Extremes," *Christian Century* 47 (Oct. 15, 1930): 1241–42; "Glimpses from Soviet Russia," *New Leader* 11 (Sept. 13, 1930): 5.

12. Henry Sloane Coffin to RN, undated, Niebuhr Papers; Fox, 112; Handy, 55, 114, 173–75; Peggy L. Shriver to Christopher Niebuhr, Nov. 29, 1989 (on endowing of Dodge chair in 1892; copy in author's possession); "Intellectual Autobiography," Kegley and Bretall, 9; *Union Theological Seminary in the City of New York: Catalogue: 1928–29*, 26–27; 1929–30, 21; 1930–31, 20–21; 1931–32, 22; 1932–33, 22; 1933–34, 20 (dates are for years of announced courses).

13. Interview with Ursula M. Niebuhr, Mar. 23, 1987; Ursula's gift to Reinhold was entitled *Meditations of St. Augustine, His Treatise of the Love of God, Soliloquys and Manual.* Her account of how she and RN met appears in *Remembering Reinhold Niebuhr: Letters of Reinhold and Ursula M. Niebuhr*, ed. Ursula Niebuhr (San Francisco: HarperCollins, 1991), 17–22.

14. "An American Approach to the Christian Message," in *A Traffic in Knowledge: An International Symposium on the Christian Message*, ed. W. A. Visser 't Hooft (London: SCM Press, 1931), 54–55, 64–65, 72–75, 80, 83–85.

15. "Race Relations in a Depression," *Detroit Times*, Aug. 8, 1931, 16; "The Lesson of the Past Decade," *Christian Century* 48 (Dec. 30, 1931): 1646.

16. Ursula M. Niebuhr to author, Jan. 13, 1989 (on RN's friendship with Gaylord White and on his summering in Heath in 1932); CRSW, 29.

17. CRSW, 28, 86; 80–81; 30, 37–41, 43–44, 48; 44.

18. MMIS, xxiii, 3–4; xii; xiii, 24–25, 214, 245; 79; xii, xxiii.

19. MMIS, 114; 8, 117–18; 163, 181, 189; 193; 205–7.

20. MMIS, 47, 91, 93; 18, 87, 97, 107; 240, 250, 252.

21. MMIS, 4. The theological element in Niebuhr's thought of the early 1930s, more explicit in his essay for Visser 't Hooft's symposium of 1931 than in *Moral Man and Immoral Society*, is obscured by his retrospective statement in 1939 that his development during the previous ten years involved "a gradual theological elaboration of what was at first merely socio-ethical criticism"; see "Ten Years That Shook My World," *Christian Century* 56 (Apr. 26, 1939): 542.

22. James H. Smylie, "Reinhold Niebuhr: Quadragesimo Anno," *Religion in Life* 42 (Spring 1972), passim; *Times* (London) *Literary Supplement*, Mar. 16, 1933, 187–88; *New Statesman and Nation* 5 (Apr. 8, 1933): 456; *Reinie: The Life and Times of Reinhold Niebuhr*, British Broadcasting Company, 1965 (Crossman's comment recorded in this film); H. Richard Niebuhr to RN, probably January 1933, Niebuhr Papers; "Optimism and Utopianism," *World Tomorrow* 16 (Feb. 22, 1933): 180; MNHC, 22. For further discussion of this book, see Langdon Gilkey, "Reinhold Niebuhr as a Political Theologian," in *Reinhold Niebuhr and the Issues of Our Time*, ed. Richard Harries (Grand Rapids: Wm. B. Eerdmans Publishing Co., 1986), 158–68.

23. Bingham, 162–63; "Thomas for President," *World Tomorrow* 15 (July 1932): 195; "The Stakes in the Election," *Christian Century* 49 (Nov. 9, 1932): 1379–81; "Ex Cathedra," *World Tomorrow* 16 (Aug. 1933): 458.

24. "Hitlerism—A Devil's Brew," *World Tomorrow* 16 (April 19, 1933): 369; "The Germans: Unhappy Philosophers in Politics," *American Scholar* 2 (Oct. 1933):

414; "The Opposition in Germany," *New Republic* 75 (June 28, 1933): 169; "Hitlerism," 369; "Why German Socialism Crashed," *Christian Century* 50 (Apr. 5, 1933): 452–53; "The Germans," 411.

25. "Why German Socialism Crashed," 451–52; "The Opposition in Germany," 170; "The Germans," 411; "Germany Must Be Told!" *Christian Century* 50 (Aug. 9, 1933): 1014–15; David A. Rausch and Carl Hermann Voss, "A Heritage of Prophetic Ministry," *Christian-Jewish Relations* 20 (Summer 1987): 10.

26. Wilhelm and Marion Pauck, *Paul Tillich: His Life and Thought* (New York: Harper & Row, 1976), 133–43; "Eternity in Our Time" (rev. of Tillich's *The Religious Situation*), *World Tomorrow* 15 (Dec. 21, 1932): 596.

27. "A Prophet Come to Judgment" (rev. of Lippmann's *A Preface to Morals*), *World Tomorrow* 12 (July 1929), 313–14; rev. of Ortega y Gasset's *The Revolt of the Masses*, *World Tomorrow* 15 (Nov. 16, 1932): 477–78; "Events and the Man" and "Trotsky's Classic" (rev. of Trotsky's *History of the Russian Revolution*), *World Tomorrow* 15 (July 1932): 210, and 16 (Feb. 1, 1933): 116–17; "The Germany of Hitler" (rev. of Hitler's *My Battle*), *World Tomorrow* 16 (Oct. 26, 1933): 598.

28. *REE*, 53, 180–89; 129–30; 168–74; 74; 243–44; RN to Ronald H. Stone, Apr. 27, 1971 (copy in author's possession); "The Ablest Interpreter of Marx" (rev. of Hook's *Towards the Understanding of Karl Marx*), *World Tomorrow* 16 (Aug. 1933): 476. For further analysis of this book, see Gilkey, "Reinhold Niebuhr as a Political Theologian," 168–81.

29. *LNTC*, 46–47 (1923); "Must We Do Nothing?" *Christian Century* 49 (Mar. 30, 1932): 415–17; "Why I Leave the F.O.R.," *Christian Century* 51 (Jan. 3, 1934), in *LJ*, 254–59.

30. Sydney E. Ahlstrom, "Continental Influence on American Christian Thought since World War I," *Church History* 27 (Sept. 1958): 256–72; "Farewell Talk to Students," May 9, 1960, Niebuhr Tape Collection (N31); George Casalis, *Portrait of Karl Barth* (Garden City, N.Y.: Doubleday & Co., 1963), 53–57; "The Churches in Germany," *American Scholar* 3 (Summer 1934): 347; W. A. Visser 't Hooft to RN, Apr. 10, 1931, Niebuhr Papers; "Barthianism and Political Reaction," *Christian Century* 51 (June 6, 1934), in *EAC*, 153; "A Theology of Revelation" (rev. of Brunner's *The Divine Imperative* and other books by him), *New York Herald Tribune Books*, May 16, 1937, 20.

31. Ursula M. Niebuhr, rev. of Wilhelm and Marion Pauck's *Paul Tillich: His Life and Thought*, *Religious Studies Review* 3 (Oct. 1977): 200; Paul Tillich, "Sin and Grace," in *Reinhold Niebuhr: A Prophetic Voice in Our Time*, ed. H. R. Landon (Greenwich, Conn.: Seabury Press, 1962), 39; *ICE* [i].

32. "Marx, Barth, and Israel's Prophets," *Christian Century* 52 (Jan. 30, 1935), in *EAC*, 156–58, 161–63.

33. *ICE*, 105; 29; 31; 65, 90, 218; 76, 84–85.

34. *ICE*, 107–8, 119–20; 163–64; 182; 171–73, 180–81; 183; 201; 223, 234–35.

35. Wilhelm Pauck, rev. of *ICE*, *Radical Religion* 1 (Winter 1936): 33–36; "Reply to Interpretation and Criticism," Kegley and Bretall, 434; *ICE*, preface for 1956 edition (New York: Meridian Books, 1956), 9.

36. Harry Emerson Fosdick, "The Church Must Go Beyond Modernism," in *The Riverside Preachers*, ed. Paul Sherry (New York: Pilgrim Press, 1978), 39–48.

37. "The Pathos of Liberalism" (rev. of Dewey's *Liberalism and Social Action*), *Nation* 141 (Sept. 11, 1935): 303–4; *MMIS*, xiii–xv.

38. "The Fellowship of Socialist Christians," *World Tomorrow* 17 (June 14, 1934): 297; Merkley, 99; Fox, 158; "Radical Religion," *RR* 1 (Autumn 1935), 3–5; "The International Situation," *RR* 1 (Spring 1936): 8–9.

39. "The Political Campaign," *RR* 1 (Autumn 1936): 6; interview with Robert B. Birge, a graduate of Yale who was associate secretary of Dwight Hall on the campus in 1936–37 and a student at Union from 1937 to 1940 (on RN's speech for FDR, which he heard); Fox, 177; "The National Election," *RR* 2 (Winter 1936): 4; "Roosevelt's Merry-Go-Round," *RR* 3 (Spring 1938): 4; RN to Arthur M. Schlesinger, Jr., Apr. 15, 1954, Niebuhr Papers. In 1936 RN voted for FDR, apparently through the American Labor Party, which supported him on the ballot in New York; Christopher Niebuhr to author, May 29, 1990.

40. "Pawns for Fascism—Our Lower Middle Class," *American Scholar* 6 (Spring 1937): 147, 149, 152; "Unhappy Spain," *RR* 2 (Summer 1937): 3–4; "The Moscow Trials," *RR* 2 (Spring 1937): 1–2; rev. of Trotsky's *The Russian Revolution Betrayed*, *RR* 2 (Summer 1937): 39–40; "America and the War in China," *Christian Century* 54 (Sept. 29, 1937): 1195–96; "Brief Comments," *RR* 2 (Summer 1937): 6 (on Ford and the Wagner Act).

41. "The Blindness of Liberalism," *RR* 1 (Autumn 1936): 4–5; *ICE*, 11.

42. Ursula M. Niebuhr, "About the Books Used by Reinhold and Ursula Niebuhr," unpublished reminiscence (Jan. 1987), 3, Union Theological Seminary Archives; Ursula M. Niebuhr to author, Dec. 30, 1987 (on RN's use of Przywara's *Augustine Synthesis*); *MMIS*, 69–70; "The English Church: An American View," *Spectator* 157 (Sept. 4, 1936): 373–74; "Intellectual Autobiography," Kegley and Bretall, 437.

43. "The Ultimate Issues" (rev. of Barth's *Church Dogmatics*, vol. 2, pt. 1), *New York Herald Tribune Books*, Sept. 27, 1936, 17; rev. of Tillich's *The Interpretation of History*, *RR* 2 (Winter 1936): 41–42; "The Contribution of Paul Tillich," *Religion in Life* 6 (Autumn 1937): 574–81.

44. "A Theology of Revelation" (see note 30); *NDM*, 2: 64. David Cairns's introduction to Brunner's *God and Man* (London: SCM Press, 1936) includes an account of the Barth-Brunner controversy.

45. "Vital Modern Religion" (rev. of Temple's *Nature, Man and God*), *New York Herald Tribune Books*, July 28, 1935, 15; "Secret of Creative Action" (rev. of Gilson's *The Spirit of Medieval Philosophy*), *New York Herald Tribune Books*, Oct. 25, 1936, 22; RN to William Scarlett, Apr. 4, 1937, Niebuhr Papers.

46. "English and German Mentality—A Study in National Traits," *Christendom* 1 (Spring 1936), 465–67; *Do the State and the Nation Belong to God or the Devil?* (Burge Memorial Lecture; London: SCM Press, 1937), in *FP*, 85, 90; *Remembering Reinhold Niebuhr*, 118.

47. John C. Bennett, "Breakthrough in Ecumenical Social Ethics: The Legacy of the Oxford Conference on Church, Community, and State (1937)," *Ecumenical Review* 40 (Apr. 1988): 132–46; W. Lance Martin, "Joseph Houldsworth Oldham: His Thought and Its Development," Ph.D. diss., St. Andrews University, Scotland, 1967, 292–324; "Militant Program Urged for Religion," *New York Times*, July 14, 1937, 12; *CPP*, 203–26 (RN's Oxford address; also in *ERN*, 79–92); Bingham, 284.

48. Myles Horton, *The Long Haul: An Autobiography*, with Judith and Herbert Kohl (New York: Doubleday, 1990), 60–62; "Ex Cathedra," *World Tomorrow* 17 (June 14, 1934): 290; Sherwood Eddy, 155–58; Bingham, 206–10; "Meditations from Mississippi," *Christian Century* 54 (Feb. 10, 1937): 183–84.

49. William Scarlett, with RN, "The Social Gospel," talk at Episcopal Theological School on Apr. 17, 1962, Niebuhr Tape Collection (N55); *LNTC*, 46–47 (1923); *BT* [v]; *Remembering Reinhold Niebuhr*, 119, 129; *BT*, 32; H. Richard Niebuhr to RN, probably Dec. 1937, Niebuhr Papers.

50. "Intellectual Autobiography," Kegley and Bretall, 3; "Sects and Churches," *Christian Century* 52 (July 3, 1935), in *EAC*, 41; "Worship and the Social Conscience," *RR* 3 (Winter 1937), in *EAC*, 48–51.

51. Interview with E. Clarendon Hyde, a student at Union from 1937 to 1940, June 11, 1986 (on RN's classroom manner); interview with Victor Obenhaus, Mar. 23, 1989 (on RN's rapport with students and rising enrollment in his classes as compared with Ward's); *Union Theological Seminary in the City of New York: Catalogue:* 1934–35, 74; 1935–36, 71; 1936–37, 75; Edmund Fuller, *Brothers Divided: A Novel* (New York: Bobbs-Merrill Co., 1951).

52. Roger L. Shinn to author, Sept. 10, 1991 (on RN's office in Room 701); interview with Ursula M. Niebuhr, Mar. 23, 1987 (on RN's study habits and Thursday evening gatherings); Bingham, 286; interview with E. Clarendon Hyde, June 11, 1986 (on RN's quoted remark).

53. John C. Bennett, "The Contribution of Reinhold Niebuhr," *Religion in Life* 6 (Winter 1937): 268–83.

CHAPTER FOUR

1. Stanley Jaki, *Lord Gifford and His Lectures: A Centenary Retrospect* (Edinburgh: Scottish Academic Press; Macon, Ga.: Mercer University Press, 1986), 2–14, 23–26, 43–65.

2. RN to William Scarlett, Aug. 28, 1937, Niebuhr Papers; telephone interview with Carl Hermann Voss, Apr. 2, 1989 (on Tillich's comment, made to Voss). RN's footnotes in *The Nature and Destiny of Man* are the best evidence of the scope of his reading from 1937 to 1942.

3. RN to Emil Brunner, Mar. 10, 1938, Brunner Papers, University of Zurich (copy provided to author by Werner Kramer on behalf of the Brunner family); Emil Brunner to RN, Mar. 23, 1938, Niebuhr Papers; Stone 121–2. Brunner's letter was translated from the German for the author by Luverne Walton, professor of German at the University of Missouri, July 10, 1987.

4. Henry Sloane Coffin to RN, July 16, 1938, Niebuhr Papers; *Union Theological Seminary in the City of New York: Catalogue:* 1938–39, 71; 1939–40, 67; Roger L. Shinn to author, Nov. 15, 1989 (on versions of Gifford Lectures as courses at Union); Gifford Lectures engagement calendar, Niebuhr Papers; Fox, 188; *Remembering Reinhold Niebuhr*, 144–46; John Baillie, "Niebuhr's Gifford Lectures," *Union Review* 2 (Mar. 1941): 7–8.

5. RN to William Scarlett, two undated letters of early and late May 1939, Niebuhr Papers; RN to Lydia and Hulda Niebuhr, May 21, 1939, Niebuhr Papers; *Remembering Reinhold Niebuhr*, 153–58; "Leaves from the Notebook of a War-Bound American," *Christian Century* 56 (Dec. 27, 1939): 1607.

6. Review of Cochrane's *Christianity and Classical Culture, University of Toronto Quarterly* 10 (July 1941): 505–10.

7. "Kierkegaard's Message" (rev. of Kierkegaard's *Concluding Unscientific Postscript*), *New York Herald Tribune Books*, Nov. 30, 1941, 33; rev. of Kierkegaard's *The Sickness Unto Death, C&S* 7 (Spring 1942): 41–42.

8. "A Faith for History's Greatest Crisis," *Fortune* 26 (July 1942): 99; Henry Sloane Coffin to RN, June 17, 1942, Niebuhr Papers; *Remembering Reinhold Niebuhr*, 340.

9. *NDM* 1:1–12.

10. *NDM* 1:12–18.

11. *NDM* 1:18–25.

12. *NDM* 1:26–122.

13. *NDM* 1:123–49.

14. *NDM* 1:150–77.

15. *NDM* 1:178–86.

16. *NDM* 1:186–207.
17. *NDM* 1:208–27.
18. *NDM* 1:228–40.
19. *NDM* 1:241–64.
20. *NDM* 1:265–300.
21. *NDM* 2:1–34.
22. *NDM* 2:35–97.
23. *NDM* 2:98–156.
24. *NDM* 2:157–83.
25. *NDM* 2:184–204.
26. *NDM* 2:204–12.
27. *NDM* 2:213–43.
28. *NDM* 2:244–64.
29. *NDM* 2:265–86.
30. *NDM* 2:287–98.
31. *NDM* 2:299–321.
32. Bernard Iddings Bell, "On Human Nature" (rev. of *NDM*, vol. 1), *New York Times Book Review*, Apr. 6, 1941, 41; Paul Tillich, rev. of *NDM*, vol. 1, *C&S* 6 (Spring 1941): 34–37; W. H. Auden, "The Means of Grace" (rev. of *NDM*, vol. 1), *New Republic* 104 (June 2, 1941): 765–66; Ursula M. Niebuhr, "Memories of the 1940s," in *W. H. Auden: A Tribute*, ed. S. Spender (New York: Macmillan Publishing Co., 1975), 104–6, 108, 112.
33. Robert L. Calhoun, rev. of *NDM*, vol. 1, *Journal of Religion* 21 (Oct. 1941): 473–80; John C. Bennett, "Current Theological Literature," *C&C* 1 (Aug. 11, 1941): 2; Calhoun, rev. of *NDM*, vol. 2, *Journal of Religion* 24 (Jan. 1944): 59–64; Joseph Haroutunian, rev. of *NDM*, vol. 2, *C&S* 8 (Spring 1943): 36–39.
34. Lowell H. Zuck, director of Eden Archives, to author, Dec. 6, 1991 (on date of RN's D.D. degree from Eden); "Citation of Nine Honored at Yale Yesterday," *New York Times*, June 10, 1942, 17. Besides Eden, Yale, Oxford, Harvard, and Princeton, the following institutions gave RN honorary doctorates: Grinnell College, Wesleyan University, University of Pennsylvania, Amherst College, New York University, Glasgow University, Hobart College, Muhlenberg College, Dartmouth College, University of Manchester, Occidental College, New School for Social Research, Columbia University, Franklin and Marshall College, American University, and Jewish Theological Seminary; for most of these degrees, see various editions of *Who's Who*.
35. Among historical works cited by RN are those of Jaeger, Cassirer, Lovejoy, Cochrane, and Becker (*NDM* 1:6–7, 61–62, 88–89; 2:14–15, 310).
36. Emil Brunner, "Some Remarks on Reinhold Niebuhr as a Christian Thinker," Kegley and Bretall, 32–33; "Reply to Interpretation and Criticism," Kegley and Bretall, 431; Stone, 254; interview with Roger L. Shinn, Mar. 24, 1987 (on the context of RN's reply to Brunner, overstating his indebtedness); *NDM* 2:64, 124, 188–91, 196–97, 251, 255–56 (on various books of Brunner).
37. Henry Sloane Coffin, *A Half Century of Union Seminary* (New York: Charles Scribner's Sons, 1954), 150; Ursula M. Niebuhr to author, Oct. 18, 1989.
38. RN to William L. Savage, June 1, 1946, Niebuhr Papers.
39. Jaki, 43–62; "Reply to Interpretation and Criticism," Kegley and Bretall, 347. The points quoted appear in *NDM* 1:219 and 2:49.

CHAPTER FIVE

1. "Anti-Semitism," *RR* 3 (Summer 1938): 5; RN to William Scarlett, Sept. 16, 1938, Niebuhr Papers; "After Munich," *RR* 4 (Winter 1938): 1; "The *London Times* and the Crisis," *RR* 4 (Winter 1938): 32.

2. *Remembering Reinhold Niebuhr*, 145; Eberhard Bethge, *Dietrich Bonhoeffer: Man of Vision, Man of Courage*, trans. E. Mosbacher and others (New York: Harper & Row, 1970), 543–44, 555–57; "To America and Back," in *I Knew Dietrich Bonhoeffer*, ed. W. Zimmerman and R. G. Smith (New York: Harper & Row, 1966), 165; "Dietrich Bonhoeffer," *Union Seminary Quarterly Review* 1 (Mar. 1946): 3; "The Death of a Martyr," *C&C* 5 (June 25, 1945): 6–7; Preface to Dietrich Bonhoeffer, *The Cost of Discipleship* (New York: Macmillan Co., 1949). RN's paraphrase of Bonhoeffer's 1939 letter, in the 1945 piece cited above, was reprinted as the original in an edition of Bonhoeffer's works, *The Way to Freedom*, ed. E. H. Robertson, vol. 2, p. 246. The original letter is not in the Niebuhr Papers, and RN told Larry Rasmussen—an authority on Bonhoeffer appointed to the Niebuhr chair at Union Seminary in 1985—that he lost it; interview with Rasmussen, June 10, 1991.

3. "The Ambiguity of Human Decisions," *RR* 4 (Summer 1939): 3–4; "Leaves from the Notebook of a War-Bound American," *Christian Century* 56 (Oct. 25, Nov. 15, and Dec. 27, 1939): 1298, 1405, and 1607.

4. "Winston Churchill and Great Britain," *C&C* 15 (May 2, 1955): 51; Walter Johnson, *William Allen White's America* (New York: Henry Holt, 1947), 525.

5. Robert M. Miller, *American Protestantism and Social Issues, 1919–1939* (Chapel Hill, N.C.: University of North Carolina Press, 1958), 337–44.

6. *Why the Christian Church Is Not Pacifist* (London: SCM Press, 1940); *CPP*, 4–6, 10–11, 26, 28–31 (also in *ERN*, 102–19 and *RNTPL*, 237–53).

7. *CPP*, 44, 56–59, 61.

8. Harold Bosley, "Illusion of the Disillusioned" (rev. of *CPP*), *Christian Century* 58 (Jan. 1, 1941): 14–6; W. H. Auden, "Tract for the Times" (rev. of *CPP*), *Nation* 152 (Jan. 4, 1941): 24–25. RN's Ware Lecture is in *CPP*, 177–202 (also in *ERN*, 3–17); his address to the Oxford Conference is in *CPP*, 203–26 (also in *ERN*, 79–92).

9. Donald L. Miller, *Lewis Mumford: A Life* (New York: Weidenfeld & Nicolson, 1989), 394, 402; "Waldo Frank, Pilot" (rev. of Frank's *Chart for Rough Waters*), *Nation* 150 (May 11, 1940): 600–601; "Challenge to Liberals" (rev. of Mumford's *Faith for Living*), *Nation* 151 (Sept. 14, 1940): 221–22; "An End to Illusions," *Nation* 150 (June 1940), in *CPP*, 167–68.

10. "Willkie and Roosevelt," *C&S* 5 (Fall 1940): 5–7; "Lewis and the C.I.O.," *C&S* 5 (Winter 1940): 6–7.

11. "The War Situation," *C&S* 6 (Winter 1940): 3.

12. "Niebuhr Launches New Journal," *Christian Century* 58 (Jan. 22, 1941): 133; "A Christian Journal Confronts Mankind's Continuing Crisis," *C&C* 26 (Feb. 21, 1966): 11–13; telephone interview with John C. Bennett, Apr. 17, 1989 (on meetings of *C&C*'s editorial advisers); "The Christian Faith and the World Crisis," *C&C* 1 (Feb. 10, 1941): 4–6.

13. "The Lend-Lease Bill," *C&C* 1 (Feb. 10, 1941): 2; "Hitler Tells Us Not to Interfere; Will Torpedo Aid Ships, He Says; Lend-Lease Bill Goes to House," *New York Times*, Jan. 31, 1941, 1.

14. "Union for Democratic Action," *C&S* 6 (Summer 1941): 6; Steven M. Gillon, *Politics and Vision: The ADA and American Liberalism, 1947–1985* (New York: Oxford University Press, 1987), 9–11; Alonzo L. Hamby, *Beyond the New Deal: Harry S. Truman and American Liberalism* (New York: Columbia University Press, 1973), 36–37.

15. "The Crisis Deepens," *C&C* 1 (May 5, 1941): 1–2; "New Allies, Old Issues," *Nation* 153 (July 19, 1941): 50–52; "Ideologies," *New Leader* 24 (Aug. 16, 1941): 4; "Japan and Economic Sanctions," *C&C* 1 (Aug. 25, 1941): 2.

16. "Repeal the Neutrality Act!" *C&C* 1 (Oct. 20, 1941), in *LJ*, 177–79; Charles C. Morrison, "Is Neutrality Immoral?" *Christian Century* 58 (Nov. 12, 1941): 1399–1401; "Momentous Decision by a Narrow Margin," *C&C* 1 (Dec. 1, 1941): 1–2; "We Are at War," *C&C* 1 (Dec. 29, 1941): 2; "History (God) Has Overtaken Us," *C&S* 7 (Winter 1941), in *LJ*, 293.

17. Ursula M. Niebuhr to author, Feb. 3, 1987 (on RN's use of remuneration for book reviews); rev. of Eliot's *The Idea of a Christian Society*, *RR* 5 (Winter 1940): 38–40; "Croce on History" (rev. of Croce's *History as the Story of Liberty*), *Nation* 152 (June 14, 1941): 699–700.

18. "Sorokin on Culture" (rev. of Sorokin's *The Crisis of Our Age*), *Nation* 153 (Dec. 20, 1941): 648; William Scarlett to RN (telegram), Dec. 22, 1941, Niebuhr Papers; Bingham, 253–55.

19. "Mann's Political Essays" (rev. of Mann's *Order of the Day*), *Nation* 155 (Nov. 28, 1942): 583–84; "The Historian as Prophet" (rev. of Burckhardt's *Force and Freedom*), *Nation* 156 (April 10, 1943): 530–31.

20. "Man Proposes but God Disposes," *C&S* 7 (Autumn 1942): 9; *Town Meeting: Bulletin of America's Town Meeting of the Air* 8 (Aug. 27, 1942): 12–13; "In the Battle and Above It," *C&S* 7 (Autumn 1942): 3.

21. "My Sense of Shame," *Hadassah Newsletter* 19 (Dec. 1938): 59–60.

22. Transcript of address to 44th annual convention of the Zionist Organization of America, Sept. 9, 1941, Zionist Archives and Library, New York City; "Jews after the War," *Nation* 154 (Feb. 21 and 28, 1942), in *LJ*, 132–42; Daniel Rice, "Correspondence Essay—Felix Frankfurter and Reinhold Niebuhr: 1940–1964," *Journal of Law and Religion* 1 (1983): 338.

23. Carl Hermann Voss and David A. Rausch, "American Christians and Israel," *American Jewish Archives* 40 (Apr. 1988): 41–43, 52–54; Hertzel Fishman, *American Protestantism and a Jewish State* (Detroit: Wayne State University Press, 1973), 72–76.

24. "The Supreme Court and Jim Crowism," *C&S* 6 (Summer 1941): 8–9; "Negroes and the Railroads," *C&S* 9 (Winter 1943): 11; "The Evacuation of Japanese Citizens," *C&C* 2 (May 18, 1942): 2–4.

25. "The Bombing of Germany," *C&S* 8 (Summer 1943): 3–4; David Astor, "The Man Who Plotted against Hitler," *New York Review of Books*, Apr. 28, 1983, 16–21; "Germany," *Worldview* 16 (June 1973): 16; "Group Here Urges Integrity of Reich," *New York Times*, Nov. 15, 1941, 6; Introduction to Jon B. Jansen and Stefan Weyl, *The Silent War: The Underground Movement in Germany* (Philadelphia: J. B. Lippincott Co., 1943), 9–10.

26. "Russia and the West," *Nation* 156 (Jan. 16 and 23, 1943): 82–83; "Marxism in Eclipse," *Spectator* 170 (June 4, 1943): 518.

27. "Tensions in British Politics," *Nation* 156 (June 26, 1943): 889; "Letter from Britain," *C&C* 3 (July 12, 1943): 2; Ursula M. Niebuhr to author, June 3, 1988 (on RN with Murrow and Laski during air raid, as related to her by William Shirer, who was with them); *Remembering Reinhold Niebuhr*, 172–73, 180–81, 184; Alzina Stone Dale, *T. S. Eliot: The Philosopher-Poet* (Wheaton, Ill.: Harold Shaw, 1988), 140–41; Carl Hermann Voss, "Niebuhr: 20th Century Prophet," *Advance* 136 (July 1944): 12; "England Teaches Its Soldiers," *Nation* 157 (Aug. 21, 1943): 208–10; "Understanding England," *Nation* 157 (Aug. 14, 1943): 175–77.

28. Christopher Niebuhr to author, Dec. 19, 1988 (on stone cottage); Christmas letter of Harold Wilke, ca. 1980, quoting a letter from Ursula Niebuhr in reply to his questions about the "Serenity Prayer" (copy provided to author by Wilke on Dec. 30, 1985). The prayer as quoted from RN's own words appeared in "To Be Abased and to Abound," *Messenger* 16 (Feb. 13, 1951): 7. Richard Fox has dem-

onstrated that it was in fact RN who composed the prayer and not the eighteenth-century German theologian Friedrich Oetinger, in whose name a German translation was published; see Fox, 290. Ursula Niebuhr gives 1943 as its date in *Justice and Mercy*, unnumbered page after title page.

29. Handy, 181–82, 204–6; interview with Ursula M. Niebuhr, Mar. 23, 1987; RN to William Scarlett, Oct. 2, 1942, Niebuhr Papers. For more on the Harvard invitation, see Daniel Rice, "Correspondence Essay—Felix Frankfurter and Reinhold Niebuhr," 339–40.

30. "White Man's Burden," *C&S* 6 (Summer 1941): 3–5; "Anglo-Saxon Destiny and Responsibility," *C&C* 3 (Oct. 4, 1943), in *LJ*, 184–88; "Christian Otherworldliness," *C&S* 9 (Winter 1943): 12.

31. *CLCD*, xi.

32. *CLCD*, xi, 7, 9–11, 40–41; 19–20, 61–63; 27–28; 23, 25–27, 42–43, 45–46, 51–54.

33. *CLCD*, 60, 112–13; 23, 32–33; 90, 104; 76, 113; 105.

34. *CLCD*, 124, 129–30, 134, 138–39, 143, 148–50.

35. *CLCD*, 155–58; 162–65; 173–74, 176; 172, 175, 177, 180; 186–87.

36. Arthur M. Schlesinger, Jr., rev. of *FH*, *C&S* 14 (Summer 1949): 26; interview with Russell Kirk, Nov. 1, 1986; James I. Loeb, "In Appreciation of Reinie," *ADA World*, Sept. 1971, 7.

37. "Is the Bombing Necessary?" *C&C* 4 (Apr. 3, 1944): 1; "The Climax of the War," *C&C* 4 (May 29, 1944): 1; "Editorial Notes," *C&C* 4 (Oct. 2, 1944): 2.

38. "Social Justice in a Defense Economy," *C&S* 6 (Spring 1941): 6–7; "A Fourth Term for Roosevelt," *New Statesman and Nation* 25 (May 15, 1943): 315–16; [Socialist] *Call*, Sept. 8, 1944, 5, quoted in Murray B. Seidler, *Norman Thomas: Respectable Rebel* (2d ed.; Syracuse, N.Y.: Syracuse University Press, 1967), 221, 223–24; *CLCD*, 113; *NDM* 2: 262. As to when RN abandoned socialism in favor of the New Deal, see William H. Becker, "Reinhold Niebuhr: From Marx to Roosevelt," the *Historian* 35 (Aug. 1973): 539–50, which argues persuasively that his conversion was final by 1943.

39. Bingham, 218–19; "Dr. Niebuhr Takes Liberal Party Post," *New York Times*, July 28, 1944, 10; "Election Insights on Our Civilization," *C&S* 10 (Winter 1944): 7.

40. "Archbishop Temple," *C&C* 4 (Nov. 13, 1944): 1.

41. Rev. of Myrdal's *An American Dilemma*, *C&S* 9 (Summer 1944): 42; "Editorial Notes," *C&C* 4 (Sept. 18, 1944): 2 (on Myrdal's book); "The Collectivist Bogey" (rev. of Hayek's *The Road to Serfdom*), *Nation* 159 (Oct. 21, 1944): 478, 480; "Concerning the Devil" (rev. of de Rougemont's *The Devil's Share*), *Nation* 160 (Feb. 17, 1945): 188–89.

42. Roger L. Shinn, *Wars and Rumors of Wars* (Nashville: Abingdon Press, 1972), 15–181; Nathan A. Scott, Jr., to author, Mar. 19, 1990 (on RN's memorial service for Shinn); interview with Roger L. Shinn, Mar. 24, 1987.

43. "The Conference of the 'Big Three,' " *C&C* 5 (Mar. 5, 1945): 1–2; "Is This 'Peace in Our Time'?" *Nation* 160 (Apr. 7, 1945): 382–83.

44. "The Death of the President," *C&C* 5 (Apr. 30, 1945), 4–5.

45. "Soberness in Victory," *C&C* 5 (May 28, 1945): 1; "Our Relations to Japan," *C&C* 5 (Sept. 17, 1945): 5, 7; "The Atomic Bomb," *C&S* 10 (Fall 1945), in *LJ*, 233.

CHAPTER SIX

1. "Russia and the West," *C&S* 10 (Summer 1945): 5–6; "The Russian Enigma," *C&S* 11 (Winter 1945): 5–6. On RN's role as journalist during this period, see

Charles C. Brown, "Niebuhr, Reinhold," in *The Harry S. Truman Encyclopedia*, ed. R. S. Kirkendall (Boston: G.K. Hall & Co., 1989), 255.

2. "I Was an Hungred and Ye Gave Me No Meat," *C&C* 5 (Jan. 7, 1946): 6; Roger L. Shinn to author, Oct. 25, 1990 (on FSC's sending food to Europe); CARE receipts, Niebuhr Papers; "The Victory of British Labor," *C&S* 10 (Fall 1945): 8; "Editorial Notes," *C&C* 6 (Feb. 4, 1946): 2.

3. "The Conflict between Nations and Nations and between Nations and God," *C&C* 6 (Aug. 5, 1946), in *LJ*, 161, 164.

4. "The Nonchalance of Faith," *C&S* 11 (Winter 1945): 9.

5. "Isolation of a Culture," *Messenger* 11 (Nov. 26, 1946): 6; "Germany," *World-view* 16 (June 1973): 18; Theodor Heuss, "German Character and History," *Atlantic Monthly* 199 (Mar. 1957): 103; "A Report on Germany," *C&C* 6 (Oct. 14, 1946): 6–7.

6. "The Fight for Germany," *Life*, Oct. 21, 1946, 65–68, 70, 72.

7. "Mr. Wallace's Errors," *C&C* 6 (Oct. 28, 1946): 1–2; "The American Labor Movement," *C&S* 12 (Winter 1946): 7; Gillon, 11–20; Bingham, 257; "Front of Liberals Urged by Bowles," *New York Times*, Jan. 4, 1947, 16; "130 Liberals Form a Group on Right," *New York Times*, Jan. 5, 1947, 5; Langdon Gilkey, "*Reinhold Niebuhr: A Biography:* A Critical Review Article," *Journal of Religion* 68 (Apr. 1988): 274.

8. Gillon, 21–23, 26, 28; Hamby, 147–54, 159–64; "The Organization of the Liberal Movement," *C&S* 12 (Spring 1947); 8, 10.

9. Walter Mallory, executive director of the Council on Foreign Relations, to RN, Nov. 20, 1946, and RN to Mallory, Dec. 6, 1946, Niebuhr Papers; interview with Kenneth W. Thompson, June 5, 1991 (on RN's attendance at CFR meetings); "The Illusion of World Government," *Foreign Affairs* 27 (Apr. 1949), in *WCAR*, 86, 89, 95–97, 99; "Can We Organize the World?" *C&C* 13 (Feb. 2, 1953), in *LJ*, 216.

10. "A Living Process" (rev. of Becker's *Freedom and Responsibility in the American Way of Life*), *Nation* 161 (Nov. 17, 1945): 526–27.

11. Rev. of Morgenthau's *Scientific Man versus Power Politics*, *C&S* 12 (Spring 1947): 33–34. Morgenthau's comment on Niebuhr appears in his notes to ch. 7 of the book.

12. "Theologian and Church Statesman," in *This Ministry: The Contribution of Henry Sloane Coffin*, ed. R. Niebuhr (New York: Charles Scribner's Sons, 1946), 118, 120, 129; Handy, 208–9, 211–14, 228, 237.

13. *DST*, 154–55, 166–67, 171 (also in *ERN*, 237–49); Arthur M. Schlesinger, Jr., "Niebuhr's Vision of Our Time" (rev. of *DST*), *Nation* 162 (June 22, 1946): 754; interview with Schlesinger, Mar. 25, 1987 (on hearing RN preach in 1940, before meeting him through ADA).

14. Telephone interview with John C. Bennett, Apr. 17, 1989 (on RN's many callers and Nola Meade's office); interview with Ursula M. Niebuhr, Mar. 23, 1987 (on move to Knox Hall); Roger L. Shinn, quoted anonymously in Coffin, *A Half Century of Union Seminary*, 150–52.

15. Roger L. Shinn to author, Nov. 15, 1991 (on RN's role in Union's joint doctoral program with Columbia and his relation to its political science faculty); interview with Shinn, June 9, 1991 (on RN's membership in the Philosophy Club— some of whose members, besides RN, Shinn knew); *Remembering Reinhold Niebuhr*, 309; Wilhelm and Marion Pauck, 183–86; "Our Pilgrimage from a Century of Hope to a Century of Perplexity," *Current Religious Thought* 8 (Nov. 1948): 25–26. On RN and the Philosophy Club, see also James Gutmann, Columbia University Oral History Project, recorded May 26, 1976, esp. p. 196. RN's Ohio State address was given on Oct. 15, 1948, as noted in *Addresses and Proceedings of the*

Seventy-fifth Anniversary, 1948–49 (Columbus, Ohio: Ohio State University Press, 1951), 6.

16. William Scarlett, with RN, "The Social Gospel," talk at Episcopal Theological School on Apr. 17, 1962, Niebuhr Tape Collection (N55); *To Will One Thing*, ed. W. Scarlett (St. Louis: Christ Church Cathedral, 1948), 3; RN to William Scarlett, Jan. 18, 1949, Niebuhr Papers. RN's Religious News Service column was carried by *Episcopal Churchnews*, the *Lutheran*, and the *Messenger*, a magazine of his own denomination.

17. Rev. of Brunner's *Justice and the Social Order*, *C&S* 11 (Summer 1946): 41–42; rev. of Bennett's *Christian Ethics and Social Policy*, *C&S* 12 (Winter 1946): 41.

18. "Editorial Correspondence," *C&C* 7 (Mar. 3, 1947): 6, and (Mar. 14, 1947): 6; "European Impressions," *C&C* 7 (May 12, 1947): 3–4; RN to Ursula M. Niebuhr, Mar. 16, 1947 (letter in possession of Ursula Niebuhr); *Remembering Reinhold Niebuhr*, 239–40.

19. "European Impressions," *C&C* 7 (May 12, 1947): 2; "American Power and European Health," *C&C* 7 (June 9, 1947): 1; "Editorial Notes," *C&C* 7 (Aug. 4, 1947): 2.

20. "America's Precarious Eminence," *Virginia Quarterly Review* 23 (Autumn 1947): 482; "America's Wealth and the World's Poverty," *C&S* 12 (Autumn 1947):3; "The Marshall Plan," *C&C* 7 (Oct. 13, 1947): 2; "Amid Encircling Gloom," *C&C* 8 (Apr. 12, 1948): 41; "No Time for Hysteria," *Messenger* 13 (Apr. 13, 1948): 6; "The Italian Elections," *C&S* 13 (Summer 1948): 7; "The 'Third Force' in Europe," *Messenger* 13 (Mar. 2, 1948): 6; "Catholic Politics in Europe," *Messenger* 11 (Sept. 3, 1946): 7.

21. Introduction to Waldo Frank, *The Jew in Our Day* (London: Victor Gollancz, 1944), 10–11, 14; "Chaim Weizmann" (rev. of *Chaim Weizmann*, ed. M. Weisgal), *Nation* 160 (Jan. 13, 1945): 51; Fishman, (see ch. 5, note 23), 78–80; U.S. Department of State, *Hearings of the Anglo-American Committee of Inquiry*, Jan. 14, 1946, 141, 155.

22. Fishman, 80–84, 89–92; telephone interview with Carl Hermann Voss, June 9, 1990 (on RN's ACPC-sponsored speeches); "The Palestine Problem," *Messenger* 11 (Aug. 20, 1946): 6; "A New View of Palestine," *Spectator* 177 (Aug. 16, 1946): 162; "Stephen S. Wise: A Leonine Figure" (rev. of Wise's *Challenging Years*), *New York Times Book Review*, Nov. 6, 1949, 6.

23. "The Partition of Palestine," *C&S* 13 (Winter 1948): 3–4; Bayard Dodge, "Peace or War in Palestine," *C&C* 8 (Mar. 15, 1948): 27–30, RN's editorial note, 30.

24. "The Future of Israel," *Messenger* 13 (June 8, 1948): 6; "Christians and the State of Israel," *C&S* 14 (Summer 1949): 3–5; "$800,000,000 Asked for Arab Refugees," *New York Times*, Dec. 19, 1951, 1, 20.

25. "Faith for a Lenten Age," *Time*, Mar. 8, 1948, 71; "The Struggle of the Church," *Messenger* 12 (Sept. 16, 1947): 7; Paul Abrecht, rev. of Richard Fox's *Reinhold Niebuhr*, *Ecumenical Review* 38 (Apr. 1986): 238–39.

26. RN to William Scarlett, Aug. 3, 1948, Niebuhr Papers. RN's paper for the Amsterdam Assembly series, "God's Design and the Present Disorder of Civilization," appears in *Man's Disorder and God's Design* (New York: Harper & Brothers, 1948), 13–28 (FP, 103–18).

27. *The First Assembly of the World Council of Churches*, ed. W. A. Visser 't Hooft (New York: Harper & Brothers, 1949), 21–24, 236–58.

28. *The First Assembly of the WCC*, 32–33, 178–79; Karl Barth, "No Christian Marshall Plan," *Christian Century* 65 (Dec. 8, 1948): 1331; W. A. Visser 't Hooft, *Memoirs* (London: SCM Press, 1973), 101; "Amsterdam Assembly Address,"

Niebuhr Tape Collection (N63); *CRPP*, 105–17 (published version of RN's Amsterdam address; also in *ERN*, 93–101). Published and recorded versions of the address are here blended.

29. *The First Assembly of the WCC*, 173; "The World Council at Amsterdam," *C&C* 8 (Sept. 20, 1948), in *EAC*, 307–8, 310; "The World Council of Churches," *C&S* 13 (Autumn 1948), in *EAC*, 297–300; "The Cult of Freedom in America," *C&C* 9 (Feb. 7, 1949): 4–7 (for text of WCC report on church and society, see *The First Assembly*, 74–82).

30. "We Are Men and Not God," *Christian Century* 65 (Oct. 27, 1948), in *EAC*, 174–75; Karl Barth, "Continental vs. Anglo-Saxon Theology," *Christian Century* 66 (Feb. 16, 1949): 201–4; "An Answer to Karl Barth," *Christian Century* 66 (Feb. 23, 1949), in *EAC*, 175–77, 179–80; Hugh T. Kerr, "Theological Table-Talk," *Theology Today* 6 (July 1949): 235–37.

31. "For Peace, We Must Risk War," *Life*, Sept. 20, 1948, 38; "The Battle of Berlin," *C&S* 13 (Autumn 1948): 5.

32. Gillon, 46; "The Presidential Campaign," *C&C* 8 (Nov. 1, 1948): 137; RN to William Scarlett, Nov. 8, 1948 (on RN's voting for Truman), Niebuhr Papers; "The American Scene," *C&S* 14 (Winter 1948–49): 3; "The New 'Fair Deal,'" *C&S* 14 (Spring 1949): 6–7.

33. "The Sin of Racial Prejudice," *Messenger* 13 (Feb. 3, 1948): 6; "Sports and the Race Issue," *Messenger* 14 (Feb. 1, 1949); 6; "Fair Employment Practices Act," *C&S* 15 (Summer 1950), in *LJ*, 145–48; "Distribution of Income in the U.S.A.," *C&S* 16 (Summer 1951): 8; "Halfway to What?" *Nation* 170 (Jan. 14, 1950): 26–28.

34. Gillon, 65; "The North Atlantic Pact," *C&C* 9 (May 30, 1949): 65; Michael J. Hogan, *The Marshall Plan* (London: Cambridge University Press, 1987), 258–59; "President Names 7 to UNESCO Session," *New York Times*, Sept. 3, 1949, 4; "Peace through Cultural Cooperation," *C&C* 9 (Oct. 17, 1949): 131–33; "The Theory and Practice of UNESCO," *International Organization* 4 (Feb. 1950): 3–11; Dean Acheson, *Present at the Creation* (New York: N.W. Norton & Co., 1969), 461. Acheson's source of the RN quotation is "The Conditions of Our Survival," *Virginia Quarterly Review* 26 (Autumn 1950): 491.

35. "The Dilemma in China," *Messenger* 14 (Jan. 4, 1949): 4; "The Plight of China," *C&S* 14 (Winter 1948–49): 5; "Communism in China," *C&S* 15 (Winter 1949–50): 6; *MMIS*, 191.

36. "At Our Wit's End," *Messenger* 14 (Dec. 6, 1949): 9; "The Hydrogen Bomb," *C&S* 15 (Spring 1950), in *LJ*, 235–37.

37. "A Protest against a Dilemma's Two Horns," *World Politics* 2 (Apr. 1950): 338–41, 344; "Our Position in Asia," *C&S* 15 (Summer 1950), 6–7.

38. "New Light on the Old Struggle," *C&S* 15 (Fall 1950): 3–4; "The Peril of Hysteria," *C&S* 15 (Fall 1950): 5; "Editorial Notes," *C&C* 10 (Nov. 27, 1950): 154, and (Dec. 25, 1950): 170; "Hybris," *C&S* 16 (Spring 1951): 4, 6; "The MacArthur Episode," *C&S* 16 (Summer 1951): 3; "The Two Dimensions of the Struggle," *C&S* 11 (May 28, 1951): 65–66.

39. "Our Relation to Asia," *Messenger* 16 (Oct. 23, 1951): 7 (also in *Lutheran* 34 [Oct. 17, 1951]: 21); "The Poverty of Asia and Communism," *C&S* 16 (Winter 1950–51): 6–7; "Editorial Notes," *C&C* 7 (July 7, 1947): 2; "The Triumph in India," *Messenger* 12 (July 8, 1947): 6; "Gandhi and Non-Resistance" (rev. of Fischer's *The Life of Mahatma Gandhi*), *New Leader* 33 (Sept. 16, 1950): 20–21.

40. "To Moscow—and Back" (rev. of *The God That Failed*, ed. R. Crossman), *Nation* 170 (Jan. 28, 1950): 88–90; Sara Alpern, *Freda Kirchwey: A Woman of "The Nation"* (Cambridge, Mass.: Harvard University Press, 1987), 210–15.

41. "The 'Super-Theologians' Meet" (reports of RN and Henry P. Van Dusen on WCC meeting), *Union Seminary Quarterly Review* 7 (Jan. 1952): 25–27; "Trans-atlantic Tension," *Reporter* 5 (Sept. 18, 1951): 14–16; "Socialized Medicine in Britain," *C&S* 14 (Autumn 1949), in *LJ*, 84–86.

42. "American Conservatism and the World Crisis," *Yale Review* 40 (Mar. 1951): 387; "An Interview with Reinhold Niebuhr" (conducted by John Cogley), *McCall's* 93 (Feb. 1966): 168; "The Perils of War and the Prospects of Peace," *C&C* 11 (Oct. 15, 1951): 130.

43. Ursula M. Niebuhr, "About the Books Used by Reinhold and Ursula Niebuhr," unpublished reminiscence, Jan. 1987, 3, Union Theological Seminary Archives.

44. *FH*, 1, 4–5, 38, 46–47, 53, 99.

45. *FH*, 55, 58–62, 64–65; 68, 70, 85, 89, 94–95.

46. *FH*, 114; 103, 126–27, 130–31, 128–29; 131, 135; 149–50; 238–41; 237.

47. *FH*, [v]; Lynn Harold Hough, "Niebuhr on the Meaning of History" (rev. of *FH*), *Pastor* 12 (July 1949): 2–3; Perry Miller, "The Great Method" (rev. of *FH*), *Nation* 169 (Aug. 6, 1949): 138; Daniel Jenkins, rev. of *FH*, *Union Seminary Quarterly Review* 4 (May 1949): 51–52; Arthur M. Schlesinger, Jr., rev. of *FH*, *C&S* 14 (Summer 1949), 26–27.

48. "Dr. Niebuhr to Address Group Here," *Richmond News Leader*, Jan. 27, 1950; "How Faith and Reason Are Related," Niebuhr Tape Collection (N2). RN lectured there on Jan. 28, 1950.

49. Interview with Ursula M. Niebuhr, Mar. 23, 1987 (on auspices of the lecture); RN to John C. Bennett, undated letter of mid-1950, Niebuhr Papers (on engagement at Aspen in July); "Augustine's Conception of Selfhood," Niebuhr Tape Collection (N1).

50. *CRPP*, [i], 120–23, 125, 138, 146. RN's Carroll lecture must have been given before his stroke, but the date is elusive.

51. "Backwoods Genius" (rev. of Miller's *Jonathan Edwards*), *The Nation* 169 (Dec. 31, 1949): 648; "Swiss Theologian" (rev. of Barth's *Dogmatics in Outline*), *New York Times Book Review*, Sept. 10, 1950, 43.

52. H. Richard Niebuhr, *Christ and Culture* (New York: Harper & Brothers, 1951), [vi]; Carl Hermann Voss to author, Oct. 19, 1990 (on Niebuhr brothers); Hulda Niebuhr, *The One Story* (Philadelphia: Westminster Press, 1949).

53. "Hazards and Resources," *Virginia Quarterly Review* 25 (Spring 1949): 194; "Germany and Western Civilization," in *Germany and the Future of Europe*, ed. Hans Morgenthau (Chicago: University of Chicago Press, 1951), 8; "Let Anyone Who Thinks that He Stands . . ." *Messenger* 16 (Dec. 18, 1951): 7; *IAH*, vii–ix; "Dr. Reinhold Niebuhr Gives Green Lectures," *Westminster Report* [Fulton, Mo.] 32 (May 1949): 2; rev. of Curti's *The Growth of American Thought*, *C&S* 8 (Fall 1943): 36; rev. of Parkes's *The American Experience*, *C&S* 13 (Winter 1948): 26.

54. *IAH*, 24, 28; 28, 53; 48–49, 79; 29; 22–23, 97–98; 89, 103.

55. *IAH*, 38–39, 69; 112–16; 123–27; 171–74.

56. Peter Viereck, "Freedom Is a Matter of Spirit" (rev. of *IAH*), *New York Times Book Review*, Apr. 6, 1952, 1; E. Harris Harbison, rev. of *IAH*, *Theology Today* 9 (Oct. 1952): 419–21; Anthony West, "Night and Fog" (rev. of *IAH*), *New Yorker* 28 (May 3, 1952): 130; William Leuchtenburg, "Niebuhr: The Theologian and the Liberal" (rev. of *IAH*), *New Leader* 35 (Nov. 24, 1952): 23–24; Morton White, "Of Moral Predicaments" (rev. of *IAH*), *New Republic* 126 (May 5, 1952): 18–19; Arthur M. Schlesinger, Jr., "Niebuhr and Some Critics" (rev. of *IAH*), *C&S* 17 (Autumn 1952): 25–27; Crane Brinton, "The Problem of Human Evil in History" (rev. of *IAH*), *New York Herald Tribune Book Review*, Apr. 6, 1952, 5; Herbert Agar, "America's

Philosopher" (rev of *IAH*), *Spectator* 189 (Dec. 12, 1952): 819–20; Henry F. May, "A Meditation on an Unfashionable Book," *C&C* 28 (May 27, 1968): 120–22; George F. Kennan, "In the American Mirror" (rev. of Arthur Schlesinger's *The Cycles of American History*), *New York Review of Books*, Nov. 6, 1986, 3.

57. Interview with Ursula M. Niebuhr, Mar. 23, 1987 (on RN's illness); Christopher Niebuhr to author, Oct. 10, 1988 (on Fitch's taking over RN's classes); RN to William Turner Levy, May 23, 1952, Union Theological Seminary Archives; *Remembering Reinhold Niebuhr*, 373; RN to faculty and trustees of Union Theological Seminary, June 24, 1952, Niebuhr Papers; telephone interview with John C. Bennett, Apr. 17, 1989 (on gift of typewriter to RN).

CHAPTER SEVEN

1. RN to Adlai Stevenson, Mar. 21, 1952, and Feb. 28, 1956, Niebuhr Papers; Stevenson to RN, Jan. 23, 1957, Niebuhr Papers; Bingham, 304; William Lee Miller, *Piety on the Potomac* (Boston: Houghton Mifflin Co., 1964), 153.

2. "Theology and Politics," *Lutheran* 34 (July 9, 1952): 10; "Christian Faith and Political Controversy," *C&C* 12 (July 21, 1952), in *LJ*, 60–61; "The Republican Victory," *C&C* 12 (Nov. 24, 1952), in *LJ*, 64–65; *CRPP*, 58–59; "The Task of American Liberalism," *ADA World* 8 (May 1953): 1.

3. "The Korean Peace," *C&S* 18 (Autumn 1953): 3–4; "Editorial Notes," *C&C* 13 (Apr. 27, 1953): 50; "Is Tyranny Changing in Russia?" *C&S* 19 (Autumn 1954): 6; "World's Ultimate Peril Remains," *Episcopal Churchnews* 118 (June 7, 1953): 12.

4. "Coronation Afterthoughts," *Christian Century* 70 (July 1, 1953): 771; "Democracy and the Party Spirit," *New Leader* 37 (Mar. 15, 1954), in *LJ*, 70; "Catholicism and Democracy," *Messenger* 18 (Oct. 6, 1953): 7 (also in *Lutheran*, 36 [Oct. 28, 1953]: 25); "The French Do Not Like Us," *C&S* 19 (Winter 1953–54): 9–11.

5. "The Moral and Spiritual Content of the Atlantic Community," *Five Years of the North Atlantic Alliance: A Symposium* (New York: American Council on NATO, 1954), 25–30.

6. "Will We Resist Injustice?" *C&C* 13 (Apr. 13, 1953): 41; "Beria and McCarthy," *New Leader* 37 (Jan. 4, 1954): 4; "Dear Editor," *New Leader* 37 (Jan. 25, 1954): 27; "The Spread of Infection," *C&S* 19 (Spring 1954): 5–6.

7. "Law and Custom," *Messenger* 19 (June 29, 1954): 7 (also in *Episcopal Churchnews* 119 [July 25, 1954]: 7); "The Supreme Court on Segregation in the Schools," *C&C* 14 (June 14, 1954), in *LJ*, 149–51.

8. "Why They Dislike America," *New Leader* 37 (Apr. 12, 1954): 4–5; "America and the Asians," *New Leader* 37 (May 31, 1954): 3; "Frustrations of American Power," *New Leader* 37 (Nov. 29, 1954): 7.

9. "Editorial Notes," *C&C* 14 (July 26, 1954): 98–99; "The Case for Coexistence," *New Leader* 37 (Oct. 4, 1954): 5–6 (also in *Alternatives to the H-Bomb*, ed. A. Shub [Boston: Beacon Press, 1955], 30–36); "Frustrations of American Power," 8.

10. "The Sources of American Prestige," *New Leader* 38 (Jan. 31, 1955): 6; "The Anatomy of American Nationalism," *New Leader* 38 (Feb. 28, 1955): 17; "The Limits of American Power, *New Leader* 38 (May 30, 1955), in *LJ*, 193; "A Glimpse into the Future," *C&S* 20 (Autumn 1955): 4; "The New Face of the Communist Conspiracy," *C&S* 21 (Winter 1955–56): 3; "The Change in Russia," *New Leader* 38 (Oct. 3, 1955): 18.

11. "Varieties of Religious Revival," *New Republic* 132 (June 6, 1955): 13–16; "Religiosity versus the Christian Gospel," *Messenger* 20 (Jan. 11, 1955): 7 (also

in *Lutheran* 37 [Jan. 12, 1955]: 12); "The Role of Religion in 'Americanization,'" *Messenger* 20 (Sept. 6, 1955): 7 (also in *Lutheran* 37 [Sept. 14, 1955]: 12).

12. "The Abundance of Things a Man Possesses," *Messenger* 20 (Aug. 16, 1955): 7 (also in *Lutheran* 37 [Aug. 24, 1955]: 12); "Favorable Environments," *Messenger* 18 (Aug. 18, 1953): 6.

13. "The Race Problem in America," *C&C* 15 (Dec. 26, 1955): 169; "Nullification," *New Leader* 39 (Mar. 5, 1956): 4; "What Resources Can the Christian Church Offer to Meet Crisis in Race Relations?" *Messenger* 21 (Apr. 3, 1956), in *LJ*, 153.

14. Handy, 217–23, 230–31, 233, 237–38, 241, 243–46, 253–54; leaflet entitled *"the claims of the world . . ."* published by Union Theological Seminary in New York, 1962.

15. Handy, 220, 227; Robert T. Handy to author, Jan. 31, 1992 (on RN's move to Room 409, next to Handy's office); telephone interview with John C. Bennett, Apr. 17, 1989 (on RN as dean and vice president of Union); James M. Ward to author, Feb. 24, 1989 (Ward, a student at Union from 1950 to 1955, became an Old Testament scholar at Perkins School of Theology); interview with Ursula M. Niebuhr, Mar. 23, 1987 (on afternoons with students); interview with Roger L. Shinn, Apr. 12, 1991 (on RN in refectory).

16. Handy, 252–53; John A. Hutchison, "Two Decades of Social Christianity," in *Christian Faith and Social Action*, ed. J. Hutchison (New York: Charles Scribner's Sons, 1953), 5; telephone interview with Wayne H. Cowan, Apr. 24, 1989; Cowan, "In 25 Years You Pick Up a Lot of Memories," *C&C* 39 (Sept. 17–Oct. 1, 1979): 210, 233; Felix Frankfurter to RN, May 14, 1955, Niebuhr Papers.

17. RN to William Scarlett, July 15, 1956, and an undated letter of the later 1950s, Niebuhr Papers; interview with Ursula M. Niebuhr, Mar. 23, 1987 (on the house at Stockbridge, her position at Barnard, and the poodles); RN to Leah Scarlett, Dec. 5, 1957, Niebuhr Papers.

18. Handy, 250–51; "Christian Faith and Humanism," Niebuhr Tape Collection (N4). Niebuhr's lecture—originally entitled "What Is the Difference between Christian and Secular Humanism?"—was given on Jan. 14, 1952; Phyllis Conley, of Union Seminary's Development Office, to author, May 20, 1987.

19. "The Hazards and the Difficulties of the Christian Ministry," *JM*, 129–31, 134; "Talk to Students on Theological Education," Niebuhr Tape Collection (N30). RN gave the former on Mar. 29, 1953; the latter on Sept. 25, 1955.

20. Emil Brunner to RN, Oct. 19, 1952, Niebuhr Papers; Lesslie Newbigin and others to RN, Aug. 29, 1953, Niebuhr Papers; RN to William Levy, June 3, 1955, Union Theological Seminary Archives; Ursula M. Niebuhr to author, June 1, 1990 (on Eliot's having tea with the Niebuhrs). Eliot during his visit christened the Niebuhrs' black poodle, then a puppy, Alexandria, but for complex reasons W. H. Auden later rechristened it Winnie, as Ursula explained in the letter cited above.

21. Alan Paton, *Journey Continued: An Autobiography* (New York: Charles Scribner's Sons, 1988), 149–50. The papers and discussions at the Kent seminar were published in *The Christian Idea of Education*, ed. Edmund Fuller (New Haven, Conn.: Yale University Press, 1957).

22. Carl Hermann Voss, rev. of *Reinhold Niebuhr: His Religious, Social, and Political Thought*, ed. Kegley and Bretall, *Advance* 148 (May 16, 1956): 23–24; "American Academy of Arts and Letters Elects Four," *New York Times*, Dec. 6, 1958, 18.

23. Wilhelm and Marion Pauck, 160–61, 176–79; "Biblical Thought and Ontological Speculation in Tillich's Theology," in *The Theology of Paul Tillich*, ed. C. Kegley and R. Bretall (New York: Macmillan Co., 1952), 216, 218–19, 222, 225;

rev. of Tillich's *Biblical Religion and the Search for Ultimate Reality, Union Seminary Quarterly Review* 11 (Jan. 1956): 59–60.

24. Ursula M. Niebuhr, "Notes on a Friendship: Abraham Joshua Heschel and Reinhold Niebuhr," in *Abraham Joshua Heschel: Exploring His Life and Thought,* ed. J. Merkle (New York: Macmillan Publishing Co., 1985), 38; "The Mysteries of Faith" (rev. of Heschel's *God in Search of Man*), *Saturday Review of Literature* 39 (Apr. 21, 1956): 18.

25. *Union Theological Seminary in the City of New York: Catalogue:* 1952–53, 81; 1953–54, 81; 1954–55, 81; 1955–56, 82; 1956–57, 84; 1957–58, 88; 1958–59, 89; 1959–60, 90; Donald L. Scruggs to author, Dec. 9, 1990 (Scruggs, a student at Union from 1958 to 1961, became a political scientist at Stephens College); W. Lance Martin to author, Jan. 12, 1988 (Martin, a student at Union from 1959 to 1962, became a minister at First United Methodist Church in Pasadena); "The Scope of Christian Ethics," Niebuhr Tape Collection (N32).

26. "Lectures in Christian Ethics," recorded from Feb. 4 to May 10, 1960, Niebuhr Tape Collection (N33–52); quotations from N35, N36, N46, N48, N52.

27. "A Third of a Century at Union," *Union Seminary Tower* 7 (May 1960): 3.

28. *PSA*, 13.

29. RN to Richard A. Brown, Stevenson for President Committee, Mar. 22, 1956, and RN to Adlai Stevenson, Oct. 31, 1956, Niebuhr Papers; "The New International Situation," *C&C* 16 (Nov. 12, 1956): 150; "The Cardinal and the Commissar," *New Leader* 40 (Oct. 21, 1957): 5–6.

30. "The New International Situation," 151; "The Middle East and Hungary," *New Leader* 39 (Nov. 26, 1956): 7–8.

31. "The Situation in the Middle East," *C&C* 17 (Apr. 15, 1957): 42; "The Disaster of U.S. Policy," *New Leader* 41 (Aug. 18–25, 1958): 9; "Our Stake in the State of Israel," *New Republic* 136 (Feb. 4, 1957): 9–12.

32. "Why We Are Losing to the Russians," *New Leader* 41 (Jan. 13, 1958): 7; "The Conquest of Space," *New Leader* 40 (Nov. 25, 1957): 7; "Neither Adam Smith nor Karl Marx," *New Leader* 40 (Dec. 23, 1957): 9; "A Rich Nation in a Poor World," *C&C* 18 (Mar. 31, 1958): 38–39.

33. "A Predicament We Share with Russia," *New Leader* 41 (Apr. 21, 1958): 10.

34. Joseph L. Rauh, Jr., to RN, Feb. 19 and Apr. 5, 1957, and typed message to ADA by RN, Feb. 28, 1957, Niebuhr Papers; Resolution of the Tenth Anniversary Convention of Americans for Democratic Action Honoring Reinhold Niebuhr, Mar. 29–31, 1957, signed by Joseph L. Rauh, Jr., Niebuhr Papers.

35. "Implications of the Elections," *C&C* 18 (Nov. 24, 1958): 161; Arthur M. Schlesinger, Jr., *The Crisis of the Old Order* (Boston: Houghton Mifflin Co., 1957), [v]; "The Meaning of Labor Unity," *New Leader* 38 (Mar. 28, 1955): 9; "Those 'Right to Work' Laws," *American Federationist* 64 (Feb. 1957): 14; "The Teamsters and Labor's Future," *New Leader* 40 (Aug. 26, 1957): 4.

36. "Djilas Dissects Communism" (rev. of Djilas's *The New Class*), *New Leader* 40 (Sept. 9, 1957): 17–18; "Stalin—Deity to Demon," *C&C* 16 (Apr. 16, 1956): 42; "Mr. Khrushchev and Post-Stalin Russia," *C&C* 19 (Mar. 2, 1959): 17; "Changes in the Kremlin," *C&C* 17 (Aug. 5, 1957): 107.

37. "'Art of the Possible,'" *New Leader* 42 (Sept. 21, 1959): 4; "A Khrushchev Visit to America?" *C&C* 19 (Aug. 3, 1959): 113–14; "Something Ventured, Nothing Gained," *New Leader* 42 (Oct. 19, 1959): 9; "Coexistence under a Nuclear Stalemate," *C&C* 19 (Sept. 21, 1959): 122; "The Test of the Christian Faith Today," *Christian Century* 76 (Oct. 28, 1959): 1242.

38. RN to William Scarlett, Dec. 27, 1955 (on RN's reading Gunther's book), Niebuhr Papers; "The Decline of Britain and France," *C&C* 17 (Feb. 18, 1957): 11; "France's Malady," *New Leader* 41 (Mar. 31, 1958): 17–18; "Will de Gaulle Save France?" *New Leader* 41 (June 30, 1958): 6–7; "France's Fifth Republic and Its General," *New Leader* 43 (Feb. 15, 1960): 12–13.

39. "Imperialism in Perspective," *New Leader* 43 (Nov. 14, 1960): 53; "The Cold Comfort of a 'Mystic Unity,' " *C&C* 20 (May 16, 1960): 65–66.

40. "Macmillan and the Peace," *New Leader* 42 (May 11, 1959): 8–9; "Failure at the Summit," *C&C* 20 (May 30, 1960): 73.

CHAPTER EIGHT

1. "Frontier Fellowship," *C&S* 13 (Autumn 1948): 3; Hutchison, "Two Decades of Social Christianity" (see ch. 7, note 16), 1–2, 4; "Christian Faith and Social Action," ibid., 233–34, 241 (also in *FP*, 127–29, 136).

2. *CRPP*, 89–94 (also in *ERN*, 214–17); 71–72; 38; 43–44; 105–17 (also in *ERN*, 93–101); 119–46 (also in *ERN*, 123–41); 15–32; 175–203 (also in *ERN*, 218–36).

3. *CRPP*, [i]; Ludwig Freund, rev. of *CRPP*, *Annals of the American Academy of Political and Social Science* 293 (May 1954): 191; Harry R. Davis, rev. of *CRPP*, *Christian Scholar* 37 (Mar. 1954): 67–68; T. S. Eliot to RN, Aug. 19, 1953, Niebuhr Papers; T. S. Eliot, *To Criticize the Critic* (New York: Farrar, Straus & Giroux, 1960), 144.

4. *SDH*, 189; *IAH*, 89; "The Case for Coexistence" (see ch. 7, note 9), 6; "The Democratic Elite and American Foreign Policy," in *Walter Lippmann and His Times*, ed. M. Childs and J. Reston (New York: Harcourt, Brace & Co., 1959), 173; "Liberalism: Illusions and Realities," *New Republic* 133 (July 4, 1955): 11; RN to Ludwig Freund, quoted in editor's footnote to Freund's rev. of *SDH*, *Modern Age* 1 (Summer 1957): 107. On the Burkean element in Niebuhr's thought, see Vigen Guroian's excellent essay, "The Conservatism of Reinhold Niebuhr: The Burkean Connection," *Modern Age* 29 (Summer 1985): 224–32.

5. "A Superb Portrait of FDR" (rev. of Burns's *Roosevelt: The Lion and the Fox*), *New Leader* 39 (Dec. 10, 1956): 11–12.

6. "Our Country and Our Culture," *Partisan Review* 19 (May–June, 1952): 303; "Culture and Civilization," *Confluence* 1 (Mar. 1952): 68, 73, 76.

7. Commission on Freedom of the Press, *A Free and Responsible Press* (Chicago: University of Chicago Press, 1947), passim; "The Role of the Newspapers in America's Function as the Greatest World Power," in *The Press in Perspective*, ed. R. D. Carey (Baton Rouge, La.: Louisiana State University Press, 1963), 39, 44, 46; "The Democratic Elite and American Foreign Policy," 168, 173–76, 188.

8. "Television's Peril to Culture," *American Scholar* 19 (Spring 1950), 137–39; Introduction to Wilbur Schramm, *Social Responsibility in Mass Communication* (New York: Harper & Brothers, 1957), xvi–xx.

9. "Sex Standards in America," *C&C* 8 (May 24, 1948): 65–66; "Sex and Religion in the Kinsey Report," *C&C* 13 (Nov. 2, 1953): 138–40.

10. "Human Creativity and Self-Concern in Freud's Thought," in *Freud and the 20th Century*, ed. B. Nelson (New York: Meridian Books, 1957), 259–60, 266, 268–69, 275.

11. *FH*, 75–76; "The Problem of Justice and the Power of Love," *United Church Herald* 2 (Jan. 1, 1959): 13.

12. *SDH*, ix, 4; 9, 11–12; 33, 39; 41, 45, 48–49, 53–55, 60; 62–66.

13. *SDH*, 75–77; 77–78, 85–87, 90–93; 97–98; 98–99; 100, 105–6; 115, 126, 132, 136.

14. *SDH*, 163; 159–60; 174–76, 180–81; 178–79, 181–82; 238–39.

15. *SDH*, [v], ix; Will Herberg, "The Three Dialogues of Man" (rev. of *SDH*), *New Republic* 133 (May 16, 1955): 28–31; James Luther Adams, "A Drama of Ideal Types" (rev. of *SDH*), *C&S* 20 (Autumn 1955): 23–24; J. Harry Cotton, "Dialogue with God" (rev. of *SDH*), *Interpretation* 10 (Jan. 1956): 100–102; John Baillie to RN, Feb. 20, 1956, Niebuhr Papers.

16. "Democracy, Secularism, and Christianity," *C&C* 13 (Mar. 2, 1953), in *CRPP*, 97; "The Question of Secularism," *Messenger* 19 (Apr. 6, 1954): 7 (also in *Lutheran* 36 [Apr. 14, 1954]:11).

17. *PSA*, 1–6, 13.

18. *PSA*, 25, 30, 32, 34–36.

19. Robert T. Handy to author, Jan. 31, 1992 (on the occasion and date of Niebuhr's address, attended by Handy, as recorded in the minute book of Union's faculty social meetings kept in the Union Theological Seminary Archives); "To Professor Reinhold Niebuhr, the Seminary Israel Institute of the Jewish Theological Seminary of America confers upon you this Citation for Distinguished Service . . . March 29, 1955," Niebuhr Papers; *PSA*, 86–87, 91–92, 95–97, 100, 105–8.

20. *PSA*, 123–36, 144–45.

21. *PSA*, [v]; Robert E. Fitch, "Essays by Niebuhr" (rev. of *PSA*), *New Leader* 41 (June 23, 1958): 25; telephone interview with Carl Hermann Voss, Dec. 9, 1990 (on reactions of Jews and Christians to Niebuhr's address); *Journal of the Central Conference of American Rabbis*, Apr. 1958, 18–32; Introduction to Waldo Frank, *The Jew in Our Day* (London: Victor Gollancz, 1944), 9; "The Problem of a Protestant Social Ethic," *Union Seminary Quarterly Review* 15 (Nov. 1959): 11.

22. "A Note on Pluralism," in *Religion in America*, ed. J. Cogley (New York: Meridian Books, 1958), 45–46, 48–50; "Dangerous Decision," *Lutheran* 30 (July 21, 1948): 19; "Religion and Education," *Religious Education* 48 (Nov.–Dec. 1953): 371–73; John C. Bennett, *Christians and the State* (New York: Charles Scribner's Sons, 1958), passim; RN to John C. Bennett, Dec. 6, 1957, Niebuhr Papers.

23. "Not Argument but Witness Is Required," *Messenger* 21 (Mar. 6, 1956): 7 (also in *Lutheran*, 38 [Mar. 21, 1956]: 25); "A Landmark in American Religious History," *Messenger* 22 (June 18, 1957): 11, 13.

24. *SNE*, ix–x; interview with Roger L. Shinn, Apr. 12, 1991 (on RN's knowledge of ancient civilizations); RN to William Scarlett, Nov. 5, 1958, Niebuhr Papers.

25. *SNE*, 7, 8, 13, 61; 36–37, 44; 53, 57–59.

26. *SNE*, 66; 70, 76–78, 84; 96–97, 102, 108–11, 117, 119–20, 126–27; 123.

27. *SNE*, 181, 150–81; 181; 150; 198.

28. *SNE*, 190, 194–95; 199–200; 202–15; 263–66.

29. *SNE*, 13–14, 228, 242–43, 252–54; 267; 269; 280–81; 282; 228–29, 235–36; 282–83; 285; 298.

30. *SNE*, [vii]; Arnold Toynbee, "There's Hope for the Future if There Is a Future" (rev. of *SNE*), *New York Times Book Review*, Aug. 30, 1959, 6, 30; Hans Kohn, rev. of *SNE*, *American Historical Review* 65 (Apr. 1960): 574; Arnold Wolfers, rev. of *SNE*, *Political Science Quarterly* 76 (June 1960): 291; Samuel P. Huntington, "Patterns of Political Order" (rev. of *SNE*), *New Leader* 43 (Feb. 29, 1960): 28; Robert Strausz-Hupé, "History's Value in a Nuclear Age" (rev. of *SNE*), *Saturday Review* 42 (Aug. 29, 1959): 12, 28; Kenneth W. Thompson, rev. of *SNE*, *United Church Herald* 2 (Oct. 29, 1959): 30; Thompson, "The Modern International Relevance of Reinhold Niebuhr," unpublished paper prepared for a colloquium in New York sponsored by the Carnegie Council on Ethics and International Affairs (1987), 4, 19.

31. Hans J. Morgenthau, "The Intellectual and Moral Dilemma of History," *C&C* 20 (Feb. 8, 1960): 5; Kenneth W. Thompson, *Masters of International Thought* (Baton Rouge, La.: Louisiana State University Press, 1980), 84–88; Morgenthau, "The Influence of Reinhold Niebuhr in American Political Life and Thought," in *Reinhold Niebuhr: A Prophetic Voice in Our Time,* ed. Harold R. Landon (Greenwich, Conn.: Seabury Press, 1962), 103–5, 109. For a careful comparison of Niebuhr's thought with Morgenthau's, see Robert C. Good, "National Interest and Moral Theory: The 'Debate' among Contemporary Political Realists," in *Foreign Policy in the Sixties: Essays in Honor of Arnold Wolfers,* ed. R. Hilsman and R. C. Good (Baltimore: Johns Hopkins Press, 1965), 271–92.

CHAPTER NINE

1. "Humphrey for President?" *New Leader* 41 (Dec. 29, 1958): 5; "Catholics and the Presidency," *New Leader* 43 (May 9, 1960): 3; *Remembering Reinhold Niebuhr,* 317; Arthur M. Schlesinger, Jr., *A Thousand Days* (Boston: Houghton Mifflin Co., 1965), 58; Fox, 271–72; "The Eisenhower Era," *New Leader* 43 (Oct. 3, 1960): 4; "The Election and the Next President," *C&C* 20 (Nov. 28, 1960): 169–70. The Niebuhrs resided at 340 Riverside Drive from June 1960 to January 1963, and thereafter at 404 Riverside Drive until June 1968, when they moved to Stockbridge, Massachusetts.

2. "President Kennedy's Cuban Venture," *C&C* 21 (May 15, 1961): 69–70; "Communist Dogma and Latin America," *New Leader* 44 (May 29, 1961): 17.

3. "Berlin and Prestige in Europe," *New Republic* 145 (Sept. 18, 1961): 17–19.

4. "Our Stake in the Common Market," *C&C* 22 (Feb. 19, 1962): 13–14; "Boulder in the Currents," *Spectator* 209 (Oct. 5, 1962): 490; "The Peril of a New Napoleon," *C&C* 23 (Mar. 4, 1963), 22–23.

5. "The Case for Congo Unity," *New Leader* 45 (Jan. 8, 1962): 3–4; "Katanga and Primitive Anti-Communism," *C&C* 21 (Jan. 22, 1962), 245; "Woe Unto Them That Spoil," *C&C* 22 (Oct. 1, 1962): 159–60; "The Rising Tide of Color," *New Leader* 44 (Jan. 23, 1961): 16.

6. "The Gravity of Our Contest with Communism," *C&C* 21 (July 24, 1961): 130; "Well-Tempered Evangelism," *New Republic* 144 (June 26, 1961): 11–12; "Reflections on Democracy as an Alternative to Communism," *Columbia University Forum* 4 (Summer 1961): 10–13, 16.

7. "The Unintended Virtues of an Open Society," *C&C* 21 (July 24, 1961): 132, 135, 137–38.

8. "Morality at the Shelter Door," *C&C* 21 (Nov. 13, 1961): 197; "Nuclear Dilemma" (rev. of *Nuclear Weapons and the Conflict of Conscience,* ed. J. Bennett), *Union Seminary Quarterly Review* 17 (Mar. 1962): 239–41; "American Hegemony and the Prospects for Peace," *Annals of the American Academy of Political and Social Science* 342 (July 1962), in *FP,* 215.

9. "Cuba: Avoiding the Holocaust," *C&C* 22 (Nov. 26, 1962): 204–5; "The Cuban Crisis in Retrospect," *New Leader* 45 (Dec. 10, 1962): 8.

10. "The Test Ban Agreement," *C&C* 23 (Sept. 16, 1963): 155.

11. "Prospects for the South," *New Leader* 44 (June 19, 1961): 3.

12. "The Mounting Racial Crisis," *C&C* 23 (July 8, 1963): 121–22; RN to William Scarlett, Sept. 4, 1963, Niebuhr Papers; "The Meaning of the Birmingham Tragedy," Niebuhr Tape Collection (N60). The Niebuhr-Baldwin dialogue was broadcast on Sept. 22, 1963.

13. "John Fitzgerald Kennedy, 1917–1963," *C&C* 23 (Dec. 9, 1963): 221; "The Kennedy Legacy: A Tentative Assessment," *New Leader* 46 (Dec. 9, 1963): 8.

14. "The Struggle for Justice," *New Leader* 47 (July 6, 1964): 10–11; "Revolution in an Open Society," *New Leader* 46 (May 27, 1963): 7.

15. "The Politics of Nostalgia," *New Leader* 47 (July 20, 1964): 3–4; "Triumph of Primitivism," *New Leader* 47 (Aug. 17, 1964): 5–6; "30 Receive Freedom Medal at the White House," *New York Times*, Sept. 15, 1964, 3; "Protestant Individualism and the Goldwater Movement," *C&C* 24 (Dec. 14, 1964): 248.

16. "Civil Rights Climax in Alabama," *C&C* 25 (Apr. 5, 1965): 61; Foreword to *Mississippi Black Paper* (New York: Random House, 1965), [ii–iii].

17. "Man, the Unregenerate Tribalist," *C&C* 24 (July 6, 1964): 134; "A Question of Priorities," *New Leader* 51 (Jan. 15, 1968), in *FP*, 265.

18. "The Negro Minority and Its Fate in a Self-Righteous Nation," *Social Action* (United Church of Christ) 35 (Oct., 1968): 53–55, 57, 63–64 (also in *Social Progress* [United Presbyterian Church] 64 [Sept.–Oct. 1968]).

19. "Our Relations to Catholicism," *C&C* 7 (Sept. 15, 1947), in *EAC*, 220–26; "The Rising Catholic-Protestant Tension," *C&C* 9 (Aug. 8, 1949), in *EAC*, 233–37; "The Pope's Domesticated God," *Christian Century* 67 (Jan. 18, 1950), in *EAC*, 238–43; "The Increasing Isolation of the Catholic Church," *C&C* 10 (Sept. 18, 1950), in *EAC*, 244–46; "A Protestant Looks at Catholics," *Commonweal* 58 (May 8, 1953): 119.

20. "A Plea for Tolerance," *Atlantic Monthly* 216 (Aug. 1962): 73–77.

21. "*Pacem in Terris*: Two Views," *C&C* 23 (May 13, 1963): 81, 83.

22. "Further Reactions to Vatican II," *C&C* 23 (Jan. 20, 1964), 259; "The Drama of the Vatican Council," *C&C* 24 (Jan. 11, 1965): 278; "Toward New Intra-Christian Endeavors," *Christian Century* 86 (Dec. 31, 1969): 1665.

23. "The Quality of Our Lives," *Christian Century* 77 (May 11, 1960): 571; interview with Donald L. Scruggs, June 11, 1967 (Scruggs is a political scientist at Stephens College).

24. "Reply to Interpretation and Criticism," Kegley and Bretall, 431; "The Concept of 'Order of Creation' in Emil Brunner's Social Ethic," in *The Theology of Emil Brunner*, ed. C. Kegley (New York: Macmillan Co., 1962), 265–71; "Martin Buber: 1878–1965," *C&C* 25 (July 12, 1965): 146–47.

25. "The Problem of the Modern Church: Triviality," *C&C* 22 (Dec. 10, 1962): 228; "The Regents' Prayer Decision," *C&C* 22 (July 23, 1962): 125–26; James F. Findlay, "Religion and Politics in the Sixties: The Churches and the Civil Rights Act of 1964," *Journal of American History* 77 (June 1990): 66–92; "Prayer and Justice in School and Nation," *C&C* 24 (May 25, 1964): 93.

26. "The Recession in Church-Going," *Berkshire Eagle*, Apr. 12, 1965, 18.

27. "An Interview with Reinhold Niebuhr," *Commonweal* 85 (Dec. 16, 1966): 320–21; "Faith as the Sense of Meaning in Human Existence," *C&C* 26 (June 13, 1966), in *FP*, 3, 8.

28. Bingham, "Postscript" in 1972 edition; interview with Ronald H. Stone, June 18, 1987; RN to Ronald Stone, Dec. 15, 1965 (copy in author's possession). RN's seminar met weekly during most semesters from the fall of 1963 through the spring of 1968, first at the seminary and later at his home, according to Union Seminary catalogs and Stone. Files of Union's registrar show that he last taught it in the spring of 1968; though announced for the next fall, it was canceled because of his bad health; Roger L. Shinn to author, June 18, 1991. In publisher's blurbs for *The Democratic Experience*, Hans Morgenthau commended it as "a penetrating and original analysis of the pre-conditions of a democratic society," and Arthur Schlesinger, Jr., described it as a "wise and enlightening book" which "throws fresh light on the vital question of democracy's future"; Niebuhr Papers. Reviewing *A Nation So Conceived*, David M. Potter concluded that, while "Niebuhr has

said some things which no student of American history can afford to overlook," it "is not, regrettably, in *A Nation So Conceived* that he has said them"; *New York Times Book Review*, May 19, 1963, 22.

29. *MNHC*, 15, 31–32, 43–44, 53–54, 59–62, 65–67; 39; 68, 76–77, 79.

30. *MNHC*, 23–24; 118–19; 107–9, 119.

31. *MNHC*, [i], 28–29; Gordon Harlan, "A Realist's View" (rev. of *MNHC*), *Christian Century* 83 (Jan. 5, 1966): 15–16; René de Visme Williamson, rev. of *MNHC*, *American Political Science Review* 60 (Sept. 1966): 707–8; Roger L. Shinn, rev. of *MNHC*, *Union Seminary Quarterly Review* 21 (Mar. 1966): 350–51.

32. "Can Democracy Work?" *New Leader* 45 (May 28, 1962): 9; "The Problem of South Vietnam," *C&C* 23 (Aug. 5, 1963): 143; "Dilemma of U.S. Power," *New Leader* 46 (Nov. 25, 1963): 11.

33. "Johnson and the Myths of Democracy," *New Leader* 47 (May 25, 1964), in *FP*, 250–51; "From Bad to Worse in Vietnam: Pretense and Power," *New Leader* 48 (Mar. 1, 1965): 7; "Consensus at the Price of Flexibility," *New Leader* 48 (Sept. 27, 1965): 19–20.

34. "Reinhold Niebuhr Discusses the War in Vietnam," *New Republic* 154 (Jan. 29, 1966): 16; "The Peace Offensive," *C&C* 25 (Jan. 24, 1966): 302.

35. [Wayne H. Cowan], "About This Issue" and "It Takes a Heap," *C&C* 26 (May 30, 1966): 107, 113; [Cowan], "We Made It," *C&C* 22 (Feb. 19, 1962): 14; Hubert H. Humphrey, "A Tribute to Reinhold Niebuhr," *C&C* 26 (May 30, 1966): 120–23. Humphrey's speech was written with the assistance of William Lee Miller and Ernest W. Lefever; interview with Miller, June 5, 1991. The full text was printed as a brochure distributed by Humphrey.

36. Hubert H. Humphrey, *The Education of a Public Man: My Life and Politics* (Garden City, N.Y.: Doubleday & Co., 1976), 316–33, 347–52; "Vietnam and the Imperial Conflict," *New Leader* 49 (June 6, 1966): 16; "Vietnam: The Tide Begins to Turn," *C&C* 26 (Oct. 17, 1966): 221.

37. "Foreign Policy in a New Context," *New Leader* 50 (Feb. 27, 1967), in *FP*, 258; "Escalation Objective," *New York Times*, Mar. 14, 1967, 46; Foreword to *Martin Luther King, Jr., John C. Bennett, Henry Steele Commager, Abraham Heschel Speak on the War in Vietnam* (New York: Clergy and Laymen Concerned about Vietnam, 475 Riverside Drive, 1967), 3; Theodore Draper, *Abuse of Power* (New York: Viking Press, 1967), dust jacket; Gillon, 196–97; RN to William Scarlett, Apr. 7 and July 24, 1967, Niebuhr Papers.

38. "A Time for Reassessment," *C&C* 28 (Apr. 1, 1968): 55–56; "Fighting an Intractable Dwarf," *New Leader* 51 (Aug. 5, 1968): 12; RN to William Scarlett, Oct. 5 and Nov. 6 and 19, 1968, Niebuhr Papers.

39. Ronald H. Stone, "An Interview with Reinhold Niebuhr," *C&C* 29 (March 17, 1969), 50.

40. "The Presidency and the Irony of American History," *C&C* 30 (Apr. 13, 1970): 70; "Indicting Two Generations," *New Leader* 53 (Oct. 5, 1970): 13–14.

41. "Caribbean Blunder," *C&C* 25 (May 31, 1965): 113–14; "Roosevelt and Johnson: A Contrast in Foreign Policy," *New Leader* 48 (July 19, 1965): 7.

42. "Adlai Stevenson: 1900–1965," *C&C* 25 (Aug. 9, 1965): 169–70.

43. "The Army in the New Nations," *C&C* 26 (May 2, 1966): 83.

44. "David and Goliath," *C&C* 27 (June 26, 1967): 141.

45. "Reactions to Man's Landing on the Moon Show Broad Variations in Opinion—Some Would Forge Ahead in Space, Others Would Turn to Earth's Affairs: Reinhold Niebuhr," *New York Times*, July 21, 1969, 7; "The President's Error," *C&C* 29 (Sept. 15, 1969): 227.

46. "The King's Chapel and the King's Court," *C&C* 29 (Aug. 4, 1969), 211–12.

47. " 'Redeemer Nation' to Super-Power," *New York Times*, Dec. 4, 1970, 47.

48. [Roger L. Shinn], "A Prophet among Us," *C&C* 31 (June 28, 1971): 126; Fox, 292–93; Christopher Niebuhr to author, Aug. 27 and 29, 1991.

49. "Reinhold Niebuhr Is Dead, Protestant Theologian, 78," *New York Times*, June 2, 1971, 1, 45 (also in June 3 morning ed.); "Reinhold Niebuhr," *New York Times*, June 3, 1971, 38; Kenneth W. Thompson to author, July 13, 1991; Thompson, *Masters of International Thought*, 31–32; Hubert H. Humphrey to author, June 25, 1971; [Roger L. Shinn], "A Prophet among Us." Kennan was 67 when calling Niebuhr "the father of all of us" as recalled by Thompson, but did not remember doing so when interviewed by Richard Fox at the age of 76 (see Fox, 238). Thompson, in recalling Kennan's appeal to him to write a memorial, stated: "He was speaking from the soul, not worrying about his own status." Kennan's phrase, more often quoted as "the father of us all," was circulating by the late 1950s and appears in an article by Thompson in *The Journal of Politics* 20 (Aug. 1958): 447. When researching her biography of Niebuhr, June Bingham contacted Dean Acheson, who said he thought the phrase was Kennan's; it is so cited in her book (see Bingham, 368); telephone interview with June Bingham Birge, June 9, 1991. Walter LaFeber quoted Kennan's phrase in *America, Russia, and the Cold War* (1967) on p. 54; the *New York Times* did so in its obituary and editorial, cited above.

50. Interview with Nathan A. Scott, Jr., June 5, 1991; Carl Hermann Voss, rev. of Kegley and Bretall, *Advance* 148 (May 16, 1956): 23; Arthur M. Schlesinger, Jr., "Prophet for a Secular Age," *New Leader* 55 (Jan. 24, 1972): 11–13.

51. "Prayer at the Service of Thanksgiving for Reinhold Niebuhr, Nov. 1, 1971, prepared and delivered by John C. Bennett," copy provided to author by Ronald H. Stone, who spoke at the service. Marilyn Cook, secretary to the president of Union Seminary, sent Stone the copy on Nov. 24, 1971.

CHAPTER TEN

1. Interview with Kenneth W. Thompson, June 5, 1991; Thompson, "The Modern International Relevance of Reinhold Niebuhr," unpublished paper prepared for a colloquium in New York sponsored by the Carnegie Council on Ethics and International Affairs, 1987, 15; telephone interview with Claude Heckscher, who served as the last secretary of the Reinhold Niebuhr Memorial Foundation, Nov. 12, 1991; Roger L. Shinn to author, Sept. 10, 1991 (on naming of Reinhold Niebuhr Place). James Loeb, Jr., was the chief fund-raiser for the Reinhold Niebuhr Memorial Award; others who served on the board awarding it included John C. Bennett, June Bingham, Joseph Rauh, Arthur Schlesinger, Jr., and Nathan Scott, Jr.; interviews with June Bingham Birge, Nov. 10, 1991, and Nathan Scott, June 5, 1991. The city councilman who led in renaming the west end of 120th Street was Henry J. Stern; Handy, 324.

2. William Lee Miller, *Yankee from Georgia: The Emergence of Jimmy Carter* (New York: Times Books, 1978), 201–40; photocopied pages of Carter's copy of *Courage to Change*, provided to author by June Bingham Birge; Jimmy Carter, "Volunteerism: Community, Nation, World," Rublee Lecture Series, Stephens College, Columbia, Mo., Nov. 12, 1991. Miller in his book argues persuasively that Carter's interest in Niebuhr is authentic. Carter invoked Niebuhr on love and justice in response to a question from the audience following his address.

3. "The Impact of Protestantism Today," *Atlantic Monthly* 181 (Feb. 1948): 61; Roger L. Shinn, *Forced Options: Social Decisions for the 21st Century* (New York:

Harper & Row, 1982; 3d ed.: Cleveland: Pilgrim Press, 1991); "From Progress to Perplexity," in *The Search for America*, ed. H. Smith (Englewood Cliffs, N.J.: Prentice-Hall, 1959), 145.

4. J. Harry Cotton, "Dialogue with God" (rev. of *SDH*), *Interpretation* 10 (Jan. 1956): 102.

5. T. S. Eliot, *The Idea of a Christian Society* (London: Faber & Faber, 1939), 61–62; Lynn Harold Hough, "Niebuhr on the Meaning of History" (rev. of *FH*), *Pastor* 12 (July 1949): 3.

6. "Reinhold Niebuhr, 1892–1971," *UTS Journal*, Jan. 1972, 15. This tribute in the minutes of Union Theological Seminary, anonymously published, was composed by Roger L. Shinn, who then held the Niebuhr chair at Union; Shinn to author, May 7, 1987. The quoted passage is the final paragraph of *CLCD*, 189–90.

APPENDIX B

1. New York: Macmillan Co., 1956; 2d ed., New York: Pilgrim Press, 1984.

2. Arthur M. Schlesinger, Jr., to author, Apr. 24, 1990.

3. "The Ethics of Loyalty," *Confluence* 3 (Dec. 1954): 485–6.

4. Chicago: University of Chicago Press, 1975. This symposium also appeared as vol. 54 (Oct. 1974) of the *Journal of Religion*.

5. The first was published by Seabury Press (Greenwich, Conn.: 1962) and the second by A. R. Mowbray & Co. (London: 1986) and Wm. B. Eerdmans Publishing Co. (Grand Rapids: 1986).

6. New York: Oxford University Press, 1960.

7. RN to William Scarlett, Apr. 30, 1960, Niebuhr Papers; Will Herberg, "Niebuhr's Three Phases" (rev. of Harland's *The Thought of Reinhold Niebuhr*), *Christian Century* 77 (Aug. 10, 1960): 926.

8. New York: Charles Scribner's Sons, 1961; 2d ed., 1972.

9. Robert Lee, "It Adds a Dimension" (rev. of Bingham's *Courage to Change*), *Christian Century* 79 (May 16, 1962): 630; Martin E. Marty, "Thinker and Doer" (rev. of Bingham's *Courage to Change*), *New York Times Book Review*, Dec. 17, 1961, 4; August Heckscher, "Mentor of a Post-war Generation of Liberals" (rev. of Bingham's *Courage to Change*), *New York Herald Tribune Books*, Dec. 17, 1961, 12.

10. Nashville: Abingdon Press, 1972.

11. James F. Childress, rev. of Stone's *Reinhold Niebuhr: Prophet to Politicians*, *American Political Science Review* 67 (Sept. 1973): 999–1000; Franklin Sherman, rev. of Stone's *Reinhold Niebuhr: Prophet to Politicians*, *Worldview* 15 (Oct. 1972): 58–59; Roger L. Shinn, rev. of *Reinhold Niebuhr: Prophet to Politicians*, *Union Seminary Quarterly Review* 27 (Summer 1972): 250; John C. Bennett, rev. of Stone's *Reinhold Niebuhr: Prophet to Politicians*, *Religious Education* 67 (Sept. 1972): 403–5.

12. Louisville, Ky.: Westminster/John Knox Press, 1992. This book, described to the author by Roger Shinn after reading the manuscript, is scheduled for publication in the fall of 1992; thus reviews have not appeared as *Niebuhr and His Age* goes to press.

13. Montreal: McGill-Queen's University Press, 1975.

14. C. F. Stoerker, "Paradoxical Role" (rev. of Merkley's *Reinhold Niebuhr: A Political Account*), *Christian Century* 93 (Mar. 3, 1976): 201–2.

15. New York: Pantheon Books, 1985; paperback ed., San Francisco: Harper & Row, 1986.

16. "The Definitive Reinhold Niebuhr," *Time*, Jan 20, 1986, 71; Langdon Gilkey, "*Reinhold Niebuhr: A Biography*: A Critical Review Article," *Journal of Religion* 68 (Apr. 1988): 263. Among other reviews were the following: Harvey Cox, "In the Pulpit and on the Barricades," *New York Times Book Review*, Jan. 5, 1986, 1, 24–25; David Brion Davis, "American Jeremiah," *New York Review of Books* 33 (Feb. 13, 1986): 7–9; William E. Leuchtenburg, "Preacher of Paradox," *Atlantic Monthly* 257 (Jan. 1986): 93–95. Henry F. May, "The Prophet and the Establishment," *Reviews in American History* 14 (Sept. 1986): 467–73; and Donald Meyer, *Journal of American History* 73 (Dec. 1986): 719–20. Unlike *Time*, these reviewers did not claim that Fox's *Niebuhr* was definitive—indeed, Fox himself insisted that it was not—but, except for one substantive criticism by Davis, all were completely uncritical.

17. Gilkey, 272.

18. John C. Bennett to author, Jan. 2, 1987.

19. Richard Harries, "A Fine Sense of Sin" (rev. of Fox's *Reinhold Niebuhr: A Biography*), *Times* (London) *Literary Supplement*, Dec. 9, 1988, 1363.

20. Gilkey, 274, 276.

21. Richard John Neuhaus, "Theologian and Activist" (rev. of Fox's *Reinhold Niebuhr: A Biography*), *Commentary* 81 (Mar. 1986): 62.

22. Gilkey, 267.

23. "The Fight for Germany," *Life*, Oct. 21, 1946, 72.

24. Roger L. Shinn, "Reinhold Niebuhr: A Reverberating Voice," *Christian Century* 103 (Jan. 1–8, 1986): 17.

25. Interview with Nathan A. Scott, June 5, 1991; Arthur M. Schlesinger, Jr., "Prophet for a Secular Age," *New Leader* 55 (Jan. 24, 1972): 13.

26. Gilkey, 266.

27. Interview with Arthur M. Schlesinger, Jr., Mar. 25, 1987; *Remembering Reinhold Niebuhr*, 356, 358, 360.

28. "Christian Faith and Humanism," lecture at Union Seminary on Jan. 14, 1952, Niebuhr Tape Collection (N4).

29. Neuhaus, 64; "Letters from Readers," *Commentary* 86 (May 1986): 16–19; *Reinhold Niebuhr Today*, edited with a foreword by Richard John Neuhaus (Grand Rapids: Wm. B. Eerdmans Publishing Co., 1989).

30. Gilkey, 276.

31. London: Chapman & Hall, 1989; Harrisburg, Pa.: Morehouse Publishing Co., 1990.

32. The incident, involving two or three students who ran up a flag symbolic of revolution, occurred on May 1, 1934 (see Handy, 185; Bingham, 166; and Fox, 159, 311). Carl Hermann Voss, then president of the student body at Union, recalls that it was a prank, following which he said facetiously to Niebuhr, "You're partly responsible," because of his part in the leftish atmosphere of the time, but Voss points out that no one ever proved that any of the culprits was inspired by Niebuhr's writings; Carl Hermann Voss to author, Feb. 19, 1992.

33. San Francisco: HarperCollins, 1991.

34. Martin E. Marty, "Reinhold Niebuhr's Private World" (rev. of *Remembering Reinhold Niebuhr*), *Christian Century* 108 (July 10–17, 1991): 690–91; Roger L. Shinn, "Reinhold Niebuhr in His Letters" (rev. of *Remembering Reinhold Niebuhr*), *Christianity and Crisis* 51 (Nov. 18, 1991): 373–76.

35. Minneapolis: University of Minnesota Press, 1963 (in Pamphlets on American Writers series).

36. Philadelphia: J. B. Lippincott Co., 1970 (in The Promise of Theology series).

37. Waco, Tex.: Word Books, 1977 (in Makers of the Modern Theological Mind series).

38. William Lee Miller, "The Irony of Reinhold Niebuhr," *Reporter* 12 (Jan. 13, 1955): 11–15.

39. John C. Bennett, "The Greatness of Reinhold Niebuhr," *Union Seminary Quarterly Review* 27 (Fall 1971): 3–8.

40. Arthur M. Schlesinger, Jr., "Prophet for a Secular Age," *New Leader* 55 (Jan. 24, 1972): 11–14.

41. Vigen Guroian, "The Possibilities and Limits of Politics: A Comparative Study of the Thought of Reinhold Niebuhr and Edmund Burke," *Union Seminary Quarterly Review* 36 (Summer 1981): 189–203.

42. Franklin Littell, "Reinhold Niebuhr and the Jewish People," *Holocaust and Genocide Studies* (published in Great Britain) 6 (1991): 45–61.

43. John C. Bennett, "Niebuhr, Reinhold," in *Encyclopaedia Britannica*, 15th ed. (1974); Roger L. Shinn, "Niebuhr, Reinhold," in *Encyclopedia Americana*, 1982 ed.; Robert T. Handy, "Niebuhr, Reinhold," in *Encyclopedia of American Biography*, ed. John A. Garraty (New York: Harper & Row, 1974).

Bibliography and Other Sources

੨**

An indispensable research tool for any study of Niebuhr is D. B. Robertson's *Reinhold Niebuhr's Works: A Bibliography* (Boston: G. K. Hall, 1979; rev. ed., Lanham, Md.: University Press of America, 1983). Its main section lists, by year, upward of 2,750 articles, essays, reviews, editorials, and prefaces written by Niebuhr over six decades. Another section lists numerous writings about him, including essays, book reviews, and dissertations. It is rather complete, but scholars continue to discover additional items.

Niebuhr's principal works, anthologies of his writings, selected works about him, and related secondary literature are listed below, followed by descriptions of the Reinhold Niebuhr Audio Tape Collection and the Reinhold Niebuhr Papers.

BOOKS BY REINHOLD NIEBUHR

Does Civilization Need Religion? A Study in the Social Resources and Limitations of Religion in Modern Life. New York: Macmillan Co., 1927.

Leaves from the Notebook of a Tamed Cynic. Chicago: Willett, Clark & Colby, 1929.

The Contribution of Religion to Social Work. New York: Columbia University Press, 1932.

Moral Man and Immoral Society. New York: Charles Scribner's Sons, 1932. Also published in Japanese and Korean translations.

Reflections on the End of an Era. New York: Charles Scribner's Sons, 1934.

An Interpretation of Christian Ethics. New York: Harper & Brothers, 1935. Also published in Japanese translation.

Beyond Tragedy: Essays on the Christian Interpretation of History. New York: Charles Scribner's Sons, 1937. Also published in German and Polish translations.

Christianity and Power Politics. New York: Charles Scribner's Sons, 1940.

The Nature and Destiny of Man: A Christian Interpretation. Vol. 1, *Human Nature.* New York: Charles Scribner's Sons, 1941. Vol. 2, *Human Destiny.* New York: Charles Scribner's, 1943. Also published in German, French, Dutch, Japanese, and Chinese translations.

The Children of Light and the Children of Darkness: A Vindication of Democracy and a Critique of Its Traditional Defense. New York: Charles Scribner's Sons, 1944. Also published in German, Dutch, Czech, and Japanese translations.

Discerning the Signs of the Times: Sermons for Today and Tomorrow. New York: Charles Scribner's Sons, 1946. Also published in German, Dutch, and Czech translations.

Faith and History: A Comparison of Christian and Modern Views of History. New York: Charles Scribner's Sons, 1949. Also published in German, French, Swedish, and Japanese translations.

The Irony of American History. New York: Charles Scribner's Sons, 1952. Also published in French, Spanish, and Japanese translations.

Christian Realism and Political Problems. New York: Charles Scribner's Sons, 1953.

The Self and the Dramas of History. New York: Charles Scribner's Sons, 1955. Also published in Japanese translation.

Pious and Secular America. New York: Charles Scribner's Sons, 1958. Also published in German translation.

The Structure of Nations and Empires: A Study of Recurring Patterns and Problems of the Political Order in Relation to the Unique Problems of the Nuclear Age. New York: Charles Scribner's Sons, 1959. Also published in German translation.

A Nation So Conceived: Reflections on the History of America from Its Early Visions to Its Present Power. With Alan Heimert. New York: Charles Scribner's Sons, 1963.

Man's Nature and His Communities: Essays on the Dynamics and Enigmas of Man's Personal and Social Existence. New York: Charles Scribner's Sons, 1965. Also published in Japanese translation.

The Democratic Experience: Past and Prospects. With Paul E. Sigmund. New York: Praeger Publishers, 1969.

Most of Niebuhr's major books have appeared in British editions, and the more durable ones have been made available in the United States as paperbacks or reprint editions.

ANTHOLOGIES OF REINHOLD NIEBUHR'S WRITINGS, ADDRESSES, AND SERMONS

Love and Justice: Selections from the Shorter Writings of Reinhold Niebuhr. Edited with an introduction by D. B. Robertson. Philadelphia: Westminster Press, 1957.

The World Crisis and American Responsibility: Nine Essays. Edited with an introduction by Ernest W. Lefever. New York: Association Press, 1958.

Essays in Applied Christianity. Edited with an introduction by D. B. Robertson. New York: Meridian Books, 1959.

Reinhold Niebuhr on Politics: His Political Philosophy and Its Application to Our Age as Expressed in His Writings. Edited with an introduction by Harry R. Davis and Robert C. Good. New York: Charles Scribner's Sons, 1960.

Faith and Politics: A Commentary on Religious, Social and Political Thought in a Technological Age. Edited with an introduction by Ronald H. Stone. New York: George Braziller, 1968.

Justice and Mercy [sermons and prayers]. Edited with an introduction by Ursula M. Niebuhr. New York: Harper & Row, 1974.

Young Reinhold Niebuhr: His Early Writings, 1911–1931. Edited with an introduction by William G. Chrystal. St. Louis: Eden Publishing House, 1977.

The Essential Reinhold Niebuhr: Selected Essays and Addresses. Edited with an introduction by Robert McAfee Brown. New Haven, Conn.: Yale University Press, 1986.

Reinhold Niebuhr: Theologian of Public Life. Edited with an introduction by Larry Rasmussen. London: Collins, 1989; Minneapolis: Augsburg Fortress Press, 1991.

A Reinhold Niebuhr Reader: Selected Essays, Articles, and Book Reviews. Edited with an introduction by Charles C. Brown. Philadelphia: Trinity Press International, 1992.

SELECTED CRITICAL, BIOGRAPHICAL, AND INTRODUCTORY WORKS

Bingham, June. *Courage to Change: An Introduction to the Life and Thought of Reinhold Niebuhr.* New York: Charles Scribner's Sons, 1961; 2d ed., 1972.

Durkin, Kenneth. *Reinhold Niebuhr.* Outstanding Christian Thinkers series. Harrisburg, Pa.: Morehouse Publishing Co., 1989.

Fackre, Gabriel. *The Promise of Reinhold Niebuhr.* The Promise of Theology series. Philadelphia: J. B. Lippincott Co., 1970.

Fox, Richard W. *Reinhold Niebuhr: A Biography.* New York: Pantheon Books, 1985; paperback ed., San Francisco: Harper & Row, 1986.

Harland, Gordon. *The Thought of Reinhold Niebuhr.* New York: Oxford University Press, 1960.

Harries, Richard, ed. *Reinhold Niebuhr and the Issues of Our Time.* London: Mowbray, 1986; Grand Rapids: Wm. B. Eerdmans Publishing Co., 1986.

Kegley, Charles W., and Robert W. Bretall, eds. *Reinhold Niebuhr: His Religious, Social, and Political Thought.* Library of Living Theology series. New York: Macmillan Co., 1956. 2d. ed., edited by Charles W. Kegley. New York: Pilgrim Press, 1984.

Landon, Harold R., ed. *Reinhold Niebuhr: A Prophetic Voice in Our Time.* Greenwich, Conn.: Seabury Press, 1962.

Merkley, Paul. *Reinhold Niebuhr: A Political Account.* Montreal: McGill-Queen's University Press, 1975.

Niebuhr, Ursula M., ed. *Remembering Reinhold Niebuhr: Letters of Reinhold and Ursula M. Niebuhr.* San Francisco: HarperCollins, 1991.

Patterson, Bob E. *Reinhold Niebuhr.* Makers of the Modern Theological Mind series. Waco, Tex.: Word Books, 1977.

Scott, Nathan A., Jr., ed. *The Legacy of Reinhold Niebuhr.* Chicago: University of Chicago Press, 1975.

———. *Reinhold Niebuhr.* Pamphlets on American Writers series. Minneapolis: University of Minnesota Press, 1963.

Stone, Ronald H. *Professor Reinhold Niebuhr.* Louisville: Westminster/John Knox Press, 1992.

———. *Reinhold Niebuhr: Prophet to Politicians.* Nashville: Abingdon Press, 1972.

SELECTED SECONDARY LITERATURE CITED OR CONSULTED

Becker, William H. "Reinhold Niebuhr: From Marx to Roosevelt." *Historian* 35 (Aug. 1973): 539–50.

Bennett, John C. "Prophet, Not without Honor." *Messenger* 11 (Apr. 29, 1946): 8–11.

———. "The Contribution of Reinhold Niebuhr." *Union Seminary Quarterly Review* 24 (Fall 1968): 3–16.

———. "The Greatness of Reinhold Niebuhr." *Union Seminary Quarterly Review* 27 (Fall 1971): 3–8.

———. "Niebuhr, Reinhold." *Encyclopaedia Britannica.* 15th ed. (1974).

Braun, Theodore C. "The Professor as Pastor." *United Church Herald* 14 (Aug. 1971): 43.

Brown, Charles C. "Niebuhr, Reinhold." In *The Harry S. Truman Encyclopedia*, edited by Richard S. Kirkendall. Boston: G.K. Hall & Co., 1989.

Chrystal, William G. *A Father's Mantle: The Legacy of Gustav Niebuhr.* New York: Pilgrim Press, 1982.

———. "Possessing Your Inheritance: Elmhurst College, the Evangelical Synod, and the Niebuhrs." *In Thy Light* [published by Elmhurst College] 1 (Summer 1986): 1–10.

———. "Samuel D. Press: Teacher of the Niebuhrs." *Church History* 53 (Dec. 1984): 504–21.

Coffin, Henry Sloane. *A Half Century of Union Seminary.* New York: Charles Scribner's Sons, 1954.

Eddy, Sherwood. *Eighty Adventurous Years: An Autobiography.* New York: Harper & Brothers, 1955.

Gilkey, Langdon. "Reinhold Niebuhr: A Biography: A Critical Review Article." *Journal of Religion* 68 (Apr. 1988): 263–76.

Gillon, Steven M. *Politics and Vision: The ADA and American Liberalism, 1947–1985.* New York: Oxford University Press, 1987.

Good, Robert C. "The National Interest and Political Realism: Niebuhr's 'Debate' with Morgenthau and Kennan." *Journal of Politics* 22 (Nov. 1960): 597–619.

Greenlaw, William A. "The Nature of Christian Truth: Another Look at Reinhold Niebuhr and Mythology." *Saint Luke's Journal of Theology* 19 (June 1976): 195–202.

Guroian, Vigen. "The Conservatism of Reinhold Niebuhr: The Burkean Connection." *Modern Age* 29 (Summer 1985): 224–32.

———. "The Possibilities and Limits of Politics: A Comparative Study of the Thought of Reinhold Niebuhr and Edmund Burke." *Union Seminary Quarterly Review* 36 (Summer 1981): 189–203.

Handy, Robert T. *A History of Union Theological Seminary in New York.* New York: Columbia University Press, 1987.

———. "Niebuhr, Reinhold." In *Encyclopedia of American Biography*, edited by John A. Garraty. New York: Harper & Row, 1974.

Littell, Franklin. "Reinhold Niebuhr and the Jewish People." *Holocaust and Genocide Studies* [published in Great Britain] 6 (1991): 45–61. The 1990 Niebuhr Lecture at Elmhurst College.

Marty, Martin E. Foreword to *Leaves from the Notebook of a Tamed Cynic*, by Reinhold Niebuhr. San Francisco: Harper & Row, 1987. Reprint: Louisville, Ky.: Westminster/John Knox Press, 1990.

———. "The Lost Worlds of Reinhold Niebuhr." *American Scholar* 45 (Autumn 1976): 566–72.

Miller, William Lee. "The Irony of Reinhold Niebuhr." *Reporter* 12 (Jan. 13, 1955): 11–15.

———. "In Strange Company." *New Republic* 186 (Apr. 21, 1982): 27–30.

Nichols, James Hastings. "Reinhold Niebuhr: Prophet in Politics." In *The Responsibility of Power: Historical Essays in Honor of Hajo Holborn*, edited by Leonard Krieger and Fritz Stern. Garden City, N.Y.: Doubleday & Co., 1967.

Pauck, Wilhelm and Marion. *Paul Tillich: His Life and Thought.* New York: Harper & Row, 1976.

Rice, Daniel. "Correspondence Essay—Felix Frankfurter and Reinhold Niebuhr: 1940–1964." *Journal of Law and Religion* 1 (1983): 325–426.

Schlesinger, Arthur M., Jr. "Prophet for a Secular Age." *New Leader* 55 (Jan. 24, 1972): 11–14.

———. "Reinhold Niebuhr's Long Shadow." *New York Times*, June 22, 1992: 12A.

Shinn, Roger L. "A Prophet among Us." *Christianity and Crisis* 31 (June 28, 1971): 126–27.

———. "Reinhold Niebuhr, 1892–1971." *UTS Journal* [published by Union Theological Seminary], Jan. 1972: 15.

———. "Niebuhr, Reinhold." In *Encyclopedia Americana.* 1982 ed.

Thompson, Kenneth W. "Reinhold Niebuhr: From Theology to Political Prudence." In *Masters of International Thought* by Thompson. Baton Rouge, La.: Louisiana State University Press, 1980.

REINHOLD NIEBUHR AUDIO TAPE COLLECTION

Consisting of recorded lectures, sermons, and addresses, the Reinhold Niebuhr Audio Tape Collection, developed in cooperation with Ursula Niebuhr and Union Theological Seminary in New York, is on cassettes distributed by Union Theological Seminary in Virginia (not to be confused with Union Seminary in New York). Among the more memorable of the sixty-four cassettes available are Niebuhr's "Amsterdam Assembly Address" (1948); his lectures "Augustine's Conception of Selfhood" (1950), "How Faith and Reason Are Related" (1950), and "Christian Faith and Humanism" (1952); and his sermon "Our Lord's Conception of the Providence of God" (1952). Another feature of the collection is a sequence of twenty-one lectures on the history of Christian ethics, delivered by Niebuhr at Union Seminary just before his retirement in 1960. Among other valuable items is his "Talk to Students on Theological Education" (1955).

For a complete list of cassettes available, with an order form, write The Reinhold Niebuhr Audio Tape Collection, Union Theological Seminary in Virginia, 3401 Brook Road, Richmond, Virginia 23227. These tapes, especially the earlier ones, reveal Niebuhr's extraordinary gifts and power as a speaker and preacher.

THE REINHOLD NIEBUHR PAPERS

The largest and most valuable collection of Reinhold Niebuhr's papers is deposited in the Manuscript Division of the Library of Congress. An initial gift by Niebuhr himself in 1966 has since been augmented by others, including a deposit by June Bingham of letters she gathered while researching her book and a series of gifts from Ursula Niebuhr over the years, including a large deposit in 1990. Of some ten thousand items now in the Niebuhr Papers, there are approximately six thousand pieces of correspondence, among them a great many letters that have lasting interest. Especially valuable are Niebuhr's many letters to William Scarlett from 1937 to 1971. Other significant correspondence includes letters to or from Samuel Press, William Savage, Charles C. Morrison, Henry Sloane Coffin, H. Richard Niebuhr, Emil Brunner, John C. Bennett, Adlai Stevenson, Arthur Schlesinger, Jr., T. S. Eliot, and John Baillie. Mrs. Niebuhr's latest gift adds not only her correspondence with Reinhold (much of it published in her volume of letters, *Remembering Reinhold Niebuhr*) but also exchanges with Dietrich Bonhoeffer, Lewis Mumford, and George Kennan, among others. She intends to give more in due course. The Niebuhr Papers also include much organizational and institutional correspondence, files on his Detroit years, lecture outlines, biographical miscellanea, and photographs—the last a gift of June Bingham.

Much of Reinhold Niebuhr's correspondence, including some with individuals named above, is in archives of institutions on both sides of the Atlantic where his friends have deposited their papers. Additional materials are in the archives of Elmhurst College, Eden Theological Seminary, Yale University, and Union Theological Seminary.

Index